The NOMINEE

The
NOMINEE

A Political and Spiritual Journey

LESLIE H. SOUTHWICK

United States Court of Appeals for the Fifth Circuit

University Press of Mississippi / Jackson

Willie Morris Books in Memoir and Biography

www.upress.state.ms.us

The University Press of Mississippi is a member
of the Association of American University Presses.

All photographs courtesy of the author unless otherwise noted
Frontis: Photograph of Leslie Southwick, 2007; courtesy of Ben Nichols

First printing 2014
∞
Library of Congress Cataloging-in-Publication Data

Southwick, Leslie H., 1950– author.
The Nominee : a political and spiritual journey / Leslie H. Southwick.
p. cm. — (Willie Morris books in memoir and biography)
Summary: "President George W. Bush nominated Leslie H. Southwick in 2007 to the federal
appeals court, Fifth Circuit, based in New Orleans. Initially, Southwick seemed a consensus nominee. Just days before his hearing, though, a progressive advocacy group distributed the results of
research it had conducted on opinions of the state court on which he had served for twelve years.
Two opinions Southwick had signed off on but not written became the center of the debate over the
next five months. One dealt with a racial slur by a state worker, the other with a child custody battle
between a father and a bisexual mother. Apparent bipartisan agreement for a quick confirmation
turned into a long set of battles in the Judiciary Committee, on the floor of the Senate, and in the
media. In early August, Senator Dianne Feinstein completely surprised her committee colleagues
by supporting Southwick. Hers was the one Democratic vote needed to move the nomination to
the full Senate. Then in late October, by a two-vote margin, he received the votes needed to end
a filibuster. Confirmation followed. Southwick recounts the four years he spent at the Department of Justice, the twelve years on a state court, and his military service in Iraq while deployed
with a Mississippi National Guard Brigade. During the nomination inferno Southwick maintained
a diary of the many events, the conversations and emails, the joys and despairs, and quite often,
the prayers and sense of peace his faith gave him—his memoir bears significant spiritual content.
Throughout the struggle, Southwick learned that perspective and growth are important to all of us
when making decisions, and he grew to accept his critics, regardless of outcome. In The Nominee
there is no rancor, and instead the book expresses the understanding that the difficult road to
success was the most helpful one for him, both as a man and as a judge"— Provided by publisher.
Includes bibliographical references and index.
ISBN 978-1-61703-912-6 (hardback) — ISBN 978-1-61703-913-3 (ebook) 1. Southwick, Leslie
H., 1950– 2. Judges—United States—Biography. 3. United States. Court of Appeals (5th Circuit)—Officials and employees—Selection and appointment. 4. Judges—Selection and appoint-
ment—United States. 5. Political questions and judicial power—United States. I. Title.
KF373.S635A3 2013
347.73'2434092—dc23
[B]   2013028384

British Library Cataloging-in-Publication Data available

For Thad Cochran
Whose enduring friendship kept the journey alive

For George W. Bush and Bennie Thompson
Whose diverse obstacles made the journey hard

For Dianne Feinstein and Trent Lott
Whose miraculous rescues gave the journey success

Each provided exactly what I needed.

And with respect
For Bob Galloway, Charles Pickering, and Mike Wallace
Each deserved success.

Contents

Acknowledgments

I begin my expressions of gratitude by identifying two people whose roles were fundamental. One made me want to be a Fifth Circuit judge, and the other gave me the chance to become one.

The idea of being a judge on that court was a seed planted by Charles Clark, the Fifth Circuit judge for whom I worked during my second year after law school. The seed was slow to germinate because it seemed impossible, and still does, to be as good a judge as he. His retirement created the first vacancy that I pursued. The journey, hence the book, are his fault.

Much later, President George W. Bush gave me the opportunity to complete my long quest. I was not his first or second choice, but my gratitude is not diminished by his selecting good nominees before me. He did finally choose me, and I will always be profoundly in his debt.

There were many individuals who played vital roles in my becoming a judge. I considered naming others, but a complete list would be too long. Instead of identifying them here, I hope the book will speak for itself as to whom my gratitude obviously extends. My dedication of the book to several individuals is a good place to begin but not to end.

My remaining acknowledgments will focus on those who assisted with this book. Senators Thad Cochran and Trent Lott agreed to review the manuscript. I told them that the book was intended to express what I knew and felt at the time about my travails. My knowledge was often incomplete or in error, and my feelings were my own. A significant part of my story is how I was not fully aware of all that was occurring. That ignorance remains in the narrative. Senator Dianne Feinstein was indispensable in my becoming a judge. She then helped again by reviewing some of what I wrote. Senator Arlen Specter may have been as critical to my success as were these three other senators. Sadly, he is now deceased. May he rest in peace.

A few colleagues, friendly rivals, even fellow travelers on the treacherous confirmation road, were given the entire manuscript. Former Judge Charles Pickering, Mike Wallace, Judge Tyree Irving, former Acting Attorney General Peter Keisler, and former Chief Judge Roger McMillin, were generous with their time and insights.

Two Senate and Bush Administration staff members helpfully examined the manuscript for errors: Gregg Nunziata on Senator Specter's Judiciary Committee staff (for whom in 2007 I often used the email salutation "the Great One" because he was that for me), and White House Legislative Affairs wunderkind Harold Kim. He was great too. Other current or former Senate staffers who helped in different ways were Brad Davis (Cochran), Eric Haden (Feinstein), and Hugh Gamble (Lott).

The book gives context for my struggles by explaining the difficulties faced by some of those considered by President Bill Clinton for Fifth Circuit seats. I am exceedingly grateful for the selflessness of the following in agreeing to relive the disappointments and give me corrections and additions to their stories: Jorge Rangel, Alston Johnson, and Bob Galloway.

All my Fifth Circuit colleagues were asked to review their sections of the appendix and, for a few, relevant discussion in the text. My most detailed description of a selection for a Fifth Circuit vacancy other than ones I pursued is that of Mississippi colleague Grady Jolly. Grady discussed his nomination with me and gave me feedback on my first draft. Others who looked over that section and made suggestions were Harry Allen, Wayne Drinkwater, Lanny Griffith, Keith Heard, former Judge Walter L. Nixon Jr., Mike Retzer, and Ken Starr. Providing important research assistance from the library at Mississippi State University was Manuscript Coordinator Mattie Sink Abraham.

Those who reviewed what I wrote were exceedingly helpful, but the final product is my own. Surely some disagreed with my emphases and certainly did not share my perspective. Where the narrative errs or irritates, the fault is mine.

Always quick with a document or details about current or prior judges was Fifth Circuit Executive Greg Nussel. His knowledge of events and, though seldom needed, where to look for what he did not know, was essential. Fifth Circuit Librarian Charlie Pearce, his successor Sue Creech, and librarians Marian Drey, Amy Hale-Janeke, Brent Hightower, and Rosie Tominello answered my occasional historical inquiries by examining the Fifth Circuit archives and other resources.

Materials at other libraries were needed to fill in details for the appendix and elsewhere. Particularly helpful, and I am surely overlooking others, were John Cannan at the Library of Congress, Rodney A. Ross at the National Archives, Steven Saltzgiver at the Federal Judicial Center, Kelly Barton at the Ronald Reagan Presidential Library, Elizabeth Myers at the George Bush Presidential Library, Leigh McWhite at the University of Mississippi, and Anne Webster and Grady Howell at the Mississippi Department of Archives and History. Liliana Vivanco, archivist and librarian for the *Stars and Stripes* newspaper, generously and quickly found an article.

A few rather odd questions about a 1969 basketball game and two of its players were answered by Ron Mears, an Assistant Sports Information Director for Rice University, with supplemental information provided by the Fifth Circuit Librarian in Houston, Tina Ting.

Helping in special ways were Chief Judge Sidney Fitzwater of the United States District Court for the Northern District of Texas, Chief Judge Brian Jackson of the Middle District of Louisiana, Southern District of Mississippi Judge Tom Lee and his wife Norma Ruth, Judge Jay Zainey of Louisiana's Eastern District, Adam Aft of Washington, D.C., Lloyd M. Green of New York City, Joe Magliolo of Dallas, and Ed Whelan, President of the Ethics and Public Policy Center in Washington, D.C. Not to be forgotten for his contribution is Joe Lee of the Dogwood Press.

And a special thanks to Jean Becker, the chief of staff to the first President George Bush.

Several photographs were acquired through delightfully prompt searches by far-away strangers. From the Fox News Network, the assistance came first from Lesley West, who left abruptly for the happy occasion of the birth of her daughter, and then from Miriam Otero. Daniel Herbster provided photographs he had taken of a press conference. Susan O. Nelson with Newscom was able to locate the photograph used on the cover after unsuccessful inquiries elsewhere had nearly caused me to abandon the search. Ben Nichols, whose former Photo Images Studio took the frontispiece photograph in 2007, found and sent the image to me. Blair Latoff, whom I got to know as a Senate staffer during my confirmation, sought out several photographs. Dana Terry with Mississippi College School of Law graciously offered her time to take the photo of La'Verne Edney and me.

Individuals at the University Press of Mississippi have been superb in demonstrating initial interest in the book, then helping turn my rough manuscript into the completed book. Among them are Editor-in-Chief

Craig Gill, Managing Editor Anne Stascavage, Senior Production Editor Shane Gong Stewart, and Editorial Assistant Katie E. Keene. The Press gave the manuscript to copy editor Bill Henry, who repaired defects of many sorts and brought clarity throughout the book.

To all of these and, embarrassingly, to those I will have overlooked until sometime after my last revision can be made, I express the most heartfelt thanks.

◆ ◆ ◆

Writing a book is a team effort. I just identified some incredibly important individuals. In addition, my family provided constant encouragement and patience. My wife Sharon not only had to put up with the selection and confirmation ordeal—filled with more "woe is me" days than appear in this book—but she also then assisted in my reliving it when I disappeared almost daily after supper into my study to write. Children Philip and Cathy were grown and gone, now with their own spouses Mary and David, but they endured the inferno with me and were exceedingly encouraging then and later during the writing of this book. Without them, I neither could have made it to the end of the journey nor would it have been worth doing so.

Thank you, one and all.

The
NOMINEE

Introduction

In January 2007, I was nominated by President George W. Bush to a seat on the United States Court of Appeals for the Fifth Circuit from Mississippi. In early May, and continuing for almost six months, I became in news reports and opposing senators' speeches and too many other places "the controversial judicial nominee." That phrase represented the essence of who I was to people newly aware of me, in the way that others who for a brief time appear repeatedly in the news are given memorable short descriptions preceding their names as a reminder to the reader, such as "gold-medal gymnast," or "shark-attack victim," or "suspected drive-by shooter."

My struggle for confirmation was not in the category of a trial in which a finding of guilt or innocence would lead to incarceration or freedom. My honor was under siege, my ambitions might have been thwarted, but defeat in the battle thrust unhappily upon me would have left me standing, not abandoned by family and friends, and able to continue my profession. I discuss difficulties, but I am aware that many people have faced far worse. When I write about misery, or being discouraged, or feeling unfairly treated, the context should be remembered.

The comforts of life teach little, as enjoyable as they are. My confirmation trials got me the closest I have ever been to a sense of what it means to have a "dark night of the soul." That is a phrase used by a sixteenth-century Spanish priest now known as Saint John of the Cross, who was referring to a spiritual crisis that can lead to the necessary full acceptance of our need for God. The ten months of the experience were lived in a furnace of criticism, leading to a sense of being wronged, to occasional anger, and to constant uncertainties. I was broken down, opened up, and, by grace, allowed a better understanding of my motivations and temptations and therefore those of others. With the individuals who most bitterly opposed me, I share a flawed humanity.

Those ten months followed sixteen years of striving, falling short, then having new chances come to me for a nomination to the court. I view my experiences in the long, always uncertain journey over many years of seeking to become a judge on the United States Court of Appeals through a lens that sees God's hand when others might see coincidence, or luck, or nothing at all.

The story that follows is not proof of anything. It is story about faith, about its ebbs and flows, about events in my life that I believe were the workings of God. The Bible tells us in Hebrews 11:1 that "faith is the realization of what is hoped for and evidence of things not seen." My sense of the realities of my experience is not the only rational explanation. It is not reason based at all. I believe; therefore I find the story to be evidence of things not seen.

I will also say what I do not believe. God does not decree cancers or car wrecks or winning and losing judgeships. He will use the situations that arise in our lives, though. There will be misery from the natural order of the universe. To believe in God is not to be insulated from that natural order. Yet within each human experience is the opportunity for God to give us what we need. It may not be what we want, though. I did get what I wanted, but in my view the success was not because God willed it. He did will me to learn from the experience. I did.

I describe my too-frequent failures to maintain charity to all during the journey. My failures were particularly wicked when someone else was nominated. Part of me was hoping there would be no confirmation and I would get another chance. Each time, I coveted what another had received. I can only ask for forgiveness from God and man for that.

No observer of what occurred during those ten months in 2007 could be more biased than I am. The difficulty of being objective is one major lesson of this struggle. When I fail to be objective, as I often will, I hope at least to show an openness to the views of others. The biases arising from my perspective make me realize that I have no basis on which to judge the motivations of others. Surely many opposed me because they genuinely perceived my record as disqualifying. Others may not have accepted the validity of the criticisms but opposed me all the same. My supporters may also have had their varying attitudes. Who was right about me is not something I can judge.

Much of what occurred in my experience of being selected for a judgeship was outside my seeing and hearing and reading. I have tried to relate what I knew at the time. The message in all the words that follow is not that this is the exact story in all its relevant details. The message is that I trusted in the Lord. I expected a miracle. I received one. Maybe more than one.

Fifth Circuit Judge Jerry Smith told me a few years ago that all who are on the court have their own involved stories of what had to occur to allow their appointments. For each person who prevailed in a judicial quest, there are many others who failed. Each of their stories are as worthy of recounting as mine. I write without any sense of having an especially worthy tale. But I do have a story, carefully recorded along the way, which may be useful.

Brief summaries of all nominations to the Fifth Circuit appear in an appendix. They give a context for what recent nominees have faced. It has not always been like this.

◆ ◆ ◆

Much of the book is drawn from what might be called a diary. There was no bound book with blank pages waiting for my penned observations. Instead, when I sought to have my name submitted in 1991 by Mississippi's two U.S. senators for consideration by the president for a judicial vacancy, I started keeping notes on a legal pad about meetings, phone calls, and other relevant events. The very first note is about the phone call I received from Mississippi when I was living in Washington, D.C. My friend let me know that one of the Fifth Circuit judges from Mississippi had announced his retirement. My quest failed that time, and my note making stopped, too.

Before the decade was over, though, new possibilities arose. By then, I was maintaining a word-processing computer document into which I dropped summaries of phone calls and copies of e-mails and letters. I also have files with the actual letters and handwritten notes. During the year I spent in Iraq, the principal communication with home was by e-mail. Those were saved to a file, too. So some but not all of what follows draws from contemporaneous material.

For reasons of clarity, conciseness, and importance, I edit out large sections, short phrases, and much else from the diary without indicating the omissions. On the other hand, when I am writing words that were not in the diary (and much of what follows never was), that will be clear.

◆ ◆ ◆

Certain words are convenient labels for the decision points in the process of becoming a federal judge. I try throughout the book to use the following terms in a fairly precise way.

A recommendation is what occurs before a president's formal action under the U.S. Constitution. There have been times, for example, when the home-state senators all but select a judge. Still, technically they are only making a recommendation. Other politicians, bar associations, and private citizens also seek to influence the choice by making recommendations to the senators or sending them directly to the White House. Self-recommendation is not unheard of, either.

One or more individuals will be selected by the administration (when the president personally becomes involved may vary). It is usually then that background investigations will be conducted by the FBI and perhaps by the American Bar Association.

A nomination is the formal act of the president to designate the one person whose name is submitted to the Senate to be considered or, at times, ignored. The ABA investigation during the George W. Bush administration occurred after the nomination.

If a nominee is to move beyond just the honor of the thing, there must be a hearing by the Senate Judiciary Committee. There, the nominee is questioned, sometimes harshly, sometimes encouragingly, and other witnesses may appear.

After a hearing, the nominee must receive a vote to be reported out of the committee and onto the floor of the Senate. If there is no reporting of the nominee to the floor, the nomination dies at the end of that Congress.

Filibuster, cloture, and *rejection* are among the words to describe Senate actions that can occur before or as a substitute for approval. Much more about those later.

Confirmation is the formal act of the U.S. Senate to approve a nominee. The Constitution refers to this as the Senate's "advice and consent" to a nomination.

Notification of the president is a formality of the Senate after a confirmation.

Appointment is the final act by the president. He signs a commission of office, later framed by the grateful new judge. The president's signing of the commission is the act of appointment.

Even after all these steps, the judge is still not in office. That requires the recommended, selected, investigated, nominated, interrogated, reported, filibustered, clotured, confirmed, notified, and appointed individual to take the oath of office and sign some documents. The best word for the last part of the process is "hallelujah." One acquaintance delayed taking his oath for ten weeks. More often, only a few days elapse. For the only time, this step is at the discretion of the judge-to-be. There may be other projects to finish before the oath of office is taken.

◆ ◆ ◆

I wrote this book to close the experience once and for all. Perhaps by holding up the events for me to see one last time, I can gain a better perspective. Only if I forgive those who believe firmly they were right to oppose me can I fully release the emotional shackles that confine me still.

Similarly, I have firm beliefs about the correctness of my actions. Nonetheless there are those who surely still see me as a deeply flawed judge. From those who believed I gravely erred in my earlier career, I trust some understanding of my perspective can also come.

This book, then, is at its most basic level a plea for reconciliation among those who battle in judicial wars. It looks back on one man's journey. Perhaps the lessons it taught me can be beneficial when others look forward to the journeys still being taken.

1

The Final Day

It was 4:30 a.m. on Wednesday, October 24, 2007. No need to keep looking at the clock. I had not slept much and definitely would not start now. I had spent the night at the Andrews Air Force Base visiting officer quarters in suburban Washington. Even a Mississippi National Guardsman like myself could get a room when vacancies were available. I arrived on Monday. It was my sixth time staying at Andrews since President George W. Bush had nominated me in January to be a judge on the United States Court of Appeals for the Fifth Circuit. The trips were to convince U.S. senators, one at a time, to confirm me. On Thursday I would leave Andrews for the last time, confirmed or defeated.

The night before, when returning to the room from my day in the world of senators, I was surprised to learn that C-SPAN was not one of the channels available on the room's television. My disappointment was mild, though. Missing the strongly condemnatory half of the two-hour debate in the Senate on my nomination more than offset also missing the supportive half. Later I could selectively watch a video of the contest.

Last night's debate occurred exactly twenty years after a Senate struggle came to a close on a more important judicial nomination, that of Robert Bork to the U.S. Supreme Court. He was voted down. I decided to consider the coincidence to be a good omen that on the twentieth anniversary of the rejection of one controversial nominee, the Senate would by at least a narrow margin act fairly toward another. Yet what would be fair? If I had learned anything from the past year, and maybe from the past sixteen years of desiring this appointment, and being considered three times before, and now finally having the nomination, it is that we all view the world from our personal perspectives. The roll call on which I needed sixty senators to end the filibuster was to begin at 11:00 a.m. When the time came, from how many senators' perspectives would I deserve a vote?

Harold had called me at Andrews last night, the marvelous Harold Kim, who was the White House Legislative Affairs shepherd of my often seemingly lost confirmation hopes. He said that I needed to meet with Colorado senator Ken Salazar at 7:30 a.m. Another meeting was already scheduled for 9:30 a.m. with Delaware senator Tom Carper. I was told that Senator Salazar would ask for a letter to be given him before the vote that would explain some employment issue. Harold knew no specifics. Before going to bed, I called my wife, Sharon, in Jackson to ask her to find on our computer and e-mail my previously written explanations regarding the only opinions from my ten years on the Mississippi Court of Appeals that I could imagine might be the subject. A computer would need to be found after the meeting to draft something quickly. I wanted as much of a head start as I could get to writing a letter under the time pressures of the morning.

Andrews Air Force Base was an economical and comfortable place to stay for someone frequently journeying to Washington, but it was hardly convenient to Capitol Hill. Around 5:15 a.m., I left the room to walk three-quarters of a mile to a Metro bus stop across the street from the Andrews front gate. A light rain had started, so I had dressed casually and carried my suit in a hanging bag. The 5:47 bus was on time. Along with only a few other riders, it took me the two miles to the beginning of the Green Line on Washington's Metrorail at the Branch Avenue station. Riding the train, I skimmed one of the free newspapers handed to riders entering the station. I was both disappointed and relieved not to be mentioned. The less attention given, maybe the less pressure on senators. Maybe.

I got off at the Archives station, went up the escalator to the street, and walked across Pennsylvania Avenue in the predawn. The now-heavy rain eerily distorted the lights on the Department of Justice building, which was my destination. The rain was a troubling omen for the events that were to end before noon. I kept thinking of omens.

I could not easily get into the building, as it was too early for the usual access. Fortunately, I was not long delayed at the vehicle entrance, under my umbrella, explaining to the guard whom to call to authorize my entry. Up I went to the third floor, my long-ago haunt when I was a deputy assistant attorney general in the first President Bush's administration. The Civil Division was now headed by one of the most considerate people I had encountered during my confirmation journey. He was Assistant Attorney General Peter Keisler, head of the Civil Division under Attorney General

Al Gonzales. A month earlier, Gonzales had resigned. Peter had just been named acting attorney general, while retired federal judge Michael Mukasey awaited confirmation as Gonzales's successor. Peter had made his Civil Division office available for me, since he had moved upstairs to the fifth-floor office for the attorney general. I dried off, changed clothes, and found my wife's e-mail. Within fifteen minutes, all that needed to be done this morning at the Justice Department was done. It was time to find Harold, waiting in his car to take us to meet Senator Salazar.

We were at Salazar's office in the Hart Senate Office Building a little before 7:30. The senator was late. That was not mentioned. The senator said he had been the presiding officer for the previous night's debate. He had listened to all the speeches, but he had been most impressed by Senator Dianne Feinstein's positive opinion of my character. She had read excerpts from a letter I had sent her in early August. That too made a favorable impression.

This morning, the senator did not want to discuss employment law. Instead he wanted me to explain my employment of law clerks on the state court of appeals. A fact often mentioned in the months of debate was that I had hired three African American clerks. Salazar said that kind of hiring would not be accidental. I told him I had not previously articulated my reasoning, perhaps not even fully to myself. It was my belief, though, that my hiring of recent law school graduates for these research and writing positions should be the result of casting as wide a net as possible. I wanted the best clerks to assist me, the most intelligent, the best writers. Those decisions could be affected by the potential I saw in an applicant.

I had confidence in each of the three clerks at the time I hired them. La'Verne Edney had been an unpaid law student extern at the state court my first summer as a judge. I was impressed—with her work, with her conscientiousness, with her. That fall she applied to begin as a clerk in the year after she graduated. She had done well at law school. I had applicants who had done better by some measures, but she deserved the chance. I hired her, and she proved to be a splendid clerk. Patrick Beasley and Gale Walker came in later years. Both were students in classes I taught as an adjunct professor at Mississippi College School of Law in Jackson. That familiarity again gave me a confidence that proved justified.

Senator Salazar asked if I would continue to hire minorities for my staff if I were confirmed later that day. I told him I would continue the same approach to finding talented clerks, but I did not want to make any specific commitment. He seemed satisfied and wanted me to write a letter to him that he could see before the vote. It would cover most of the same ground as the letter sent in August to Senator Feinstein regarding other issues, but something needed to be added about my hiring practices. We talked for thirty minutes, but he had to go to a regularly scheduled prayer meeting with other senators. I hoped his seeking divine guidance would be beneficial for me, but that thought was presumptuous, if not sacrilegious. I thanked him for his willingness to meet and left with Harold to find a computer to prepare a letter.

The Republican staff for the Senate Judiciary Committee had an office in the Hart Building, close to Senator Salazar's office. Elizabeth Hays generously allowed me to take over her office. I had an hour until my meeting with Senator Carper. The earlier letter to Senator Feinstein was downloaded from a Web page where it had been posted by someone interested in judicial confirmations. That was the quickest way to get a digital copy from a computer in a Senate office building. By the time I finished the new letter, the morning half of the debate on my confirmation had begun. The only thing I saw on a television was a Democratic senator from New Jersey, saying something particularly condemnatory about my record. I quickly forgot the details, but the image of disgust on his face lingers in my memory. Another unpleasant memory of the journey.

The letter had to be shown to the White House Counsel's Office, which also sent a copy to the Justice Department. This aspect of the confirmation experience would arise from time to time, where my words had to be reviewed by others. It was both helpful and irritating, but the helpfulness was usually the dominant aspect. The letter was finalized and delivered to the senator.

My 9:30 meeting with Senator Carper was much different from my other meeting that morning. The senator was accompanied by at least four aides, and it was they who asked the questions. The questions—with the vote almost in sight—explored in depth the two cases that had become controversial over the last six months, ones that an outside group had identified as disqualifying only days before my May hearing. I was startled by this kind of questioning with the vote ninety minutes away. Near the end of the meeting, as the time drew near for the senator to go to the floor, I got exasperated with a staff member's question. It fairly elaborately suggested a different way a legal issue in one of the two cases might have been viewed. I should have answered his question. Indeed, over the past few months, I had answered at least two hundred questions in my separate meetings with twenty different Democratic senators in their offices, almost always being asked about the same two cases, always answering them respectfully and, usually, thoughtfully.

Instead, at this meeting with the actual vote so near and so uncertain, I stopped listening as Carper's aide continued on his lengthy course. When he finished, my response was that I did not recall considering the suggested alternative when the case was under review years ago. Consequently, I told him it hardly seemed to matter what I thought of it now. Unstated was my knowledge that the critical question at the moment was whether the personal criticisms of me had any substance. If some unconsidered alternative now seemed a better way to have decided a specific legal issue, what relevance was that to the question before the Senate? The grades the senators were giving me were not on my legal reasoning. They were on my character.

I do not recall pushing back verbally at any other questioner in all the hours of interrogation I had undergone since my first visit to a senator in July. With the vote to be held so soon, I would have thought I could maintain my discipline just a few minutes longer. In fact, this was the very last question I would be asked. Likely it was precisely because the vote was the next scene in this drama that something within me required one mild protest in my last opportunity to do so. These interrogations over the last several months had not been pleasant. I had often felt frustrated about the kinds of questions being asked, yet I answered them. But this morning my self-discipline was breaking down. I needed Carper's vote, but pride, wounded and silly pride, is what caused me to answer this way. Pride is said to go before a fall.

I expect that this question became the last because Senator Carper realized, even if I did not, that I had reached the end of my capacity to deal with these efforts to find a darkness in my soul. After a few comments, he asked everyone else to leave, which included all his aides and also my ally Harold Kim. Once the others left, the senator and I stood facing each other, a close handshake's distance. He still had not decided what he would do. He wanted to give what we had discussed a little more thought and to pray about it. He also thought I would be confirmed. Did he really? The senator said some other things, too, and I left convinced about the goodness of this thoughtful man. I hoped there was reason for him to feel positive about me, as well, independently of whether he voted for me. But I sure hoped he would vote for me.

After my two meetings, the number of my handlers increased. They had been needed. White House associate counsels Kate Todd and Cheryl

Stanton joined Harold to take me to the congressional subway that whisks members of Congress from the office buildings to the Capitol. My companions had the authorizations necessary to ride and take me along, too. I had taken that trip many times since being nominated in January, but I realized this was the trip to see how the struggle would end.

We got off the train beneath the Capitol, then rode an elevator up to the floor for the Senate chamber. We walked to the large and rococo Senate Reception Room just off the Senate floor, with a vaulted ceiling painted with murals, an intricately patterned tile floor, ornately framed paintings of five historic senators, and a few benches and chairs along the side. Through a door on the far side was an office for vice presidential staff. Today I was taken to that office, a place I had been several times before. There, in late June, I had met Pennsylvania GOP senator Arlen Specter. He and perhaps three of his staff sat down with me to discuss the two opinions that were the subject of the attacks. He asked one of his staff some questions about what the staffer had found. Specter was shown the key parts of the opinions that were made controversial, which he studied. The Senator then wonderfully asked his staff person, "Is that all there is?"

Those are my five favorite words of the entire experience.

On another trip, sitting in the reception room, I had discussed my credentials with South Carolina GOP senator Lindsey Graham. In the course of his expressing strong support for my confirmation, we compared our experiences as military lawyers. Also in the staff office, back on August 1, I had spent four hours writing the letter to Senator Feinstein on the long night before the Senate Judiciary Committee vote that would decide to report me to the floor. My miracle worker surprisingly supported me and made the course of the next three months possible. But this morning I needed more than just one miracle vote.

I was escorted into the staff office. Many people were there, including vice presidential staff, the invaluable Harold, and the two associate White House counsels, Kate and Cheryl. A closed-circuit monitor showed the proceedings on the floor. Senator Reid was saying something negative. I turned the sound off. A few minutes later, Harold turned it back on. The proceedings were too personal, too epochal to me, to start watching and listening before I had to. But now I left the controls alone. Too many had done too much for too long for me to object.

My meetings and letter drafting, beginning at 7:30 and lasting almost to 11:00, had kept me away from the debate that had begun at 9:00. I missed the superb, the bad, and the really ugly. What was frequently shown in television stories later that day were remarks by New York senator Charles Schumer, one of the sharpest intellects in the Senate and a member of the Senate Judiciary Committee. I never met him, though I had wanted to. Still, I will say that as a New Yorker, he is harsher and more dismissive than is considered polite down South.

The part of Schumer's remarks that was often shown was that Southwick "may be a good man and I certainly don't think he is a racist, but his words have to be seen in context. Like it or not, when he is nominated to the Fifth Circuit, he is carrying 200- some-odd years of bigotry that has existed in this country, and particularly in this circuit, on his back."[1] Assigning to me the obligation of carrying the weight of history I found to be surprisingly revelatory. My biased view on the troubles I was encountering made them appear much more to do with history than with me.

After I had been in the room only a few minutes, Senator Salazar came in to say he had a problem with the ending of the letter I had sent two hours earlier. He was carrying the letter with something on the last page circled. He wanted me to make one change. Here, now, with so much at stake, another matter I had hoped was closed had reopened. I discussed his concerns and what would satisfy them. We quickly worked on some additional language. Replacement phrasing was typed out for the closing paragraph. He gave the copy back after writing "Perfect!" He still did not commit, but I optimistically concluded that this literally last-minute exercise was not just for the sake of having a better copy to file away.

Finished with the latest crisis, I saw on the television monitor that the speeches were over. Senate Democratic leader Harry Reid was discussing the procedure ahead. I knew all too well that sixty votes were required to invoke cloture, that odd supermajority procedure that ends a filibuster and allows an actual vote. If cloture were voted, Senator Reid announced, the Senate would turn immediately to a vote on whether to advise and consent on the nomination. For that, only a majority of those voting would be necessary.

Senator Reid finished. The senator presiding, Ben Cardin of Maryland, called for a reading of the resolution on which the vote would be taken. It was read. Senator Cardin picked back up on his script: "The question is, Is it the sense of the Senate that debate on the nomination of Leslie Southwick to be United States Circuit Judge for the Fifth Circuit shall be brought to a close? The yeas and nays are mandatory under the rule. The clerk will call the roll."

I walked to a window looking out from the east side of the Capitol, not far from the madding crowd in the reception room, and called my wife Sharon. I told her where I was, what was occurring, and that I loved her. I hope I said that last phrase, anyway. Emotions were heightened, and it is the kind of thing I would have said. But the memories are blurred.

The roll call started. Names of senators were read alphabetically, with very few voting at the first opportunity. About sixty-five senators were considered possibilities. I needed sixty. Senator Mary Landrieu of Louisiana said no. "*No?*" was my internal cry of dismay. I had been told she would vote for me. Bill Nelson of Florida also said no, another senator on whom I had been depending. How many more votes would slip away? Senator Dianne Feinstein voted for me, after being the sole Democrat to vote for me in committee, after giving a warmly supportive speech last night, after doing everything I could have asked and then doing some more. God bless her. Senator Joe Lieberman voted aye, too. God bless them both.

The vote would take twenty-five minutes. When the time to vote ended, the presiding officer would ask whether there were senators who still wished to vote or to change their votes. If he heard no one, he would read the totals in favor and opposed. The Senate, the president who had named me, those who had worked hard for and against me, my friends, my family, and I too would finally know whether all that had occurred had led to success.

What occurred had started much earlier. The journey had been so long, and had seemingly stopped so many times, that had I been able to reflect on all that had brought me to that moment and place, with success or failure both possible, I would have been even more numb emotionally.

Perhaps the beginning of what was ending on this morning in October 2007 had occurred on a morning in July 1991. It was then I learned that the judge for whom I had worked right out of law school would retire. I sought to replace him. Success did not occur then, or during the Clinton presidency when that first vacancy was finally filled by someone from Louisiana, or at the end of the Clinton years when the next vacancy was filled by no one, not even in the early stages of the George W. Bush administration when a Mississippi federal trial judge was nominated for a new vacancy, or once that judge had withdrawn after a four-year ordeal and someone else was nominated. I was recommended by Mississippi senators for a Fifth Circuit vacancy in 1991, 2004, and 2007, and for a trial judgeship in 2004 and 2006, was nominated once for each, but had yet to be confirmed. As a Jackson newspaper said, in a friendly tone, I had often been the bridesmaid, but never the bride. Though named Leslie, I am a male. The newspaper knew that—I think.

The first nomination was in June 2006. Finally, I had a nomination after the previous times when I had not been a Republican president's choice. The selection was for a trial judgeship. My troubles seemed over. Instead, that year I was one of many who never got a vote on the Senate floor. At least I had been unanimously voted out of the Judiciary Committee. Then in 2007, when I was finally nominated for the Fifth Circuit, I became the target of opposition only two days before my Judiciary Committee hearing.

The roller-coaster ride of my judicial nomination and confirmation experience is the subject of what follows. My exhilaration or anxieties peaked and plummeted as the events unfolded. The means to maintain emotional balance became best articulated after I was selected by the president for a trial court judgeship in March 2006. After seeing the words on a placard at church, I printed and put on my desk the lines from Proverbs 3:5, "Trust in the Lord with all your heart, and rely not on your own understanding. In all your ways be mindful of him, and he will make straight your paths."

That verse became increasingly important as that year ended without confirmation and I began the even more difficult path of the circuit nomination. I was satisfied that even if the path did not take me where I desired, my life was playing out in the way that was best.

I tried to internalize a version of this passage just before the Senate Judiciary Committee vote in August 2007. On July 19, two weeks before the committee voted, I wrote my former law clerk Patrick Beasley that "Proverbs 3:5 says to trust in the Lord with all my heart, and I will add to that, one should also expect a miracle. That is the way I feel, most of the time."

Trust in the Lord, and expect a miracle.

2

Beginnings

The voyage that was arriving at its destination on that October day was the result of people and events that influenced my life long before President Bush nominated me. Some provided opportunities that set my course or gave me obstacles that redirected me. Others shaped my interests. There were companions who traveled with me. A few parts of my background made the voyage difficult. I cannot identify all the influences, but I can try to give some understanding of what led me that October morning to be in a room off the Senate floor.

My hometown is Edinburg, Texas, which is in the very southern tip of the state. The arid but irrigated and agricultural area is called the Magic Rio Grande Valley by local boosters. My father was Lloyd M. Southwick, born in 1906 in Moville, a small community in northwest Iowa. Dad got out of the cold Midwest when he graduated from medical school. After a one-year stop in Dallas, he moved to the southern tip of Texas in 1931. We almost never visited Iowa during winter.

My mother was Ruth Tarpley, born in 1910. Her parents were teachers who lived in Johnson Station, a small town between Dallas and Fort Worth. In about 1922, the family moved when Granddad was hired as school district superintendent in the Valley town of Weslaco.[1]

Mom and Dad were married in 1934. I have twin older brothers, Lloyd and Larry, born six months after the December 7, 1941, attack on Pearl Harbor and on the day the pivotal battle of Midway began in the Pacific. By then, Dad had been on active military duty for months. He served throughout the conflict in North Africa and Italy. He returned in 1946, but he never talked to me about the war. He was a general practitioner, surgeon, and deliverer of babies. My sister Linda was born in 1949, and I came the next year. Briefly in high school, I also had what was almost my own twin brother. Philip Boole was born in Edinburg four months before I was. His parents had just come from England on a one-year teachers' exchange program. My father delivered Philip and was his godfather. When we both were seventeen, Philip returned from England to live with us and attend a year of high school. A few years earlier, his older sister Penelope had also lived with us for a year.

In 1966 Dad died unexpectedly from a heart attack early one January morning at home. Mom had already begun coursework for a master's degree in biology from Texas A&I College in Kingsville. She drove a hundred miles each way to classes, twice a week, as I recall, studying as she went. She received her degree in 1969 and began teaching biology at Pan American University in Edinburg. In 1972 she married a formerly confirmed bachelor ten years older than she, James McHugh Flanagan, whom we called Mr. Jim. He came from Johnstown, Pennsylvania, and was a newspaper man, State Department official, English teacher, and dignified man of letters who did not quite know what to make of the rougher-edged Southwick family.

My major interest in high school was playing the trombone. My best friends were fellow trombone players James Williams and Carl Estrada. I practiced enough that our neighbors, though the closest one was a quarter mile distant from our rural home, would comment on the nighttime noise to my parents. During each of my last three years of high school, I was chosen for the Texas All-State Band through local, then regional, competitions. Andy Russell and Paul Draper, two years ahead of me in Edinburg High School, would between them be the first chair all-state trombone player for four years. Their achievements were hugely inspiring, but the highest I reached was seventh chair at All-State in my senior year.

I loved my experiences in band, but I did not want to concentrate on music in college. Government and politics were my fascination. In high school, I followed national elections closely and could name most governors and senators from around the country. The equivalent to me of today's rock stars were the six Republican victors pictured in November 1966 on the covers of the *Newsweek* and *Time* magazines that reported on the just-completed elections.[2] Both covers showed newly elected senators Edward Brooke of Massachusetts, Mark Hatfield of Oregon, and Charles Percy of Illinois, and governors Ronald Reagan of California, Nelson Rockefeller of New York, and George Romney of Michigan. For a time, it was my goal to be on such covers one day. That goal, and the magazines, both faded away in the decades ahead. Not on the cover but far more important to my future, George Bush received mention inside one of the magazines for his first election victory, which was for Congress.

Both of my older brothers had attended Rice University in Houston. I did the same, beginning in August 1968. I majored in history and political science. For three summers, I worked in South Dakota. The first two were at the Mount Rushmore National Memorial, and in the third year I worked for the Flaig Brothers construction firm, which built new houses in nearby Rapid City.

The first political event I ever attended was in 1968. I heard presidential nominee Richard Nixon speak at Hermann Park in an outdoor amphitheater across Main Street from the Rice campus. My only "campaigning" was to display a psychedelic-orange Nixon poster on my wall in the dorm. People could laugh at its unconvincing effort to make Nixon appear "hip." My warmhearted but politically opposite roommate for two years, Roger Hurst of St. Louis, may have laughed quietly. Twenty years after we started college together, on December 21, 1988, Roger was one of the 243 passengers on Pan Am Flight 103, which fell in pieces near Lockerbie, Scotland, after a terrorist's bomb exploded. Roger was going home to New York to be with his wife and children for Christmas after a business trip. In college, we did not consider the fragility of life, that chance might one day strike one of us down in an instant while the other lived for decades more.

In the fall of 1970, my third year at Rice, I worked on my first political campaign. George Bush (the father) was running for the U.S. Senate in Texas. He was young, moderate, dynamic. I worked in Bush's state headquarters in Houston, not too far from Rice. I enjoyed making phone calls, folding and stuffing letters, and stapling yard signs alongside other volunteers. I did not get to know George Bush at that time. I did not even meet him, unless it was at the "victory" party (he lost) on election night at the Shamrock Hilton Hotel. I found out later that the hotel is where my future wife worked for a time, but not that night. The 1970 campaign began my involvement with Bush family politics, the rest of which occurred after I moved to Mississippi.

I met my future wife, Sharon Polasek, during my sophomore year at Rice. One of my roommates, George Zodrow, was dating her sister, Pat. In the style of the time, she had long, straight hair, a wonderful smile, and a calm view of life. Before my Rice years were over, I wanted my years with Sharon to be just beginning.

After I graduated from Rice in 1972, I attended law school at the University of Texas. Before I could start, though, I had a physically challenging summer working with my future father-in-law, Johnnie Polasek. Both he and his wife, Annie Pechanec Polasek, were descendants of Czech immigrants who had entered America through Galveston in the late nineteenth century. Johnnie installed central heat and air-conditioning in new homes in southwest Houston. For a summer, I joined him, being paid more than I was worth, being treated like the family I had not yet become, and learning lessons about the benefits and pains of daily physical labor. Running metal ducts with fiberglass insulation wrapped around the outside was a sweltering and itchy job.

In August 1972, I started at the University of Texas School of Law. A memorable professor was Charles Alan Wright. He was brilliant, aloof or perhaps shy, and during my second year he was busily defending President Nixon in some of the Watergate cases. One morning he began his class of one-hundred-plus students with a few sentences referring to his need to write a brief in one case. Most of us realized at about the same time what he was going to ask. Hands shot up all over the classroom. Mine was with the large number who were a half-second late. He was not looking my direction, anyway. The first person he spotted, or so he said, got to assist him in the work.

Sharon and I were married in August 1973, after my first year of law school and just before the beginning of her first year of teaching elementary school in Austin. I graduated in 1975. I spent each of my first two years out of school as a law clerk for judges. The first clerkship was for presiding judge John F. Onion Jr. on the Texas Court of Criminal Appeals in Austin. Another young lawyer, John Potter, was his longer-term research assistant. My work for Judge Onion was a vital credential when I was being considered for the next clerkship. I owe Judge Onion my later career. Indeed, writing this book has made me well aware of how each new opportunity in my life arose because of a previous opportunity that had been seized. I have been boosted up on the shoulders of many. John Onion's shoulders were absolutely necessary.

◆ ◆ ◆

In April of my third year of law school, the school newspaper printed an article about students who would have federal judicial clerkships after graduation.[3] Seven of my classmates would work with Fifth Circuit judges.

One, Jay Nelson, would clerk with Fifth Circuit judge Charles Clark in Jackson, Mississippi. I asked Jay how he had gotten the clerkship. He said that Judge Clark took one of his three clerks each year from the University of Texas, relying on professor Charles Alan Wright to make a recommendation. I would be clerking for Judge Onion the same year Jay would be with Judge Clark. I decided to apply with Judge Clark for the next year.

Professor Wright gave me a strong endorsement, gaining me an interview. I recall only two minor but personal questions Judge Clark asked. Was I interested in the clerkship only because of its salary (about $17,000 per year)? I was not. Did I smoke? I did not. On November 6, 1975, the judge called me at the Court of Criminal Appeals to offer a position. I immediately accepted.

Judge Clark was tall and handsome, courtly even, with white, wavy hair, almost always with a smile. It was frequently said that no one looked more like a judge than he. He acted like one too, never speaking disrespectfully of anyone, not telling inside stories about his colleagues. He was a peacemaker, fair-minded, a man who had found his calling as a judge.

Sharon and I moved to Jackson to start the clerkship in late July 1976. My two co-clerks were John Henegan of Mississippi and Andy Wistrich of California. We researched and wrote memos on the cases the judge would hear when he traveled every month or two to New Orleans, one time to Atlanta, and once to Dallas. We also discussed each of the cases with him the week before argument. Once we got back to Jackson, we drafted opinions based on his guidance.

Clerkships were only for one year. After being in Mississippi for several months, both Sharon and I were seriously considering staying. That spring, Sharon attended a Lenten meeting held by her Catholic Church, a church I had not yet joined. There she met Ed Brunini Sr., the senior partner of one of the largest law firms in the state. Gracious man that he was, Ed started a conversation with the person who probably knew no one there, Sharon. He learned about my clerkship and that we were considering staying in Jackson. The next day, I received a call from one of his associates, Holmes Adams, asking if I wanted to interview. The call led to a twelve-year career with Brunini, Grantham, Grower, & Hewes, keeping us in Mississippi and giving me a solid foundation in the practice.

During my work at the firm, I was rarely in court. My interest in oil and gas law led me into that part of the practice, principally as a title attorney and, less frequently, as a litigator. Untold numbers of days were spent researching land records in courthouses in south Mississippi counties where most of the oil and gas exploration occurred. I handled three cases in the Mississippi Supreme Court and one in the Fifth Circuit, winning all of them with the help of others. A perfect batting average is possible only when there are not many plate appearances. Partners most responsible for showing me the way were John Grower, Jack Welsch, Newt Harrison, and Ed Brunini Jr.

In the early 1980s, Newt introduced me to the last judge of the U.S. District Court in the Panama Canal Zone. The court existed from 1914 until 1982. Unlike the life-tenure federal judges in each state, the sole federal judge in the canal zone had an eight-year term. In July 1978, President Carter appointed Robert H. McFarland of Bay Springs, Mississippi, as that court's last judge. He resigned a year later due to the death of his thirty-two-year-old daughter, Dr. Susan Anne McFarland. The judge wrote to the president that he and his wife had been in Panama and unable to be with Susan in Mississippi as she succumbed to a chronic illness. "This traumatic experience" convinced him to stay close to his remaining family. No new judge was named before March 31, 1982, when the district court ceased to exist under a 1979 treaty with Panama.[4]

Judge McFarland's quickly relinquishing what I would try so hard for many years to gain was an instructive statement about life's values. Similarly, the most important events of these early years in Mississippi for Sharon and me were not related to jobs. First was the birth of our son, Philip, who joined us in 1978. Doubling the joy, our daughter Catherine was born in 1984, completing the family. I can sincerely say that all the events in my professional career described in this book are nothing compared to the joy that Sharon, Philip, and Cathy have given me. That career too often caused me not to give them the time and attention I should have.

Philip's getting old enough to notice that I was attending a Methodist church and Sharon a Catholic one caused us finally to resolve which one of us would leave the church of our parents. We tried for a while going to St. Andrew's Episcopal Cathedral in downtown Jackson. After hearing the similar prayers and seeing the similar rituals to those in the Catholic Church, I really had no answer for Sharon's question: "If you are willing to do this, why not become a Catholic?" Now that I have been Roman Catholic for close to thirty years, I am extremely glad that I made the change.

Most attractive to me about the Catholic Church is that it does not bend readily to the winds of the modern world. My Christian obligation as a judge is to fulfill my oath to uphold the Constitution and the laws of the country, which means following what higher human authority says those laws mean. The Catholic Church is opposed both to abortion and to the death penalty. It recognizes an inherent and unalterable value for human life among the innocent and not yet born, as well as among the heinously guilty. Current law permits the taking of life in both situations. If I cannot fulfill an oath that I took to enforce the law, then I no longer need to be a judge.

◆ ◆ ◆

Practicing law occupied most of my time, but I was soon also involved in Mississippi politics. Ten years before we moved to Mississippi, I became interested in the state's politics. In early October 1967, I read in *Time* magazine that Rubel Phillips was trying to be elected as the first Republican governor since Reconstruction by seeking support from black voters. A Phillips television ad claimed that the two "races are bound together so closely that neither can rise significantly without lifting the other." *Time* speculated that Phillips, whose cause had seemed hopeless, might now be able to win by capturing the nearly two hundred thousand black and moderate white voters.[5] I was thrilled that in the state symbolizing some of the greatest resistance to change, a Republican was trying to lead the way. On election night, I could not find the Mississippi results on any radio broadcast that reached south Texas. It was several days later before I learned Phillips had lost badly. I believe some seeds of my desire to become part of political change in Mississippi were sown in 1967 by Rubel Phillips and a *Time* magazine article.

I was intrigued and encouraged anew in 1975 when Republican Gil Carmichael ran for governor. He courted minority voters, had the endorsement of the only black legislator, Democrat Robert Clark, and among other initiatives urged adoption of a new state constitution.

My growing openness to practicing law and being involved in change in Mississippi was shown in the concluding paragraph of my July 10, 1975, cover letter for the clerkship application I sent to Judge Clark:

> I would like to state one other fact, one which does not augment my side of the scale but does reveal one of the reasons for my interest in this clerkship. This point is my desire to practice law in Mississippi. The seriousness of the interest is tempered by caution, since what I know of the state comes only from some recent books and the comments of one friend from

Mississippi. It seems a state of recent, manifold, though not completed advances, of people who still retain certain venerable moral/religious values while acquiring refreshingly new social views. Perhaps not the "best of all worlds," but still it may be one in which a young person, a fledging attorney to choose a random example, could enjoy desirable change while not rejecting all that is past.

Judge Clark never mentioned the letter, but it was awkwardly personal. Still, he offered me a clerkship. His offer came two days after Carmichael's narrow defeat in the November election.

My first volunteer political work in Mississippi was for congressman Thad Cochran in 1978. Longtime U.S. senator James O. Eastland announced that he would not run for reelection. No Republican had been elected to statewide office since Reconstruction, but this year appeared to offer real promise. Also running in the GOP primary was state senator Charles Pickering. Both contenders would play prominent roles in my quest to become a Fifth Circuit judge decades later. Thad was the victor in the primary. A formidable Democratic opponent remained, respected former district attorney Maurice Dantin. A black independent, Charles Evers, also was running. With 45 percent of the vote, Thad Cochran made history and replaced Eastland in the Senate.[6]

I got to know Thad and some of the people close to him. Thad was forty, soft-spoken with a sharp intellect, a handsome man with southern mannerisms of courtesy and humility. He would be eclipsed in public recognition by others, including the later junior senator Trent Lott. Thad was an old-style senator, not overly partisan, finding friends among ideologically opposite colleagues. Key for me is that he never forgot my help in 1978.

My strongest political identification was as an ally of the first George Bush. My work in Houston on his 1970 Senate campaign made me a lifelong supporter, but I never developed a close relationship with him. When Jimmy Carter took office in January 1977, Bush resigned as CIA director and returned to Texas. I wrote in May, encouraging him to run for Texas governor. Bush responded with one of his famous handwritten notes.[7] He would not run in 1978. "As to '80—I'm keeping open whatever options a baseless, ex-Ambassador, ex-spook, ex-Congressman might have. If I do anything nationally, ever, I enthusiastically accept your offer of help."

George Bush is known and loved for his small courtesies to so many people from all stations in life. The notes, the remembering of names and faces, the socializing with people no matter their varied backgrounds, created an enthusiastic legion of supporters wherever he went. A young lawyer from Oxford, Mississippi, who became a good friend of mine, Lanny Griffith, had the same reaction after meeting Bush in 1978. The Bush campaign let us know of each other. Lanny became executive director of the state party in March 1979, a position from which he gave me wise political advice.

In 1978, Bush established the Fund for Limited Government to raise money for his political activities. I contacted the fund to make a contribution. A twenty-eight-year-old Texas political operative named Karl Rove responded. I contributed and had an exchange of letters and phone calls with Rove over the next few months. Rove passed along to Bush my offer to help Bush if he got into the 1980 presidential race. Bush wrote another note. "I am not now a candidate, but I'm doing the things I ought to do if I want to be one next year. And I will take you up on your offer if I run. Let's keep in touch and thanks again." Bush wrote again in late 1978, saying that "things are moving forward. I will make a very early final decision (first quarter of 1979). All signals look 'go.'"

Bush announced on May 1, 1979. In early June, I tried to contact Rove and see what needed to be done in Mississippi, but he had left the Bush effort to work for newly elected Texas governor Bill Clements. Bush campaign political director David Keene responded instead. He said the campaign would focus on Iowa and New Hampshire for a while longer. In December 1979, I flew to Washington to meet with Keene. Considering the paucity of volunteers in Mississippi, I was likely only minimally checked out before being anointed as the state campaign manager. I remember the list of supporters the campaign gave me as being rather short, perhaps containing only the name of the politically active and well-liked Miki Cassidy of Marks. I sent a memo to the executive committee for the strongly Democratic Brunini law firm, seeking clearance for this role. Committee chairman Leigh Allen returned the memo with his drawing of a happy face and the words "No problem."

The Mississippi presidential primary was not until June. The campaign had a few highs. Jerry Gilbreath, a thirty-one-year-old lawyer in Laurel and one of only four Republicans in the state House of Representatives, became campaign chairman on February 6, 1980. We urged Bush supporters to attend a Lincoln Day dinner to be held in Jackson on February 12. Former president Gerald Ford was the featured speaker, but a straw poll was also a draw. Governor Reagan was considered the strong favorite, with Thad Cochran–endorsed former Texas governor John Connally in a competitive second place. Instead Bush received 29 percent. That put him in second place behind Reagan's 37 percent, and 3 percent ahead of Connally.[8] The straw poll gave us a needed boost.

The high of the campaign nationally was Bush's winning the Iowa caucus on January 21. The low came with a dismal second-place finish in the New Hampshire primary on February 26. Bush ended up being the last GOP opponent to Reagan, with the second-highest vote total and number of primary victories. On May 26, Bush finally withdrew from the race. The GOP primary was on June 3, and we no longer had a candidate. For the only time in state history, the Republicans (but not the Democrats) chose their delegates to the national convention by voting for them individually on the primary ballot. The Reagan and the Bush campaigns had several delegate candidates in each of the five congressional districts. We encouraged votes for Bush delegates as a signal that Bush should be nominated for vice president. The signal was not sent. The highest vote for a Bush delegate was 13 percent in the north Mississippi district. Our candidates there got about 375 votes each, while the Reagan delegate candidates averaged 2,700. The lowest was 5 percent in the southwest Mississippi district. I am the candidate who set the floor, with a grand total of 337 votes in my first political race. The four Reagan candidates in the same district averaged 6,000.[9]

Bush was not finished for the year, though. In the week before the national convention, Bush came to Mississippi for the first time that year. On a Wednesday night, July 9, with the national convention to start five days later, Bush attended a fund-raising dinner in Jackson to retire some of his campaign debt. I was finally able to meet and spend some time with him. Chesley Pruet, an oilman from El Dorado, Arkansas, organized the event, along with his daughters and sons-in-law, Ann and Rick Calhoon, and Paula and Randy James, who lived in Jackson. These and other prominent Mississippians became my friends because of George Bush, then assisted me in my later endeavors. Such is the cycle of politics.

The next morning's opportunities to be with Bush were allocated carefully. Mr. Pruet, Rick, and Randy breakfasted with Bush at the Walthall Hotel. Rick still remembers that Bush ordered grits. Ann and I took him from there to the airport. Ann was pregnant, so still another Pruet family member participated. I was the intruder that morning. We left Bush at the airport, where a reporter was waiting. "No interviews," Bush said.[10] With his prospects for the vice presidency clear but fragile, silence was best.

The next week, Reagan very publicly considered former president Ford as his running mate. Ford told a reporter that Reagan was discussing a role for him that was almost a copresidency. Not long after those overly bold statements, Governor Reagan went to the convention to announce George Bush as his choice. The Reagan-Bush ticket won a landslide victory in November.

Bush's selection was the most significant event in creating my own later political and judicial opportunities. It put George Bush on his way to the presidency, his namesake son on his own course, and allowed me to play a more significant role in future Mississippi politics than I otherwise would. I am very grateful to President Ford for suggesting he might be a copresident.

◆ ◆ ◆

Soon after President Reagan took office, I had my first minor involvement in a Fifth Circuit selection battle. The need for a new judge became known on January 29, 1981, when J. P. Coleman of Mississippi announced he would resign as chief judge of the Fifth Circuit on February 2, then would retire as an active judge as soon as the new administration "decides its procedures for filling vacancies." He retired on May 30.[11] Describing how the new judge was selected will provide a tame preview of what lay ahead for me. Importantly, the two key officials who disagreed over the selection—Thad Cochran and Trent Lott—were also involved in every judicial contest in which I competed. They usually disagreed about me, too—until it mattered most.

Senators dominated the selection process for judges in their states. In 1981, Senator Cochran was the first Mississippi Republican to have that power since 1881, when the term ended of the most recent prior GOP senator, Blanche K. Bruce. Not long after Thad learned of Judge Coleman's plans, he contacted his good friend Grady Jolly, a forty-three-year-old founder of a Jackson labor-law firm. Thad said he was considering recommending Grady as Coleman's successor and wanted to be sure Grady wanted to be on the court. He did. Perhaps by March, Grady was Thad's choice.

Grady was a longtime Cochran supporter and had worked on Republican Charles Pickering's failed 1979 race for attorney general. He was not, though, a consistent Republican. One untimely example of Grady's lack of GOP fealty occurred while he was being considered for the judgeship. In a June 23, 1981, special election to replace a GOP congressman who had resigned, Grady supported Democratic state senator Ed Ellington of

Jackson. Senator Ellington, a longtime friend of Grady's and Thad's, was one of several Democratic candidates. Republicans were united behind Jackson businessman Liles Williams. Both lost. During the week after the June election, it became public that Grady was Thad's choice to be the new judge. A Republican complained, "We just got through fighting Grady Jolly in the Fourth District campaign . . . and Thad turns around and nominates him for the biggest piece of patronage we have ever had." Grady's bipartisan inclinations were hardly unusual. Democrats' century-long, total control of the state was being challenged, but few voters were unwavering Republicans. Revealingly, after Thad won in 1978 and before the Reagan-Bush ticket carried the state in 1980, Democrats in 1979 won all nine statewide races, including the race for governor, and also won 166 of 174 legislative seats. Most races had no GOP candidate.[12]

Grady's GOP credibility needed some tending, and I was among those asked to assist. John Hutcherson, a partner at the Brunini firm who was a friend of Grady's and Thad's (and also an Ellington supporter), asked me to write the senator on Grady's behalf. My letter, coming from the 1980 "Bush guy," was to be one of many from Republicans that Thad could use as evidence of GOP support for his choice. I had met Grady, liked him, and was willing to help. I wrote to the senator on June 22 to say I was impressed by Grady's integrity and intellect. On July 2, Thad responded: "I'm recommending Grady today to the Attorney General and the President."

Grady is a genial man, mischievous in his humor, and a smart lawyer who enjoyed being "in the center of a good fight" in law and politics. Unfortunately for Grady, Senator Cochran had supported John Connally, not Reagan, for the 1980 GOP nomination. An early and vigorous Reagan supporter was Congressman Lott, and he was selected in January 1981 by his House Republican colleagues as the party whip. To take Judge Coleman's place, Lott recommended his political supporter and good friend Harry R. Allen of Gulfport, a superb attorney, age forty-eight, who in 1979 had been one of the defeated GOP legislative candidates. In 1983–84, he would serve as chairman of the state GOP finance committee. Allen clearly was a stalwart Republican. Lott contacted Allen around May 1 to ask if he would be interested in the judgeship. He was. Later I got to know Allen well and became convinced he too would make an excellent judge. On July 2, both recommendations became public. Cochran met that day with attorney general William French Smith to urge Grady's selection. Lott said he had "some time ago" urged Allen's selection. The administration was also considering other lawyers. Senators had near autonomy in selecting district judges, but the White House also wanted input from Reagan state campaign leaders and state party officials before it selected nominees for circuit courts of appeals.[13]

Once Allen knew Lott wanted to recommend him, he met with Thad to be sure the senator did not believe he alone should be making suggestions. Thad confirmed that the White House wanted other recommendations. Even so, Allen—who wanted to avoid widening party divisions—said he would have declined Lott's offer had he known Thad was going to recommend Grady. The party had been badly split by the 1976 battle between Ronald Reagan and President Ford for the GOP nomination. National committeeman Clarke Reed had made long-term enemies by switching his support to Ford after initially backing Reagan. Mike Retzer, who became party chairman in 1978, was a Reed ally. Bitterness and distrust remained for the 1980 race, as I experienced in my work for Bush. Congressman Lott and other leaders of the state Reagan campaign tried to oust Reed and Retzer at the May 1980 state party convention, targeted Retzer again in December 1980, but failed each time. Divisions were again on display on August 10, 1981, when Vice President Bush flew to Gulfport to speak at a party dinner. Local GOP leaders knew Reed and Retzer would be at the dinner, but did not include them in the group to welcome Bush's plane. The two went to the airport anyway, jumped a fence, and joined the others. They were not even named on the printed dinner program, and it had a lot of names. One person whose name did appear prominently in the program was Harry Allen, shown as a member of a small steering committee. Allen decided his competition with Grady was creating a perilous new flash point for the party, which clearly had plenty. Allen called Cochran on August 20 to say he was withdrawing. Congressman Lott, who reportedly believed Grady was insufficiently conservative, gave notice that he was not ready to concede and would offer other names.[14]

By October, after the intervention of the administration and state party leaders, a compromise was announced. The choice was fifty-three-year-old federal district judge Walter Nixon of Gulfport. Democratic president Lyndon Johnson had appointed Nixon in 1968, but he "'met the test' of a Republican philosophy" that satisfied GOP leaders. A GOP philosophy was the best that could be offered, as the state had no federal district judges with Republican backgrounds. Party Chairman Retzer said that Cochran and Lott would accept Nixon. Indeed, "all elements of the party 'were involved to a greater or lesser extent [in the negotiations]. Everyone's feelings were considered.'" Lott conceded that Thad would select Nixon's successor as district judge. Grady would have been named, putting him in line to become the district's chief judge in March 1983 when the current chief turned seventy. Though Thad neither talked to Nixon nor agreed to substitute him for Grady, he let the administration know he would not oppose the selection.[15]

Retzer told me that as he tried to facilitate a compromise, he had the benefit of access to Ken Starr, who was a young assistant to Attorney General Smith. Retzer's contact with Starr was Wayne Drinkwater, who served with Starr as a law clerk to chief justice Warren Burger from 1976 to 1977. Wayne lived in Greenville, Mississippi, as did Retzer and Clarke Reed. Wayne told me that Starr first called because of the administration's frustration that the state's Republicans could not agree on a choice. He wanted Wayne's views on Grady and Harry Allen.

Lott said the White House first suggested Nixon as a candidate and "continually came back to Nixon in subsequent talks." He expected Nixon would be nominated if he wanted the job. Judge Nixon did not recall, thirty years later, talking to Cochran, Lott, or Retzer about the seat. He was told by someone involved in the process that President Reagan would call him if he agreed to be named. There are those who believe Judge Nixon was never seriously interested in giving up the autonomy of being a district judge to join an appellate court of fourteen judges. On October 15, forgoing a presidential call, Judge Nixon announced publicly that his love of trial work made him want to remain a district judge. He declined "the magnanimous offer of our great President to elevate me" to the Fifth Circuit.[16]

Chairman Retzer said he was unaware that Nixon had aligned himself with the Republicans until seeing him at the Bush dinner in Gulfport on August 10. Sharon and I were there too, sitting with state GOP executive director Lanny Griffith. Before Bush appeared in the banquet hall, Lanny was summoned from our table for a private meeting with Bush. I was painfully envious. Lanny returned with vice presidential cuff links as a memento. He passed them around our large table for everyone to see, but they disappeared before getting back to Lanny. It wasn't me. Lanny would be a key leader in the 1988 Bush campaign. The vice president may already have been taking his measure.

On the day Judge Nixon declined, Senator Cochran again wrote the president to urge that Grady Jolly be selected. He thanked the president for having met with him in mid-July to discuss Grady, noted "the length of time involved and the clear superiority of this recommendation over any other possibility," and asked that Grady be nominated as soon as possible. Lott also reacted to the collapse of the Nixon compromise. On October 27, Lott sent President Reagan five new names: state chancery judge James Arden Barnett of Jackson and attorneys Hunter Gholson of Columbus, Ernest Graves of Laurel, Frank Montague Jr. of Hattiesburg, and George E. Morse of Gulfport. Barnett had been the defeated Republican nominee for a Mississippi Supreme Court seat in November 1980. That credential might be significant, as another pioneering Republican judicial candidate had recently been rewarded: Will Garwood of Austin had lost his 1980 race for the Texas Supreme Court and was nominated in September 1981 to the Fifth Circuit.[17]

A few weeks after Lott's letter, there was a report that White House chief of staff James Baker, while in Jackson on November 12 for a GOP dinner, had warned Chairman Retzer that the deadlock could cause the seat to be filled by someone from another state. In mid-February 1982, still with no one chosen, a columnist speculated that President Reagan did not want to "step into the middle of a standoff between" Cochran and Lott. Three days after the story, Congressman Lott again wrote the president to recommend Judge Barnett in particular, but Montague and Morse "would also be acceptable to me." Explaining the delay in selection, Retzer, who was allied more closely with Cochran than with Lott, said, "The main problem is not Jolly, but that 'Lott wants to be No. 1 here. Power—that's the name of the game.'" It certainly was partly a power struggle, a common Washington event.[18]

What may have settled the issue was that by February, Senate Judiciary Committee chairman Strom Thurmond finally informed the administration that any nominee who was not acceptable to Senator Cochran would not be approved. The competition was over by mid-March, when President Reagan told Lott that Grady would be named. After an FBI background check was completed, Grady was nominated on July 1. At his hearing on July 14, he answered four brief questions from GOP senator Charles Grassley, then went on his way. His confirmation was unanimous on July 27.[19]

Grady's success required the persistence of Senator Cochran, the withdrawal of at least one other strong candidate, avoiding being shifted to a district court nomination, overcoming the insistence of a powerful politician for someone else, and an eventual acceptance by others of the prerogatives of a senator from the nominee's home state. To succeed twenty-five years later, I would need all of that, but incredibly more so in all respects.

◆ ◆ ◆

Long before I became interested in following Grady's path, a different opportunity for public service presented itself. In late 1984, Governor Bill Allain appointed ex-governor and now fully retired Fifth Circuit judge J. P. Coleman to be chairman of the Constitution Study Commission. On November 15, 1985, Governor Allain wrote letters to numerous Mississippians inviting us to join the commission. Along with 350 others, I accepted.

Over a year's time, with periodic meetings, we quickly decided on the need for a new state constitution, then drafted one. The final draft was approved by the commission on December 18, 1986. The state legislature then had the authority to continue or to kill the reform effort. In January 1987 the Senate approved a bill that would require a referendum on the November ballot on whether to hold a constitutional convention. When the House revealed reluctance, I wrote a column for the local paper discussing the risks that opponents were raising and arguing they were minimal and could be controlled. The House of Representatives was just a handful of votes shy all session of a majority to call for a referendum. The House leadership strongly opposed the measure. The final try came on the last day of the session. The House voted 61–57 to adjourn without voting on the referendum.[20]

The commission was one more, and a substantial one, of my commitments away from private law practice. My billable hours dropped dramatically in 1986 when I was spending so much time on the constitution commission. My partners were displeased. Before too long, both the firm and I would have to decide whether my career would continue at the Brunini firm.

The final two political campaigns in which I volunteered were in the late 1980s. I was the county chairman in 1987 for Jack Reed, who I believe was the greatest governor Mississippi never had. He was a businessman from Tupelo. He had been a persuasive and courageous proponent of public education in his area in the 1960s and 1970s, when integration of schools was at its most contentious. Former governor William Winter, a progressive Democrat, wrote two decades later: "No person in my lifetime has done more to inspire and try to lead our state in the way it should go than Jack Reed."[21] I agree. Reed lost, but it was close.

Overlapping the 1987 Reed campaign were the beginning stages of the 1988 Bush presidential race in Mississippi. The vice president came to the state for some political event almost every year beginning after his inauguration in 1981. I was always involved with those visits. I was no longer one of just a handful of people supporting an obscure candidate, as had been the case in 1980. Instead Bush was the favorite for the 1988 nomination.

In 1987, Lanny Griffith became Bush's coordinator for the entire South, probably the key region for the Bush campaign. Over time, the Mississippi volunteer leadership was put in place. A Jackson businessman, Julius Ridgway, who was a major fund-raiser for the party, was named chairman. Mike Retzer was finance chairman. Titles are inexpensive, and the one given to me was chairman of the state steering committee. Someone who would help bridge the divide with conservatives who did not quite trust Bush was former state party chairman Charles Pickering. He had recently been president of the Mississippi Baptist Convention. I had gotten to know him in 1979, when I helped in his nearly successful campaign for attorney general. He agreed to become state cochairman with Julius, a pairing that made a solid political statement.

George W. Bush was probably the most frequent campaigner among the Bush sons. I was with him several times during the campaign. He was a delightful person to be around, funny and a little irreverent, charming, focused on the task of helping his father be elected. I drove him around Jackson to various events in my car. Considering he was a future president, I should have washed the car. Bush, future Fifth Circuit judge Rhesa Barksdale, and I went on an early-morning five-mile run through downtown Jackson during that campaign. I was not used to that distance and started to lag with a mile or two left to go. The future president and judge did not let me fall too far behind before they circled back to make sure I did not need emergency medical attention. I was not sure, but I expressed confidence and told them to go on without me.

Another run came after the national convention. Vice presidential nominee Dan Quayle came to Jackson for a evening campaign event. Rhesa Barksdale again took the initiative as he had with George W. Bush. He suggested to Senator Quayle that since we knew he was a runner, perhaps the next morning he would like to go for a run. Whether he really wanted to go running or not, being agreeable is what candidates need to be. Quayle was agreeable. Senator Cochran was, too. Early in the morning, with more Secret Service than I was used to having while running, we went to the Chastain Junior High School dirt track and spent some quality time going around in 440-yard circles.

Election night, 1988, is a vivid memory. I had started with George Bush in 1970, saw him lose a U.S. Senate race and then ten years later a presidential one. Ronald Reagan breathed new life into Bush's national hopes by choosing him as vice president. The 1988 campaign was long and difficult. Bush seemed near defeat many times. After going to a few of the candidate parties at a downtown hotel, I went home for the final results. Sitting on the floor in our bedroom, leaning against the bed, I heard George Bush declared the president-elect.

3

The Bush Administration

I was tempted but undecided about whether to try to follow Bush to Washington. It was a difficult decision to leave private law practice for the uncertainties of a political position in Washington. Sharon was unenthusiastic. She did not want to move, to sell or rent the home we had built just four years earlier, to find schools for Philip and Cathy, and otherwise to have an upheaval for what I assured her was only temporary duty. We discussed the possibility several times.

As I struggled with whether I should pursue the opportunities that would likely be there, I found myself listening more than coincidentally often to a song by Roger Whittaker, which contained the lines "I met a man who had a dream he had since he was twenty / I met that man when he was eighty-one."[1] Being part of government in Washington had been a dream for years. I did not want to defer that dream and one year find myself to be the person in the song.

My first postelection trip to Washington was in December 1988. I talked with Lanny and others at the transition office. There was a brief visit there with George W. Bush, who was surely being importuned by hundreds of individuals whom he met in his constant campaigning for his dad. I kept in touch with him. He made contacts for me and for many others.

I was most interested in becoming the director of the Peace Corps. Soon, though, President Bush named Georgia state senator Paul Coverdell to be director. I then sought the deputy director spot. In February, I flew to Atlanta to meet Paul before he moved to Washington. He was a wonderful man, and we seemed to hit it off. Eventually I was offered the position of general counsel. Before then, though, I had accepted an offer in mid-May to be a deputy assistant attorney general in the Civil Division of the U.S. Department of Justice.

A few months before going to Washington, I went to a three-day Catholic retreat in Jackson. It was an opportunity to focus on spiritual matters. At one point, I was alone outside, with a wooded area on the other side of a fence from where I was sitting. I wrote on a piece of paper some words, perhaps "going to Washington," that represented the decision I had made. I wadded up the paper and threw it over the fence into the woods, trying to make that act the equivalent of discarding the decision I had already made and letting God guide me. I had not totally immersed myself in the experience, because the littering bothered me. But I recall a great deal of peace in the feeling that I really had released my own plans and thereby opened myself to his.

I felt then, and more so over the next few days, that going to Washington was acceptable in God's eyes as a new course in my life. Psychologists would have explanations regarding self-justification. Since I know there is a God, his wanting to give me guidance if I will only be open to it is entirely unremarkable. Being open is the struggle. It would have been embarrassing to change my mind after all that had occurred. I had accepted the offer and told my extended family and the law firm. An article had appeared in the newspaper. Still, I believe that I would have stayed in Jackson had that been my sense of the direction I was being led after "throwing away" the ambition.

Sharon, Philip, and Cathy would remain behind for one school year as I began my work for the Justice Department on August 1, 1989. Sharon probably hoped that I would get enough after a year and go home. If not, she would join me.

I shared with many of the other new appointees a tremendous excitement about joining the Bush administration. I felt that we were a team who could do great things. I expect those are the feelings of most supporters who go to Washington with the candidate whose success they have so emotionally embraced for years. I had no idea what to expect at the Department of Justice. My title, deputy assistant attorney general, gave meaning to the adage that the longer the title, the less the authority. But I would learn that I had lucked into one of the best possible positions for my interests and my future.

The attorney general when I started was Dick Thornburgh. He resigned in August 1991 and was succeeded by his deputy, Bill Barr. I got to know both men and found them to be skilled lawyers and conscientious public servants. The assistant attorney general in the Civil Division was Stuart M. Gerson, a superb attorney at a large Washington law firm. Barbara Fisher was my secretary, and Rosalie Bern and Toni Rice were the others in the front office. They provided invaluable institutional knowledge that allowed new political appointees to learn our way. The career management staff of the 120-lawyer Federal Programs Branch that I supervised were some of the best lawyers I ever met. Dave Anderson, Denny Linder, Brook Hedge, and Vince Garvey were incredibly skilled career attorneys who impressed me with their legal knowledge and insights. I also had responsibility over the Consumer Litigation Branch, in which John Fleder and later Gene Thiroff held sway. I have great admiration for the lawyers with whom I worked at the Justice Department.

There were three other new deputy assistant attorneys general, in charge of other branches of the Civil Division. Patricia Bryan had been at the White House Counsel's Office. Her sharp intellect and high-level legal experience taught me much about the big leagues of legal practice that I had entered. Steve Bransdorfer, a longtime political ally of former president Gerald Ford from their mutual hometown of Grand Rapids, was an excellent lawyer who had been president of the Michigan Bar and ran unsuccessfully for state attorney general in 1978. Rick Valentine was a lawyer who had worked, as it was put, "on the Hill" for much of his career. The one career deputy assistant attorney general was Stuart Schiffer. He had outlasted several administrations. He was remarkably incisive and knowledgeable, as well as incredibly humorous. I greatly admired and liked him. Rounding out the front office was Lloyd Green, who had been opposition-research counsel for the Bush national campaign. He served as counselor to the assistant attorney general until late 1991, then was succeeded by Tim O'Rourke, a young lawyer from a large Washington firm. In my prejudiced view, it was an excellent team.

Many of my memories of working at the Department of Justice center on key cases on which I worked. The lawyers of the Federal Programs Branch in the Civil Division defended governmental departments and agencies when their activities were challenged in court. If the government did it, someone would likely sue about it, and we were the ones to defend it.

The lawsuits could be exciting. One of the first federal programs under legal challenge after I got to the department was NASA's imminent launch of the space shuttle *Atlantis*. In its cargo bay would be the *Galileo* spacecraft, to be launched once the shuttle was in orbit. *Galileo* was to journey to Jupiter, to arrive in 1995. To travel so long a distance, the spacecraft was plutonium fueled. An environmental group argued that if this shuttle blew up in the atmosphere as had the *Challenger* in January 1986, it would spread radiation across an enormous area and cause widespread deaths and irreversible harm to the environment. On October 10, 1989, the district judge refused to stop the launch. It occurred on October 18 without incident.[2]

The first court argument that I presented for the department was to defend new legislation intended to correct the financial recklessness that had been occurring in the savings and loan industry. The Financial Institutions Reform, Recovery, and Enforcement Act was passed after Bush took office. It greatly tightened the regulation of savings and loans. Many S&Ls that were in compliance under the old rules brought suits challenging the legality of the changes. One of the institutions that sued was the Long Island Savings Bank. The attorney it hired, Lloyd Cutler, was the prominent senior named partner in a major Washington law firm. In 1994 he would be President Clinton's second White House counsel. A later savings and loan lawsuit caused me to negotiate with Bernard Nussbaum, President Clinton's first counsel.[3]

On December 8, 1989, in a courthouse in Brooklyn, I made the argument on behalf of the government while Cutler argued for Long Island. We wanted the case to be the vehicle for determining the constitutionality of tightening the accounting regulations. The trial judge, though, never entered a decision. Later, Long Island dismissed the case and brought suit in the Court of Federal Claims, seeking damages for the change in accounting rules.[4]

Early in my tenure, I was involved in a variety of disputes arising from prosecutions brought by the independent counsel who had been named because of the Iran-Contra affair. The most famous of the defendants was Oliver North. By the time I was at the Justice Department, the target was retired admiral John Poindexter, a former national security adviser. Poindexter subpoenaed former president Reagan to testify. The assistant attorney general, Stuart Gerson, was recused from the case. That placed me in charge of the case for the Civil Division. After several hearings, we had to accede to having President Reagan deposed as an alternative to testifying at trial. The deposition was held in a Los Angeles courtroom on February 16–17, 1990. United States District Judge Harold Greene from Washington presided, available immediately to resolve objections. The courtroom was sealed. Only individuals who were connected with the case and had the proper security clearances were allowed in. An associate independent counsel, Dan K. Webb, and Poindexter's own lawyer handled the questioning. I was there to protect the interests of the government in national security, with individuals from the CIA and State Department with me to help me understand if a question was straying into a problem area. David Anderson of Federal Programs also was there. The videotaped deposition took six hours on the first day and concluded on the next.[5]

President Reagan had his personal attorney present, future solicitor general Ted Olson. I became Ted's great admirer in this process, as he is an extremely able, public-spirited, and decent man. His wife Barbara was on the airliner that terrorists crashed into the Pentagon on September 11, 2001, making that tragedy more personal to me than it would otherwise have been.

Several significant lawsuits arose from the preparations to oust the Iraqi army from Kuwait. Fifty-three congressmen and one senator sued the president to prevent his using American troops in Kuwait without a declaration of war. The suit was dismissed in December 1990. The court held that until Congress had taken some step as a body, such as voting to prohibit the presidential action, the claim was not yet ready to be resolved.[6] Congress later voted its approval and ended the issue.

I was an active participant and occasional courtroom advocate in these and numerous other lawsuits. On selection of Fifth Circuit judges, though, I was only a spectator most of the time. The president named four and left four vacancies. I failed in my pursuit of one that no one filled.

President Bush made his first Fifth Circuit nominations on November 17, 1989. The president named my friend Rhesa Barksdale for one vacancy and Jacques Wiener of Shreveport for another. They were both confirmed unanimously on March 9, 1990. I had a very small role in Barksdale's consideration. In February and May 1989, I met with Murray Dickman, an assistant to the attorney general, to explore working at the Justice Department. At both meetings, I also urged Barksdale's nomination. I sent follow-up letters each time, discussing my interests and also mentioning Barksdale. Two days after I began work at the DOJ in early August, I sent a memo to Dickman summarizing Barksdale's career and attaching his résumé. Barksdale earned that nomination, but I like to think my efforts helped in some unknowable way.

Concerns about racial diversity were voiced when President Bush nominated Barksdale after earlier nominating Charles Pickering for a district judgeship. The Jackson newspaper did a feature story on them, headlined "Judges: White, Protestant, Male." The story said these characteristics were standard for federal judges across the nation. An NAACP leader, Cleve McDowell, candidly noted that a significant problem was that Republican senators and presidents wanted to name conservatives. "Being realistic," McDowell said, there were not that many black attorneys who were conservative or "active in the Republican party."[7] Later federal judicial vacancies in Mississippi were also filled by white males, and the insistence for racial diversity would keep growing.

Two vacancies from Texas arose in 1990. A Texas legal newspaper reported in January 1991 that President Bush had settled on his choices, and FBI investigations were under way. One was U.S. District Judge Emilio Garza of San Antonio. He was nominated in April 1991 and quickly confirmed. The other reported selection was John E. O'Neill, a forty-three-year-old partner in a defense firm in Houston. He had also been considered for the Fifth Circuit during Reagan's second term. In February 1992, O'Neill was reportedly still a possible nominee, but he was never nominated. He later said he did not know if the ABA had been the problem, but he understood that certain members of the Senate Judiciary Committee thought he lacked "judicial temperament."[8]

O'Neill had at least two moments of fame that penetrated well beyond legal circles, one before and one after his consideration for the Fifth Circuit. In 1971 he was a young navy veteran home from Vietnam, where he had served on "swift boats." He was outraged that another swift boat veteran, John Kerry, was accusing service members of committing war crimes. On June 30, 1971, O'Neill and Kerry debated each other on the nationally broadcast Dick Cavett show. Later O'Neill became a highly successful attorney in Houston. Kerry entered politics in Massachusetts. Over thirty years after their first battle, they were antagonists again when Senator Kerry gained his party's presidential nomination. O'Neill wrote a highly critical book about Kerry's Vietnam record, called *Unfit for Command: Swift Boat Veterans Speak Out against John Kerry.* The book and related television advertisements were well-known during the 2004 election.[9]

John Kerry would not be president, and John O'Neill would not be a Fifth Circuit judge. Their highly public battles contributed in different degrees to each man's disappointment.

President Bush made his last successful nomination to the Fifth Circuit on June 27, 1991, when he named the well-respected Houston lawyer Hal DeMoss. DeMoss was the President's longtime friend, active in Bush campaigns beginning in the 1960s and ending with a six-month leave of absence from his large law firm to work on the 1988 campaign. His confirmation was delayed because Supreme Court Justice Thurgood Marshall announced his resignation the day DeMoss was nominated. Clarence Thomas monopolized the Senate's attention on judicial selection until his confirmation on October 15. DeMoss was then easily confirmed on November 27.[10]

I watched these nominations, except for Barksdale's, as an outsider. Two weeks after DeMoss's nomination, though, I started down the same road as had the others. A journey of a thousand miles begins with one step, or so, roughly translated, did the Chinese philosopher Lao-tzu say in about 550 BC. My first step toward the goal a thousand miles away of being a judge on a federal court of appeals was prompted by a phone call on July 10, 1991. This is the point at which I started to keep my diary about my Fifth Circuit journey. Once the note taking began, I returned to it whenever a new chapter was reached in the story with such an uncertain ending.

My first note was this: "7-10-1991. Pete called—Clark's resignation in paper." Pete was my friend Pete Perry, in whose condo I had stayed for nine months when I was first in Washington and who had moved back to Mississippi a few months earlier. He called to tell me about the front-page story in the morning's *Jackson Clarion-Ledger*.[11] United States Court of Appeals Judge Charles Clark would resign from the Fifth Circuit. Much later, I was given a copy of the July 5 letter that Clark sent to his colleagues and his two senators. Clark wrote, "Emy and I have decided that I will resign from the court I love on January 15, 1992," and join a large Jackson law firm.

The next entry, the same day as the phone call, was this: "7-10-1991. LS [that's me] called Thad and Trent and Lanny." Senator Cochran received the first call. He thought it was worthwhile for me to pursue this. We set up a meeting. With that invitation in the bank, I called Senator Lott's office. Surprisingly, I was able to meet with both of them the next day. I guess they were in a hurry, which was fine with me. Lanny Griffith was by then an assistant secretary at the U.S. Department of Education. He knew every Mississippian who would be considered for the vacancy, and he was conflicted because of all his friendships. But he gave me good advice.

"7-12-1991. Met with Thad 10:00 a.m. and [staff member] Haley Fisackerly. Met with Trent 1:30 p.m." Both senators were in the Russell Senate Office Building, about ten blocks from the Justice Department. I do not remember either meeting being particularly substantive, though I did discuss some of my experiences at the Department of Justice that might indicate a capacity for handling the kinds of legal issues that would come before a federal appellate judge.

In October, I finally learned what seemed to be the final result. In fact, though, it was not even the end of the first chapter. "10-4-1991. Thad Cochran—Called to say it was Judges Henry Wingate and Glen Davidson. Thad would not oppose me if I got it [i.e., if the president nominated me even though I was not on the list]. He understood if I kept after it."

The next day I sent Thad a note saying that his news had made it difficult when we talked to figure out what to say. A short typed note allowed me to collect my thoughts. "What was appropriate and accurate is that there are always large numbers of people, many of them friends and good political allies as I believe we are, who want the same thing from you. Making everyone happy is never a possibility. I do not envy you on having to make these kinds of decisions."

This response was an effort to model something that made a strong impression on me in 1978. John Warner, a former secretary of the navy, was better known at that time as the husband of the actress Elizabeth Taylor. Of course, he later became an ex-husband. In June 1978 he narrowly lost the GOP nomination for the U.S. Senate from Virginia to Richard Obenshain. Warner immediately announced he would contribute to and campaign for the winner. His subsequent actions proved his support was not simply perfunctory. On August 2, Obenshain was killed in a plane crash. Warner's uncommon grace in defeat was critical to making him acceptable as the replacement nominee. He won in November.[12] In each of my many defeats over the years, I sought to emulate Warner by recognizing the good qualities of the person who bested me.

I am pretty sure that my message of understanding and acceptance was sincere. One of my concerns about being in Washington was captured in a saying that I first heard when I was at the Justice Department: with every appointment, the president makes nine enemies and one ingrate.

In time, I learned the issue remained open. I was told the Justice Department was insisting on more names. It did not seem that the first two names were unacceptable, but the administration did not want a precedent that two names were enough.

"10-23-1991. Barbara Drake [a Justice Department lawyer working on judicial selection] called at 9:30 to say the senators let her know that they would be willing (pleased?) to have me considered. Told Sharon, she *was* very pleased. Question still is whether I am the only new name."

There was considerable secrecy, but eventually I learned that four more names joined those of district judges Henry Wingate and Glen Davidson. In addition to me, the other new recommendations were Jackson attorneys Mike Allred and Mike Wallace and ex-congressman and former state trial judge Webb Franklin. To be chosen from that list would be extremely difficult.

Another friend in the Civil Division who was a truly admirable man was pursuing his own federal judicial appointment back in Michigan. Steve Bransdorfer had the same-level position as mine but oversaw a different branch of the Civil Division. He had begun the selection process for that vacancy shortly before I did. He had already been interviewed and shared with me his recollections of the questions. We talked at some length on multiple occasions.

At that time, interviews for the circuit judgeship nominations were held at the Department of Justice. My interviewers were a quartet of luminaries. The solicitor general Ken Starr, who himself had been a U.S. circuit judge before resigning to take his present post, was on most observers' list of possible U.S. Supreme Court nominees. His chief deputy was John Roberts, a future chief justice of the United States. The third was as impressive as the other two, but not as well known. Tim Flanigan would in a few months become the head of the most prestigious section of the Justice Department, the Office of Legal Counsel. He is a brilliant, honest, godly man. The fourth was Tony Schall, who in 1992 became a judge on the Federal Circuit Court of Appeals.

It was a Murderers' Row of high-powered interviewers, but each was a friendly acquaintance. I received every courtesy from them. Each interviewed me separately, thirty minutes apiece, starting at 9:30. I walked from one office to the next, with no break in between. The one question I will mention came from John Roberts: "Which three people would you like to see on Supreme Court?" With an apology for sounding clumsily ingratiating toward the next interviewer, I listed Ken Starr first. I should have named John Roberts, too. I also named Fifth Circuit judges Rhesa Barksdale and Patrick Higginbotham. I still believe all three were excellent choices.

Surprisingly, perhaps, no one asked, and never would in all my interviews for a judgeship over the next sixteen years, what my views were on abortion.

While I was making my own pursuit, I learned on November 6 from Steve Bransdorfer that he had been told the previous day that he would not be nominated. All of Steve's friends at the Justice Department—everyone who knew him—were disappointed. He was a gentle, patient, engaging fellow, just a lovely man, who would in less than a year return to Grand Rapids to practice law with his sons. His advice to me about the kinds of questions to expect at the interviews had been invaluable.

Another person who was helpful because of her knowledge, judgment, and friendships was Deputy Assistant Attorney General Patricia Bryan, who supervised the Appellate Branch of the Civil Division. Her office was adjacent to mine, connected by an interior door that opened frequently—from my side. She had been at the White House Counsel's Office during the Reagan presidency and knew key people there as well as in the Justice Department.

I had been interviewed on Halloween. Through Justice Department channels, I learned that the last of the six who had been recommended was interviewed on November 15. I heard different predictions and alleged insider information from different people. A friend from the Department of Energy, Barry Hartman, told me he thought it was "between Wallace and me. John Roberts high on Wallace because he was Rehnquist's clerk. Barry said 'this is a tough one.'"

I made only occasional entries about spiritual faith in my notes. I was aware of that and mentioned it. "12-4-1991. Hope I am not showing lack of faith. Thought about those who do not go to doctor with sick children, but rely on prayer alone. Tension between letting God work alone, and giving God actions through which he can work, finally re-analyzed to a decision I would do what I thought would help, looking for God to guide me." The tension between the sayings of "letting go and letting God" and "doing all I can and letting God do the rest" always seemed to work out where I did everything I could.

In December, I decided to contact George W. Bush. "12-9-1991. George W. Bush (9:30 a.m.)—was in Dallas. I told him my understanding is six people [were recommended], came down to two; Boyden Gray decided on Wallace. George said he would call Boyden right away." The results of that phone call were immediate.

"12-10-1991. [Associate Counsel] Lee Liberman called. Said it is hard when White House Counsel folks don't know someone very well. Boyden Gray, Lee, and others did not know me well, and they would like to interview me. She stated this was unusual, but since I was part of the administration, they were willing to do it. Said she, Gray, and Mark Paoletta would have lunch with me, probably in the White House mess. Her secretary would call back with date and time."

An embarrassing misstep had to occur before we met, though.

"12-13-1991. Claire, Lee Liberman's secretary. She said 'three people were waiting for me for lunch at White House.' Turned out no one had let me know; would reschedule." Good grief, this was a debacle, standing up the White House counsel during the one interview I would have with them. No one had ever called to schedule the interview, but would they believe that?

"12-16-1991. Pat Bryan—Mentioned this disaster to Pat, and she said they are so disorganized at White House Counsel that this is no surprise. Even if it had been my fault, they probably would think it was theirs." Pat's comments might have been mainly to reduce my worry about the awkwardness of the missed lunch, but I found comfort in her words.

"12-18-1991. Boyden Gray, Lee Liberman, Mark Paoletta—Met at Lee's office at noon in Old Executive Office Building. Then walked to White House to Boyden's office. Talked generally [at lunch] about executive branch tussles with Congress, independent agencies, why I want to be judge. Lee after lunch said they wish to move on this very fast to see if can get it through."

At the lunch, someone mentioned U.S. district judge Ricardo Hinojosa of McAllen, Texas (a city seven miles south of my hometown of Edinburg). The White House was urging him to accept nomination to the Fifth Circuit, but he would probably decline. He did. Similarly, a few years earlier, Thad told Mississippi district judges William Barbour and Tom Lee that he wished to recommend them for the Fifth Circuit, but neither wanted the position. Judge Lee explained his refusal by telling Thad "how much I enjoy being a trial judge, which includes the association with lawyers and people and which contrasts with a circuit judgeship in which there is involved more of a secluded, 'ivory tower' existence." District judge Walter Nixon rejected a similar promotion before Grady Jolly was nominated in 1982. Much later, I would face the opposite choice (being moved from a circuit judge nomination to one for district judge) and state the opposite preference. I did not welcome the "ivory tower" isolation, but it did not deter me, either.[13]

Finally, the word came. "1-22-1992. Lee Liberman told me it would be Wallace. Mike had more trial and appellate experience. He also had strong Senator backing, which would be critical during this tough confirmation period. I thanked her, said this must not be the most enjoyable part of job. She said it was not, and Barbara Drake or a letter usually covers it. But because of 'all I had done for President,' they felt she should call."

It was done. I called Mike that afternoon and congratulated him. He was a far more experienced litigator and a stunning intellect. My credentials for the position were legitimate, but I had not yet done enough in my legal career to justify my selection over Mike.

I soon told Judge Clark, whose retirement had started all of this. He said he was not giving up on my nomination. He then used a quaint phrase that almost became a mantra for me through all the travails of the years ahead: "There is many a slip between cup and lip." He meant it in terms of Mike Wallace, but it was true for everyone over the next decade and a half. A long and difficult struggle would seemingly end, but then that person was either not nominated or not confirmed. Then the issue would return for another struggle.

On January 24, reporter Kenneth Jost called from the *Legal Times* newspaper. He had learned, perhaps accurately, perhaps not, that the final two under consideration for the Fifth Circuit vacancy were Mike and me. The two-day-old call from Liberman was fresh in my mind. I let Jost know that I was no longer under consideration. I did not want a story indicating I was one of two remaining possibilities when the choice had actually been made. People who saw such a story would then congratulate me, and I would need to correct them. The brief story that appeared in the January 27 issue was solely about Mike, contained his picture, and identified him as "the leading candidate" to be nominated. My name was not mentioned. I called Jost to thank him.[14]

The disappointment on the judicial nomination left me wanting to find something else. I was disappointed, frustrated, ready for a change, but floundering in deciding what made sense. In April, I met with Martha Goodwin and Nancy Miller at the White House Personnel Office and explained my interests. One possibility was the position of general counsel at the Department of Energy. A few weeks earlier, the personnel office had sent an initial group of résumés to the department. They had not planned to send any more but would be "glad" to send mine.

On May 15, I had an interview with Linda Stuntz, the deputy secretary of energy. It was a comfortable, relaxed conversation, and the first hurdle seemed cleared. Over the next few weeks, I received encouraging information about my chances. On June 8, I met with Secretary of Energy James Watkins, who was a retired navy admiral. Stuntz was there too. This meeting was not so relaxed, though it was pleasant enough. One question, based on phone calls they had made, was whether I would be sufficiently forceful in manner to deal with the inevitable conflicts with other departments and with Congress. Admirals would want aggressive subordinates. My manner may best be described as "laid-back," but I told them of my confidence that I would be as assertive as the occasion required. Whatever confidence I had felt was gone after the interview.

On June 22, I heard from Stuntz that the other candidate had been chosen. It was a "very close" decision, and she said that the admiral was a little more comfortable with the other finalist.

Mike Wallace was having his own tough journey to the Fifth Circuit. Senator Cochran was quoted in March as saying, "This will be a controversial nomination."[15] President Bush sent the names of his judicial selections to the American Bar Association before their nominations. In time, it became clear that Mike's ABA rating would be negative. I heard through a friend that Mike and four other criticized Bush picks were discussed one last time by the rating committee during the ABA's annual meeting in August. Results were never publicized. Senator Cochran gave me a fair summary at one point by saying that Mike had run into a "buzz saw of criticism." Mike was never nominated.

Just days before the election, I joined hundreds of other political appointees on the White House lawn to greet the presidential helicopter as it brought Bush back from his last campaign swing. Tim Flanigan was there too. He said the judicial selection committee would move quickly in the next year on all vacancies if President Bush won reelection. Of course, Bush did not win.

Ironically, getting nominated in 1992 may have been the easy part. Among those nominated for judgeships was my interviewer, John Roberts, who was nominated on January 27, 1992, for the D.C. Circuit. A friend at the Justice Department, John Smietanka of Michigan, was also nominated that day for a Sixth Circuit judgeship, as was District Judge Sidney A. Fitzwater of Dallas for the Fifth Circuit. A November 1991 nominee for the Tenth Circuit was Frank Keating, a friendly acquaintance who served as general counsel at the Department of Housing and Urban Development.[16] In 1994, Frank was elected governor of Oklahoma after he, like Roberts, Smietanka, and Fitzwater, never even got a vote in the Judiciary Committee. The Senate moves glacially when it must.

After President Bush lost the race for reelection, the *Legal Times* labeled winners and losers in the legal arena. It considered John Roberts a loser: he came "within a whisker of a lifetime appointment to one of the judiciary's most prestigious posts—only to lose it through no apparent fault of his own."[17] That evaluation, though reasonable, was not prescient.

As a result of not being confirmed in 1992, Roberts likely had substantial earnings in private practice before being appointed by the next President Bush to the D.C. Circuit in 2003. When nominated for chief justice in 2005, he only had to defend two years of judicial opinions, not thirteen. In hindsight, he likely was a 1992 winner.

4

The Mississippi Court of Appeals

On Inauguration Day 1993, as Bill Clinton stood on a platform at the Capitol to be sworn in, I was packing a U-Haul trailer to return to Jackson. A moving van had already taken almost everything back to Mississippi when Sharon, Philip, and Cathy went home the previous June.

My final few years at the Brunini firm had not been successes in billable hours. Instead of cultivating and acquiring clients, I had focused on politics and, for much of 1986, a gubernatorially appointed commission to prepare a new state constitution. Clearly I was no profit center. At some stage before the 1992 election, I called the firm's managing partner. I said that regardless of the election outcome, I would be returning to Jackson in early 1993. I would like to go back to the firm but only if made a full partner again. Nothing was requested during that call. After Bush lost, I called again. I was asked whether I planned to leave again. My answer, which I should not have given because I was not certain, was that this time I would stay. The partners would discuss my request and let me know. Up to that time, no one had ever left the firm and then returned. On December 2, I was told the firm "could not meet my terms." I wrote that comment on the message slip from my secretary that had let me know the managing partner returned my first call. It was, fittingly, a pink slip. Though not surprised, I worried about what to do.

One opportunity followed from my getting to know the Peace Corps director four years earlier. In Washington, I occasionally saw Director Coverdell and his assistant Molly Dye, as I liked them both. Coverdell resigned in October 1991 to run successfully for a U.S. Senate seat from Georgia. After the 1992 election, Coverdell offered to name me his counsel in his Washington office. I was touched by his thoughtfulness, as I had not sought the position. I declined, though, because I wanted to go home to Mississippi.

I had lived easier years than 1992. In January, I learned that the Fifth Circuit nomination had slipped away. In June, seemingly-in-my-grasp selection as general counsel of the Department of Energy had been embarrassingly fumbled. President Bush lost the November election, ending my renewed Fifth Circuit hopes. Then the Brunini firm said no. The saying that there was nowhere to go but up may have occurred to me. If it did, I was likely uncertain that it was true.

On December 11, 1992, I met with Governor Kirk Fordice. He had been elected in 1991 as the first Republican governor since Reconstruction. Andy Taggart, a friend for ten years and one of the most faith-filled men I know, was his chief of staff. Andy smoothed my reception. The position of counsel for the Department of Human Services was offered. I did not accept. Instead I used the opportunity of a sabbatical to pursue a far-fetched idea with which I had toyed for years. Mississippian John Grisham's recent bursting on the scene as a novelist—his first big commercial success, *The Firm*, had been published in 1991—may have been one of the reasons I decided to take time off and write a novel. Despite constant advice given to novelists to write about something they know, over a four-month period I wrote a novel of historical fiction set in Russia. A fine book, or so I thought, but no publisher was interested.

With rather amazing good fortune, something for which I might actually be suited had been in the news since I had come home from Washington. In the spring 1993 legislative session, a state intermediate appeals court with five judgeships was created. The legislation provided that the first judges would be elected at the November 1994 elections, a year and a half later. With the novel finished, I started meeting with possible supporters about a race for the court of appeals. This book is mainly about the difficulties of being appointed to a federal judgeship. The difficulties I now describe of being elected to a state judgeship seemed almost easier.

A supportive business group was the Business and Industrial Political Education Committee, or BIPEC, whose director was Dick Wilcox. It had been formed to coordinate business efforts for the election of state legislators. It had only recently become interested in judicial campaigns. The plaintiffs' lawyers had similar interests, so 1994 was a contentious election year.

The person who would become my campaign manager, Ken Stribling, in addition to having an excellent political mind, was an excellent state representative. We got a written endorsement from former president Bush and used it and his photograph prominently in the campaign. It was important in this wide-open election that I stand out from all the others who were running. Thad Cochran would generously participate in two fund-raising receptions with me.

On January 31, 1994, I made a formal announcement. Former Fifth Circuit judge Charles Clark, fully retired as a judge and working in a Jackson law firm, stood by me when I announced and then made some remarks. Ed Brunini Jr. was my chairman. Lawyers in my old firm were generous in sharing the treasure of time and funds. Harry Walker, the president of the bank in whose building the firm had been located for decades, was my finance chairman. Harry and his wife Dearie were contemporaries. Harry had risen in the bank as I progressed as a lawyer. Andy Taggart was a constant and superb adviser. Pete Perry, my old housemate, and Clinton Graham, a longtime comrade in politics, were other confidants. We met frequently, along with Ken Stribling, to figure out what needed to be done. Later in the campaign, Henry McCullum of Prentiss introduced himself and offered to work in the black community in the district. I agreed, and he made a valuable addition to the team. In 1999, Henry would be elected sheriff in his home county. Even Lanny Griffith, involved with far bigger matters in a lobbying firm with Haley Barbour in Washington, graciously served as a sounding board and helped with fund-raising. Lanny, Andy, and Clinton were all former executive directors of the state Republican Party, so I had some highly skilled assistance.

I drew no Republican primary opponent. My early start and strong identification with the Republican Party caused many of the traditional party workers and financial backers to join my campaign. My November opponent at that point was Bobby DeLaughter. He was an assistant in the district attorney's office in Jackson and was unopposed in the Democratic primary.

The Jackson newspaper story on my announcement mentioned DeLaughter prominently.[1] DeLaughter was leading the prosecution of Byron De La Beckwith, on trial in 1994 for the third time in the 1963 slaying of civil rights leader Medgar Evers. The film *Ghosts of Mississippi* (1996) tells the story of the case, with Alec Baldwin starring as DeLaughter. No doubt Bobby would be a formidable opponent. I wanted to do my part to keep the contest as friendly as possible. He would do the same. I wrote him on the day after I announced: "You got almost as much publicity as I did out of my announcement yesterday about your plans to run for the Court of Appeals. I'll try to help you out a little less often in the future."

DeLaughter would no longer be my opponent if changes made by the legislature on April 6 to the entire judicial election system were approved by the Department of Justice under the Voting Rights Act. Under the proposed revisions, two judges would be elected from each district, not just one. The revisions also dropped party primaries in all judicial elections. Instead everyone who filed for a judgeship would be on the November ballot. The top two finishers for a seat would compete in a runoff two weeks later if no candidate got a majority. Under that system, I would be running against a district attorney from south Mississippi, Richard Douglass; a state representative from Mount Olive, Joe Warren; and a former Jackson state representative, DeWayne Thomas. DeLaughter would have two competitors for the other seat. Summer would come and go without any decision from the Justice Department.

While I was seeking a state appellate judgeship, someone was named to the Charles Clark vacancy that had eluded everyone in 1992. On Wednesday, June 8, 1994, President Clinton nominated Louisiana Supreme Court justice Jim Dennis to the Fifth Circuit Court of Appeals. The previous day, Republican primary voters had officially nominated me for the Mississippi Court of Appeals. Jim and I each had tough campaigns ahead.

I was concerned about being seen as a big-city, Republican, coat-and-tie lawyer. I decided to walk the entirety of the principal north–south highway in my district, other than the interstate, and then on a west–east highway. It was hard and sweaty work, perhaps making me appear a little foolish, but likely giving me a more human image. The nickname tried out for a while was "Walkin' Les." It did not catch on, unsurprisingly, other than for one friend who still uses it.

The seat of the southernmost county in the district was Magnolia. Heading north from there, I would walk ninety miles along U.S. Highway 51 to reach Jackson. Early Monday morning, August 22, on the county courthouse steps in Magnolia, I talked briefly with a television reporter. Then I was off. I developed a practice of going into businesses, talking to people who were outside their homes, but not going door to door. I would never have completed the journey had I done that. This first day, Ken Stribling drove the van with a large vinyl sign tied to the side, announcing "Southwick, Court of Appeals," in large letters. A smaller banner tied below the first one read "Walking Ahead." My schedule was rigid because

Ken had placed half- or full-page advertisements in the local newspapers along the route, announcing that I would be in their communities on certain dates. It was daunting, knowing that I was going public with this kind of detail when I was not positive I could walk the walk.

Ken would go ahead of me a mile or two, park off the roadway but position the vehicle so that a driver from either direction would see my name on the banner, either just before or just after seeing me on the highway walking. At the end of that first day, I had made it to the north boundary of the first county, for sixteen miles. I took a piece of chalk from the van and marked a line across the roadway to designate where to start the next day. I had walked a little later than intended to get to that spot. I was about to be late for a dinner meeting scheduled by one of my local supporters, McComb attorney Norman Gillis. After my sweaty walk, I was in no odor to be meeting prospective supporters. There was not enough time to get back to where I was staying that night.

Ken and I drove back to the home of someone who, having seen my advertisement in the paper, had that afternoon been outside waiting in a lawn chair to encourage me. I figured that if she had enough interest to do that, perhaps she would allow me to use her shower. She did not mind, apparently. Having cleaned up and expressed my thanks and embarrassment, I was on my way to dinner. It could have been worse, but still I was thirty minutes late. I would have to do better.

Sometimes I stayed in supporters' homes, people such as Chuck Nelms in Brookhaven, and Tommy Jolly in Monticello. Also hosting me were Olen Bryant and his wife Evelyn in Hazlehurst. I knew them both, but Evelyn better because she had been a secretary at Brunini when I was there. On Friday night, I was on the outskirts of Jackson. That night I slept in my own bed. On Saturday morning, I had seven final miles to go before reaching the grounds of the Capitol.

The next morning, I went back in the van to the previous night's stopping point, to begin the final leg. My arrival at the post office was timed to meet a group of friends. We walked the last half mile together, through downtown Jackson on a Saturday morning to the Capitol. Crews from local television stations were there to catch the final steps. The van pulled in ahead of me, allowing my banner with the Southwick name to be the backdrop for the remarks I made at the end of my walk.

A cameraman filmed a close-up of my shoes as I walked the final fifty yards. He may have realized how much this campaign initiative depended on my feet. I was walking about fifteen miles a day, and the blisters became serious by the second day. I had been jogging for years, but my feet were not prepared for this. An old friend, Paul McDade, who among his many talents was a Boy Scout leader, started to be my trainer every morning. He would use Scout remedies such as moleskin and special ointments, bandage my feet, and send me on my way. Paul would fix me up until I figured out how. It is incredibly humbling to have someone working on your feet, reminding me of Jesus at the Last Supper. Paul was a strong Christian and saved me in this critical way.

Other forms of campaigning went on for a few weeks to allow my feet to heal. On Labor Day, I went to Natchez and spent the night with some new friends, Kenneth and Cindy Drane. The next morning, I went to a bluff overlooking the Mississippi and gave my remarks to a few supporters and members of the press. Then I was off. A newspaper reporter rode in the van driven by Kenneth for a few blocks, writing that it was "stocked with water, bananas and plenty of shoes."[2]

That same day, the rules of the campaign changed. The Justice Department had finally cleared the way for the election changes to take effect. My opponents now were Richard Douglass and Joe Warren. A fourth contender, DeWayne Thomas, dropped out because of the late start he would be getting on a campaign.

I arrived in Laurel on Thursday, September 15. There was a good crowd, and there were reporters to spread the word. Success. I managed to earn a story and photo on the front page of the newspaper of every county through which I walked except for one. Many of the people I met probably had the reaction of one woman quoted in a news story who seemed to be leaning my way: "He must be very interested in the job to walk that many miles."[3]

On Wednesday, November 2, six days before the election, I was the speaker at a Rotary luncheon in Natchez. I discussed beginning my walk in mid-August in Magnolia. On the second or third day out, with the hot August sun on me, I saw buzzards circling over the roadway ahead. Surely they were too far away to have me as their target. Lessons learned included the power of mind over body. In fifteen days on the highway, I walked over two hundred miles. I learned to set ambitious goals but meet them one step, literally, at a time. Don't think about finishing the entire walk, just reach the top of the next hill.

Election night 1994 was the first one in which I was anxious about my own vote totals. For three decades, I had watched the returns of many candidates in whom I was interested. Sharon and I decided, or maybe I decided and she agreed, that we would not watch the returns. The results would come in slowly, the outcome would be doubtful, and I needed a distraction. So all four of us went to the movies. We saw *Little Giants*, a comedy about peewee football with Rick Moranis and Ed O'Neill. It started at 7:00, just as the polls closed. We got home around 9:15. I learned that I had the lead but was well short of 50 percent.

The results were Southwick, 47,581 (42.4 percent); Douglass, 43,897 (39.1 percent); and Warren, 20,869 (18.5 percent). I did not expect to win without a runoff, but the closeness of the vote was a huge disappointment. Douglass and outside groups supporting him had spent a comparable amount of money to me, his funding primarily from plaintiffs' lawyers, while my funding had come from businesses and defense lawyers. I kept making speeches and made one more television advertisement that we ran for the last three days. On November 22, I won with 21,760 votes, or 56 percent, to Douglass's 17,076, or 44 percent.[4] We did not go to the movies this time. Instead, we all went to a shopping mall. The family was all quite thankful on Thanksgiving two days later.

Jim Dennis made some progress for the Fifth Circuit while I was out walking. He and five district court nominees received a hearing on September 14, 1994, the day before I finished my walk from Natchez to Laurel. Alabama senator Howell Heflin, presiding at the hearing, asked Dennis five perfunctory questions, to which he gave brief answers. Heflin said that confirmation would likely "run smoothly," and the process was being expedited for all six nominees.[5]

Heflin was right about the five district court nominees, but not about Dennis. In late October, GOP senator Orrin Hatch reportedly told committee chairman Joe Biden that if Dennis were voted out of committee, "Republicans would use delaying tactics to block a vote" on the floor.[6] Republicans asserted that Dennis was too liberal. He also had not provided copies of all his speeches and lectures as requested by the committee. Dennis was left in committee, never receiving a vote. I thought that objections by the Mississippi senators to nominating a Louisiana judge to the Clark seat likely also played a role.

In the November election, the Republicans gained a majority in both houses of Congress. Justice Dennis would have to be nominated again at the beginning of the next Congress. His troubled journey went into the new year. Mine had successfully ended. Even my feet had recovered.

◆ ◆ ◆

A Mississippi Court of Appeals was created because the state's sole appellate court, the Mississippi Supreme Court, could not keep up with an ever-increasing number of appeals. The court was created by the legislature in 1993. All cases would still be appealed to the supreme court, but that court would divide up the workload. The concept was that about half the appeals would be assigned to us. A few categories of cases could not be heard by the court of appeals, including appeals from convictions involving the death penalty.

By statute, the supreme court chief justice named our chief judge. Our first was John Fraiser. He had for a few years been one of three appointed state supreme court magistrates. Only two of the new judges had previously been elected to a judgeship. James Thomas was a trial judge, and Billy Bridges had been one for years but had been defeated for reelection in 1990.

Four had been legislators. Oliver Diaz and Leslie King were serving in the House of Representatives when they were elected. Frank Barber, the other judge elected from my district, had been a state senator. So had chief judge John Fraiser. Tom Coleman, the son of former governor and Fifth Circuit judge J. P. Coleman, had been a district attorney. The judges other than myself who had not previously served in elective office were New Albany attorney Roger McMillin and Jackson law professor Mary Libby Payne. The person I knew best before the campaign, a superb lawyer from Meridian named Greg Snowden, lost narrowly. He would have won handily when he was the Republican nominee in a strongly Republican district in a strongly Republican election year. Before the election, though, the Justice Department approved the changes to the election rules. Greg later became a powerful legislator. Life can seem unfair, but then it may surprise.

During its first year, the court of appeals decided 535 cases, all with written opinions. Just over half the cases decided in 1995 were criminal appeals. Included were reviews of convictions for murder, assault, rape, driving under the influence, and most other crimes. The remainder of the appeals was an assortment of civil matters, such as appeals from decisions about benefits for injured workers, divorces and other domestic disputes, personal injury cases, and a few estates. Some of the appeals from the backlog we had been given were over four years old.

My dearest friend and most congenial colleague was Roger McMillin. We thought very similarly about issues, and I learned just how much I enjoyed legal discussions from the ones I had with him. He was about my

age, soft-spoken, so considerate of others, seeking peace among his colleagues. I thought him the best lawyer on the court, finding the true issue
often missed by the rest of us. In time, my friendship with Tom Coleman
became almost as close.

A delayed colleague was Jim Herring, the first judge to come to the
court by gubernatorial appointment. On January 31, 1997, just two years into
the life of the court, chief judge John Fraiser resigned. Jim was appointed
to replace him as a judge, but the new chief was Judge Bridges. Jim was
gracious and thoughtful. Several times, he and his wife Beverly had us all
to their Victorian home in Canton, north of Jackson. Had he stayed longer
on the court, he would likely have been named chief judge because of his
leadership skills and the other judges' great fondness for him.

In the strange workings of politics, the person who defeated Jim at
the 1998 election, Tyree Irving, also became a dear friend. Tyree is African
American and a former Democratic national committeeman, whose life
experiences and politics were perhaps further from my own than those
of any other member of the court. Jim Herring, on the other hand, was a
former Democrat who became a Republican and eventually chairman of
the Mississippi Republican Party.

When Tyree defeated Jim in 1998, I wrote Tyree a letter of welcome. It
explains my view of what those in elective office not only are required to
do but usually will want to do.

November 16, 1998

Dear Judge-Elect Irving:

Congratulations on your victory.

You and I will soon be working together, a result of your diligent efforts over
the last six months. You may not know anything of my background, but to
put it simply, we have traveled in different political circles. Despite that, I
have every hope and reason to expect that we will be congenial colleagues.

It is certainly true that Jim Herring is a friend of mine. Yet to have a friend
defeated and then to work well and collegially with the victor are parts of
political life. You wanted his position and went out and earned the right to
replace him. I honor you for that, congratulate you for your success, and
sincerely extend a welcome to the court.

Even before I was well settled in, a perceived opportunity to move up to the state supreme court appeared. Chief Justice Dan Lee was nearing the end of his second eight-year term. I wondered if he would run again. In the early spring of 1996, I asked to meet with him to discuss his plans. At that time, he believed he would seek another term. A second supreme court position would be on the ballot in the same central district for the court, held by Justice Fred Banks. I met with him too, and he said he would seek reelection. His judicial philosophy was different from mine, but he was an excellent judge. If he ran, I promised not to run against him.

The filing deadline for the court was May 10, 1996, a Friday. On Monday of that week, I called Chief Justice Lee to ask if he was still planning to run. He was and urged me to be patient. He tried to convince me that I had a good chance of being appointed in a few years, as he planned to resign midterm. I told him that I would run, and that I was sorry to be challenging him. The chief justice said that several people had called to say that they would not run if he did, but he felt obligated to let them know he was being challenged.

No one besides Lee had yet filed, but after our phone call, several did. Two people filed within hours of my conversation, a local state trial judge, Chet Dillard; and Bill Waller Jr., who was in private practice in Jackson. I filed on Thursday, May 9. On the last day, three more joined the race. They were county judge Gerald Hosemann from Vicksburg; a plaintiff's attorney from Philadelphia, Ed Williamson; and court of appeals judge Billy Bridges, of neighboring Brandon.

Bill Waller Jr. was clearly going to be formidable. He was in private law practice in Jackson with his father, former governor William Waller Sr. Winners of large-district judicial elections are those who at the end of the campaign are the best known, or, as it is said in politics, have the most name identification. Waller was starting ahead of where the rest of us could only hope to end.

There was uncertainty among my advisers about doing another walk. Something I did not mention to others as an alternative way to draw attention was to learn how to fly an ultralight aircraft, schedule events at which I would arrive in the plane, and land near whatever crowd had been drawn by the idea. The plan was a variation on Lyndon Johnson's 1948 U.S. Senate campaign, when he drew huge crowds who wanted to witness the novelty of a helicopter.[7] Eventually I decided that the ultralight plan was too dangerous to myself and others. Instead, I was back on foot along the highway. The first part of the walk was thirty-five miles through the

Mississippi Delta in the middle of the summer. The west-to-east route was 140 miles, from Vicksburg to the Welcome to Alabama sign. My one paid campaign worker was Scott Corlew. He was a law student, industrious, and the son of a good friend who would decline consideration for the Fifth Circuit in 1999.

Bill Waller led the ballot with 33 percent, while my court of appeals friend Billy Bridges was the other candidate in the runoff with 23 percent. I came in third, with 20 percent of the vote. Maybe I should have learned how to fly an ultralight. The morning after, I sent an e-mail to the judges and court staff. "I am alive and well, satisfied with my effort, impressed by Judge Bridges' effective campaign, and just glad that it is over." That was all quite true. Waller won the runoff easily.[8]

On the court of appeals, I participated in the decision of almost seven thousand cases. Every case was initially considered by a three-judge panel. A written opinion had to be produced by the panel and, once the panel agreed, circulated to all the other judges on the court. I often felt too little informed about a case that came from another panel, and spent much time familiarizing myself with some of them. I thought we should seek a rules change from the supreme court so that we could issue final decisions as three-judge panels, but the full court never agreed to make the request.

The serious work of being an appellate judge is reading briefs, conferring in three-judge panels on the cases, drafting opinions, and circulating them among the other judges on the panel and finally to the full court. From the beginning, I had indispensable help. My first hire was of a judicial assistant. Willie Rainer had worked for several years at a large Jackson law firm. Most recently she had been the secretary for my friend, Andy Taggart. I was extremely fortunate to have her.

At first, each judge had only one law clerk. There too I got lucky. A December graduate of the University of Mississippi Law School, Whit McKinley, had a clerkship starting in August with a justice of the state supreme court. He was available until then. With their help, I wrote more opinions for the court than any other judge that year. I just barely bested James Thomas, who wrote one fewer. In eight of my first ten years on the court, ended by an eighteen-month leave of absence, I was able to lead the group. I hope quality did not suffer.

I told myself from the beginning of my service that one way to measure my fairness is to reflect occasionally on recent decisions and determine how often I ruled in a way that was contrary to what might be my preconceptions. The question was on my mind when I read the first opinion my good friend Jim Herring wrote after being appointed. If ever there was a situation in which I just wanted to express approval, it was with a new colleague and good friend's first new opinion.

The case was a high-profile prosecution on the Mississippi Gulf Coast. Melissa and Shannon Garrison, along with Shannon's boyfriend, were accused of smothering the mother of the two girls one night in her bed. The reason was that the mother was trying to stop the older girl's overnight stays with the boyfriend. Shannon was seventeen at the time of the murder. She confessed and implicated both her boyfriend and her sixteen-year-old sister, Melissa, for having helped her plot and carry out the murder. The appeal we heard in 1997 was by the younger sister, Melissa. The first three times she had been tried, the jury could not reach a verdict. News accounts I read of the trials indicated that she was dressed to look as young as possible, and as cute, with pigtails as one feature of her appearance. A number of reasons made it difficult to convict her.

At the fourth trial, the prosecutor for the first time offered a transcription of Shannon's statement when she pleaded guilty. The jury returned a guilty verdict, and Melissa was sentenced to life in prison. I believed Shannon's statement was self-serving and was inadmissible under hearsay rules. After a couple of discussions with my friend and brand-new colleague, Jim Herring, we remained in disagreement. I was overly dramatic when I started my dissent this way:

> The purpose of criminal trials is to permit the jury to reach the truth, as imperfectly as humans are capable of knowing truth. Evidentiary rules have been established to define the evidence that can properly be presented to a jury, and that which cannot. Some of those rules are of rather modern origin, but some have been of such long standing as to be set out in our constitution. One of the most fundamental rules is the right of confrontation protected by the Sixth Amendment. Because I believe Melissa Garrison's right to confront the witnesses against her was violated, I respectfully dissent.

This controversial murder case was just the kind that elected judges least wanted to write to reverse. Still, Roger McMillin and Tom Coleman joined my dissent. The Mississippi Supreme Court unanimously reversed our court, agreeing that Shannon's statements were inadmissible.[9]

What often intrigued me were intricate legal issues regardless of the factual settings. For example, questions arose about how federal regulation of grade crossings affected the liability of a railroad for a collision between one of its trains and an automobile. We held that the federal approval of a minimal warning—a simple crossbuck sign—at that particular crossing foreclosed claims that a better warning was needed, but certain other claims about how difficult the train was to see at night were not foreclosed.[10] In another case, I dealt with unsettled issues about the liability of a grocery store owner for failing to prevent a mentally ill patron from attacking another patron; the outcome partly depended on the meaning of a confusingly written state statute that had been a compromise between business interests and plaintiffs' lawyers.[11] I also wrote an opinion in a slander case that on further review by the supreme court was reissued as that court's opinion.[12] That was the first time such an adoption occurred.

With likely unappreciated boldness, I suggested in a concurring opinion that the state supreme court was not abiding by the constitution's limits on its authority. I recognized much more of a role for the legislature in establishing rules that litigants had to follow than did the supreme court.[13] I was sufficiently concerned about the separation of the powers of the three branches of state government that I wrote two overly lengthy law journal articles on the question.[14]

◆ ◆ ◆

On April 9, 1996, my second year on the state court, U.S. Supreme Court justice Antonin Scalia spoke in Jackson at an event sponsored by the Christian Legal Society at Mississippi College School of Law. He made national news with his remarks. As the Jackson newspaper put it the next day, he "delivered a message of faith rather than law" to seven hundred people at the First Baptist Church for a breakfast gathering.[15] I was one of those in attendance.

Scalia said that those who believe themselves sophisticated often reject religion owing to their faith in science or reason. "We must pray for the courage to endure the scorn of the sophisticated world" and, like St. Paul, be "fools for Christ's sake." He encouraged the audience by saying it is possible to "be sophisticated and believe in God."[16]

He mentioned a story from 1992 about a Catholic priest in Lake Ridge, Virginia, near Washington. I was living in the area at the time and had seen the news reports. Father James Bruse at St. Elizabeth Ann Seton Church was the center of stories that drew the faithful and the skeptics alike to him. A statue of the Virgin Mary at Father Bruse's church seemingly shed tears when he was near it. The priest also said he was experiencing the five wounds of Christ, which are called the stigmata. His hands, feet, and side bled as had Christ's when he was crucified.

Even Christians can have difficulties with such stories. Among the skeptics was a *Washington Post* reporter. The reporter witnessed the weeping statue. He looked closely at the statue and saw water forming at the corner of one eye. He saw no wires, no "battery-operated tear ducts." After going over what he saw and the lack of a rational explanation, the reporter wrote: "Proof positive you can be seeing and still not believe you're seeing it."[17]

Scalia was saddened by the reporter's rejection. Faced with something so real and so inexplicable, a person too much of, in, and for this world will choose not to believe. Scalia said he believed in miracles. He described the *Washington Post* story on the weeping statue as "strangely ambivalent," and he thought that if the reporters could not explain the phenomenon, why were they not "absolute converts"? The so-called worldly wise reject faith, from miracles such as this to the more fundamental elements of Christianity such as Easter and the ascension of Christ into heaven.[18]

> A general belief in God is one thing, . . . [but] it is quite another matter to embrace the miracles of the Virgin birth of Christ, His raising the dead and His own ascension from the grave. Yet it is "irrational" to reject miracles a priori. One can be sophisticated and believe in God. Reason and intellect are not to be laid aside where matters of religion are concerned. What is irrational to reject [is] . . . the possibility of miracles and the Resurrection of Jesus Christ, which is precisely what the worldly wise do.[19]

His speech was so memorable partly due to his using the word *cretin*. The word generally means someone with marked mental deficiencies. Scalia said the word was derived from a term used in eighteenth-century French to refer derisively to Christians as feebleminded. "To be honest about it, that is the view of Christians taken by modern society. Surely those who adhere to all or most of these traditional Christian beliefs are to be regarded as simple-minded."[20]

Scalia's point about the ridicule faced by Christians was powerfully made. Scalia himself was scorned. In a front-page story the next morning, the *Washington Post* said that his comments were "revealing and out of the ordinary, even for arguably the court's frankest, most publicly confrontational justice." A *Post* editorial cartoon depicted him as a simpleton, reading his Bible on the bench and fuming about his "worldly wise guy" colleagues. I felt sorrow for the cartoonist. Scalia is courageous. The secular world felt that a belief in God was for Sundays, and increasingly not at all. Faith surely was not for Supreme Court justices to be embracing so provocatively.

In Jackson, Scalia got a standing ovation. He also soon got a letter from me. I wrote that his remarks about facing ridicule reminded me of the phrase "muscular Christianity," which believers in this world need. "This to me demands meekness in promoting self-interest, but courage in standing for Christianity in all the varying ways that daily arise. As you beautifully discussed, the muscle is often needed just to brave the silent ridicule of sophisticates, 'good people' in most senses." I also wrote that his comments about Father Bruse caused me to take the clippings I still had of the *Washington Post* and the *Washington Times* articles into the office to show my law clerk who had heard the speech. The *Washington Times* had not been skeptical and detailed without condescension some history of the stigmata. Its wonderful title was "Do You Believe in Miracles?"[21]

Justice Scalia wrote back to thank me for my comments and to ask for copies of the articles. He said a *Washington Post* columnist had questioned his recollection of the disbelief his paper's reporter had shown. I gladly obliged.

My personal faith may reflect significant cretinous tendencies. I pray so. One of my earliest childhood memories comes from when I was four or five, visiting the Hobby Haven store a few weeks before Christmas in nearby McAllen, Texas. I saw on a shelf a plastic rifle with a scope, the kind of weapon a cowboy would need to shoot the desperadoes he encounters. My mother did not want to buy it. For some reason, though, the plastic rifle was essential to me.

Every night over the remaining weeks until Christmas, with a child's view of what is proper to pray for, I silently asked in the privacy of my bedroom for that toy rifle for Christmas. A few days before the day, the whole family flew to Grandma Southwick's house, over a thousand miles away in Iowa. The morning arrived, a white Christmas. Going downstairs for breakfast, none of us was allowed into the study where the fireplace, the tree, and the presents awaited. After breakfast, a quick breakfast, the time came.

I entered, looked under the tree, saw no package that was the right shape, and was disappointed. Then I looked at the fireplace. Leaning against it, unwrapped, was the toy I had prayed for. No one claimed to have bought it for me. It was the only unwrapped gift. Of course there was no gift tag. Why would there be? I knew who had sent it. It was the secret between me and the one who heard my prayer.

This boyhood experience provides a helpful lens through which my reaction to many later experiences can be viewed. I am convinced that God is real, that he is willing to intervene in our lives at times and in ways that do not always meet our expectations or our desires. How he intervenes is usually through the actions of others, but not always.

I accept that outright miracles occur. It is consistent with my view of reality that my 1950s Christmas gift could have been received in the very way that I believed at the time. God heard the request, placed the order himself, and without human interaction caused the delivery to be made. I am uncomfortable admitting that, but I want to explain in the best available way that my faith does accept that very little things not only can, but do, occur in extraordinary ways.

Yet with maturity or worldliness or, worst of all, unbelief intruding, I confess that there are rational explanations for what occurred. That the gift was unwrapped and untagged would mean that something happened besides my request in the store, and my mother's going back later to buy the object of my clear desire. She or someone in the family may themselves have heard the prayer one night and decided to create this belief in my mind. I remember a conviction that no one could have known that I was praying for the rifle. I could have been wrong. As an adult, I asked my mother and my sister whether they had any recollection of the Christmas gift. Neither admitted any.

However the unwrapped gift came to be leaning on the fireplace, my receiving it was a faith experience. I feel certain that God heard my words and acted on them, perhaps through the rational way I suggested, or perhaps not. But this fervent prayer was heard by God.

Some will inevitably compare my account to the comical absurdities of the movie *A Christmas Story* from 1983, when nine-year-old Ralphie had to have a Red Ryder BB gun. There are embarrassing similarities. Fans of older movies may see the manner in which I reflect on this story from my childhood as a troubling allusion to Orson Welles's 1941 movie *Citizen Kane.* In the main character's dotage, a snow sled from his youth becomes the one thing the rich man treasures. The comparison may even be apt to the extent that my gift represents an innocence unsullied by the complications of adulthood.

Once I decided to write about the gift, I tried to identify the object of my long-ago desires. It may have been the Lone Ranger Click Rifle, with, as the box excitedly announced, a "TELESCOPIC sight." Internet searches are amazing, if inconclusive. God knows, of course.

Many would say that if there is a God, surely toy guns are not among his gifts. I fear trivializing God's role in my life by using this child's example of faith. If I am willing to believe *that* was God's interaction, the rest of what I write must be childish, too. I take the risk of that reaction because I try to maintain a childlike faith in God.

5

Clinton's Fifth Circuit Choices

Controversies about circuit judge nominations used to be extremely rare if not quite nonexistent. The first circuit court judge positions were created in 1869. The first nomination to the Fifth Circuit not to be approved was made in 1881, the second in 1943, and the third in 1979. Then, what had been gaps of multiple decades between defeats became much shorter. A Reagan nominee failed in 1987, then a Bush nominee never got a vote in 1992. After the failure of only five nominees in the first 125 years of the Fifth Circuit, five more would be blocked in the next 15 years. President Bill Clinton had three of his nominees stopped. George W. Bush had two, while two others had to overcome filibusters. This book's appendix gives more details on this history.

These recurring frustrations increased the resentments in both political parties. To appreciate the environment in which I found myself when seeking a nomination from President George W. Bush, the experiences of President Clinton's Fifth Circuit nominees are instructive.

Clinton took office on January 20, 1993. Three months later, Texas senator Bob Krueger, recently appointed by governor Anne Richards to succeed new secretary of the treasury Lloyd Bentsen, recommended four Texans to President Clinton for the four vacancies. They were U.S. district judges Robert Parker of Tyler and George Kazen of Laredo, Texas Court of Criminal Appeals judge Morris Overstreet (the first African American to be elected to statewide office in Texas), and Corpus Christi lawyer Jorge Rangel.

Rangel told me in 2009 that President Clinton offered to nominate him in 1993. The problem was Rangel's service as the Fifth Circuit representative on the ABA Committee that investigated and rated nominees.

Committee members pledged not to accept a judicial nomination until being off the committee for a year. The rule did not restrict the president, of course. Rangel was the one with an obligation. He resigned from the ABA Committee on April 27, 1993. At some point the White House requested a waiver of the one-year rule, but the ABA responded it likely would not give one. On August 20, Rangel sent a letter to President Clinton. He explained the hurdles presented by the ABA and that he was unwilling to proceed. Thanking the president, he withdrew.[1]

The importance of Senator Krueger's recommendations for the Fifth Circuit lessened after he lost in a special election in June to Republican Kay Bailey Hutchison. By September, news reports said that President Clinton had asked for a background check on former Texas Court of Criminal Appeals judge Pete Benavides. Clinton and Benavides had become friends during the 1992 campaign. A "Democrat source" said that Clinton himself identified Pete as a possible appointment. "The President is very fond of him."[2] Those who know Pete usually are.

Leaders in both Louisiana and Mississippi were also trying to get at least one seat. The White House reportedly considered two Mississippians. One was Supreme Court Justice Fred Banks. He had been NAACP counsel in the state, then was a trial judge before beginning his service as the second African American on the state Supreme Court in 1991. Another possibility was the acting dean of the University of Mississippi Law School, Carolyn Ellis Staton. Louisiana Democratic senators Bennett Johnston and John Breaux recommended state court of appeals judge Carl Stewart, who had been on that court since 1991. He would be the second African American Fifth Circuit judge and the first since the Fifth Circuit split in 1981. Justice James L. Dennis, who had served on Louisiana's supreme court since 1976, was also recommended.[3]

On January 27, 1994, President Clinton made three nominations: Pete Benavides and Robert Parker of Texas, and Carl Stewart of Louisiana. The Clark seat remained without a nominee until Jim Dennis was nominated on June 8, 1994. Judges Benavides and Stewart were confirmed on May 6, 1994, and Judge Parker was confirmed on June 15. Dennis was not confirmed in 1994. In the November elections, the Republicans gained a Senate majority.

On January 31, 1995, the president nominated Dennis again. In May, Senators Cochran and Lott sent a letter to Judiciary Committee chairman Orrin Hatch, complaining that Dennis had been named to a Mississippi seat. They also said Dennis wrote opinions that are "unresponsive to the crime problems from which our communities are suffering." Senator Breaux met in June with both Mississippi senators to get them to relent. They would not.[4]

On July 20, 1995, despite the Mississippi objections, the committee unanimously reported Dennis favorably to the full Senate. Three days later, the *New Orleans Times-Picayune* published an article suggesting that Justice Dennis should have recused himself in a recent appeal. On September 28, Mississippi senator Cochran moved to send the nomination back to the committee to examine the recusal issue. In the ensuing debate, both Mississippi senators spoke on the recusal matter and also insisted the seat was for someone from their state. The two Louisiana senators spoke in favor of confirmation. Chairman Hatch said the recusal question was insignificant, that the committee had already examined it, and that Dennis should be confirmed. But "if the motion to recommit is granted, that is going to be it for Justice Dennis." The motion to recommit failed on a 46–54 vote. Dennis was then confirmed unanimously. Senator Hatch urged President Clinton to nominate a Mississippian for the next Louisiana vacancy on the Fifth Circuit.[5]

Three more vacancies arose in the Fifth Circuit during Clinton's second term. The first was due to the January 23, 1997, retirement of Will Garwood of Austin. Jorge Rangel was nominated on July 24, 1997. Texas senator Phil Gramm allegedly believed Rangel, as the Fifth Circuit representative on the ABA committee that evaluated judicial nominees, had been critical of some of Gramm's recommendations to the first President Bush. Gramm met with Rangel and said he was concerned because Rangel had never served as an appellate judge. Had he been nominated for a U.S. District Court, Senator Gramm indicated he was far more likely to support him.[6]

Judiciary Committee chairman Hatch was following the practice of allowing the senators from a nominee's home state to veto the selection. Unless those senators returned a "blue slip" on the nominee, a hearing would not take place.[7] Senators Gramm and Kay Bailey Hutchinson did not return their blue slips on Rangel. Democrats sharply criticized the practice of a home-state-senator veto. The practice was a constant no matter who was in power, though. It was again a controversy in the last two years of the George W. Bush presidency, but the two political parties' roles were reversed.

In September 1997, two months after his nomination, Rangel met with Senator Gramm's committee that advised Gramm on judicial prospects.

The impasse remained. In May 1998, each senator met with Rangel at his request. Still, the senators never gave their approval for a hearing. The day after Congress adjourned on October 21, 1998, Rangel wrote to President Clinton, indicating that he wished to withdraw. Rangel said there was "a season for everything, and the time has come for my family to get on with our lives and for me to get on with my work."[8]

President Clinton next nominated Enrique Moreno of El Paso. His name was sent to the Senate on September 16, 1999. Moreno was the youngest of three children born in 1955 to a steelworker in a plant in Chihuahua City, Mexico. The family moved to El Paso when Enrique was still an infant. There his father worked as a carpenter and his mother as a seamstress. He attended Harvard as an undergraduate and law student, then returned to El Paso. He was a solo practitioner for much of his career and won some particularly notable jury verdicts on behalf of injured plaintiffs.

Moreno received a unanimous well-qualified rating from the ABA. He also appeared before the same advisory panel with whom Rangel had met. In a statement submitted to a Judiciary Committee hearing conducted by Democratic senator Leahy in 2002, Moreno said, "I was later advised that of the thirty-one members of this advisory group, ten members recommended against my confirmation, five recommended in favor of my confirmation," and the other sixteen did not vote. *Texas Monthly* reported that Senator Hutchison said some members of the panel found Moreno too vague in his answers. The author of the article believed that to be an obvious pretext.[9]

As a result of the vote by the panel, Senators Gramm and Hutchinson wrote Moreno on May 5, 2000, saying they could not support him. Senator Gramm said that he considered Moreno "a fine man and a good lawyer." The committee, though, had found Moreno not to be experienced enough "to be fully engaged and effective on a court one notch below the United States Supreme Court." Gramm was open to considering him for a trial judgeship, but not for the appellate court.[10]

The final nominee to the Fifth Circuit by President Clinton was to fill the vacancy caused by the retirement of John M. Duhé Jr. of Louisiana, on April 7, 1999. On April 22, 1999, President Clinton nominated Baton Rouge lawyer H. Alston Johnson III. He was managing partner in the Baton Rouge office of Phelps Dunbar, a large regional law firm. Clinton and Johnson had met as high school students in 1963, when they were both delegates to Boys' Nation in Washington, the event at which a well-known photograph was taken of the teenage Clinton with President Kennedy. They continued their friendship when they were both undergraduates at Georgetown University.[11]

Johnson became one of several circuit court nominees waiting for a hearing. Reading about this period reminds me of the experience two presidential terms later, when George W. Bush's circuit court nominees as a group, spread across the country, kept wondering who would be given the next ticket for a hearing. There were not many tickets. A critical problem for Johnson was that his nomination became tied to the prospects of a Mississippi candidate promoted by Senate majority leader Trent Lott for the final vacancy on the Fifth Circuit.

That final vacant seat was that of Henry Politz of Shreveport. He wrote President Clinton on February 10, 1999, that he would retire exactly six months later. This vacancy and the one for which Alston Johnson was nominated were the first Louisiana openings on the Fifth Circuit since Mississippi lost the Charles Clark seat to Louisiana in 1995. Senator Hatch, as chairman of judiciary, had insisted in 1995 that Mississippi later get recompense. Now it was time.

I did not learn of Politz's plans until seeing an article in a legal newspaper in mid-May.[12] The Politz vacancy is the one for which I would be nominated in 2007. My Judiciary Committee hearing was only a few days short of eight years after I saw the news story. *Eight years.* They were years in which I serially pursued nomination, fell short, dealt with the disappointment, later had hopes revived, and started over. I should have learned not to be anxious about tomorrow.

Because of my well-known past activities as a Republican, I did not ask the senators to recommend me. On June 25, 1999, I wrote Senator Cochran: "My interest remains strong regarding that court. Nonetheless, I believe this is not the time. Instead, I would like to give a vote of confidence to two other people." I first encouraged him to consider Mike Wallace, "a man of exceptional legal ability." Mike was a more prominent Republican than I was, but I thought he would want to try. I then described court of appeals judge Roger McMillin. "I have never failed to be impressed by his ability, fairness, and hard work." The state "court's loss would be offset by his gaining a larger stage on which he could make his exceptional contributions as a judge."

The senators were looking elsewhere, however. They agreed that an excellent lawyer from the Gulf Coast, Bob Galloway, should be nominated to the Politz vacancy. The senators chose well. For this book, Bob generously provided me a summary of his experience. I drew on a few other sources, as well, including a conversation with Senator Lott.[13]

At some stage, likely not long after Judge Politz wrote President Clinton, Senator Lott began pursuing the vacancy for our state.[14] Senator Lott much later told me that the first three Mississippi lawyers he asked all declined. These were University of Mississippi Law School professor Guthrie Abbott, Jackson lawyer John Corlew, and Pascagoula lawyer Roy Williams.

In the spring of 1999, while in a deposition, Bob Galloway received a call "out of the blue" from Senator Lott. Lott said Galloway was his choice for a Fifth Circuit vacancy. Galloway accepted. They had been fraternity brothers at Ole Miss, with Lott a year ahead of Galloway. They were not particularly close, and Galloway was not an identified Republican. Considering what Lott was trying to accomplish—to get a Democratic president to nominate Lott's choice for so important a court—the respect and the distance between Lott and Galloway were both advantageous. Galloway does not recall ever talking to Senator Cochran or his staff. Majority Leader Lott had the helm.

Galloway's nomination depended on Senator Lott's skills as a deal maker. The deal Lott was structuring was to allow a vote for a Louisiana nominee in exchange for Mississippi getting a new judge, too. Lott's plan was to persuade President Clinton to nominate Galloway, and in return Lott would allow confirmation of Clinton's great friend Alston Johnson. Nominated in April 1999, Johnson was still waiting for a hearing.

On July 7, 1999, Galloway received a call from Mark Childress. He was a senior White House counsel responsible for identifying, investigating, and gaining Senate approval of presidential nominees. Childress acknowledged that Galloway's nomination would require a Louisiana-Mississippi package deal, but President Clinton had not yet indicated whether he would agree. An associate White House counsel, Sarah Wilson, would immediately send Galloway the paperwork that needed to be completed. Coincidentally, I knew Wilson from the time we were both in the Civil Division. Fittingly for my book's focus, Clinton nominated her for a judgeship on January 3, 2001, then, on the day before he left office on January 20, gave her a recess appointment.[15]

In August, Galloway was interviewed in Washington by Wilson and two or three other lawyers. Back in Mississippi, he filled out the forms he was given. He was told to send them to Wilson, unsigned. Galloway did so in September. Toward the end of that month, Childress called to say that the president wanted to "go forward with the next step of the process." Wilson then called, requesting updated and signed forms to be sent immediately. She also said the president was asking the American Bar Association to conduct its investigation. On October 18, 1999, Harry Hardin for the ABA interviewed Galloway. No final report was ever issued because Galloway was never nominated. Not long after the interviews, Galloway understood from Hardin that the ABA evaluation would not create any problem for his nomination.

Everything was in place for Galloway's nomination to be made and linked to Johnson's, but Galloway heard only silence. One of the reasons might have been that the organization to which many black Mississippi lawyers belonged, the Magnolia Bar Association, opposed Galloway. A "dear friend" letter was sent on Magnolia Bar letterhead, dated March 9, 2000, but unsigned, opposing Galloway.[16] "President Clinton is considering nominating Robert Galloway" for the Fifth Circuit. It then starkly noted, "Galloway is a white male." Mississippi, which has the "largest population of African-Americans in the country, has no African-Americans on the [Fifth Circuit] bench." Nothing negative about Galloway as a person or lawyer was stated.

In May 2000, a New Orleans newspaper reported that Galloway might be nominated if Lott agreed to the confirmation of four Democratic nominees. Senator Breaux was trying to meet with President Clinton to tell him that Johnson would never be confirmed on those terms. Because Galloway was not Lott's first choice, Breaux saw little incentive for Lott to make that trade.[17]

The impasse was never broken. Bob Galloway never got a nomination, and neither Alston Johnson nor Enrique Moreno ever got a hearing or confirmation. The coda to Galloway's experience occurred after George W. Bush's election. Galloway spoke to Lott's chief of staff Gottshall to say he remained interested. Galloway realized, and remembered Gottshall saying as much, that there now was less need for someone with few Republican ties. Considering the controversies ahead, that opinion may have been shortsighted.

All of Clinton's four Fifth Circuit nominations were confirmed in his first term, but none were in the second. Among the others from around the country who were nominated but waited in vain for a hearing was Elena Kagan, nominated on June 17, 1999, for the D.C. Circuit. Like John Roberts in 1992, she was not confirmed, had the two terms of the next president intervene, and then, when her party was back in power, was selected for the Supreme Court.[18]

Each political party uses statistics to explain how the other party's obstruction of judges is worse than its own. It is fair to compare what occurred in the Senate during the last two years of three recent presidents' service, when the party opposing the president had a majority. During 1991–92, the last two years of the first Bush presidency, 31 circuit court nominations were submitted, and 20 were confirmed. That is 65 percent. In 1999–2000, President Clinton's last two years, only 15 of 34 circuit nominations were confirmed, or 44 percent. Then, in 2007–8, President Bush submitted 23 circuit court nominations; 10 were confirmed, or 43 percent. Among the 23 were three nominations that were withdrawn and three new ones offered.

In 2002, with a Democrat-controlled Senate, a hearing was held titled "Setting the Record Straight" about nominations.[19] Both Rangel and Moreno testified. Testimony about Republican nominees who experienced similar frustrations was also given. What was set straight was that the two parties act very similarly. When the political party in opposition to the president has control of the Senate during the two years leading up to the next presidential election, the Senate gets the slows. And perhaps each new Senate is a little slower than the previous one.

6

A Hesitant Application

Several judicial nominees of the next president, George W. Bush, encountered more than the usual resistance. To designate one of them as having the most contentious struggle would be too bold. It is safe, though, to identify Charles Pickering's nomination to the Fifth Circuit as a clear finalist for that designation. Pickering was nominated for the Henry Politz seat, the one for which Bob Galloway had been considered, the one to which I would be nominated in 2007.

At the beginning of the four-year Pickering battle, I was on the outside, trying to break into the discussion. I did not know when I began that the initial discussion was all but over. As the postelection struggle continued in Florida over who had carried the state and would become the next president, I was in frequent conversations with my best friend on the state court, chief judge Roger McMillin. On December 12, 2000, the Supreme Court ruled in favor of Bush.

On December 13, Roger e-mailed me: "My most gut-wrenching question, which I dread asking and which can permissibly be answered by 'None of your business,' is this: What does this apparent Bush victory do to the makeup of this Court?" I replied:

> You have touched on a matter of great delicacy and even uncertainty. Should I pursue a federal judgeship, considering that it might leave you with no strong comrade in arms? It is my present inclination to do so, with the concern that integrity—do the right thing, good of all over interests of self, all that which we aspire to do but often fall short—suggests that I stay.
>
> Your ally, friend, and fellow-traveler on the road,
> LeS[1]

The next day, Roger sent me word that Senator Cochran was scheduled to speak at the dedication in Oxford of the portrait of a federal judge
who was retiring. I replied by e-mail: "With all the other people who will
be in line to talk to Thad about various things, I was reluctant. Still, it probably is best for me to go. Whenever I get into the supplicant mode, I am
reminded of the Janis Joplin line in a song—'Oh Lord, won't you buy me a
Mercedes-Benz?' It is not a happy reminder."[2]

I went to the dedication, but Senator Cochran had canceled. So instead
of talking to him in person, and instead of telephoning him, on December
18 I wrote him a letter.

> This is a job application. A new Republican administration must bring you a
> swarm of them. Here is mine.
>
> I would like to be considered for a Fifth Circuit vacancy when the new
> President Bush evaluates the appointment. In my 1999 letter about Roger
> McMillin and Mike Wallace, I restated my interest in a Fifth Circuit judge-
> ship but said that then was not the proper time.
>
> I would appreciate hearing from you if you have an opportunity to
> discuss this.

Because I did not hear back, I finally called on January 10. It was way
too late. My passivity was the problem, as my notes reveal.

> Called Doris Wagley in Sen. Cochran's office. I said that I wanted to be sure
> that Senator Cochran got my letter about the Fifth Circuit and to find out
> if there would be any reason to go up and see him. She said that [someone]
> would get back to me. She said to be careful what I ask for, I might get it.
> Sounds good to me.
>
> Thad called. He did not know of my interest and may not have seen
> the letter. Charles Pickering will be recommended to President Bush. Thad
> and Trent have already discussed it, and that was their decision. Trent did
> not mention my name during the discussion, though there were some other
> names. He encouraged me to call Trent.
>
> Thad generously said he and Trent may have "jumped the gun," and
> made a choice prematurely. I asked for his favorable consideration if there
> is another opportunity, and he said that he would be sure I am considered
> should there be a new look at the selection.

In less than a month, it became clear that not being included on the
senators' list was near fatal to my being considered by the White House.

I did not consider the issue finished, as the president had not yet agreed. Bush was not even president yet. I persisted, but the Senate majority leader considered the matter settled. Later on the same day as my call to Thad, I tried to reach Trent. I was only able to talk to a friend of mine on his staff, Chip Reynolds, and told him of my interest in the Fifth Circuit.

A friend from the first President Bush's Justice Department, Tim Flanigan, one of the 1991 interviewers, was now the deputy White House counsel. I called him on January 31, congratulated him, and asked for any candid suggestion on what I should do. He told me that main thing was to shore up the senators. "Not absolute, but sure helps." I told him I would try to go see them. Tim responded, "Call him when I come up, and he will try to see me."

Though I felt some progress was being made, I learned otherwise when I saw the next day's local paper. The headline on the front page blared: "Pickering Pick for Fifth Circuit."[3] The story concerned the recommendation of the two senators to the president, not his nomination by the president. With their choice being made public, though, it greatly increased the difficulty for me to change the direction now set in motion. It was a positive story about him, with no criticisms. One of the founders of an interracial Christian organization, Dolphus Weary, called Pickering a man with a "caring heart." A prominent black attorney from a small town south of Jackson, Carroll Rhodes, said that Pickering "understands that there have been differences in the past and that there needs to be reconciliation—that's good for the federal judiciary."

Despite the poor prospects, I still had a trip scheduled to meet with the Mississippi senators, people I knew at the White House, and some others. My friends John and Julie Hamre agreed to put me up for a few nights. John had been one of the other college students at Mount Rushmore when I worked there in 1969 and 1970. He is one of the most intelligent, articulate, and godly men I know. He was the best man at Sharon's and my wedding. John worked on Senate committee staffs and was the deputy secretary of defense during President Clinton's second term. He now heads one of best-known think tanks on international affairs, the Center for Strategic and International Studies.

In Washington, my first meeting was on February 12 with Tim Flanigan.

11:00 a.m. Tim said that the key was Trent Lott. Mentioned that they wanted names, and an appellate judge did not even need to be on a senator's list, but at least when it came to Trent Lott's prerogatives [as senate majority leader] they would not try to override him. He did not want to be pessimistic, but I needed to get Trent to move favorably.

Lanny Griffith. 2:00 p.m. Talked over situation, especially problem with Trent. Explained that Thad essentially told me the process was over before I called, not only for the Fifth Circuit but also for a district judge vacancy that I did not even know existed. Lanny did not have any advice. Need to figure out if there is anything that he can do.

Thad Cochran. 3:00 p.m. [Cochran aide] Brad Prewitt participated. Thad and the other Republican senators had just been given at noon a letter from [White House counsel] Al Gonzales that the president wanted "input" on appellate judges and three names on district judges. Thad mentioned that he and President GHW Bush had a similar conversation years ago. [Thad disagreed with both presidential efforts to diminish senatorial influence.] Thad said he had gone to meeting with Trent (pre-Christmas?) with my name and some others written down that should be considered. Trent had no reaction to my name, but said that he wanted Pickering.

Thad said that if Judge Pickering were not nominated, I would be his next choice. Brad suggested some people I should meet, and Thad told him to take me around. That afternoon and the next day, I met people who could be helpful. I had not known any of them. I got in to see Senator Lott's chief of staff Billy Gottshall for a brief meeting. I also met with a few staff members for other senators, and some members of outside groups. One of the meetings was with Leonard Leo of the Federalist Society. I went by myself to meet him and Shara Haden, who worked with him. "Leo thought the White House was making selections right now on whom to interview. The process is moving quickly."

"February 14, 2001. [Karl Rove deputy] Chris Henick. 11:00. Went to Old Executive Office Building." We met in his office for a while, then Chris took me across the street to White House to make the rounds. "I met Karl Rove, to whom I mentioned the interest in the judgeship and that the senators had recommended someone else. Then went by White House Counsel's office, and checked on Gonzales. But he was in a closed-door meeting."

No clear answers from my visit, but I had useful meetings and was tremendously encouraged. Once I was back in Jackson, the results of my efforts began to appear.

February 21. Chris Henick called. Had just left judicial selection meeting, involving the Attorney General, associate White House counsels, and Karl

Rove plus others. I said that Thad had indicated a willingness to accept me if Pickering was not nominated. Chris asked in the meeting that [scheduling an interview with me be delayed] for 24 hours until he has had a chance to talk to Thad at least. But the idea is that I would go up next week and interview with the counsel's office. Perhaps what Thad says could change that. Chris thought my seeing Rove last week was very important, as he was a real advocate for me today.

February 23, 2001. Chris Henick called. I told him I felt like the defendant and he was the jury about to announce the verdict. Chris was not able to reach Thad, but talked to Mark Keenum. Mark then talked to Thad. The senator fully backs Judge Pickering, but if the White House ends up objecting, Thad has a different candidate. Mark was not sure about the name, he said, "Les . . . ," and Chris chimed in, "Leslie Southwick?" "Yes, that's the guy," said Mark. At Wednesday's meeting [of the judicial selection group], Nick Calio, Assistant to the President for Legislative Affairs, and Jack Howard, [a former Lott aide and] Deputy Director of the White House Office of Legislative Affairs, said Trent really needs to be told before I go up. That will be done Monday.

Noel Francisco is the associate counsel who is looking at the Fifth Circuit. He or someone else had already done some work on me, looked at some of my writings. Noel will call to extend the invitation. I thought the only thing that could change that is if Trent made it clear that any nomination of me would be useless. Chris indicated that when the [judicial selection] meeting ended Wednesday, I was to be invited up for an interview. No one else was under consideration. Again he said that if my goal of going up there last week was to get into the mix, I had exceeded my goal.

After three encouraging weeks, reality set in. "March 2, 2001. Chris Henick called. He said Nick Calio thought it would be crazy to name anyone except Pickering. It sounds as if no one ever talked to Lott. When there are meetings with judicial selection, my name always comes up. Still looks as if I would be interviewed and not just a courtesy. Chris mentioned that if not for now, then maybe later. Most pessimistic yet."

"March 3, 2001. Sent fax to Chris and Tim on whether it will be damaging overall to name me, and if that is the decision I can accept it. Not a surrender, just a reflection." I also copied onto the notes for this day this passage from *Julius Caesar*, act IV, scene iii: "There is a tide in the affairs of men / Which, taken at the flood, leads on to fortune, / Omitted, all the voyage of their life / is bound in shallows and miseries." I felt the tide was missing me.

Occasionally—well, more than occasionally—I would write down passages like this: "March 16 (Friday). Nothing. Silence. Zip. Chris, Tim, Noel, senators." I will not repeat other versions, but they reflected my anxieties about having the process silently move beyond me. The end to the silence finally came. "April 4, 2001. Noel Francisco. 3:58 p.m. Apologized for the long delay in calling. I said that no apology was needed, as I expect what I am told was largely out of his hands. 'To a certain extent, that is true.' He said that due to forces that we knew were there all along, it was decided to go a different direction. I thanked him for letting me know."

On May 9, President Bush held a ceremony in the East Room of the White House to announce his first eleven circuit judge nominees. They stood alongside him on risers in three rows. For most of this president's two terms, many of his nominees would not be received in the Senate with enthusiasm. Perhaps some of the nominees in the East Room already had their anxieties.[4]

Two of those who would have the most difficulty were on the front row—Miguel Estrada for the D.C. Circuit, and Priscilla Owen for the Fifth Circuit. Another Fifth Circuit nominee, Joy Clement, was on the second row, but her journey would be comparatively painless. Future chief justice John Roberts was also on the second row, nominated for the D.C. Circuit nine years after the first President Bush had done the same.

Of the East Room eleven, only the two who had first been nominated as federal judges by President Clinton were confirmed by October. Joy Clement of New Orleans was the only other one approved before the year ended. Of the other eight, two were confirmed by that Congress, which ended in November 2002. Three were finally confirmed in 2003, including John Roberts. The ninth and last of the group to be confirmed was Priscilla Owen in May 2005, four years after the East Room ceremony. The remaining two withdrew, one in 2003 and the other in 2006.

The risk that nominees would face such long delays began when the 2000 elections created a Senate evenly divided between Republican and Democratic senators. As president of the Senate, vice president Dick Cheney was able to cast his vote to break the tie. Republicans were thus able to organize the Senate and have GOP senators as committee chairman. The 50–50 split ended on May 24 when Vermont GOP senator Jim Jeffords announced he was becoming an independent and would align with the Democrats on organizing the Senate.[5] Instead of Republican Orrin Hatch as chairman, Jeffords's Vermont colleague, Democrat Pat

Leahy, would be chairman. Judicial confirmations became incredibly more difficult. For some, they just became impossible.

Judge Pickering's support among the senators and the administration was strong. He was an experienced and respected judge, a leader of the state's Baptists, a man of courage from the civil rights era, who, though a child of segregated times, fought in court and in politics against the Klan. He was a conservative and compassionate man. He was also considered to be pro-plaintiff in his rulings. One of the best known of the state's plaintiff lawyers, Dickie Scruggs, allegedly told national Democrats that Pickering was as good a judge as this administration would possibly name. Though Scruggs was Trent Lott's brother-in-law, his statements were likely sincere.

On May 25, two weeks after the East Room announcements and the day after the Jeffords switch, Judge Pickering was nominated. I learned of the selection early the next morning. After picking up the newspaper at the bottom of our driveway, I opened it to scan the headlines while walking back up. I stopped abruptly. "Pickering Nominated for Federal Post," the headline blared. The story said that Jeffords had "thrown the fates of Pickering and other nominations by President Bush into question." Both Cochran and Lott expressed optimism that Pickering would be confirmed.[6] My walk back up the driveway was a slow one.

7

Becoming a Soldier

As I worried and then despaired about my personal ambitions, others were making plans for war. The attacks of September 11, 2001, created a new perspective. This tragedy in so many lives made my pursuit of judicial office seem frivolous and selfish.

This was one of those rare events in which adults at the time can easily remember where we were when we learned. I was walking down the fire escape of the Court of Appeals Building, taking the shortest route to the street so that I could walk to the class I was teaching at Mississippi College Law School a few blocks away. Coming in from the parking lot was one of my law clerks, Patrick Beasley. He asked if I had heard about a pilot crashing a plane into the World Trade Center. The news was all so inexact—what kind of plane, was it an accident, was this something momentous or not? We were all learning as that day and future days went by.

I could not have been more inspired by a leader than I was by President Bush in the months ahead. I listened with patriotic fervor to the speeches he gave to rally the country. I felt pride in him and in our country. No apology was needed for that pride. His addresses during services at the National Cathedral on September 14, then to a joint session of Congress on September 20, were among the most effective and appropriate I had ever heard an American leader give. George W. Bush was the right man in the right place at the right time.

The president helped us with our resolve. Small symbols of that common purpose were all the flags that appeared. That walk back and forth to the law school took me past an office building that edged its front flower beds with American flags. That was just one example. We needed to be united. Briefly, so very briefly, we were.

The continuing functioning of government was part of the necessary proof of the strength of our resolve. Mississippi Supreme Court justice Mike Mills had been nominated for a district judgeship. Before 9/11, his hearing had been scheduled for September 13. All airlines were grounded, but Judiciary Committee chairman Pat Leahy wanted to show that after postponements for two days, the committee "is back at work." Leahy got word to Mike through Senator Cochran that he should come up. Mike and his wife Mona drove all night to attend his hearing.[1]

My immediate interest after 9/11 was to go on active duty in the army. I had not served when I was younger. Ten years earlier, though, I had started the process to join the U.S. Army Reserves. I will describe why—to the extent I am sufficiently self-aware to do so.

Vietnam was the first American war in which I could have served, but I never did. I remember as a high school senior walking into the cafeteria with a classmate and saying I was considering enlisting after we graduated in May 1968. It is a strong memory because it was momentous to admit that to anyone, and it is an uncomfortable memory because nothing came of it. When I turned eighteen, I had a student deferment from the military draft. That left me free from the draft as long as I was a student and as long as the draft rules did not change.

In late November 1969, Congress authorized the first draft lottery since World War II. I was a Rice University sophomore when the lottery by birth date was held on December 1. Three hundred sixty-six blue plastic capsules, each containing a slip of paper with a different month and day written on it, were drawn one at a time from a large glass bowl in the Selective Service System auditorium in Washington. Males born from 1944 through 1950 all had their draft status set by that first lottery. My birth date was in the 216th capsule drawn. The top third was almost certain to be drafted, the bottom third certain not to be. I was in the ambiguous middle third. In 1970 the draft reached the first 195 birth dates.[2] Each year, the number of men drafted declined, and the draft was abolished in 1973. I was never called.

On the night of the lottery, I went to a Rice basketball game on campus. Tipoff was one hour after the lottery began and thirty minutes before it ended. Rice guard Tom "Boom-Boom" Myer and his costar Gary Reist each scored a team-high twenty-one points in a "furious, but way-too-late rally" to lose the game by three points. Within a few days, the story in student gossip channels was that Myer had an even better night in the lottery because his birth date was the last capsule drawn. I did not know until writing this book if that were true. It was.[3] If Myer had been told during the game that he was number 366, that could have started the late rally.

I was attracted to military service. My father had served during all of World War II as a medical doctor. I felt a need to answer the nation's call to arms. At Rice, I considered joining the ROTC. Yet I remained just an observer. One of the reasons for my reluctance was that if I volunteered, my obligation would be a year longer than if I were drafted. I wanted to participate on my terms—a self-centered, conditional patriotism.

As the military made clear it would not demand my services, I drifted along without taking any initiative. I supported the war as long as it went on, regretted how we let it end, and felt I had not performed a duty. After Vietnam came several brief and successful military actions, such as the incursions into Grenada and Panama. I thought these were undertaken in good faith and with patriotic intentions, whatever reasonable disputes there might have been as to their necessity.

I became even more sensitive to failing to live my beliefs when U.S. senator Dan Quayle, after he was nominated for vice president in 1988, was condemned for having joined the Indiana National Guard during the Vietnam War. I strongly disagreed with the criticism, as service in any military capacity is honorable. I saved an article from soon after Quayle's nomination containing a list of the few members of Congress who had military service.[4] That I had done so little despite my beliefs was a goad that worked on me.

When Saddam Hussein invaded Kuwait in the fall of 1990, some of the political commentators ridiculed politicians who strongly backed the use of military force but had not served in Vietnam despite being the right age to have done so. Critics labeled them "chicken hawks" or "war wimps."[5] The criticism was political, but the contrast between my word and deed was awkward. Yet again, I was supporting others going to war although I had not served. I had a conversation about my sense of guilt with army colonel Bill Aileo, who was assigned for a year to the Justice Department. He told me of a program in the reserves that would allow me to train every summer but would not require monthly weekend drills. My goad met opportunity.

On the day that the air war began, January 15, 1991, I mailed my paperwork to the army. Several trips to nearby Walter Reed Army Hospital for physical examinations, including one for a bad back, delayed my acceptance. So did getting an age waiver. Years later, I would see in my official army records that one of the reviewers recommended denial of the waiver, figuring that by beginning at age forty-one, I would not serve long enough to be worth the training. Finally I was cleared for service. In January 1992, long after the brief Persian Gulf War ended, I received a commission as a first lieutenant in the Army Judge Advocate General's Corps. Later I joined a regular army reserves unit, began drilling a weekend each month and having two or three weeks of more intensive training in the summer. In 1997, I shifted to the Mississippi Army National Guard.

An officer in the military receives a commission, signifying appointment as an officer. My father's 1941 commission and mine from 1992 hang side by side in my office. Each says it is executed "for the President" by the army's adjutant general. In November 2000, the first president George Bush, eleven days after the election that was still unsettled between his son and vice president Al Gore, attended an event at Mississippi State University to honor Bush's great friend Sonny Montgomery. I arranged with former congressman Montgomery, whom I did not know well but who had always been gracious to me, to ask the former president to sign the commission. Congressman Montgomery also gave the former president a letter from me explaining my late-in-life beginning of military service.

Dear Mr. President:

Your mind and heart are filled with many things right now. Your son certainly must be uppermost, and your good friend Sonny Montgomery is also receiving your justified attention at the special event honoring him. I am, no doubt, intruding, but perhaps briefly enough.

I received this commission while you were President. Until 1991 I had never been in the military. When Desert Shield began, I yet again felt guilty about not having served. So in 1991 I sought and received a commission in the Army Reserves.

To have your signature on the document would be a tremendous honor.

The former president kindly signed my commission.

Less than ten months later, the military commission, even if it had not been personally signed by the president, became one of my most treasured possessions. That is because it made me eligible to participate in the military response to the 9/11 attacks.[6] I was serving in a JAG unit at the state Guard headquarters on September 11, 2001. For the next six months, I pursued a temporary tour of active duty that would allow me to become part of the fight.

One of my earliest post-9/11 contacts was with Greg Maggs. His wife, Janice Calabresi, was a friend from my Washington days. Besides being a law professor at George Washington University and a former U.S. Supreme Court clerk, Greg was a JAG in the army reserves. On 9/11, the Washington streets were closed soon after the attacks. Greg joined the thousands walking home that night, his walk being to Arlington from the law school near the White House. On Wednesday, September 19, I sent him the following e-mail:

> Greg, I hope that you and your family escaped any direct effects of last week's outrage. If not you directly, then surely people you know were affected. Your work at the Pentagon [as his army reservist duty] for several years may have put you in a close working relationship with some of those who did not survive the attack. It is all so tragic.
>
> It looks extremely unlikely that the National Guard unit that I am in here, which is the State [Headquarters], will be called up. What I am wondering is whether there is a need and opportunity for individual JAGs to volunteer for active duty. For now, I am trying to find out if there is a way to be useful. The biggest problem, but hardly the only one, is the potential need to resign my judgeship. There are far greater sacrifices that others have already made.
>
> Perhaps you know where I can look at the national level. Would you let me know if you have any information on how to find out about opportunities?
>
> The best of luck to you. We are all living in most difficult times.[7]

Greg responded, indicating he too was volunteering to do something on active duty or part-time as a reservist. Nothing yet.

I contacted the full-time Mississippi National Guard JAG, Lieutenant Colonel Eddie Pearson, and got useful guidance. I also contacted various people in Washington who might be able to help from that end. One was the former chief army lawyer, an officer who is called the Judge Advocate General, or in army jargon, TJAG. General Nardotti had been one of a dozen witnesses to the beginning of my military service when I was sworn in at the Pentagon as a commissioned officer in February 1992. General Nardotti was only three years older than I, yet he had experienced most of a long military career—including being seriously injured in Vietnam—before I even began. He had retired from the army after his service as TJAG and was at a large Washington law firm.

I wrote General Nardotti on October 3, saying that I was "seeking advice on how to serve on active duty during this time of national crisis." He called two days later, saying "not to become too hurried about getting involved. The 'dust has not settled yet,' and what would be available remains to be seen. He described a variety of options, but counseled patience."

General Nardotti's counsel proved exactly correct. I contacted many others during this period, including Brigadier General Tom Walker, who was an Oklahoma National Guardsman and a state trial judge. He was an adviser to the current TJAG. He said he would be in Washington in a few days and would discuss my interest with the person whom President Bush had nominated to be the army's new TJAG, Thomas Romig. General Walker's e-mail signature block had a phrase that seemed particularly apt, "Always Forward."

I also contacted Colonel Keith Hamack in TJAG Romig's office. His duties included keeping track of vacant JAG positions for reservists. He explained that a list of volunteers was being maintained and specific skills that may be demanded were being noted. He closed by saying, "I will place your name on the list and keep your bio for reference. Keep your powder dry." Martial phrases—"always forward," "keep your powder dry"—had more resonance in the weeks and months after 9/11 than they had before.

I continued the pursuit of an active-duty assignment over the next few years. When a judge advocate position opened in the 155th Armored Brigade of the Mississippi National Guard, a unit that would likely soon be mobilized, I agreed to be assigned to the position in May 2003 to improve my chances to serve. That opportunity would come, but much happened before then.

8

Mixed Judicial and Military Pursuits

Judge Pickering's initial hearing in the Judiciary Committee was on October 18, 2001.[1] It was immediately clear he would have to return. Senator Ted Kennedy said he was not trying to block the nomination, but he wanted to see many more of the judge's opinions from his eleven years on the district court. So did fellow Democrats Pat Leahy and Chuck Schumer. District judges do not write numerous and lengthy opinions that are then published.

A news article said that even though Pickering had been expected to "win easy approval," particularly since he had been confirmed eleven years earlier for the district court, the committee was "spurred by concerns raised by civil rights groups" to look more closely. The People for the American Way, the NAACP Legal Defense Fund, and the National Abortion Rights Action League were all identified as groups lobbying Democratic senators to slow his nomination. Pickering estimated he had resolved over four thousand cases and written one thousand opinions.[2] He would spend a lot of time in the coming months searching through files.

I remained busy with my state court work and the search for an active duty military assignment. I scheduled a trip for Washington in mid-November. My goal was to meet with senior JAG officers who could assist me. I chose the date so that I could also attend the annual meeting of the Federalist Society. Many well-known conservative legal thinkers, such as Robert Bork, have been active in the society. There are Democrats who seemingly view it as a conspiratorial group planning on overturning the settled legal order.

In 2007, Democratic senator James Webb's chief of staff read the society's mission statement to me and asked if it was my agenda, too. I do not remember my answer, but I do not see the society as a threat. Its value to me is as one of the competing groups that consider important concepts around which modern legal debate revolves. A meeting provides a challenging intellectual environment, not to indoctrinate but simply to educate.

The Federalist Society's Web site describes the society this way:

> Founded in 1982, the Federalist Society for Law and Public Policy Studies is a group of conservatives and libertarians dedicated to reforming the current legal order. We are committed to the principles that the state exists to preserve freedom, that the separation of governmental powers is central to our Constitution, and that it is emphatically the province and duty of the judiciary to say what the law is, not what it should be. The Society seeks to promote awareness of these principles and to further their application through its activities.

"Benign" may not be the most apt word, but "malignant" is not either. I fear that both political parties have their conventions, their standard complaints, and raise them unreflectively. To the annual lawyers' meeting I went and enjoyed it all. I did not feel brainwashed. Admittedly, the best propagandists are the most subtle.

Judge Pickering's confirmation journey was so political that the news often tested, and I often failed the tests, my ability to maintain a fair attitude about what he was suffering. "January 10, 2002. Chris Henick [Karl Rove's deputy] called. He said that at meeting recently (sounded like the judicial selection working group), the DOJ representative mentioned that Pickering was going to be in a tough fight. Democrats are going to try to use him as target on race, relive the 1950s, etc. Chris then said, 'That must be why Leslie Southwick just called me.' It got a good laugh, which he thought was a favorable sign since it at least showed that I had good name identification. He said that Tim Flanigan, Judge Gonzales, Brett Kavanaugh, Noel Francisco, and others were there. They discussed that a bad fight over Pickering would not necessarily help the next white male Mississippian named to the Court." I told Chris that I am no angel, but I could not wish this on Judge Pickering.

Pickering was scheduled for his second Judiciary Committee hearing on Thursday, February 7, 2002.[3] The day before, Mississippi's only black congressman, Bennie Thompson, and the rest of the Congressional Black Caucus urged his defeat. Representative Thompson said that any black person who testified in favor of Pickering was a Judas. Perhaps earning such enmity was U.S. district judge Henry Wingate, who sent a strong letter of support to the committee. Another possible Judas was Charles Evers, whose brother Medgar was slain in Jackson forty years earlier because of his civil rights work. On the day of the hearing, Evers wrote in the *Wall Street Journal* that Pickering was an admirable and brave man whose treatment he found to be appalling.[4]

At the hearing, Judge Pickering was called insensitive on race and women's issues. A few specific cases were criticized, including one in which he had convinced the prosecution to drop a charge against one of three men prosecuted for burning a cross in a interracial couple's yard. That charge mandated a sentence Pickering felt was out of proportion to those given the other two.[5]

In an e-mail to my friend Roger McMillin on February 9, 2002, I first wrote some details about the controversies, which seemed contrived. "What a system. Almost makes you long for a good old-fashioned election, unless you happen to be involved in one. I have finally been able to say to myself, I think honestly, that I want the Lord's will to be done whatever it might be. I hope that the outcome will include no damage to the President and that Judge P. and his family will be at peace with the decision. If all of that means confirmation, then that is what I am for."[6]

I soon contacted the judge himself. "February 18, 2002. Wrote Judge P. and wished him well. I said that I did not think all ten Democrats are going to vote against him. Just too extreme. Even the *New York Times* and *Washington Post* are saying this is character assassination."

An insightful national writer on my troubles in 2007 was Stuart Taylor Jr. In February 2002, he wrote that Pickering had "the misfortune of being the first Bush federal appeals court nominee openly targeted by liberal groups and senators."[7] In 2007, I would be the last. He said Pickering was a "decent man" and "hardly the racially insensitive 'throwback' portrayed by some of his liberal opponents." Taylor said all the vitriol was really about control of the courts: "This is a battle about power—the power to shape the liberal-conservative balance on the federal appeals courts."

A photo opportunity was given to the media of the president and Judge Pickering in the Oval Office on March 7. This "overt demonstration of presidential support for Mr. Pickering was designed to send the message that 'we will fight' for Mr. Bush's nominees, said a senior White House official."[8] From that point forward, the president warmly and publicly embraced Pickering.

The *Magnolia Report*, a Mississippi blog, linked to a story that a deal was being proposed to confirm Judge Pickering in exchange for naming black state judge Johnny Williams of Hattiesburg to Judge Pickering's district court position that he would have to relinquish to accept the Fifth Circuit. A similar compromise would later be suggested about me. No deals were ever made.

On March 14, 2002, the day for the Judiciary Committee's vote on Judge Pickering had finally arrived. The business meeting was tedious. I called it in my notes a "hearing that would never end." I was on a three-judge panel hearing an argument in the afternoon. When it was over, I checked the Internet, but there was nothing final yet. "Decided to go running about 3:45. Very sluggish, my emotions and stress had tired me. Came back, and argument still occurring at the hearing. Heard on the radio at 5:40 that Judge P. had lost. Then at 6:30 saw Judge P. with [his wife] Margaret Ann saying that he would not withdraw."

Stalemate. The headline in the next day's paper was "Senate Panel KOs Pickering." Three votes were taken, and all had a 10–9 straight party alignment defeating each motion.[9] The first vote blocked reporting Pickering to the floor with a favorable recommendation, the next stopped reporting with no recommendation, and the final refused to report with a negative recommendation.

The press speculation on a new nominee if Judge Pickering withdrew centered on the African American U.S. district judge in Jackson, Henry Wingate. The desire for more black judges from Mississippi was the principal dynamic, so Judge Wingate was an obvious replacement. Just a few days after the Judiciary Committee voted against Judge Pickering, I got a surprising e-mail from my aunt Beverly Tarpley, who lives in Abilene, Texas, about her knowledge of that speculation.

Subject: Small World Story

I have just returned from a two day [ABA] meeting in Naples, Florida. Yesterday morning, I was in the lobby of the hotel with [Mississippi College Law School dean] Richard Hurt waiting to be joined by Judge Henry Wingate. When the good judge came down, he apologized for keeping us waiting, but said he had been caught on the phone. Folks in Jackson were calling to tell him about the newspaper accounts that he was on a list of three who were reported to be in the running for appointment to the Fifth Circuit.

We congratulated Henry and then asked who the other two people were. He said "Mike Wallace and Leslie Southwick." [Dean Hurt] and I collapsed in laughter, and Henry looked puzzled until we explained the family connection. I could hardly wait to call [her husband] Dick with the news. I know it is just speculation at this time, but we have our fingers crossed. You are to be congratulated just for getting into the running.[10]

Aunt Beverly expressed fondness and respect for Judge Wingate. "I have enjoyed getting to know Henry Wingate. Apparently he takes his job very seriously and works hard."

The Jackson newspaper story my aunt had learned about in Florida came out two days after Judge Pickering had been blocked in committee.[11] It was the first newspaper article to name me in connection with a Fifth Circuit judgeship, after ten years on the quest. Former judicial colleague Jim Herring later told me he added my name to the reporter's short list. I had asked not to be mentioned back in 1992. Now that I was somewhat in view, would that help or hurt?

The same story also stated that Judge Pickering was not withdrawing. "Morning paper stated that the administration had asked Judge P. to remain as nominee. I guess it is only fair. For me not to receive any advantage from what was done to Pickering would be simple justice."

Another news article was more encouraging. On March 15, the *Magnolia Report*'s biweekly newsletter assumed that someone else would be named:

Whether or not the vacancy on the Fifth Circuit is filled with another Mississippian, or someone from Louisiana or Texas, remains to be seen. One name floating around as a possibility is Mississippi Court of Appeals Judge Leslie Southwick. Southwick is 52, twelve years younger than Pickering. He is Catholic instead of Baptist. He was a Deputy Assistant Attorney General under the first Bush Administration. As a young lawyer, Southwick clerked for Judge Charles Clark who served on the Fifth Circuit Court of Appeals. Some suggest that while Pickering was Lott's top choice, Southwick is on the list by Senior Senator Thad Cochran.[12]

I wanted Senator Cochran's reaction to Pickering's remaining the nominee. "March 19, 2002. Called Thad. He and Trent were talking yesterday about this, and decided that if Judge P. is not withdrawing, that there was no reason to recommend anyone else. I should just lie low."

In the following months, usually no word came from anyone. In July, President Bush was coming to Mississippi to participate in a campaign fund-raiser for congressman Chip Pickering. I knew the president was an avid runner. On July 29, I sent a fax to White House counsel Al Gonzales. After certifying to my ability to maintain at least an eight-minute pace, I asked that he "present my invitation for some executive exercise in Jackson [to President Bush]. A Secret Service sanctioned course could be found. It will be hot and humid, but Texans are used to such. Perhaps a three mile journey would helpfully energize the Leader of the Free World while he is here." No luck. A week later, I made a note: "August 7, 2002. Went running with Cathy at 11:00. I told her that this was a lot more fun that running with the president."

Judge Pickering was not the only Bush judicial nominee being blocked in the Senate. On July 23, 2002, Texas Supreme Court justice Priscilla Owen had her hearing. Among her burdens was to be selected for the same seat to which Jorge Rangel and Enrique Moreno had been nominated. No dish is quite so flavorful in Washington as payback. The criticisms started soon after her May 2001 nomination. One of the groups that researched Republican nominees' records for information that could be used to block them was the Alliance for Justice. In 2001 it identified cases in which she had allegedly revealed a bias favoring business interests.

Abortion also played an important role. She dissented from a decision allowing a high school senior to have an abortion without first notifying her parents. Her position was characterized as being impractical and insensitive. Awkward to her defense was that current White House counsel Al Gonzales had also been on the Texas court at the time. His opinion sharply criticized the dissenters. The American Bar Association, though, gave her its highest rating, "well qualified."

Senator Hatch opened the hearing with a strong defense. Senator Leahy criticized Republican colleagues, saying that Owen would get a fair hearing, something Rangel and Moreno "were never allowed to have before this committee." The hearing was a contentious battle among the senators. On September 5, the committee maintained its party discipline, refusing to report her to the floor on a party-line 10–9 vote. President Bush responded, "Washington is a tough and ugly town at times. Treating a fine woman this way is bad for the country; it's bad for our bench."[13]

What might change the dynamic would be for the Republicans to regain the Senate and thus be able to set the agenda. "November 6, 2002. Big night. GOP gets 51 or 52 Senate seats, depending on Louisiana." I felt the GOP majority made my nomination unlikely. Instead Judge Pickering should be named again. He had been unfairly treated over the last year and a half. A Republican Senate majority might be able to make amends.

Judge Pickering's strongest supporter had an unexpected change in course. On December 5, Senator Lott made comments at senator Strom Thurmond's one hundredth birthday party, creating a controversy that would not die. Thurmond, as the States' Rights Democratic nominee for president in 1948, had split with the regular Democrats because of President Truman's support for civil rights. Thurmond finished third in the election, but it was an important event in southern Democrats' gradual abandonment of their former party in favor of the Republicans. Senator Lott said, "I want to say this about my state: When Strom Thurmond ran for president, we voted for him. We're proud of it. And if the rest of the country had followed our lead, we wouldn't have had all these problems over all these years, either."[14] The person he was trying to embrace rhetorically may not even have heard or understood. Thurmond was leaving office, moved into a nursing home a few months later, and died in June.

Whether Trent could recover from this statement is one more event that I, regrettably, judged in terms of how it affected my prospects. "December 14, 2002. If Trent is sacrificed, does that make J. Pickering more likely—a bone tossed? Might J. Pickering say, for good of country, of my friend Trent, of whomever else, that he will not be the vehicle for additional rancor and division? Up and down emotionally, J. Pickering and myself. Please, Lord, if it be thy will."

On December 20, from his home in Pascagoula, Senator Lott announced that he was stepping down as Senate Republican leader. Not quite three years later, that Pascagoula home would be destroyed by Hurricane Katrina. Trent Lott has had some sharp blows.

There was speculation in the national press that Senator Lott's fall would take Judge Pickering with him. The incoming Judiciary Committee chairman, Orrin Hatch, expressed uncertainty in late December. "It's up to the President who's going to be re-nominated. I'm quite sure that Priscilla Owen will be re-nominated. I'm not sure whether Judge Pickering will be re-nominated."[15]

◆ ◆ ◆

The first major event of my new year had nothing to do with the Fifth Circuit. By the benefit of perseverance, but more the good fortune that

Andy Estrada, whose brother Carl was one of my best high school friends, knew somebody who knew somebody, I was going to perform two weeks of military duty at the United States Military Academy in West Point.

I went up on Sunday, January 5, 2003. The scene along the Hudson River, with the academy on a hill, snow blanketing the parade grounds and the roofs of the buildings, was beautiful and inspiring. There were sessions every day with the cadets who were in their final year at West Point. Because this is the military, the seniors have to be called something odd to the civilian ear. They are called First Years, shortened to Firsties. There were about fifteen reservists joining the JAG's in the Department of Law. The two weeks were a simulation for the Firsties of some of what they might face soon after being commissioned. The legal issues that we presented were just part of a larger array of real-world scenarios that were part of the training.

In my first week, I was in my hotel room, watching the morning news as I got ready for class. Later that day, I e-mailed Roger McMillin about what I saw. "I saw the morning TV news in my room that the President had renominated two judges who had been defeated [in the Judiciary Committee last year]. No names, but I thought that if the President got to two, he would reach J. Pickering. So I dressed quickly and went to a grocery store in the town of Highland Falls, which is the community along part of the West Point boundary. It took the *New York Times* to confirm."

The television report was referring to Judges Pickering and Owen, who had both been voted down in committee. I did not realize they were the only nominees stopped in that way. Had I known that, I could have saved myself a trip into town. The reason there were not any more is that nominees disfavored by the Democratic majority would usually not even get a hearing, much less a vote. Only Pickering and Owen were stopped by 10–9 party-line votes in committee. In the new Congress, with a 10–9 Republican majority in committee, Democrats could not prevent nominees from getting hearings or being reported to the Senate floor.

Hearings on the stalled circuit court nominees began. Priscilla Owen had a second hearing on March 13, 2003, which Republicans titled "Setting the Record Straight,"[16] less than a year after Democrats had a hearing with the same insistent title about their blocked nominees. On March 27, she became one of those reported out of committee on a 10–9 vote.

The first nominee to be subject to a filibuster was Miguel Estrada, nominated for the D.C. Circuit. At the beginning of 2003 he was forty-one, an immigrant from Honduras who arrived in this country at the age of seventeen, knowing little English. Five years later he was an honors graduate of Columbia University, which he followed by being near the top of his class at Harvard Law School.

The close working relationship between Democratic senators and various outside groups became known when memos between them were discovered on a shared Judiciary Committee computer network. A June 2002 memo to several of the senators suggested Estrada's hearing be delayed to give the outside "groups time to complete their research and the committee time to collect additional information." Memos suggested that as a Hispanic, Estrada would be politically difficult to block later for the Supreme Court. He needed to be stopped before it was too late.[17]

The first vote to end the filibuster on Estrada's nomination was taken on March 6, 2003. It would take 60 votes, but the tally was 55–44. A week later, there was another try. The vote this time was 55–42. Five days later, a third try ended with a 55–45 vote. Four more attempts were made, the last on July 30, 2003, and all failed. On September 4, Estrada had his nomination withdrawn.

After four failed tries to end the Estrada filibuster, Republicans sought a vote for Priscilla Owen. The first try was on May 1, 2003, but it failed on a 52–44 vote. Later in May, then once each in July and November, cloture was again defeated. An Alabama nominee to the Eleventh Circuit, William Pryor, was next. Cloture was sought twice for him, once in July and later in November. He received only fifty-three votes, far short of the sixty he needed.

Judge Pickering had not yet been considered by the Judiciary Committee. Because he had two hearings in the previous Congress, he did not get called back. Before the committee vote, one of the Clinton Fifth Circuit nominees who had never received a hearing or a vote, Jorge Rangel, urged senators to support Pickering. Rangel said the criticisms were unfair and described him as "compassionate, sensitive and free from bias."[18] Rangel's magnanimity speaks well of both men. On October 2, 2003, Pickering was reported out of committee with a 10–9 vote.

A filibuster greeted him. The debate on the floor and a vote on cloture were set for October 30. On the next day, the Jackson newspaper printed a front-page photograph of Judge Pickering and his family watching the Senate proceedings from his home near Laurel. Pickering was shown holding two of his grandchildren, with a television in the background showing the C-SPAN coverage of the vote. The vote was 54–43. President Bush called the vote a "disgrace."[19]

The failed cloture vote took place on a Thursday. The following Tuesday, Mississippi Republican Haley Barbour defeated the incumbent Democratic governor, Ronnie Musgrove. The national Democratic Party's opposition to Pickering, who was widely respected in the state, probably gave a slight boost to Barbour. Judicial confirmation struggles have many ripples. Pickering, a pioneer in the state's Republican Party, had the consolation that his travails likely benefited his old party.

Cloture was sought twenty times in 2003 on ten circuit court nominees. The votes were always about the same. Offering a new nominee affected almost no senator. With sixty votes needed to end debate, the most any nominee received was the fifty-five votes received five times by Miguel Estrada. The fewest was fifty-one.

Following the failure of cloture, some leading Republicans promoted the idea of Judge Pickering's being appointed by the president. These "recess appointments" were authorized by the U.S. Constitution. Because Congress would not always be in session, there would be a need for the president to fill vacancies that arose between sessions. For a limited period, the appointee could remain in office regardless of what Congress did upon its return, else the recess appointment might be so brief as not to allow for useful service. However, if Congress had not confirmed the appointee by the end of the *next* session, the appointment expired.

A headline in the Jackson newspaper three weeks after the failed cloture vote was "Leaders Pushing Recess Option for Pickering."[20] Senator Lott said that recess appointments were "not something I'm generally supportive of," but in Pickering's case, "it should be considered."

On November 13, 2003, I e-mailed Roger McMillin:

It sounds about right as the denouement to something that had its climax a long time ago. Frustrating, but Judge P. has been treated like dirt. If he wants this, then it is a way to resolve the matter with him getting something out of it, something that does not require a net five or six new GOP senators in the 2004 election. I feel the way I did a year ago. Hoping something was about to turn, then seeing the prospect of another year of going another direction. I wish I could chunk the whole thing and move on.[21]

The nomination remained too important a goal to abandon quite yet.

On January 16, 2004, President Bush gave Pickering a recess appointment.[22] He announced that he was "proud to exercise my constitutional authority to appoint Judge Charles W. Pickering to serve on the United

States Court of Appeals for the Fifth Circuit." A "bipartisan majority of senators supports his confirmation," but a minority "has been using unprecedented obstructionist tactics to prevent him and other qualified individuals from receiving up-or-down votes." Judge Pickering could serve at least until the end of the next session of Congress, which began four days later. Unless he was confirmed before that session ended in December, though, the appointment would end.

Uncharitably, I wondered how this would affect me. The morning after Pickering's appointment, I received comfort from my devotional. "The scripture reading was of having faith in the Lord in difficulties, turn them over to the Lord with quiet confidence. I will try." I mailed a note to Judge Pickering, congratulating him and expressing my sympathy for all he had endured.

Not long after Judge Pickering's recess appointment, he was quite favorably treated in a segment on the CBS television show *60 Minutes*. On March 28, 2004, reporter Mike Wallace revealed significant inaccuracies and unfairness in the characterizations that had been made of him. I thought Judge Pickering should be pleased.

To accept the recess appointment to the Fifth Circuit, Judge Pickering had to resign as a U.S. district judge. A colleague on the state court of appeals, Judge Kenny Griffis, e-mailed me to ask, "Are you in the running for his district court position?" I responded in a January 20 e-mail: "If nominated I will run; if elected I will serve." I much preferred a Fifth Circuit appointment, and I worried whether I had the set of skills to be comfortable as a trial judge. Still, I wanted to try.

The next day, Senator Cochran called. "Thad said he wanted to include me on the list of those to be considered by the White House for the district judgeship. I told him it was always a pleasure to talk with him, but this was one of the most enjoyable." A week later, Thad called again. He and Trent were signing a letter that day to send to President Bush, including my name and a few others who were being recommended for the Southern District seat. He and Mark Keenum agreed that if I got this nomination, it would put me in good position for the Fifth Circuit next year, assuming that Judge Pickering was never confirmed (and assuming that the president was reelected).

I flew to Washington on February 5. The other recommendations, whose names appeared in that day's Jackson newspaper, were Keith Starrett, a trial judge in McComb; Ermea J. Russell, a former trial judge from

Jackson and future state court of appeals judge; and Mike Randolph, an excellent lawyer and future state supreme court justice from Hattiesburg.[23]

The interview was to be at the Old Executive Office Building. I arrived a few minutes before my 2:00 p.m. appointment, and waited in the West Wing. Dabney Friedrich and two other White House lawyers questioned me. I later wrote my recollection of some of questions. "(1) Why do you want to shift from appellate to trial? (2) What do you think the biggest differences will be? (3) What is your judicial philosophy? (4) How do you interpret statutes? (5) What if Fifth Circuit panel had a decision that was the only one on point, and you strongly disagreed with it?" After I answered these kinds of questions, the others left, and Dabney asked about skeletons in my closet. None to report.

The White House moved quickly. On February 10, my birthday, I received a call from Thad's chief of staff, Mark Keenum. Mark said that Cochran had been called today and told that the selection was someone else. He was told that I looked like a strong candidate for the Fifth Circuit. Thad agreed. Keith Starrett had been chosen, and I called to congratulate him.

I sent an e-mail to my colleagues on the state court:

> Many of you are aware from an article in last Friday's newspaper that I had been recommended for a federal district judgeship. I interviewed on that Friday in Washington. Today (Tuesday) I was called and told that the appointment was going to someone else. That person has far more trial court experience than do I, and the decision makes perfect sense.
>
> No complaints. Disappointment, yes, but no basis to complain. I lost an election for the Supreme Court once, and later decided that the defeat may have been the best thing that could have happened to me. This latest forced redirection may well in hindsight prove equally a positive one.
>
> To all of you who encouraged me, I thank you. Life goes on.

In rereading these comments years later, I do not recall being disappointed. I was still in limbo, but I had probably improved my opportunity eventually, and maybe in January, to be named to my actual goal of a position on the Fifth Circuit.

I still had heard only from Mark Keenum. The official call came on February 24 from assistant White House counsel Dabney Friedrich. I said that had I been making the decision, trying as best as I can to view it objectively, I likely would have made the same choice. She said that I should not take this as any problem with my credentials, and that it was a very close decision. It was Keith's trial experience, and especially his handling of so many jury trials, that made the difference.

In my notes, I wrote: "Dabney told me twice during the conversation that my appellate record made me 'a very strong' candidate should a vacancy come up on the Fifth Circuit. The fact that the White House called makes me feel a little better about this, and having Counsel willing to tell me that the Fifth Circuit is a good fit for me is also quite encouraging. Let's hear it for Bush in '04!"

"Excuse me," I wrote in my notes, "I am nonpartisan."

As some good news, though mixed, had occurred to my interests in a federal appointment, the enjoyment of my work at the state court took a blow in late March. My closest friend on the court, chief judge Roger McMillin, decided to resign to work with an old friend, David Morris. Morris had a business that tested applicants for various kinds of positions, particularly police forces. He was pursuing a contract from the U.S. government to test Iraqi applicants for the Baghdad police force. Managing such a contract would be intriguing, exciting, and dangerous. Roger McMillin was the kind of person attracted to those features.

Roger would resign on April 30. He sent a farewell to his colleagues on April 21. I responded a few days later, one last e-mail as a colleague.

> There's not much for either of us to say. Our work together has been the conversation that we need not have now. We have spent quality years in our common quest of seeking what appellate courts should always seek— well-reasoned opinions, faithful to existing law and facts, as carefully explained as possible. We spurred each other on, drew on the strengths of the other, made each better than we would have been without the prodding and searching and even, in a very narrow way, the competition. That competitiveness was on my part a desire to have thought clearly and expressed logically, because you would gently inform me when you noticed the lack of clarity or logic. It is the opportunity to have an intellectually and personally satisfying relationship with a colleague that eases the isolation of appellate judging.

I closed with "God speed, good friend. Check in occasionally."[24]

With our chief judge gone, the chief justice of the Mississippi Supreme Court would name a new one. I would have liked to be chosen, but it was not to be. I was called a few days later by one of the few remaining original members of the court, Leslie King, and told that he had been named. I wished him well and meant it. It is the kind of position that is most enjoyed on the day it is offered. I wrote Leslie a note a few days before Roger left the court.

Dear near-Chief:

Congratulations. Chief Justice Smith made the right choice. You are by breadth of background, calm temperament, and interpersonal skills, the most suited of us all.

I will admit to hoping that the Chief Justice might stray from the obvious choice. Forgive me my hope, as I extend my best wishes.

Good luck in the cat-herding that is ahead. I am one of the herd, and will do my best to follow your lead.

Warm regards,

Leslie Southwick

9

Training and Pursuing

A week after Leslie King's selection, I learned of another reason I just would not do as chief judge. It was a long-awaited, desired, but still-feared telephone call.

"Saturday, May 8, 2004. Lieutenant Colonel Roy Carpenter called at the house at about 3:15. Sharon answered. She did not know who it was and handed the phone to me with a look of concern. Roy was calling all the JAGs to let us know we were now on alert for imminent military duty. He had no other details. I told Sharon. She said that she wished I had gotten out a long time ago. We did not talk about it much after that."

The person actually going into active military duty is often much less anxious than the family members left behind. Whatever worries I might have felt were diluted by knowing what was occurring at any particular moment. That was almost always tame compared to the speculations that someone thousands of miles away might have.

I felt caught up in something that stretched back to the beginning of our nation's history and would inevitably continue well into the future. I supported what we were trying to accomplish in Iraq, wanted at the core of my sense of who I was to serve my country in this way, and was fully aware I would be sent well beyond my comfort zone. Those realizations were just beginning.

As I was going through my anxieties about war, promotion to the Fifth Circuit, and other worldly things, Judge James E. Thomas, a good friend and another of the few remaining original members of the court, was going through something much more fundamental. He was in the hospital with extremely advanced lung cancer. I asked his secretary if I could visit.

I received word on Thursday, July 1, that he was in good enough condition for me to see him at the hospital.

I visited on July 3. A few others were there, including his wife. I stayed a little more than an hour. It was an enriching experience, to see him with such acceptance of his fate. James died the next day, the Fourth of July. It is not necessary to go to Iraq to face death.

Work on the court grew increasingly secondary as preparations for active military duty intensified. I had eight days of duty at Camp McCain in north central Mississippi. The camp was named for senator John McCain's great-great-uncle, who was born in a nearby town. I improved my skills at driving a Humvee, including in pitch dark in the woods wearing night vision goggles. My passengers more than once warned me I was drifting off the road toward the trees.

The court issued a press release on July 22 about my imminent departure on a leave of absence. Usable quotes were needed. "It's a great privilege to have served on this court since its inception in 1994. I leave with extraordinary respect for my colleagues and great appreciation for how they have supported me through the years and particularly how they have supported me in what I am about to undertake. It is also an honor to serve with the U.S. Army. It is an important mission that we have been assigned in Iraq. There is a sense of fulfillment in my military career to have this opportunity to be some small part of what we are seeking to achieve in that troubled area."

The news story about my departure made the front page of the Jackson newspaper. The headline on the continuation of the article inside the paper was "Judge: Joining Guard Unit Fulfills Southwick's Dream to Serve."[1] The reference to a "dream" bothered me. Now, years later, I realize the headline got it exactly right.

In late July, the family gathered south of Hot Springs, Arkansas, for some time at Lake Hamilton. For five days we swam, rented both a boat and jet skis, toured, and otherwise tried to have as intense a time together as we could. With the mobilization just days away, with a year in a war zone just over the horizon, I felt there was haze over the experience, an unseen, unphysical reality of future danger hovering above it all. I expect the others had similar feelings, but it was a wonderful reenergizing of our family bonds. I even received a telephone call there notifying me of my promotion to lieutenant colonel. Our time together came to an end all too soon.

The summer was spent between two worlds. Reporter Emily Wagster caught me in a reflective mood in a story that appeared on Friday, August 6.

> Without a hint of pretense in his voice, Judge Leslie Southwick harkened to Roman mythology to describe his station in life.
>
> The 54-year-old from Jackson is taking a leave from the Mississippi Court of Appeals to fulfill his military duty as a member of the 155th Separate Armored Brigade.
>
> He reports for active duty Monday in Tupelo and by midweek will move to Camp Shelby near Hattiesburg for several weeks of training. After additional training elsewhere in the United States, Southwick is expected to be in Iraq by January.
>
> Discussing the transition from civilian to military life, Southwick talked about Janus, the Roman god of gates and doors—a figure with one face pointing forward and another pointing back.
>
> "I have been looking both ways since I got the alert on May 9, both keeping in mind what I'm doing here as a judge and having to look forward (to military duty)," Southwick said. "The looking back at the court is getting less and less frequent."
>
> Southwick has packed up his office and has written his last pre-deployment opinions for the Court of Appeals.

And so it began on, as the military would say, 9 August 2004, at 0800 hours. The August 10 Tupelo newspaper pictured me dropping my duffel bag onto a pile of others. Several takes had been needed before I dropped it just right for the photo. The story closed with my saying that some people had asked if I were too old for the army. "I would like to think I am experienced. A nice word would be 'seasoned.'"[2]

By the end of the week, I had driven to Camp Shelby in southwest Mississippi, where most of our training would occur. "The first few days at Camp Shelby involved processing chores. We got some shots and went through various physical examinations, none of which were too demeaning. We also had to go through a series of stations in a large drill hall for financial and other records."

"The training so far has involved simulated and actual weapons practice, use of gas masks—fortunately not yet needed in Iraq—a little road marching (officers in the rear, where their literal missteps won't be seen by the enlisted soldiers) and other things. We have some cultural awareness briefings starting Monday, and later some land navigation training. I still have to go to the firing range, as the range for the pistol that I am issued could not be used a few days ago when others were qualifying with rifles and other weapons."

"So far I have relearned the joys of small things—shade and a wall to lean against were the major joys a few days ago as we were waiting outdoors during a particularly slow simulated weapons-fire process; earlier I would have been thrilled if I could have taken my heavy helmet off—that was a joy denied." *Not* doing the low crawl in the dirt holding a rifle over my head was another joy denied.

On the anniversary of 9/11, I mailed Philip and Cathy a somewhat preachy message. "This is Saturday morning, the third anniversary of the terrorists' attack on the Pentagon and the World Trade Center. There is certainly a basis for calm and measured disagreement regarding how best to combat this continuing terrorist threat, but there should be little basis to argue that we can ignore it. Going to Iraq seems to me a legitimate effort to strike at the heart of the problems that we face in this new century. It certainly is proving to be a difficult challenge, though."

"A few weeks ago someone mailed me a set of 1941 post cards of Camp Shelby, probably purchased on something like eBay, but he did not say. The twenty images reveal the constancies of military life—living in barracks (except maybe the officers) and occasionally in tents, training in the field, marching, and all the rest that make military life such a unique world."

This training showed us what the army thought we would encounter as JAGs in Iraq. We spent several months at Camp Shelby. About a hundred of us went to Fort Irwin in the southern California desert for ten days, preparing for the brigade's journey there later. On October 24, the full JAG section went to Charlottesville, Virginia, for classes at the Army JAG School. The JAG School training completed, Roy Carpenter and I drove to Fort Bragg, North Carolina, on Tuesday afternoon, November 3. We were to have discussions with scores of other JAGs, some who like us were about to deploy, others who had come back and could explain their experiences.

Our travel day also was election day. *The* election. It would decide the direction of the Iraqi mission. I wanted President Bush to be reelected so that we could continue the mission with energy and commitment. It was also an election that would decide my fate. Looking back now, years later, my recollections are not reliable. Yet to the extent that I could know myself, the more important matter to me was Iraq. The judgeship would be a heck of an additional benefit, though.

I had no duty that evening and just needed to be ready for an early start the next day. No winner was declared that night. The air conditioners in the hotel-like quarters were not working. With the windows open, I tossed and turned, trying to sleep. Election Wednesday 2004, I turned on the television about 5:30 a.m. The president needed one more state to be declared for him, and the mission would be accomplished. Republicans had already increased their majority in the U.S. Senate and would likely increase it some more. The broadcast fully woke me.

During a break from meetings, I was able to return my daughter Cathy's phone call. She told me Senator Kerry had conceded. Despite my saying earlier that the continuation of the Iraq mission was the most important reason for my enthusiasm for President Bush's reelection, I also clearly remember that as the next few days went by, it was my growing sense that the Fifth Circuit nomination might almost be in my grasp that really started to dominate my thoughts.

We returned to Camp Shelby. From there, I sent Cathy a letter on November 11. "Last week I went into Hattiesburg for lunch with some JAGs from Georgia, and coincidentally was in the same restaurant as Fifth Circuit Judge Charles Pickering. He wanted to be confirmed during the one-week special session, but if that failed, he would not pursue another appointment. His wife, Margaret Ann, wants just to get on with retirement. He seemed satisfied with that too."

On Saturday, November 20, the entire brigade flew to Fort Irwin in southern California, leaving quite early in the morning, as the army seems to require. After several days of training and briefings, on November 27 about a thousand of us were staged in more than a hundred vehicles on the outskirts of the base, waiting for word to start the long drive to the desert camps. Rees called when I was sitting in the back of the Humvee, about an hour before we left. He "mentioned an article on Judge Pickering in the morning paper which said Sen. Lott had tried to have Judge P. on the unanimous consent calendar along with Keith Starrett, but the Democrats balked." Starrett had been nominated on July 6 but was not confirmed until this postelection session.

Congress was scheduled to adjourn for the year on December 8. Congressman Chip Pickering, the judge's son, went to the Senate floor that day and urged the Republican leader to make one final try at getting Democrats to agree to a vote. GOP leader Bill Frist tried but failed.

That night, Judge Pickering was driving home in a rental car from Memphis in a rainstorm, having missed the connection for his flight from Washington. He learned by phone during the drive that these final efforts had not succeeded. The next day, he made a public statement. "My confirmation struggle lasted four years. Although I would prefer confirmation, I am in good spirits and at peace with the result. My faith is strong. I will continue to be involved in community and civic affairs. I will also speak out on issues relating to confirmation reform." Judge Pickering stated that at age sixty-seven, he thought it was time for a younger person to be nominated. He later wrote that the White House had assured him the president would nominate him again if he wanted to continue the journey.[3]

For two weeks I was in the desert, trying hard to leave these subordinate concerns behind and focus on my training. There was no cell phone service, which was for the best. Though the training was quite helpful, my strongest memory is of the brutal cold, shivering all one night with a miserable cold and wearing most everything I had brought with me. There was some Internet service, though not reliable. Among the people who sent me a message about Judge Pickering's announcement that he was retiring was Jackson lawyer and wonderful friend Kevin Watson. I responded:

> I just got back from a Humvee mission through a rather attractive desert setting. There is an Iraq election out here today in the training scenario, and we are providing security for voters.
>
> I have been an also-ran in the judicial races for so long that I wonder if I want emotionally to go through this again. The other two people you mentioned are strong contenders, and I doubt if I would qualify as a front-runner. I would like the appointment very much. Right now, though, other things seem more imminent and important.[4]

Two days later, I wrote Kevin again. "I got in from the desert on Friday at about 1900. We will be here until Tuesday night, and back in Camp Shelby on Wednesday. Some turn-in of equipment; washing of vehicles, clothes, and selves; going to after-action-reports; and a myriad of other activities will take up much of the time."

Fort Irwin was left behind on Tuesday, December 14. We would be at Camp Shelby for a few days before we all received ten days of leave at Christmas. My next diary entry said this: "December 17, 2004, Friday. Went back to my quarters at 0900 to get computer thumb drive. I was just sending up a prayer that I really wanted to hear from Thad, when the phone rang. My former secretary at the court, Martha Ponder, called to tell me that Dabney Friedrich [at the White House Counsel's office] wanted to schedule an interview."

"I called Dabney. They wanted me Monday afternoon if I could get there. Timing was terrific." Because I was not in charge of my life anymore, I had to get permission from the brigade commander to leave a few days earlier than had been scheduled. He agreed. I flew to Washington on Sunday, December 19. The next day would be critical.

"December 20, 2004. Snowed during night. Bitterly cold. Went for early morning run, and though wore gloves, my left hand got extremely cold." Frostbite. It would bother me for months. The White House interview was not until 4:00 p.m. I walked a good bit, just to give myself something to do as the interview loomed. "Was on Chinatown sidewalk at noon when Thad called. He wanted me to know that though there were five names submitted, he had let the White House know that I was the man he wanted. He said that Trent seemed to agree that I was the best choice. I thanked him most sincerely." Thad's call was a huge relief and gave me some optimism. Trent surely preferred Mike Wallace, but perhaps Trent saw Mike's confirmation as too difficult.

The meeting took place in the White House counsel's office. I met with outgoing counsel Al Gonzales, incoming counsel Harriet Miers, Dabney, and another young lawyer. We went into Gonzales's office. He asked how I went about interpreting statutes. I said that I looked at the words in the context of the overall enactment, and that I did not find the comments and speeches of individual congressmen to be reliable indicators. Whom did I admire on the Fifth Circuit and on the Supreme Court? I did not know many Fifth Circuit judges, as my state court work did not cause me to be reading their opinions. "I liked both Rhesa and Grady a good deal. As to the Supreme Court, I respected them all. They all seemed to be honorable people trying their best to interpret the law as they see fit. I find Scalia quite admirable but do not agree completely with him. I also like Clarence Thomas, who himself disagrees with Scalia with some frequency." I realized that such positive statements about all might not be the smartest approach, but it was how I felt.

After perhaps thirty minutes, the two young staffers left. Harriet Miers stayed while Gonzales asked me about the negatives: financial, drugs, crimes, taxes, nannies, hate groups, controversial speeches, and so on. No problems there. I asked about the effect of my deployment. Gonzales said that the group had not discussed it. I thought the interview had gone well enough, but not great.

While waiting for my plane the next day, I was called by Ana Radelat, a reporter who wrote for the *Clarion-Ledger*. She had learned that the others being interviewed were Supreme Court Justice Kay Cobb, Judge Henry Wingate, GOP chairman Jim Herring, and Mike Wallace.[5]

Over the next four weeks, I heard nothing from the White House. It was now time for me to go. Civilian concerns mostly behind me, I boarded a plane with several hundred other soldiers on January 17, 2005. I will describe my year in Iraq later. First, though, I will explain how I received the answer to the nomination question.

After a week in Kuwait, I flew with a hundred other soldiers into an air base in Iraq. From there, helicopters took soldiers to their different bases. On January 28, I finally got to Forward Operating Base Duke, in the southwestern part of the country.

A month later, I wrote family and friends about the silence I was hearing on the Fifth Circuit position. "The calendar pages keep flipping over since the vacancy for which I interviewed first came up. At times I have wondered if I should identify with those last World War II Japanese holdouts on some Pacific islands, who were told to hang on until relieved. The war ended and no one for decades let them know. So there they were, in the 1960s, still believing the conflict raged on."

All along, I thought Mike Wallace was the most likely alternative. The principal reason people who discussed the matter with me did not think he would be chosen was that he would have a difficult time being confirmed. On March 15, I wrote an optimistic letter to Sharon. After news about my recent activities, I turned to the nomination. "I will be disappointed if I am not named, but it will not be devastating. So many considerations go into an appointment like this. I have been considered before, so it is a little hard to say there is any thrill just in being considered. I will say, though, that I remain fairly optimistic." I got the answer three days later.

As I usually did, I got up about 5:30, dressed in jogging clothes, and walked to the headquarters to check e-mail that had come overnight. After turning on the computer, I discovered a message from an associate White House counsel. I got on my knees on the concrete floor to pray briefly for God's will before I opened it. There was an eight-hour time difference, so it had been sent about 4:44 p.m. on the previous day.[6]

Subject: RE: Transitions
Judge Southwick:
I hope this e-mail finds you and your colleagues well.

I'm writing to let you know that the President has made a tentative decision to move forward with another candidate. As we've discussed before,
occasionally there is a need to change course, and we genuinely hope that
you remain interested in serving.
Dabney

I had to collect myself for a few minutes; then I wrote her back. "Thank
you for letting me know. I said that the most important thing to me now
was doing a good job and getting home safely. This news challenges me on
whether that was in fact an accurate statement. I still think it was. The best
to you and all who were involved in this process. You have a difficult job."[7]

She responded: "As I have said before—in another context—the decision was a very difficult one. I am sincere when I say you should continue
to try for positions on the federal bench. I'm sorry once again to be the
bearer of bad news."[8] The "once again" referred to her telling me a year
earlier that I was not the choice for the district judgeship. I went for a jog
after sending my first e-mail. Running allowed me to reduce the immediate shock of the news. After my run, poor Dabney had to deal with the
overly raw emotions her message had caused.

"You are wonderfully kind. Both now and a year ago, you presented
the news most gently. My sense now, though, is that the dream has died.
This is the position for which my background arguably made me a viable
contender. One or more people were better. I do not know if it is in me
to ask my senators to recommend me for something else. I feel particularly awkward that I have let Senator Cochran down."[9] I meant that Thad
had done everything he could for me; the timing was propitious; what he
was seeking must be too unappealing. How could I ask Thad to try again?
"There are other dreams, and goals, and ways to serve. The desert will give
me time to sort through them. Thank you very much for writing me with
that encouragement."

After calling Sharon, Philip, and Cathy, I wrote them on March 19.
"This news was like a strong, unexpected kick to the stomach, which
knocked all the air out of me when I was told. It was only air, though, and
that is slowly coming back. There will be some soreness for a while, but no
permanent injuries. It is for the best that I can better focus on the mission.
My military duty affects many people, from those whose claims for damages I am reviewing, to those who will be benefited if we can improve the
court system in our region, to individual soldiers and commanders with
whom I work. The net result of someone else's being appointed, on all the

people affected in the many ripples that flow from that decision, is probably good."

Sharon's response to the news was beautiful. "Last night I turned to scripture readings trying to find comfort to deal with the disappointing decision. In the *Strength for Service* [daily meditation] book, I read March 18 since it was the 18th where you are. The important thing is: 'Remember that you have a home and that a light burns for you and that prayers are lifted to God for you.'"[10]

Two days later, I sent Dabney a final message, with the subject line "Sunshine in Iraq":

> Thank you for trying a couple of times to help me gain some solace in dealing with recent events. It is the nature of selection to create a few grumps. I needed a day or two to grieve, but I am on the road to recovery.
>
> In all sincerity, I trust the people who participated in this decision, from the President on down. I have no doubt that all of you considered me fairly and made the decision on a reasonable basis. Each of the others was a legitimate candidate.
>
> I hope it creates no awkwardness for me to mention that I have primarily tried to let my religious faith bring peace. Verses in a meditation book, which providentially were the daily readings when I was ready to listen, ended with these:
>
> But soon my heart spoke up from 'neath our burden,
> Rebuked my tight-drawn lips, my face so sad:
> "We can do more than this, O Soul," it whispered,
> "We can be more than still, we can be glad!"
>
> And now my heart and I are sweetly singing,
> Singing without the sound of tuneful strings;
> Drinking abundant waters in the desert;
> Crushed, and yet soaring as on eagle's wings.

Such intrusions of sentimentality are excessive in a note to you, with whom I have a professional and not a personal relation. But I did not want my final words to you to speak of the death of dreams. I may at times revert to being troubled and confused, the latter being a fairly natural state for me, but do not think that I despair. In my disappointment, I can still congratulate all of you for working so hard on these decisions. I am not yet soaring on eagle's wings, but I am starting to break into an occasional jog, singing *a cappella* and drinking the abundant waters.[11]

Within a few days, I learned that Mike Wallace had been chosen. I wrote to congratulate him.

Among the people who needed to know was my past and future secretary. On Thursday, March 24, I wrote to Martha Ponder:

> No matter what happens on this, God has something special for me, something better. Something better by His measurements, though, which are not the ones we use. Better because this trial makes me closer to Him, or more open to doing something more important in his lights. That could be just to make me a better person, more reliant on Him. In God's scheme, having a better title or better job is not a significant thing. Answers are good, but patience for His timing in giving those answers is what I must maintain.[12]

On April 6, I sent Rees a letter:

> In an [earlier] e-mail, I stated that Mike makes perfect sense as the choice. That was sincere, but realizing the merits of the selection does not mean that I have avoided being significantly disappointed. My selection also would have made some sense. Of course, this disappointment is a rather small event considering the trials that so many suffer. A soldier lost both legs a few days ago. My news is a trifle.
>
> During Palm Sunday and Holy Week, I read in my daily contemplations about the sense of abandonment that Jesus felt. A Palm Sunday meditation stated that by "abandoning the fleeting things that we think will lift us up for human status," we can better grasp a share of divine grace. There is no better description of that judicial appointment than it was a fleeting thing that would have lifted me up for human status. It was more than that, but it was that too. I can not fathom how God works, whether he causes results or just works with us once a very human outcome is reached. I had already been thinking that the failure had focused me on my unmistakable need for the Lord.
>
> I had brought a George Bush 2004 poster over here, thinking that if I were nominated and went for a Senate hearing, I would try to get other soldiers and some Iraqis to sign it with messages for the President. Then if I went by the White House while I was there, it could be delivered to him. I have sometimes descended to anger at the President after the news; no

doubt irritation will push back out occasionally even though I try not to think that way. But I still believe he is an outstanding President and Christian man. By putting the poster out now, I am trying to accept that nothing that has happened has changed his merits. I do not expect something better in the earthly sense, but I am working to gain something better in the spiritual sense.

The disappointment remains, appearing like occasional waves disturbing the otherwise calm surface of my emotions. The waves are neither as high nor as frequent as at first. I am most arduously seeking to be content in all things.

On April 23, the Jackson newspaper ran a story about the vacancy.[13] The five of us who had been recommended were named. The story focused on Mike, suggesting the reporter knew he had been selected, but no one would confirm it on the record. "Wallace, a former aide to Sen. Trent Lott, is likely to provoke the most criticism from Democrats and interest groups who opposed" Judge Pickering's nomination. Mike's selection did not become public for almost a year.

There was a chance Mike would join the list of those subjected to a filibuster. Democrats had successfully used filibusters to block floor votes on ten circuit court nominees in the previous Congress, which adjourned in December 2004. In the spring of 2005, Republicans considered changing the rules so that filibusters were not permitted for judicial nominations. That proposal was colorfully labeled the "nuclear option," though Republicans called it the "constitutional option." Democrats threatened to shut down routine business if the rule was changed. A vote on Judge Owen's nomination was scheduled soon, and it was time to consider the option, whatever its name.

Among those wanting to avoid a vote to change the rules was a bipartisan group of fourteen senators. They announced an agreement on May 23, 2005, to last for the rest of that Congress. It was big enough news that my "local paper," the *Stars and Stripes*, provided to service members in Iraq and everywhere else in the world, ran a story.[14] The senators were known as the Gang of Fourteen. The number was important. There were fifty-five GOP senators; they all usually supported the president's nominees. The forty-five Democratic senators could with a very few exceptions be expected to supported any serious filibuster. Seven Republicans could prevent a GOP majority vote; seven Democrats could give Republicans more than the sixty votes needed to end a filibuster.

The seven Republican senators agreed to oppose a change to the rules. That ended the possibility of having filibusters banned on judicial nominations. In return, the seven Democrats agreed they would not support a filibuster on the nominations of Priscilla Owen, D.C. Circuit nominee Janice Rogers Brown, and Eleventh Circuit nominee Bill Pryor. Specifically identified as not covered by the peace agreement were Sixth Circuit nominee Henry Saad and Ninth Circuit nominee William Myers. Sixth Circuit nominees Richard Griffin and David McKeague were not mentioned, apparently because Democrats had already agreed to stop obstructing them. Filibusters against future appellate nominees were to be considered only "under extraordinary circumstances."

Ten nominees had been filibustered, but three had withdrawn: Miguel Estrada in September 2003, and Judge Pickering and Ninth Circuit nominee Carolyn Kuhl in December 2004. The agreement by the Gang explicitly or implicitly resolved the fates of the remaining seven.

On May 24, cloture was voted on Judge Owen by an 81–18 vote. The next day she was confirmed 55–43.[15] In the next two weeks, cloture and confirmation were achieved for the long-delayed nominations of Brown, Pryor, Griffin, and McKeague. No vote was ever held on Henry Saad, and he withdrew on March 23, 2006. The nomination of William Myers to the Ninth Circuit remained pending throughout the remainder of the Congress, but he was not renominated in 2007. Of the ten nominees blocked by filibusters in the previous Congress, five were finally confirmed, and five were not. Whether that should be seen as a half-full or a half-empty result became the basis for both the praise and the criticism of the Gang of Fourteen agreement.

My own judicial hopes were revived a bit when I went home on leave in May. U.S. District Judge William Barbour of Jackson announced he would retire on his sixty-fifth birthday, less than a year away. While home, I contacted Senator Cochran to express interest in the new vacancy. About a month later, I received a surprising e-mail from Grant Dixton at the White House. "Judge Southwick, Harriet Miers has asked me to speak with you when your schedule permits. I know you are in Iraq, and I am happy to call you if there is a number I can call you at. Alternatively, please give me a call at your convenience."[16]

I told Dixton how to reach me via the military phone system. He did so less than two hours later. "He said that White House counsel Harriet Miers initiated the idea that I be named to the Barbour vacancy if the senators are willing. He twice said that the only judgeship available now was this one. If I indicated that I was interested, then the senators would be called. I was interested."

Later I was told that Senator Cochran had been sufficiently troubled about my being passed over for the Fifth Circuit that he called the White House Counsel to express his dissatisfaction with some vigor. His calling Miers may have had something to do with Dixton's calling me.

I expected to hear more about the district court right away, but I heard nothing until I was back in the United States six months later. Though no one ever explained, the delay likely arose because on July 1, four days before I was called, Supreme Court justice Sandra Day O'Connor announced her retirement. John Roberts was nominated on July 19 to replace her. Then on September 3, chief justice William Rehnquist died. Two days later, John Roberts's nomination was shifted to the chief justice vacancy. Harriet Miers was then nominated for the O'Connor seat on October 3 but withdrew on October 27, and Sam Alito was nominated on November 10.

10

A Year in Iraq

The events of 2005 involved far more important matters than my frustrated ambition. I had a chance to fulfill my dream of serving in the military, as so many other Americans had before me.

On January 15, I sent my last letters to Philip and Cathy before leaving Camp Shelby. "I am definitely ready for the deployment to Iraq to be under way. There is important work to be done; it should be quite interesting, and I expect looking back on the experience I will always be glad that the opportunity was available. However, it also is the kind of endeavor that will be more satisfying as something that I have done as opposed to something that I am presently doing. So I am ready to get it started, work at it, and then get home. Until then, my life is sort of on hold. I am particularly hopeful that the year will seem to your mother to have gone by quickly. I do regret leaving her alone for this period. She is a brave lady, though, and will do fine."

I wrote from overseas on January 18: "Tuesday morning in Kuwait. We arrived at the Kuwait City airport at 4:00 p.m. local time. Unloading the baggage from the plane took a while, and the seven-bus trip to take all of us to our desert base took many more hours. We did not get to our particular tent until midnight."

We had several training events at Camp Buehring in Kuwait before we left for Iraq. More weapons practice was among the most important. The JAG section had four lawyers: Lieutenant Colonel Roy Carpenter, Captain Mark Majors, Captain Bill Dreher, and myself. Bill was delayed in the United States but joined us in June. We were told to split ourselves among the brigade's six bases. The brigade was responsible for counter-insurgency operations in four of the eighteen provinces in Iraq. The most

116

dangerous base initially was at Iskandariah, within the Sunni Triangle. Captain Majors was chosen for that assignment, with Sergeant Wes Grissom and Specialist Mikie Brown assisting. Staff Sergeant Lesa Hubbard was sent without an officer to get in her way at a base called Lima in the city of Karbala. Specialist Ashley Rankin was assigned there too. In July, Lieutenant Colonel Gene Hortman and Captain Joel Jones joined us for the second half of the tour.

My safety was often on my family's mind. In January Sharon wrote to me: "I hope when you read this you are safely in place on a base. I have asked members of our small faith-group to pray for your safe journey. At Gleaners today [a charity at which Sharon worked], Gloria Martinson said, 'Don't worry. He's in God's hands.' I felt better after being reminded of that."[1]

I started a report that I hoped was reassuring. "Now I am at the first stop in Iraq. The flight here was on a C-130 transport. The fifty-two of us sat on four plastic-netting benches that stretched the length of the plane, two along the outside wall and two back to back in the middle. We were given earplugs for reasons that became obvious when the engines started up. We had boarded the back of the plane up the cargo ramp; the pallet with our duffel bags and other gear was loaded by a forklift; then the ramp was closed. The flight was ninety minutes and took us to a hub air base for military transports deep in Iraq. My stepping onto Iraqi sand for the first time was at about 0215—we stayed in the plane awhile after landing. We got to our tents about 0330, sort of slept, then got to the departure building at 0900."[2] There we waited all day without getting a flight.

The next day, this: "Amazing. I did finally make it. At noon on Friday, 28 January, we got the word to load up on a helicopter. Only ten of us per helicopter, two different helos, flying about 100 feet above the ground. The flight was over some large lakes and much barren desert. Desolate, deserted, (desperate?), must all come from the same root word. We saw some camels along the way. There was a four-person crew, a pilot and co-pilot and two gunners, one on each side of the helicopter with 50 caliber machine guns at the ready. They kept a careful watch, but it was wide open desert and water all the way. No problems. The windows were down, and the wind was really blowing in. Quite cold, but I was well-bundled."

I was assigned to a Forward Operating Base (FOB) Duke in southwestern Iraq. The Marines had been there for seven months. For two weeks they would show us how they operated, and then they would leave for home. Only a few miles from FOB Duke was the significant Shia city of

Najaf. The Marines had fought fiercely there in August 2004, defeating the Mahdi Army of the anti-American cleric Muqtada al-Sadr. Some of the worst fighting was in an enormous cemetery with large underground tombs where fighters and weapons were hidden. A negotiated truce allowed Sadr to survive. The Iman Ali Shrine in Najaf and two mosques in Karbala were sites at least twice a year for hundreds of thousands of Shia pilgrims. The pilgrims also were targets for Sunni attacks.

The Marine JAG, Major Chris Walters, was one of the key organizers of a program that followed close behind the fighting. The goal was to compensate those whose homes and other property had been destroyed. I went to the last of the periodic claims days the Marines held. We drove into town in a convoy of trucks and Humvees with open sides and canvas roofs. I was aghast. Roadside bombs and snipers were the terrifying reality of the war, making well-armored, completely enclosed vehicles vital. For my first travel by convoy to be in what we called "hillbilly trucks" took me well outside my comfort zone. For months, in this and other ways, the Marines had been making a statement after the fighting. It had worked.

In Najaf, I saw hundreds of Iraqis lined up outside a large fenced area. Inside were several portable buildings with a few American soldiers with their Iraq interpreters in each. I took one of the stations with an interpreter. Once the Iraqis were allowed in, for hours we examined their photographs and listened to their descriptions of destruction. We made decisions on the spot about whether to pay, and if so, how much. The claimants picked up their payments in American dollars before they left. No doubt some fraud was occurring, but so was much good. Najaf had been among the most violent cities. Now it was one of the calmest. The Marines' steel fist brought victory during the fighting. The velvet glove of compensation was at least a factor in securing the peace.

Major Walters was smart, innovative, and courageous. I had large combat boots to fill.

A short time later, some of our command staff needed to go to Baghdad. I wanted to talk to certain lawyers at the U.S. Embassy. I caught a ride on one of the helicopters. I described the trip in an e-mail to my siblings: "On my birthday, but not because of it, I flew to Baghdad. I left about 1:00 p.m. and returned about midnight. We arrived at a landing site adjacent to the U.S. Embassy in Baghdad. It was one of the Presidential Palaces for Saddam. I met with several lawyers who should be helpful if I am able to work on a project of helping the local Iraqi court system in the neighboring provincial capital. That is work that we are being encouraged to do, and the security situation here is good enough that it makes sense to pursue that."[3]

Back at FOB Duke, I wrote my family. "We had the departure ceremony for the Marines at 10:00 a.m. A platoon of Marines and a platoon of soldiers stood in adjacent formations. The Marines' flag and the U.S. flag were marched on, and we stood at attention saluting the U.S. flag as the national anthem was played (on a boom box). Then after a few salutes and other martial maneuvers, the Marine holding his service's flag did an about-face and marched off with his flag, and a soldier who had stood off to the side marched on with the Army flag. A brief statement was made by our commander, and we were dismissed. Pretty strong symbolism with the flags. The Marines are leaving, and we are here."[4]

The next day I wrote my sister. "My quarters are in a small trailer. No plumbing, but there is a refrigerator. The shower trailer is adjacent to it. I have a bed, a desk, a wardrobe in which to hang clothes, and even a few rugs. Rank has its privileges, as there are only three of these trailers on the base. Until the Marines left yesterday, I was in a ten-person tent. Then this metal building became available."[5]

Some terrible news brought the dangers of the war home. An Iowa National Guardsmen, Lieutenant Brian Gienau, had been at FOB Duke when I first arrived. I had spent considerable time with him because our duties overlapped. I wrote my predecessor, the Marine JAG who was now back in California, about Brian. I sent this excerpt from the *Stars and Stripes* newspaper: "The latest identifications [of casualties] reported by the military: Army 2nd Lieutenant Richard B. Gienau, 29, Longview, Iowa; died Sunday in Ramadi, Iraq, from injuries sustained when an explosive hit his vehicle; assigned to the National Guard's 224th Engineer Battalion, Burlington, Iowa."

Then I wrote, "Brian came by to see me Saturday, 26 February, to say goodbye, as he was heading out for Ramadi. I had heard Tuesday that someone in the 224th had been killed. The chances that it was anyone whom I knew were minuscule. Whoever it was would have been a tragedy. That it was Brian just made it personally affecting. I had been quite impressed with his diligence, initiative, and intelligence."[6] Unsurprisingly, many more deaths would follow.

I sent family and friends occasional reviews of events. "My first thirty days in Iraq have almost been completed, after ten days in Kuwait. The work is interesting, challenging, and I humor myself at times that part of it is meaningful. Today I went in a convoy of about 20 vehicles to a base an hour away. We had an ambulance that was taking a young girl who had been shot in the legs many weeks [ago]. I am pretty sure she was injured by fire from a helicopter gun ship. She had been treated at a Baghdad civilian hospital but was not getting better; indeed, she was in decline. So we were taking her to our facility at this base to get better care. Her mother went with her."[7]

The court project was advancing. "This afternoon I am having a meeting, along with two Civil Affairs reps including Chris Scott, in Najaf with the chief judge of the province, Judge Raheem. This is preliminary to a meeting in April with a larger group, in which an assessment team out of the U.S. Embassy will come down to meet with lawyers, judges, and court administrators. They have some money to provide, training, and other expertise. This is my first meeting with any officials in Najaf on the project."[8]

As had the Marines, we received claims from local Iraqis for damage we had allegedly caused. We did not usually pay for battle damage, but we would pay for damage from accidents. Of indispensable assistance on the claims work was my Iraqi interpreter. For security reasons, I will not name him. Silence might be the best way to show him the great respect I feel. "Quite a day, almost all on claims. But a successful one. I met for three hours this morning with the interpreter who works with me. We went through every file. The interpreter is getting one of the other locals to help him. He will start making calls and for those without phones, get messages to them to bring certain documents to the base on Tuesday."[9] The interpreter's English was excellent. He had a lot of common sense, and he was a genuinely friendly and concerned person. I had tried to learn some Arabic, but without any success.

I learned in April that our son Philip had found the woman with whom he wanted to spend the rest of his life. She was Mary Voorhies, a New York native who, after a few other stops, had ended up in Austin. They had met, at least as I remember the story, on a roof while volunteering on a Habitat for Humanity project. The first words either spoke to the other were "pass me a shingle." I did not yet know Mary, but Philip's happiness was all the proof I needed that she must be very special. Their engagement was announced to us in April, with a wedding planned for soon after I was scheduled to return.

I wrote to congratulate them and to say a little about the wonders of marriage. "Philip's mother and I have been wonderfully blessed in our marriage. If there have been difficulties, they have been minor and infrequent. We do not keep score; we do not remember disagreements. Marriage really does have to be an equal partnership, built on love and on faith. I pray that you will be at least as blessed as have we. I expect that you will be."

In late March I had to move fifty yards from my original "can" to a new one. "I had an unexpected several-hour project. The shower trailer that serves the three buildings, one of which is my little condo, was to be moved to another location. I was offered and accepted a move to the new, 'double-wide' buildings. It is three rooms. One large room as you enter, essentially the same size as my previous place. The second metal building, all joined together with the first, has a bedroom that makes up two-thirds of it and, ta-da (that's a trumpet), a bathroom for the remaining one-third. It has a sink, a shower, and this strange device I have not seen in two months. I think it is called a commode. God works in mysterious ways. I do not get the federal judgeship, but I do get a porcelain toilet. Over here, what I got is a whole lot more useful than what I did not."[10]

On May 5, I wrote Cathy about my frequent travel in well-armored Humvees, always at least four vehicles. No open-sided vehicles like the one I rode in with the Marines. At least two were gun trucks, with a person standing up inside the Humvee looking out a turret, with a 50-caliber machine gun. "Travel has to be arranged through a transportation officer who keeps track of convoys and will know if there is an available seat. Yesterday I had the luxury of a private convoy. The deputy brigade commander [Colonel Mike Thornton], whose office is near mine, has a personal security detail—a squad of soldiers and sufficient vehicles whose sole mission is to provide security in his travels. He loaned the squad to me yesterday. Once at the other base, however, I received word that something came up back at the base where I started. Colonel Thornton was gracious, but he asked that I get back just as soon as I finished with the claims. By the time I got back, someone else had picked up the mission which he had wanted to do. Some senior officers might quickly place their wishes first when a situation changes. This fellow is not that way, for which I am grateful." Colonel Thornton was humorous, profane, and a lot of fun to be with. He also was one tough soldier.

In the letter, I also discussed Cathy's big event that I was going home to attend. "Graduation. My goodness, Cathy, I can hardly believe it. You have done so much in your life so far, achieved many things, excelled in school, showed initiative, diligence, as well as intelligence. As importantly as anything, you have retained your appreciation for the central role of God in your life. I am truly proud to be your father. And I love you very much."

Home I went. I made it a few days before the Saturday graduation. Every soldier in Iraq was entitled to fifteen days' leave from the war zone. The delays of getting to the United States did not reduce the time we could be at home. It was a joyous reunion in Jackson, then Houston, with all the family. It ended too quickly, though. I arrived back at FOB Duke on May 30. I wrote Sharon: "It was absolutely, positively, beautifully enjoyable to be with you for those two weeks. They went much too quickly, but they gave me the boost to make the next part more endurable."

On July 25, I moved to the brigade headquarters at FOB Kalsu. I explained the move to my family. "My first six months in Iraq were spent as the deputy staff judge advocate, at a forward operating base in the southwest part of our area called FOB Duke. The staff judge advocate was Lieutenant Colonel Roy Carpenter. He served at the headquarters at FOB Kalsu. Being there was particularly stressful because it was in the territory in which the warring Sunni and Shia factions of Islam each lived in large numbers. Fairly frequent mortar and rocket attacks were one result. Further south, the Shia dominated and were relatively welcoming. As we got near the halfway point in the deployment, I asked if Roy would like for me to take his place at FOB Kalsu, while he took mine at FOB Duke. He did, as I would have."[11]

Among the benefits of being at Kalsu was that I was no longer working alone. A terrific soldier, Master Sergeant Chris Young, was the noncommissioned officer in charge. Sergeant Dan Caparoso and Specialist Billy Roach were there, as was Captain Bill Dreher. There was more work to do, and more hands to do it.

I explained some of the new duties to my siblings Lloyd, Larry, and Linda on July 29. "Every day there is an hour meeting at 0800, another hour-long one at 1800, and a thirty-minute (or less) meeting at 1930. Only that last meeting is strictly for me. The meeting is with those who interrogate the prisoners, and I get a summary of what has been learned from them. [Often those meetings were with Lieutenant Susan Lennon and Sergeant Bert Blasingame.] I then decide which prisoners should continue to be held and which released. A release decision gets 'vetted' with the unit that captured the person and must be accepted by the brigadier general [Leon Collins] who commands the brigade. I meet with him daily, and with his chief of staff [Colonel Bill Glasgow] three or four times a day. In addition, three days a week there is a meeting at 1000. Then there are special ones, such as the two-and-a-half-hour meeting that started at 1230 today."

One of the fascinating people I met at Kalsu was the brigade's surgeon, Colonel William N. Bernhard.[12] He was seventy-four, lived in Maryland, and volunteered for deployments. He was energetic, in great physical condition, mentally sharp, and too often called on to be a trauma specialist. Once a dump truck with hidden explosives blew up as it was trying to enter our front gate. All the medical personnel were busy that day.

My responsibilities on Sundays also changed in a powerful way. "One of the changes of being at the new base occurs almost every Sunday. The one Catholic priest [Father Samuel Giese] with the brigade resided at FOB Duke. So on Sunday, I was used to a priest-led mass. At FOB Kalsu, Sunday services are a little different. I have become the lay officiator at the Catholic service here. This was the second week that I did that. A priest comes in every other week during the week to take care of the Papists. Not to be confused with the Baptists."[13]

A friend from my Brunini law firm days, as well as the man who kept me walking during my 1994 campaign, was Paul B. McDade Jr. We wrote each other occasionally, mainly discussing religion. On August 20, I responded to one of his letters. "Your exquisite letter arrived early in the week, and I have been too humbled and overwhelmed to respond. My travels in faith have been different from yours. As in most things, I have done things moderately. I never traveled too far from good religious roots, but neither have I gotten impassioned as sometimes I wish that I would. There have been some mountaintop experiences, not too many valleys, but much of the potentially too comfortable acceptance of God's reality and blessing. It is in the fires of the furnace that purification occurs, and there have not been many furnaces. Yet."

I include this reflection because it highlights why both the Iraq experience and the fiery trials of my reaching for the goal of the U.S. Court of Appeals may have been particularly important to me. I needed to stop half-living my faith. Both experiences drew me well out of my areas of comfort, indeed, of complacency.

On August 29, Hurricane Katrina hit the Mississippi Gulf Coast with devastating effect. It also caused significant damage and power loss all the way to Jackson and beyond. Sharon was fortunate to be without power only for a day. Those from closer to the Gulf suffered greatly, and many of our troops were from that part of the state. For a time, we were dealing with examining emergency leave requests. Few were approved. Too many people were affected, and the command decision rightly had to weigh the dangers of reducing our force too greatly.

As October began, the calendar gave us new worries, as I wrote my friends Charles and Lee Jackson. "October 7. The latest from here is that we have just entered Ramadan. That is a thirty-day or so period of fasting (during daylight only, meals at night) and worship for Muslims. Our intel briefings highlight whenever there is an upcoming religious holiday, as that is when the terrorists are most likely to target large numbers of worshipers gathered in pilgrimage towns whom they can bomb. We have large numbers of people killed by a suicide bomber, then the same terrorists are waiting on the route or outside the likely hospital, and the survivors and others are attacked. This is nasty business."

The referendum on the new Iraqi constitution was another opportunity for attacks, as I wrote to Sharon. "October 16. I was glad to be here for the referendum. On this day-after there is no word on the outcome. Official results are expected on Thursday, 20 October. A fair idea of the results may be known before then. A majority nationwide is needed, but the referendum will fail if at least three provinces each reject the constitution by a two-thirds vote."

On October 28, I wrote Barney Robinson, a JAG friend who was back in Mississippi. His deployment would come a few years later. "Earlier this week I was in Baghdad to meet with Multi-National Corps–Iraq, which as you may know is the highest operational command. They retain all military justice authority on E-8s [the highest-ranking enlisted soldiers] and above, and on all the [more serious courts-martial]. I was going over the files on some officers, and an enlisted general court-martial. Felt just like working in a prosecutor's office and meeting with the DA. There is a former palace compound west of downtown Baghdad, Camp Victory, we call it, in which MNC-I is located. That is where I went. This is my third visit there, so the novelty has worn off."

Detention operations were a very closely monitored component of our mission. "I spent two hours down at the detention facility today, as we had an inspection team come in. My part seemed well-received, which was whether I was following the policies for review of the evidence and making decisions on whom to release and whom to send forward to prison."[14]

I wrote my aunt and uncle (who was a World War II veteran) about some topical humor. "A Vietnam veteran [Rhesa Barksdale] says that toward the end of his service he started to hear, and create, 'short jokes,' referring to how short was the remaining time period in country. The first one he passed along was 'I am so short that when I sit on the curb my feet don't touch the street.' I am not that short yet."[15] I loved short jokes, not for the sharpness of the humor but because they were now apt.

Though we were all getting short, some still were struck down. I wrote a letter to my old friend Kevin Watson on November 24. "We lost another soldier in the brigade last night. Counting some accidental deaths, that makes twenty-five in the brigade. I pray this is the last one. I have not been to many memorial services, but about three weeks ago I attended one here at the base. The Army has had much practice in conducting these services, and the ceremony I attended was very moving. It is a way for those who knew the soldier well to deal with their grief, to honor the person, the mission, and the sacrifice." Two more were killed before we left.

The end could not arrive until my replacement did. On November 27, I wrote my judicial mentor. "Dear Judge and Mrs. Clark, This is the Sunday after Thanksgiving, about 1600 hours. An hour ago I got a rather enjoyable telephone call. My replacement [Major Mary Card] is in Kuwait as part of the advance party for the 2d Brigade, 4th Infantry Division out of Fort Hood. It is comforting to know that the pieces are falling into place for my leaving the country."

At the end of November, something very significant happened back home in the bitterly partisan battle about Iraq. A *Wall Street Journal* column written by the 2000 Democratic nominee for vice president, senator Joe Lieberman, appeared on November 29. It was titled "Our Troops Must Stay: America Can't Abandon 27 Million Iraqis to 10,000 terrorists."[16]

The senator reported on his fourth trip to Iraq. He found real progress. In his lengthy piece, he detailed various measures about the success, though clearly mixed, of our efforts. He also wrote about the incredible importance of what we were doing. I felt compelled to contact him.

From the perspective of my base southwest of Baghdad about 35 miles, you are exactly correct. As vital as having an accurate view truly is, more impressive is that you had the patriotism to explain your counter-party perspective on this central foreign policy issue of the moment.

The challenges of constitutional writing were daunting for the Iraqis, but not more so than should have been expected. Our new chief justice wrote years ago that America's Founding Fathers were bound together in their work on nation building by the "silken cords of friendship." The Iraqis have simply the iron chains encrusted with hate that held them together after Saddam took over decades ago. The chains have been broken in many places, but much of the hate remains. The Iraqis still have to work through the essential issues of creating and preserving freedom. It is much harder in this environment, but an acceptable result is achievable with a greater degree of imperfections and distortions. We did not get it all right at first either.

I am hopeful and anxious. The potential benefits are incalculable. The difficulties are undeniable. As is said in this country, *inshallah*—if God wills it—the outcome will be good. What He wills is still being revealed. Your comments may prove to be one of the key positive events during this time of troubles in maintaining the national will. Thank you.

Christmas Day arrived with a surprise from the enemy. I did not write the family about it. I recall vividly, though, that several rockets were fired onto the base by insurgents from some hiding place. Most hit our landing strip. A Roman Catholic priest was flying in to say mass and was delayed. Some of the rockets did not explode, and those had to be carefully removed.

On the afternoon of December 26, a helicopter took me from FOB Kalsu to the former Iraqi air base Al-Taqaddum. Then, a few hours past midnight, we boarded a C-130 for a several-hour flight to Kuwait. We waited at a base in Kuwait called Camp Victory for our turn to catch a chartered flight home, staying in one of several large tents, perhaps a hundred soldiers per tent. On January 4, the word finally came to load up on buses that would take us to the airfield.

Getting on the chartered plane, it was still hard to adjust to the fact that this was it. I remember Holmes Adams, one of my few friends who had served in Vietnam, telling me about the excitement of loading up on the planes to leave while others were arriving to begin their tours of duty. So much had happened, so many anxieties had existed, so many people had been injured and killed while I remained unscathed physically and I hoped emotionally. I had served my country in this traditional way, the way my father had, and now it was all but over.

When the plane started down the runway, I tried to feel excited. I failed. The nose of the plane started to rise. There was some cheering, but it was not widespread. Perhaps being in the peacefulness of Kuwait for four or five days, being away from danger, had taken the edge off. We had already been gone from the war ever since we got to Kuwait.

We landed in Gulfport, Mississippi, on a truly wondrous day, January 5, 2006. The families were ninety miles away at Camp Shelby and were not allowed at the airport. We boarded buses to return to what had been our training base for four months. A large crowd had gathered on the open field where the bus would unload. I strained to see Sharon and finally did just before we stopped. She was holding a vinyl banner, welcoming me back. Hugging her was one of the most satisfying parts of the return. We were together again.

I was asked to give the address for the May 2006 dinner for the bar association in Jackson. This was an annual event, with several hundred people attending. I was honored and also eager. It was a chance to collect my thoughts about what I had just gone through.

I started my talk that night by recalling that it was on the day before Mother's Day in 2004, two years and one day before this night, that we got the word I was going to war. "My wife Sharon, who is the mother of our two extraordinary children, experienced her own intense challenges because of that call. The grown children were in Texas. Sharon had a house to maintain and her usual employment to continue, and then had all my responsibilities, few as there were, to the management of our lives descend on her alone. There is a old phrase, anachronistically sexist, that 'a man's gotta do what a man's gotta do.' Maybe, and the proper response for wives may be, 'yes, and a woman has to do everything else.' Sharon did everything else. What I will discuss tonight was possible because of her. It really was. Thank you."

I then described some never-before-experienced situations.

A sandstorm in March, the leading edge of which looked like a bulging, pulsing wall ten stories tall, that came across the entire desert of Iraq and made day into night for several hours.

Desert heat that reached 140 degrees—ah, but I was to feel cooled when people back here told me it was a dry heat.

Seeing crowds of young children run up to our convoys smiling and waving, some wanting candy, but all looking eager and happy for us to be there.

Having our convoy forced off a narrow road once by a herd of camels, whose smell I will not try to describe, and much more often having to weave around hundreds of sheep.

I tried to put matters in perspective:

Likely the most famous American judge who once served as a soldier was Oliver Wendell Holmes Jr. As a young man, he was in a Massachusetts regiment during the Civil War. Holmes was seriously wounded three times during his three years of service, including at Antietam and Chancellorsville.

In an 1884 Memorial Day speech, Holmes tells us something of what all soldiers to a degree experience, and why we should knowingly, willingly, and sincerely honor at Memorial Day those who paid the harshest cost that service to country can demand: "The generation that carried on the war has been set apart by its experience. Through our great good fortune, in our youth our hearts were touched with fire. It was given to us to learn at the outset that life is a profound and passionate thing. . . . We are permitted to scorn nothing but indifference, and [we] do not pretend to undervalue the worldly rewards of ambition . . . . But, above all, we have learned that whether a man accepts from Fortune her spade, and will look downward and dig, . . . the one and only success which it is his to command is to bring to his work a mighty heart."

"Our great good fortune" to be "touched by fire": with that as the measure, if I may even be considered a soldier, I was the least of all.

I then reflected that America seemed to be losing its way.

We are enlightened and sophisticated, with few beliefs, and no heroes. As I worry about the state of the modern world, though, it is almost refreshing to read that the old verities have long been under attack. G. K. Chesterton, who died in 1936, was one of the leading literary figures in England and was known for his defense and explanation of Christianity. He is given credit for writing that "he who does not believe in God will believe in anything."

It is a marvelously insightful saying. A person who is not anchored to something will find power in anything blown by a new wind. In a democracy, something similar to the epigram about those who do not believe in God will believe in anything, is that those citizens who do not believe in the basic integrity of its leaders will believe anything about them.

Holmes in his "touched by fire" speech remarked on the need to use the life-changing events of this war to make an impact on the peace. All of us who returned have that opportunity to move on with changed attitudes, with heightened awareness of what is, and is not, important. Not to let the experience change us diminishes the sacrifice.

Among the truths that I see more clearly than before is that every day is a gift; that nearly every difficulty in life can be transformed into an opportunity which has arisen from "our great good fortune"; that the motives of people with whom I disagree will almost always be at least as virtuous as my own; and that regardless of rewards of money or prestige or other earthly advantages, every moment with family is the real treasure.

I brought back with me a flag that flew at our brigade headquarters throughout the day on 9/11 last year. It had been given to my wife's family years ago at the funeral of an uncle who was a military veteran. She mailed it to me in Iraq when I learned that it would be possible to have it flown there. That it would be on the flagpole on such a significant anniversary was a surprising opportunity. Wherever my future takes me, I will in the peacefulness of my office display that flag to remind me of one of the most significant years of my life. I was among the lucky ones.[17]

11

Back Home and Breaking Through

After taking most of January off, I finally went back to the court. This was my reelection year. Deciding whether to run again would be affected by the decision on the federal judicial appointment. There still was no word from the White House.

On January 23, 2006, I e-mailed Senator Cochran's chief of staff, Mark Keenum. I wanted to be sure the senator knew I was back. Mark replied: "I hope you are still interested in serving as a federal judge. I just talked to one of my White House contacts and he confided to me that you were still very high on their list for appointment after the Alito confirmation is completed. As I learn more details I will be glad to pass them along."[1]

Because I had been called in Iraq by the White House six months earlier, it was baffling to me that I was just "high on the list."

On January 31, Judge Alito was confirmed for the Supreme Court by a 58–42 vote. With both Supreme Court vacancies filled, I hoped the rest of us would start moving. About a week later, the president finally nominated Mike Wallace. The local newspaper quite accurately said that his "nomination [was] expected to draw criticism from some of the civil rights groups that opposed Pickering's candidacy."[2] Both Senators Cochran and Lott gave enthusiastic endorsements, but the challenge ahead was daunting.

After seeing a hate-filled column about Mike Wallace in the online edition of the *Houston Chronicle*, I wrote Roger McMillin about my reactions. "And so it begins. I wonder at times what would have been said about me. I can't go through another Pickering controversy, waiting in the wings as the months slowly go by, and then the years. I need to 'move on.' I think there is an organization by that name. Maybe I need to join it."[3]

Roger answered:

In the right circumstance, people on a mission overstate the case without blinking an eye. Who could expect [various senators] and their minions to be fair in their assessment of you? There is no question that the decision model is to make the decision first and then gather the necessary evidence.

I expect there are enough court of appeals decisions out there where the nature of the case could be sufficiently distorted to cast you into the "throwback" pot based on nothing more than your vote if they were of a mind to do that.[4]

Roger would be proved precisely, painfully accurate.

On February 17, I learned that a lawyer in one of the big Jackson firms, Dan Jordan, had been selected for one of the two vacant Jackson federal judgeships. I had still heard nothing, and that was embarrassing. I typed in my notes, "Trust in the Lord with all thy heart, and do not lean on your own understandings. I so much want to call Cochran, or someone. But I turned this over to the Lord and committed to stay out of it. I will keep trying to do that."

On February 18, I wrote down some uncharitable, un-Christian thoughts. "I was an incredible fan of George W. Bush. This ordeal, this unceasing rejection and delay, has drained me. Now there is just an emptiness. There was news that he would be on the Mississippi coast tomorrow. Not long ago, I would have tried to see him. Now I do not care. There is still respect and a belief in so much of what he is trying to do, but there is no warmth about him."

"That is pique, but it also seems like the emotions that I would guess arise in a divorce. In a few painful words, my guess is that I do not matter. And that is the cruelest cut of all."

On March 6, Ken Griffis told me that he had heard from the FBI, who had questions about Dan Jordan. It seemed a new low that Dan, who had not even been in the race, had now passed me. I later read the Bible contemplations for the day, Romans 8:31, that nothing can separate me from the love of Christ. Forgive me, Lord, but I almost doubt that there is a God, for all my prayer and effort to follow him, and a constant rejection by Bush. My selfish disappointment in the president made me think of a verse, but I had to search for it. It was Psalms 146:3: "Put not your faith in rulers, or in the son of man, in whom there is no salvation."

I had bottomed out. I was self-absorbed, self-pitying, and out of patience. I was two days from the beginning of an intense nineteen-month journey.

"March 8, 2006. At 3:45 p.m., [Thad Cochran's assistant] Doris Wagley called, said, 'Hello, darling.' I did not recognize her voice, and I responded that there are so many women who call me 'darling' that I can have a difficult time figuring out which one it is. We chatted briefly, then she asked if I had 'two minutes' to speak to Sen. Cochran." I had all the time he wanted.

"After a few pleasantries, Thad said that [White House counsel] Harriet Miers had called him and said that I would be nominated for the Barbour vacancy, and Dan Jordan would be named [to Tom Lee's seat]. Miers also said that I would be seriously considered if there were another Miss. Fifth Circuit vacancy. Thad said something to the effect that he would continue to pursue a Fifth Circuit vacancy for me." I did not tell anyone at the court but went home to tell Sharon.

"March 9, 2006. Went to St. Peter's [Catholic cathedral] for 0720 mass. I did not feel that I had properly thanked the Lord for having this step occur."

In the weeks ahead, I spent much time filling out forms, preparing lists of publications, showing my key opinions, sending and receiving letters and e-mails and phone calls. Included was a set of physical and mental health questions that were to be answered by a doctor (how deranged am I for agreeing to go through what may happen to me in the Senate?), and blank fingerprint cards to be sent in after a visit to the local police station. I needed references for different stages of my career, names of neighbors at different residences, fellow students at each school. There was a lot of information to track down. Once I was nominated in June, the Senate Judiciary Committee gave me even more forms to fill out.

Starting in April, I met with FBI agents, and so did family and friends. One agent met with a neighbor on Wednesday, April 5. "FBI talked to Becky Crook. Asked all sorts of things, including how I dress when I mow the yard. She later told Sharon she had to think for a moment, then answered 'he is well-covered.'"

Though it was far from certain that I would be confirmed before my term ended, I did not want simultaneously to run for reelection and pursue the federal judgeship. I let a few weeks pass to make sure the federal appointment did not encounter early and potentially fatal problems. On April 19, I publicly announced my decision not to run again. "My future plans remain uncertain," I said in a press release, "but I believe it is time to pursue other opportunities."

On April 27, Senator Cochran called. "He thought [my nomination] could be taken care of this year, but whether it would take all year remained to be seen. 'Then the Congress would go Democratic,' he said. He thought it would be a real jolt, like 1980 when the Republicans won the Senate. Much higher hill to climb for the Senate than the House, but he thought it could happen when no one was really expecting it." I do not think in April that many people were predicting the Democratic landslide in November. Thad saw it coming.

Simultaneously, Mike Wallace's nomination was moving, but the direction was not forward. Controversy began soon after his nomination, as it would with mine a year later. A few weeks after his nomination, the Jackson newspaper's headlines read: "Wallace Nomination May End Truce on Capitol Hill."[5] His "staunch conservatism, and criticism from civil rights groups for some things he did as an aide to Mississippi Republican Sen. Trent Lott 20 years ago," threatened his approval. Also weighing Mike down was the political burden of having served as special impeachment counsel for Senate Majority Leader Lott during President Clinton's 1999 Senate trial.

On May 6, the association of black lawyers in the state, called the Magnolia Bar, voted to oppose Mike. A column by its president, Jaribu Hill, claimed that by nominating Wallace, "the president has chosen to conduct business as usual and bestow even more privilege upon those who are already overly represented as a race and gender."[6] Her column also contained specific criticisms of Mike. The organization would oppose all three Bush nominations to the Fifth Circuit from Mississippi and objected to most of the district court choices.

Reuben Anderson, the first black justice on the Mississippi Supreme Court and Wallace's law partner, wrote his own guest column. He thought President Bush "could not have picked a finer person or better lawyer." Anderson was confident about Mike's integrity and fairness.[7]

On May 9, the American Bar Association released its rating of Mike. The fifteen-person committee unanimously determined that he was "not qualified" to be on the court. The ABA committee found that he had the highest professional competence and possessed the integrity to be a federal judge. The committee believed, though, that he did not have proper judicial temperament. A White House spokesman said that "we disagree with the ABA and reject the rating. He is a well-respected attorney who would make an excellent judge."[8]

An article in a Washington newspaper gave the background on Mike's troubles.[9] "Senate leaders in both parties have been cautious in picking their judicial battles, and the bad rating could significantly damage

Wallace's hopes." At a Judiciary Committee hearing, "the ABA could detail why it gave Wallace its lowest grade." Republicans "have been pointing to the political leanings of board members and what they say is a history of tension between Wallace and Stephen Tober, the chairman of the [ABA's] Standing Committee on the Federal Judiciary." One incident occurred after Wallace had been named by Reagan to be president of the Legal Services Corporation board in the 1980s, which oversees a program for legal aid to the poor. "Tober, then president-elect of the New Hampshire Bar, accused Wallace of sandbagging him and harboring a 'hidden agenda' to set the stage for block grants through a lesser regulatory change, according to a transcript of their conversation."

Criticism of the ABA also came in a conservative political magazine, the *National Review*.

> The Mississippi lawyer is a battle-scarred veteran of the wars over the Legal Services Corporation in the 1980s. Wallace's supporters call his efforts to end liberal activism and deliver services to the poor as a Reagan appointee on the corporation's board "heroic," but his liberal adversaries saw his reform efforts differently. Among his harshest critics 20 years ago were Michael Greco, the current president of the ABA, and Stephen Tober, who now chairs the ABA's committee on judges.[10]

My feelings at the time were set out in an e-mail to my Aunt Beverly and Uncle Dick, responding to theirs about the ABA rating. "The ABA's rating of Mike Wallace, who has been a friend for many years, has been major news over here. I feel dirty, as my reaction to his bad news is an unworthy one. The feeling of those who have talked to me is that he would have had a difficult time being confirmed without this, but that this will end it."[11]

My process was moving slowly, but the next step was finally taken. On June 6, White House associate counsel Grant Dixton called me at the court at 7:55 a.m. He said that I would be nominated that day or the next. I quickly called Sharon, Philip, and Cathy. What a relief.

No one could forecast how long this would take. Since I was nominated on D-day, June 6, I facetiously told the White House Counsel's Office that I hoped my confirmation would not take more time than the Allied troops took to liberate Europe sixty-two years ago, which was the following May 9. That statement, meant to be ludicrously pessimistic, proved to be wildly optimistic.

June 7: "Thad Cochran called. He looked forward to introducing me to the Senate committee. I asked if he had a date that I could write down on my calendar. He laughed. I said that no ingratitude should be suggested for what I have received, but if there is another opening on the Fifth Circuit, I hope he would recommend me. Thad said I was his man."

Just before Thad called, my daughter Cathy and I had exchanged e-mails. I was to call her in ten minutes. While I was still talking to Thad, well after the ten minutes, she sent a one-word e-mail: "Father?" She usually calls me "Dad." I called her quickly after I got off the phone with the senator. I should not have let anyone's call cause me to forget her.

One other significant hurdle was receiving my ABA rating. The Fifth Circuit representative on the ABA committee, Kim Askew, was to be my interviewer. She had also conducted the investigation that resulted in Mike Wallace's "unqualified" rating. Dan Jordan, though, had been extremely pleased with her work on his rating. Askew worked for a large, well-regarded Dallas law firm and was a smart and skilled attorney who had always seemed open-minded about me. During our meeting on July 11, she did not seem concerned about my lack of extensive trial experience and found the time on the appellate court to compensate. We had an enjoyable and encouraging discussion.

On July 20, for Dan Jordan the possibility of becoming a district judge became a reality. He was confirmed without dissenting vote. His nomination had been on April 24, so it had taken a few days less than three months from nomination to confirmation. I had been nominated six weeks after Dan. A similar delay would have me confirmed sometime in September. I almost was.

Mike Wallace's hearing before the Senate Judiciary Committee was scheduled for July 19. A month before, GOP chairman Arlen Specter wrote the chairman of the ABA committee, asking for the ABA report supporting its rating. Specter argued that it was "fundamental fairness" that Wallace have some time before the hearing to prepare a response to the allegations. On June 30, the ABA refused, saying that Wallace was fully aware of the report's negative information. Instead the ABA would provide the testimony of its representatives forty-eight hours before the hearing. The day before Mike's July 19 hearing, with the testimony still undelivered, the hearing was postponed.

My own news from the ABA finally came on July 26. A "substantial majority," which meant between ten and thirteen of the fifteen members, of the ABA committee said I was "well qualified." The remainder said that

I was "qualified." My lack of substantial trial court experience had not hurt too much. Kim had written me first, informing me of the rating. I was extremely appreciative, despite some guilt because of what I considered to be a serious error in the evaluation of Mike Wallace.

Kim e-mailed me her congratulations, and I immediately responded. "That was an extremely gracious message. Thank you. I am hopeful that the favorable opinion of the committee will have an opportunity to be tested by my actually becoming a federal district judge. Time, and the U.S. Senate, will tell."[12]

Unfortunately for me, the Senate went into recess on August 3, not to return until after Labor Day. Once Congress did return, another long recess was already scheduled before the 2006 elections. There would not be much time for official business.

Important matters and lesser ones were brought into perspective on August 7, when I learned that Judge William Barbour's wife had died. Her name was Stewart Fair Barbour. When William retired in February 2006, opening up the position to which I had been nominated, the caption above the large photo that appeared with the local story was, "I'm going to . . . travel with my wife."[13] Most if not all of the federal judges attended her funeral in Yazoo City a few days later. The judiciary can be a family, fractious at times perhaps, but capable of coming together when necessary.

August finally ended. Schedules of weekly hearings for judges began to be announced for September. I was not announced in either the first two weeks, and I got worried and irritated. There would not be many hearings before it was too late. With the elections in November, the senators would disappear from Washington. I needed to get moving. Finally I received word that my hearing would be on September 19.

My wife could not join me at the hearing. A personal sadness had intruded. My father-in-law, Johnnie Polasek, died on August 21. He was eighty-seven, suffering from Alzheimer's for the last two years, no longer the indefatigable worker he had once been. Sharon's mother came to stay with us because she suffered a stroke a few days after the death of her husband of sixty-one years. Philip had his own schedule that kept him from going. Daughter Cathy could join me. We would stay at the Watergate Hotel, a fitting location due to my sense of history.

When I arrived in Washington, I went straight to the mock hearing at the Justice Department. I passed through the security checkpoint at the building's entrance at the same time as Paul Maloney, whom I had not seen in more than a dozen years. He sure looked familiar. We would become much better (re)acquainted. All four of us were questioned that Monday by perhaps five attorneys from the Justice Department and the White House. The questions were meant to be much tougher than we were likely actually to experience. Those selected for district judgeships did not encounter the Senate inquisitions that those seeking circuit court positions often faced. The mock hearing was awkward at times, as there was an unnecessary harshness to the questioning.

Cathy flew in later, and we met at the Watergate. That evening we went to a play at the Kennedy Center, barely a block from the hotel. The play we chose was called *Shear Madness*. To me, the title implied the play was about judicial selection, but it was not. I found its humor annoying. Likely I was not in the mood for entertainment, being too nervous about what was ahead.

At 3:00 p.m. the next day, September 19, the hearing began in the Judiciary Committee hearing room in the Dirksen Senate Office Building. The only committee member there was Kansas Republican senator Sam Brownback. One member has to attend, or else no hearing can take place. When the nominations are noncontroversial, often only one senator is present. I shared the witness table with three nominees from the western district of Michigan. I knew one of them, Paul Maloney, from the Justice Department of the first Bush administration. We had even testified together in 1990 to the House Judiciary Committee. The other nominees were Bob Jonker and Janet T. Neff. Paul was a state trial judge, Bob a young lawyer in private practice, and Janet a judge on Michigan's intermediate court. The three Michigan nominees were a carefully negotiated package. Paul and Bob were supported by Republicans. The two Democratic Michigan senators allowed them to proceed in exchange for the president's nominating Janet.

The nominees each introduced those who were with us. When my time came, I first noted that Sharon, Philip, and Mary could not attend. "I am honored beyond, I think, her understanding that my daughter Cathy has joined us today." I mentioned that she had to get up at 3:30 in the morning to catch a 5:30 flight from Houston. Senator Brownback, understandably thinking I meant she had gotten up early that morning, said: "Cathy, thank you. And we have extra coffee if you need it. [Laughter.] Welcome. Delighted."[14] I loved having her with me.

The next day's Jackson newspaper gave a report on my part of the hearing. The heading was accurate and a relief: "Southwick Confirmation Hearing Cordial."[15] The secondary heading said I was "expected to sail through process." It reported that Senators Cochran and Lott were the only witnesses for me. The only substantive question I received concerned my view of judicial restraint. "Southwick responded that he would honestly interpret the facts and the law." I was "expected to win easy approval when the Judiciary Committee votes next week. But a confirmation vote by the full Senate is not expected before Congress breaks for recess at the end of September and may be held in a lame-duck session after November's elections."

My hearing on September 19 put me one step closer to confirmation. One week later, Mike Wallace was again scheduled for a hearing.[16] Senators Cochran and Lott appeared to support him as they had me a week earlier. Also witnesses, less friendly, were Roberta B. Liebenberg of Philadelphia, who was the new chairwoman of the ABA's Standing Committee on the Federal Judiciary; Kim Askew, my new friend and the Fifth Circuit representative on the ABA's Standing Committee; and four other present or former members of the ABA committee.

A Mississippi panel, some supporting and some not, included former Supreme Court justice Reuben Anderson, prominent Jackson attorney Scott Welch, civil rights attorney Carroll Rhodes of Hazlehurst, and attorney Robert McDuff of Jackson. It got fairly basic at times, as when Texas GOP senator John Cornyn asked, "Are you a bigot?" Wallace answered, "I don't think anyone who knows me would call me a bigot."[17] Civil rights groups alleged that Wallace had "helped [Senator] Lott lobby on behalf of Bob Jones University. The then-segregated school was defending its right to take federal tax deductions in a case before the Supreme Court." Mike responded that Lott's concern "was that executive agencies follow the law. 'The fact that a discriminatory institution might benefit from that is no more an endorsement of discrimination than a lawyer endorsing murder when he defends an accused client,' he said." He described his zealous representation of Claiborne County, a black majority county. He had sought but failed to invalidate a new state statute that required property taxes paid on a newly constructed nuclear power plant in Claiborne County to be shared with all counties in the service area of the company.

Most of the criticism centered on his work as a board member and then president of the Legal Services Corporation. He argued that he was only trying to reform the agency so that it would focus on its core mission of providing legal help to the poor. On the board, he had carried out the president's desire, one with which he agreed, to prohibit the kinds of suits that took on broader issues against government.

This was the end of Mike's consideration by the committee. He never received a vote.

Mike's hearing had occurred on the Tuesday before the congressional session ended on Friday. My chance for confirmation was slipping away. On Thursday morning, the three Michigan nominees and I appeared on the committee's agenda for its morning business meeting. Four circuit court nominees and eight for the district court were on the agenda. That many nominees might not be reported at one time. In early afternoon, we learned that no meeting was even held.

Later Senator Lott's counsel gave me some encouragement. "The Committee has scheduled another Executive Business meeting for tomorrow morning. There are no guarantees that this meeting will be any more productive than other recent attempts, but they're trying. You are on the itinerary for tomorrow's session. If this doesn't fall into place, then we're going to shift our focus to the lame duck session. Obviously, the length of the lame duck session will be largely dependent on the outcome of the elections, so it's truly an unpredictable situation."[18]

On Friday, I got great news. Eight district court nominees, including the three from Michigan and me, were all voted out of committee that morning. There were now thirteen district court nominations pending on the Senate executive calendar, ready for a floor vote.

Senator Lott's counsel, Hugh Gamble, told me about a Senate procedure. I forwarded his message to my family. "My understanding of a 'hotline' message is this. The Senate Majority Leader e-mails to all senators a hotline. The senators have a limited time to indicate whether they have any objection. Those items/people to whom no objection is raised within a certain period of time can go on the unanimous consent calendar for action. Majority Leader Frist will bring up unanimous consent matters later today, maybe *very* late today. If no one objects by e-mail, and if no one raises a late objection in the Senate itself when he brings a matter up, confirmation will occur today."[19]

By the time I went to bed on Friday night, the Senate still had not gotten to us. I slept fitfully and got up at perhaps 3:00 a.m. to see what the Internet would tell me. I looked for a good while but learned nothing other than the Senate had recessed until after the election. Later in the morning, I discovered that we had not made it. I wrote my three Michigan comrades in frustration.

"The Catholic Church reading for Thursday was from Ecclesiastes 1, 'I have seen all things that are done under the sun, and behold, all is vanity and a chase after wind." When I read that two days ago, I wondered how applicable it would seem when the session was over. I thought we might have been seeing the finish line ahead, but it was just another milepost along the way."[20]

I wrote a friend about the failure. "My friends in the Senate decided to use their peremptory strikes against us all late Friday/early Saturday last week. There were thirteen district court and two circuit nominees on the unanimous consent/executive calendar before the knives came out. There has been some commentary that it all started with Sen. Feinstein striking an Idaho nominee for the Ninth Circuit [Randy Smith], then an Idaho Republican [Larry Craig] striking everyone else. Don't really know, but it makes sense in the way things in Washington make sense, which is not good sense."[21] My ability to imply anything negative about Senator Feinstein would disappear ten months later and be forever gone. I leave this one aberrant comment.

A different story appeared the next day in a Michigan newspaper.[22] "The nomination of Michigan Court of Appeals Judge Janet Neff to the federal bench is on hold because she helped lead a commitment ceremony for a lesbian couple four years ago. Sen. Sam Brownback, of Kansas, an opponent of gay marriage who has presidential aspirations, said Friday he wants to know whether there was anything illegal or improper about the ceremony in Massachusetts. He also said he wants to question Neff about her views on gay marriage and how her actions might shape her judicial philosophy." The story explained that one "senator can block a nomination from moving forward by placing a hold on it." Once Judge Neff was stopped, one of the Michigan Democratic senators promoting her put a hold on the two Republicans, Jonker and Maloney. Fairly quickly, we all were held. Other newspapers had the same story.[23]

Quite possibly these are accurate pieces of a larger story. A critical mass of holds for specific individual reasons may have led to a hold on everyone.

What was left was an election. On November 7, an angry electorate rewarded Democrats for not being the party in power. Picking up six Senate seats, they would now have fifty-one and control the Senate. My soon-to-be-former seat on the court of appeals was subject to a runoff between Ed Patten and Virginia Carlton. Two weeks later, Virginia was chosen as my successor.

On November 16, the *Clarion-Ledger* reported that Mike Wallace's nomination was doomed.[24] I was mentioned as still having an opportunity to be confirmed before adjournment. For the first time, there was this printed speculation: "It's also possible the White House may pull Southwick's nomination to the District Court and nominate him—instead of renominating Wallace—to the 5th Circuit seat when the new Congress convenes next year." The reporter, Ana Radelat, had called me the night before the article. I got the impression she thought I would know about such a plan, but I did not. It may have seemed likely, but I had been wrong too many times already. The last sentence in the article was memorable: "Southwick's possible nomination to the appellate court probably would not spark Democratic opposition."

There were two short Senate sessions, broken by the Thanksgiving holidays. The 55–45 Republican majority was still intact until adjournment, but the GOP was dispirited and uninterested in judges. No votes were taken on any district judges before Congress adjourned on December 9. In fact, on July 20 Dan Jordan was the last nominee in that Congress to be confirmed for a district court in any state. The door then shut behind him. My irritation about later nominees getting hearings ahead of me was so much senseless, self-centered fretting. None of us made it.

My 2006 district court prospects ended with a whimper. What I hoped lay ahead was a shift to a course that would lead to the Fifth Circuit.

12

The Fifth Circuit Shift

By the time this very long journey ended, I had kept three separate word-processing documents that made up my diary. The first started with the gleam in my eye in 1991 and was kept haphazardly until after the 2000 election. The second document was dedicated to what happened in 2006 about the district court, which could be described as either a lot or almost nothing. The final document covered all of 2007. It was the longest, as an eventful year was ahead.

The first entry was an e-mail I sent to Thad's counsel Brad Davis four days after Congress adjourned for the year. "I talked to Sen. Cochran [on the telephone] a little while ago. He was gracious and supportive, as always. I was hoping that he knew of some secret, unpublicized judicial confirmations, but no luck there. I am considering what to do with myself in January after I leave the state court. Some options would require more of a commitment than others. Any talk yet of what the situation will be next year?"[1] Brad responded that only guesswork was available now, but he thought I would be confirmed for the district court in the first few months of 2007.

A week after my first e-mail, I again wrote Cochran's counsel. "Among the things that Sen. Cochran and I discussed was the possibility of being nominated for the Fifth Circuit and his support for me if that opens up. Whether Pres. Bush would renominate Mike W. or seek someone else is a question. I would greatly prefer the appellate court, though the chances of never being confirmed—that is the pattern for Miss. 5th Cir nominees— are certainly much greater than for the district court. I am willing to take that chance if given it. Of course, nothing has been offered."[2]

Within two hours, I got a message to call Brad. My notes summarized the call. "Mike Wallace talked to Brad today after talking to Thad last week. Mike had been in discussions with DOJ and Counsel's Office about whether it was possible to succeed next year. He has agreed to withdraw and is working on a letter to Bush saying that. It will be released to the press. That would explain the failure of the White House to contact me. *Maybe*."

I wrote Rees that night about Mike's likely withdrawal. I first explained what I had been told. "There is a sadness in this. My dream, and that is what it is, almost certainly is no stronger, fervent, or worthy than Mike's. I feel almost ashamed to hope what I was told is true and that it redounds to my benefit. I am not the agent of his difficulties, but that is not a sufficient justification for wanting this to come to pass. Recognizing that my reactions are part of life, and of my humanity, I still feel regret. I hope he has a firm grip on his own faith. I expect he does."[3]

Two days later, Mike's withdrawal was front-page news in the *Clarion-Ledger*. A few days later, Sid Salter, the same reporter who had written about Mike's withdrawal, wrote an editorial titled "Now, Can Someone Give Wallace His Reputation Back?"[4]

With the new year came speculation about who would be next. On January 2, the *Clarion-Ledger* gave a status report on the vacancy.[5] "So far, two of the president's nominations for the seat have failed to win confirmation, and now he must come up with a third as Democrats prepare to take over Congress." Senator Lott was quoted as saying that I had "impressed" the White House. "Southwick is up for a federal judge seat in Jackson, and could possibly have to choose between the two." The others who had been recommended in 2004 were listed: Jim Herring, Kay Cobb, and Henry Wingate. Congressman Bennie Thompson suggested two black women, Judge Tomie Green of Jackson and Constance Slaughter-Harvey. A critical racial divide once again appeared.

As I waited for all of this to play out, I began teaching at Mississippi College Law School. My uncertain prospects for quick confirmation to any judgeship caused me to accept the offer to be a visiting professor there. It was extraordinarily helpful of the school, an offer initiated by a good friend, professor Matt Steffey, then accepted by the faculty and dean Jim Rosenblatt.

On January 3, Thad's counsel Brad Davis called. "He had just gotten off phone with White House Counsel's office. He was asked whether Thad was still as high on me for the Fifth Circuit as he was a year ago. Brad said Thad was. Unclear whether the White House wants to work off a list, such as the remaining four from 2004, or whether will just consider me."

The next day, associate White House counsel Cheryl Stanton called me. "She asked if I would be willing to be considered for the Fifth Circuit. I said it was my preference." Apparently there was as yet no presidential decision.

On Tuesday morning, January 9, 2007, I was at home, sitting in my study. Sharon answered the phone at about 8:00 a.m., then gave it to me. I am reminded of a time almost three years earlier when Sharon answered, was unsure of who it was, and handed me the phone for some momentous news. The previous time it was Lieutenant Colonel Roy Carpenter, telling me that I would deploy to Iraq. This time it was Cheryl Stanton. She also told me of an opportunity to go into a war zone.

Cheryl immediately got to the subject of the call. She said, as best as I remembered when writing it down later: "President Bush has decided to nominate you for the Fifth Circuit." I stopped her right then, saying I needed a moment. Sharon was standing nearby. I had to tell her. We, together, had been waiting for someone to tell me that since a time when President Bush was another man. We hugged, and then I got back on the phone.

How to respond could have been a difficult question. There was considerable risk in changing course from the almost certain confirmation for the district court. In the previous week's phone call, it was suggested I might be nominated for the district court first, secure confirmation, then proceed on this much more uncertain course. None of that was suggested on January 9.

Whatever hesitation I might have felt, it was brief. I had to seize the day, one that with such incredible difficulty and interminable delay had finally come. I accepted the offer and the challenge. Later I thought of the following occasionally heard tale as a good one to explain my instinct to accept. A sheriff came to a house, warned the man living there that a flood was coming, and told him to leave. The man said he would rely on God to save him. Later the waters got so high that the man climbed on his roof. A boat came. Again the man refused to leave because God would save him. Finally a helicopter lowered a net for him to climb onto. He waved them off. The man drowned. Arriving in heaven, he asked angrily, "God, why didn't you save me?" God replied, "I sent the sheriff, I sent a boat, I sent a helicopter, what more did you want me to do?"

Waiting for something to happen exactly the way you want it to can be fatal for the ambition. The phone call gave me a chance, one I had been praying for. Implicit in my pleas had been that I be given a safe and sure passage. Instead, I had been offered the possibility of an ugly struggle with an uncertain result. I had to accept, because this might be my only chance.

Later that day, I went to my old court to let my friends know. One person I wanted to see was Tyree Irving, but he was out. We later talked by phone. Tyree thought my only problem was the need for diversity, and he offered to help where he could. He was exactly right.

When I got home late in the morning, there was a voice mail from Thad. It was very gracious, positive, supportive. I still have the recording. This is what he said: "Good morning, Leslie, this is Thad Cochran. I was calling to give you news from the White House Counsel's Office. They let me know this morning that your nomination for the Fifth Circuit Court of Appeals has been approved, and it will be submitted to the Senate today. Congratulations, my good friend. Well-earned, well-deserved nomination, and I'm optimistic that we're going to have smooth sailing here in the Senate. I'm going to be talking to Pat Leahy and let him know of your excellent qualifications and urge him to see that the Judiciary Committee reports this favorably to the Senate at the earliest possible time. Anyway, let's stay in touch, and I'm really happy this is working out as we hoped it would. Congratulations again."

The nomination was front-page Jackson news the next day. It was not the story I wanted. Doubt started with the headline "Bush Selection of Southwick for Appeals Court Criticized."[6] Pictured was Jaribu Hill, the Magnolia Bar president who had announced her group's opposition to Mike Wallace. My nomination, she said, was "a glaring example of insensitivity of the administration" by not naming African Americans to judgeships in Mississippi. "It is high time the federal bench is diversified. It is way overdue," she said. For now, nothing besides my race was raised as a reason to oppose me. Other reasons would be filled in later.

For a few days, a handful of letters to the editor supported or criticized the criticisms. My former court of appeals colleague, Mary Libby Payne, wrote urging that my race not be held against me. She is a wonderfully kind friend. The newspaper itself wrote a remarkably supportive editorial on January 11.[7] "Southwick, of Jackson, is an outstanding nomination for the bench, with no hint of any reason for disqualification. He has an established judicial record which should stand up under any scrutiny." It mentioned the criticism of my selection. "It's not aimed at Southwick but [at] Bush. Greenville lawyer Jaribu Hill, president of the 400-member Magnolia Bar Association . . . is right that diversity on the bench is 'overdue.' But that's not the fault of Southwick, nor does it in any way reflect on his abilities or qualifications." The newspaper would maintain that editorial position throughout my long ordeal. I was quite appreciative.

Several people sent congratulations. One of the most poignant was from Mike Wallace. He said he was "delighted" at my nomination. He hoped that he and Charles "have at least managed to clear some of the land mines out of your way." I replied, "Your decision to withdraw must have been a difficult one. My desire for the position is I expect no more fervent than yours, so I can appreciate some of the feelings involved." Whether I would reach the destination remained to be seen, "but your sacrifice placed me on the starting line. I will always owe so much to you."

There were new questionnaires to answer for the Senate, and many more materials to provide. The Senate Judiciary Committee now wanted a copy of all opinions on which I had ever voted. The problem was that on my old court, although a three-judge panel initially considers a case, the other seven judges ultimately vote on the panel opinions. So the committee was asking for about seven thousand opinions. For the first five years of the court's existence, the opinions were not published and were not available outside the court itself. Because of that problem, the committee eventually agreed for the earlier time period to accept a computer disk just of my opinions.

I was worried about providing a computer disk with all my opinions, as it could be circulated widely among interest groups to search for something to use against me. It occurred to me to undertake the expense of printing all four thousand pages or so containing the opinions that I had written, send the four copies (sixteen thousand pages) that the committee wanted, and not provide a digital copy. But that was too much waste. As it turned out, nothing I had written would be a problem.

As I was trying to move ahead, Judge Pickering finished the second of two books on his experiences. The first was called *Supreme Chaos: The Politics of Judicial Confirmation and the Culture War* (2006), and the second, *A Price Too High: The Judiciary in Jeopardy* (2007). Bloodied but not bowed, disappointed but not bitter, Judge Pickering took valuable lessons from his experiences that he has shared through his writing. My goal is the same.

As I was gearing up for the new and more arduous struggle for confirmation, some of the district judge nominees who had been stalled with me in September were getting confirmed. Of the thirteen district judge nominees who got tied up in the September late-night debacle when various holds started to be placed, nine were confirmed between January 30 and March 8. The three Michigan nominees and I were the exceptions. We remained joined by delay.

In February I contacted someone whom I had not met but who had also been nominated for a circuit court. He was Peter Keisler, the assistant attorney general in charge of the Civil Division, where I had worked fifteen years earlier. He had been nominated for the D.C. Circuit on June 29, 2006, about three weeks after I had been nominated for the district court. On August 1 he received a hearing in that GOP-controlled Judiciary Committee. Senator Chuck Schumer alleged the hearing was premature, that "we are trying to break the land speed record" on a nominee. Fellow Democrat Pat Leahy said all the Democrats opposed giving Peter a hearing that soon.[8] As I fully accepted after getting to know him, the administration properly saw him as one of the star nominees who needed to be moved on through. Peter received no vote before Congress adjourned. President Bush renominated him on January 9, 2007, the same day I was named.

We became friends through the confirmation experience and our shared connection with the Civil Division. He is a lovely man. Peter is at the top of the legal profession, an incredibly smart former Supreme Court law clerk, just forty-seven in 2007, so thoughtful about others that after visiting with him, I would try to mirror his attitude until the effect wore off. Most damaging in the politics of confirmation, though, was that his extraordinary law school record had earned him the honor of clerking for Judge Robert Bork. Peter was also one of the original directors of the Federalist Society. Such credentials condemned him in the eyes of many Democrats.

On February 5, 2007, though I would not see the letter for a year, Mike Wallace wrote Senator Arlen Specter. He thanked Specter for his "steadfast support I received from you and the other Republican members of the Committee last year." Mike generously introduced me to the senator. "I was pleased to see that President Bush nominated my friend Leslie Southwick to the Fifth Circuit last month." He called my state court record "outstanding" and my prospects "wonderful" for the federal court. He encouraged the senator and the committee to give me "the same unwavering support that you gave me." That was a generous and thoughtful act.

I was not getting any criticism, yet, on the work I had done. For several months, the only complaint was that the nominee needed to be a black person. An article appeared in the *National Law Journal* of February 14, titled "Lack of Black Bench Nominees Criticized."[9] The article opened by stating that in nine of the eleven state of the South, President Bush had named no African American to the sixty-two openings for federal trial court judgeships. The new president of the Magnolia Bar, Carlton Reeves, complained that Senator Lott "has never, to my knowledge, consulted with the Magnolia Bar, and we have been in existence since 1955."

As I worried about the developing political challenge, the ABA released its rating on Friday, February 23. Kim Askew had again conducted the investigation. The committee unanimously found me "well qualified." I wrote to Philip and Cathy:

> This is the good news from Friday. The ABA published my rating. What was the death-knell for my most recent predecessor as a nominee for this seat was that the ABA gave him a "not qualified" rating, which is the lowest of the three possibilities. Mine was "well qualified."
>
> That is also the rating I got last year for the district judgeship, but it was not unanimous as it was for the Fifth Circuit. My lack of significant trial court experience was a justifiable basis for a small minority last year to rate me as "qualified."
>
> The rating is less of a benefit than it is an avoidance of a significant detriment had a lesser rating been received. Had the ABA said that I was not well qualified, there would have been additional ammunition for the opposition.[10]

My predecessor nominee, Mike Wallace, did not believe he was treated fairly in the ABA process. I respect and am fond of Mike. I also became quite fond of his ABA nemesis, Kim Askew. With great respect for her, I believe Kim and the ABA were wrong about Mike. Admittedly, though, the ABA could have been wrong about both of us.

On Sunday, February 25, I wrote down some of my thoughts. "During jog on levee at 1030, decided that I would like to use Lent as Jesus did his forty days in the desert before his public ministry began (today's readings, Luke 4:1–13). Perhaps go to confession, try to cleanse myself, give myself a good foundation for Lent and preparing for my new mission as a Fifth Circuit judge."

I feared that if I received the same treatment as had Judge Pickering and Mike Wallace, I would become embittered. I was entering into, even volunteering for, something that needed to be avoided. The Roman Catholic Church speaks of "near occasions of sin," meaning situations in which we expose ourselves to spiritual danger. I feared a federal court nomination in this climate was exactly what my church wisely cautioned me to avoid. I promised myself to remain vigilant and withdraw if necessary. I did not want to risk something eternal for an earthly bauble. I feared, though, that withdrawing might be most difficult just when it was the most necessary.

A constant worry for nominees was whether they would ever get a hearing. Once a month, some months, the committee announced which fortunate circuit court nominee was next. Peter Keisler compared it to the attitudes of the toys waiting on the shelves in the movie *Toy Story*. Each of us was eager to be the next one chosen by Chairman Leahy, who represented the character Andy in our lives. Admittedly, Leahy as Andy is not an obvious metaphor. On March 13, Thad told me that March was not my turn. Third Circuit nominee Tom Hardiman was next. Thad "felt sure I would be confirmed 'this year' (ouch!), but no idea when. He had talked to Sen. Leahy, and in leadership meetings Trent had mentioned to the Democratic leaders the importance of my nomination."

In early April, I learned that a circuit court nominee from New York, Debra Livingston, was next off the shelf. The Senate was being deliberate, but I was optimistic. One reason was that on April 9, I was given copies of two letters. One had been sent to Senator Cochran and the other to Senator Lott. The letters suggested a way to compromise on the insistence that more African Americans needed to be judges in Mississippi. The two letters were largely identical and both dated March 23, 2007. The signatories were all African Americans. They were former Mississippi Supreme Court justice Fred Banks; Magnolia Bar president Jaribu Hill; the president of the 100 Black Men of Jackson organization, Eric Stringfellow; the chairwoman of the black legislative caucus, Reecy Dickson; and the president of the state NAACP, Derrick Johnson.

The five requested a meeting with each senator to discuss the district court vacancy, the one to which I had been nominated in 2006, which had still not been filled. "Despite requests from many Mississippians that he nominate a black judge or lawyer to the U.S. Court of Appeals for the Fifth Circuit, the President recently declined to do so." They were referring to my selection. "However, there is still an opportunity to rectify the larger situation . . . by recommending one of the many qualified black lawyers or judges" for the district court.

I never spoke to the senators about the compromise. I found it an extremely encouraging sign. Because it seemed inevitable that the next district court nominee would be a black judge or lawyer, a senatorial concession in exchange for gaining support for me seemed to be costless. My perspective, though, was so self-centered that anything that eased my troubles was bound to appear correct. No agreement was made.

The weekend after Easter, I left for my third annual trip to a Catholic retreat house between Baton Rouge and New Orleans called Manresa. It is a silent retreat, where the one hundred attending do not talk at all to each other between 8:00 p.m. on Thursday evening and lunch on Sunday. One saying printed on Manresa's materials is that it is a place "where nobody speaks to anybody, and everybody speaks to God." I felt a tremendous need for the peace that comes from the quiet, the prayers, and the thirty-minute presentations several times a day by the retreat leader to his silent audience. I found this weekend "absolutely wonderful; maybe the best."

When I returned to Jackson on Sunday, April 15, I e-mailed Senator Lott's counsel Hugh Gamble with a few questions. He called me back Monday morning with a few answers. "He said that Leahy, Cochran, and Lott were together at some point last week. The Miss. Senators encouraged Leahy to give me a hearing next, and to allow me to be considered in May. No commitment from Leahy. Lott has gotten the apparent agreement of McConnell to urge that I be the next circuit nominee, as Peter Keisler has some controversies arising out of his work at DOJ."

I wrote Peter with my somewhat ambivalent feelings about being called up next ahead of him. He had been nominated for the circuit court first and would clearly make a wonderful judge. "Subject: two little Indians. Maybe I should not use ethnic terms like 'Indians,' but I feel that the two of us are the sole survivors of something, and that word came to mind. Unless nominees start to be taken out of order, it would seem that one of us will move to the plate in May or thereabouts. I hate wishing anyone to have their ordeal continue. If you are next, that is just fine. Admittedly, if I am next, that is, shall I say, finer?"[11] He responded with great friendliness, surmising that I would be next.

On April 19, I got the phone call I wanted. "At 5:45 p.m., in dining room after having walked out of the kitchen, phone rang. Sharon picked up and saw that it was a D.C. number. I asked her to answer. It was Hugh Gamble, and she handed the phone to me. He said that he would call me back in just a moment and put Sen. Lott on the phone."

"Trent called and immediately asked, 'How would you like to be confirmed by Memorial Day?' Trent indicated that Leahy, Cochran, McConnell, and perhaps one other whom he named had agreed that I would be one of the two people confirmed before Memorial Day. I asked if that meant that these people agreed that 'Leslie Southwick' would be confirmed (as opposed to just a second nominee). Yes indeed. It was a very friendly conversation, and even humorous."

I wrote these thoughts in my diary. "Thank you, thank you, thank you, Lord. This is the day the Lord has made. I will rejoice and be glad." I went from being uncertain one moment of whether I would ever get a hearing to being convinced the next that I would get a hearing, be reported, and confirmed, all in about a month. It was my turn to come off the shelf.

"It is hard for me to get my mind around the concept that I could be confirmed by May 25. Memorial Day weekend. I have several times since the call said to Sharon, 'Memorial Day.'" She knew what I meant. We both found it hard to believe that success was imminent. When Trent explained everything I had been waiting to hear for so long, I remember feeling that this must be a conversation about someone else. In a way, it was. The senators had agreed to confirm the noncontroversial 2006 nominee. In 2007 I was about to become somebody quite different.

13

The Hearing

Trent Lott was a senator who made things happen, who enjoyed the battle and loved to win. Commentators would remark about how his hair was perfectly combed and unmoving. To me, his appearance symbolized how well organized he was in all ways. Once committed to a goal, he was indefatigable. I heard him in action once in his office, speaking on the phone, cajoling and praising a Republican colleague, given sound political advice, all while trying to get the caller's vote on something. I, fortunately, became one of his final Senate projects.

Late in the afternoon of May 3, I heard from Senator Lott's counsel, Hugh Gamble. "Thirty-minute talk that was quite interesting. Sen. John Kyl asked Leahy whether there would be one circuit nominee a month as Leahy had indicated. Leahy seemed to indicate that was still his desire. Apparently I am being named by GOP senators on the committee as the one to go next. What the GOP wants is another confirmation, and I am the best choice right now. Hugh thought someone like Kennedy might be objecting, saying that we needed diversity in Miss. federal court."

Late on May 3, the Judiciary Committee posted the news that each circuit judge nominee waited to see each month, namely, who was the single circuit nominee who would move ahead.

MAY 10, 2007
Judicial Nominations
Senate Judiciary Committee
Full Committee

TIME: 10:00 AM
ROOM: Dirksen-226

OFFICIAL HEARING NOTICE / WITNESS LIST:
May 3, 2007
NOTICE OF COMMITTEE HEARING

The Senate Committee on the Judiciary has scheduled a hearing on Judicial Nominations for Thursday, May 10, 2007, at 10:00 a.m. in Room 226 of the Senate Dirksen Office Building. Senator Whitehouse will preside.

Witness List
Panel I
The Honorable Thad Cochran, United States Senator [R-MS]
The Honorable John Warner, United States Senator [R-VA]
The Honorable Carl Levin, United States Senator [D-MI]
The Honorable Trent Lott, United States Senator [R-MS]
The Honorable Jim Webb, United States Senator [D-VA]

Panel II
Leslie Southwick to be United States Circuit Judge for the Fifth Circuit

Panel III
Janet T. Neff to be United States District Judge for the Western District of Michigan
Liam O'Grady to be United States District Judge for the Eastern District of Virginia.

There it was. I was next.

On Tuesday before the Thursday hearing, I got word that all might not be well. My former law clerk Dean Korsak sent notice of a Web site posting by one of the groups that opposes most Republican circuit court nominees, the Alliance for Justice. He thought I would have known about it already, but I did not. The site listed five opinions that I had written or joined that the group found to disqualify me from further judicial service. Chiming in a few hours later was a similar group, the People for the American Way, which listed the same five cases.

I quickly became reacquainted with these newly controversial decisions. The group tossed out several to see if any would stick. Three disappeared, but the others became my twin burdens, used to crush me in the months ahead. They were written by other judges, but I had joined them.

The earlier of the two cases was *Bonnie Richmond v. Mississippi Department of Human Services*, from August 1998.[1] Richmond was a white state employee of the Department of Human Services. In 1994 she met with three other employees: Renee Elmore; Joyce Johnson, the director of the division in which these individuals worked; and a third unnamed woman. Apparently all four are white. Director Johnson asked why Varrie Richmond, a black employee, was traveling that day. Varrie Richmond was assigned to one county office but was traveling to one in a different county. The director seemed to be questioning the purpose of the trip. It appears that Bonnie Richmond, who is not related to Varrie Richmond, said, "All I can say about Varrie, she's a good ole n——," using the racial slur. Nothing further happened at the meeting regarding the statement.

The next day, Varrie Richmond spoke with Bonnie Richmond and Renee Elmore, who had heard the racial slur. Elmore said, "Guess what Bonnie said about you?" It was unclear whether it was Bonnie or Elmore who then identified the slur. Bonnie apologized during that initial conversation.

Soon the Department of Human Services went through its personnel procedures for disciplining Bonnie Richmond. The state personnel rules did not contain anything express about the use of offensive words. Instead Richmond was charged with acts "plainly related to job performance . . . of such nature that to continue the employee in the assigned position could constitute negligence in regard to the agency's duties to the public or other state employees." She was further charged with creating a "hostile, harassing and offensive environment" for the others workers in the department.

Richmond was fired. She appealed to the Mississippi Employee Appeals Board. At a hearing, Varrie Richmond, the target of the slur, testified that she found the word offensive, but "it was not like there was any real problem associated with the incident." She described herself as the kind of person to withdraw from "things of that nature," but her feelings were hurt.

Bonnie Richmond testified on her own behalf. She said the slur was used to express her sense that Varrie Richmond was unable to assert herself. She denied any racial motivation and compared it to her being called a "honky" or "redneck."

There was no other appreciable evidence from the department. Director Johnson testified that numerous phone calls were received complaining about Bonnie Richmond. When questioned about details, Johnson said she would have to check her records. No evidence was later offered.

On the general charge—a disruption in the workplace sufficiently serious that to continue Richmond would be negligent, or the creation of a hostile work environment—the hearing officer found insufficient evidence. In a part of his opinion that I did not accept, the hearing officer said that the slur indicated that the target was granted special privileges, saying little more than that she was "a teacher's pet." I expect the hearing officer may on reflection wish he had not put the matter in those terms. The hearing officer also said that Bonnie Richmond "possibly should have a letter of reprimand, but I don't think she needs to be terminated." The hearing officer did not follow up on his reprimand proposal, as the Department of Human Services was not arguing that a lesser penalty should be considered if termination was overturned.

The Employee Appeals Board itself reviewed its hearing officer's decision and issued a short opinion agreeing that she did not need to be fired. That decision was then appealed to a state trial court, which acted as the first-level appellate court. Judge James Graves reversed and reinstated the termination. James would later serve on the United States Court of Appeals for the Fifth Circuit. So two of the judges involved with the Richmond case were later nominated for the court.

That decision was next reviewed by the Mississippi Court of Appeals. Initially a three-judge panel decides an appeal. I did not sit on the three-judge panel for *Richmond*. After the panel finished with a case, the other seven judges of the court were given the opinion to review and to indicate whether we joined it. Further opinions could be written by the other seven judges who were not on the original panel. There would be two dissenting opinions.

The following comes from our court's decision, written by presiding judge Roger McMillin. He wrote: "Review of the decisions of administrative agencies and boards is substantially limited." If the department who disciplined a state employee loses at the Employee Appeals Board, that department does not have a *right* to appeal. The Department of Human Services had to ask the appellate court, Judge Graves's court in this case, to permit the appeal. He did.

After further appeal to my court, we were not to weigh the evidence, decide what witness was credible, or engage in any other such evaluation. We were simply to decide if some evidence existed to support the decision the Appeals Board made and whether legal error had occurred. These stringent rules may seem a disguise for what really happens. One senator at the hearing rejected my description of all of this, saying he was certain that judges always just get to the result they want regardless of such technical rules. He was wrong. Judges are imperfect, but I have tried my best. The army has an expression about soldiers "staying in their lane," which I mentioned at the hearing. Decisions are handled by the right soldier at the right level of command.

We affirmed on further review. What occurred was largely uncontested, the opinion noted. That included when the slur was used, the context for it, the apology the next day, and the target's dual statement that she was hurt by the words and that it was not a major problem. The only evidence of problems came from the director, who said there were telephone calls complaining. Without her records, which she did not have at the hearing, she could not say how many.

A dissenting judge, who is African American, accused the majority of wanting a race riot before we would find problems. What our procedural rules required was something in the record that we would *have* to accept as trumping everything else. The dissenter was making a decision as if he were the review board, weighing the evidence himself. That is not our role. I could not find that there was *no* evidence to support the Employee Appeals Board's conclusion. Relatedly, federal courts usually hold that a one-time use of a racial slur in the workplace does not create a hostile environment justifying a lawsuit by the person targeted.

Another dissenter would not have reinstated Richmond but argued we should send the matter back to the Employee Appeal Board to enter findings explaining why no lesser penalty was imposed. Reversal on that basis was an attractive option, but it ignored controlling law. First, neither party asked for that. Both parties were seeking all or nothing. Richmond wanted to keep her job. The Department of Human Services wanted to fire her. The hearing officer had even mentioned the possibility of a reprimand, but the agency was not requesting that.

The other reason I disagreed takes a more detailed explanation. A few years earlier, I became incredulous when researching an appeal from an administrative agency. The Mississippi Supreme Court had long ago created a nearly unique process in the country in which agencies do not need to give detailed explanations of their rulings, but courts are supposed to give these nearly blank decisions great deference. I wrote on this in a lengthy opinion in 1995 in a case involving a nurse who had lost her license.[2] The conclusion of my Nursing Board case was a plea both to state agencies to make better fact findings and indirectly to the Supreme Court to change this rule.

I could have written a concurring opinion to explain all of this in *Richmond*, as a senator nine years later suggested. But as much as I might write at times, I did not write in everything. Had the approach of the dissenting

Dad, World War II. His service inspired me to serve.

From left: Leslie, Lloyd Jr., Larry, and Linda, 1954.

Mom and Dad's twenty-fifth wedding anniversary, 1959.

Ruth Southwick Flanagan and Jim Flanagan, 1987.

From left: Philip, Mary Voorhies, David Brown, Cathy, Sharon, Leslie, and Annie Polasek, April 2010.

GEORGE BUSH
For United States Senator

George Bush, U.S. Senate, 1970.

Author, Gil Carmichael, and Judy Lewis, 1975, 1979.

Thad Cochran, Senate, 1978.

Key political campaigns
that shaped my career.

Sharon, author, Julius Ridgway, and Vice President George Bush, 1987.

Jack Reed, governor, 1987.

Part of the Texas Court of Criminal Appeals and staff, March 1976. Front, from left: Judge Leon Douglas, Presiding Judge John F. Onion Jr., Judge Truman Roberts. Judge Onion's staff includes the author, directly behind Onion; Judicial Assistant Dianne Sobotik to the author's right; and co-clerk John Potter behind and to the author's left.

Judge Clark (center), author (bottom left), co-clerk John Henegan (top right), and my trailblazer University of Texas classmate Jay Nelson (seated next to author), November 1979.

Civil Division, Department of Justice, November 1992. Seated: Assistant Attorney General Stuart Gerson. Standing, left to right: Patricia Mack Bryan, author, Colonel Tim Naccaroto, Rosalie Bern, Rick Valentine, Tim O'Rourke, Janice Calabresi, Stuart Schiffer, and Ken Zwick.

Practicing law at FOB Duke, Iraq, March 2005.

Brigadier General Leon Collins, Southwick, Governor Haley Barbour, Major General Harold A. Cross at FOB Kalsu, Iraq, Thanksgiving 2005.

Bill Dreher, Roy Carpenter, Joel Jones, author, Gene Hortman, and Mark Majors at FOB Kalsu, Iraq, July 2005.

First day of court of appeals campaign, January 31, 1994.

Cathy and author near Crystal Springs, 1994 campaign walk.

End of two-hundred-mile walk, supreme court race, August 2, 1996, near Alabama line. My friend Andy Taggart built and painted the frame for the sign. He even loaned his pickup truck.

December 1994 Mississippi Court of Appeals, back row, from left: McMillin, King, Payne, Barber, Thomas; front row, from left: Coleman, Fraiser, Bridges, Southwick, Diaz.

Bob Galloway.

Mike Wallace.

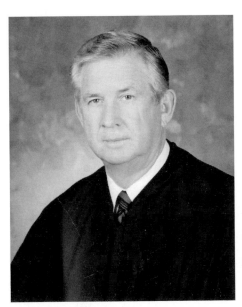

Judge Charles Pickering.

Judge Henry Wingate.

Special Assistant to President for Legislative Affairs Harold Kim.

Gregg Nunziata, on Senator Specter's Judiciary Committee staff as chief nominations counsel.

Sharon, the author, and Senator Cochran on morning of Judiciary Committee hearing, May 2007.

Fred Barnes, Mort Kondracke, Charles Krauthammer, Brit Hume, supportive but all predicting my defeat on July 18, 2007.

Senators Arlen Specter and Orrin Hatch, at press conference with representatives of several supportive interest groups, September 5, 2007. Left to right, Drew Ryun, American Center for Law and Justice (ACLJ); Ed Whelan, Ethics and Public Policy Center; Curt Levey, Committee for Justice; Jessica Echard, Eagle Forum; David Keene, American Conservative Union; Senator Specter; Carly Gammill, ACLJ; Senator Hatch; Todd Gaziano, Heritage Foundation.

Trent Lott and author in Capitol, taken
a few minutes after confirmation.

Arlen Specter and author.

MARSHALL RAMSEY

YET ANOTHER BUSH 5TH CIRCUIT NOMINEE FROM MISSISSIPPI RECEIVES A WARM RECEPTION FROM DEMOCRATS IN WASHINGTON...

Cartoon by Marshall Ramsey depicting my reception by Senate Judiciary Committee Democrats at the May 10, 2007, hearing.

President George W. Bush.

Bennie Thompson, U.S. representative for Mississippi's second congressional district.

La'Verne Edney and author.

Dianne Feinstein, U.S. senator for California.

Senators Pat Leahy, Daniel Inouye, and Thad Cochran.

Senators Cochran, Lott, and Feinstein.

Senator Dianne Feinstein, joining six Republicans senators for a press conference after my confirmation.

Being sworn in, October 30, 2007. Sharon, author, and Judge Rhesa Barksdale.

judge who thought we should remand for a better fact finding garnered more votes, I might have asked Judge McMillin to add something to his opinion about how that violated controlling authority. Otherwise I thought the point need not be explained again.

Our opinion got substantial local news coverage when it was released. A warning of the future politicization of the opinion came immediately when the Mississippi Legislative Black Caucus said it found the result "appalling." It called for abolishing the court.[3] Despite the pressure, the court denied rehearing. Changing our minds because of political pressures would have been the worst form of judging.

The case was then heard by the Mississippi Supreme Court. Its opinion was relatively brief. It agreed with the court of appeals that the Employee Appeals Board was within its discretion—it was not "arbitrary or capricious," in the legal jargon—to find that Richmond did not need to be terminated. As the court put it, this case was decided on its facts. There was "a first offense, an otherwise good work performance record, and an apology by the offending employee."

However, the court then went on to say that the Employee Appeals Board had not made "sufficient findings on the record as to why there should be no penalty." So the court remanded "in order for the board to impose an appropriate penalty less than dismissal, or to make detailed findings as to why no penalty should be imposed."

I was startled. The court referred to three of its precedents for its conclusion that better findings were required. The court is entitled to state what its prior rulings means, but I did not see such a rule in those precedents. The reversal in *Richmond* seemed to be a one-case rule, unfortunately, as there has been no trend in later cases for requiring better fact finding from administrative agencies.

After my hearing, one of the senators asked me to explain what happened next in the case. I did not know, so I found out. After receiving the case on remand, the board ordered a letter of reprimand. Richmond received her back pay for the time during which she was terminated.

Someone who wrote often and well on my behalf to rebut the criticisms of these cases was Ed Whelan, president of the Ethics and Public Policy Center in Washington. I will quote some of his analysis of the case.

> The narrow legal question that the majority opinion addressed was whether "there was evidence in the record to support" the administrative agency's conclusion that "this one use of a racial epithet, when viewed in the context

in which it was said, did not constitute sufficient basis to terminate an employee whose service, over a number of years, was shown to have been satisfactory in all other respects."

On appeal, the Mississippi Supreme Court majority agreed with Southwick's court that termination was not an appropriate remedy. . . . The Court somewhat altered the judgment that Southwick's court had reached, as it remanded the case to the administrative agency "for the imposition of a lesser penalty, or to make detailed findings on the record why no penalty should be imposed." That's the minor sense in which it's technically true that there was a unanimous reversal.[4]

Hard cases should not make bad law. I thought any other decision than the one we had reached ignored the law. I was not holding that use of the slur could not be punished; I was holding that the decision about whether termination was the proper punishment was for the board to make, not the court.

The other case was an appeal from a child custody decision by a state trial judge. Because of confidentiality concerns about the parties, the names were not used. The case was called simply *S.B. v. L.W.*[5] Our decision was handed down in 2001. There was no appeal. Again, this was a decision written by another judge on the court.

The parents were unmarried. After their daughter was born, the mother moved from the home the parties had shared. Early in the child's life, both parents worked, the father as a paramedic and the mother as a nurse.

In 1994 the mother moved into a house with another woman. As the court's opinion put it, the "mother testified that she was bisexual and admitted that her relationship with the woman was intimate." Later the mother quit her job and notified the child's father that she was moving to the Mississippi Gulf Coast, several hours away from where the parents had been living. The father sought a custody order. Until then, there had been no court involvement in the custody of the child. Their daughter had by agreement been staying most of the time with her mother.

A decision on child custody, regardless of whether it is part of a divorce or an independent matter when there has not been a marriage, is required to be based on findings as to twelve factors. These include such matters as the child's and parents' ages, the child's health, the emotional ties of the child with each parent, the employment and economic condition of each spouse, and other matters. The trial judge went through all these custody factors and found most to favor the father.

Whether reviewing an administrative agency's decision or that of a trial court, our authority is limited. "This Court does not have the authority to reverse a chancellor's custody determination unless the chancellor is manifestly wrong, clearly erroneous, or applies an erroneous legal standard." We found the correct legal standard had been applied, so the only issues were the factual analysis of each of the custody factors. We then examined the evidence.

What made the case controversial is that a section of the opinion discussed the mother's relationship with another woman. We found state supreme court rules binding on two points. One is that the fact a parent is gay or lesbian was a factor to be considered. That was law for us. To ignore it would have been lawless. Second, there was also U.S. Supreme Court authority, announced in 1986, that supported the position.

A dissenting judge argued it was improper to consider the sexual preference of a parent in making the custody decision. The writer of the dissent, James Thomas, sadly now deceased, is someone for whom I had a great deal of affection and respect. But this time I think he was seriously in error. What he advocated was for us to overrule the state supreme court. The only relevant U.S. Supreme Court authority supported the law as the majority stated it. He believed "the wealth of authority" from other states proved his approach was better.

I saw his opinion, which was joined by one judge, as perhaps reflecting where the state supreme court would take the law, either on further review of this case or in another. The U.S. Supreme Court in 2003—two years after our decision—overruled its 1986 decision that had seemed fully to support the rules the state supreme court had adopted for these kinds of issues. The decision was *Lawrence v. Texas*, which I will mention later.

I could be wrong, but it seems to me that many of my critics did not argue all that strongly that there was much wrong with the result. The law was there, and we were obligated to apply it despite the politics. The greater concern was that the phrase "homosexual lifestyle" was used, and it was deemed insulting. It is difficult to stay current with the proper vocabulary in an area of law and culture that is undergoing substantial change. It was interesting to see this particular criticism pretty soundly rebutted, as in 2001 it was a widely accepted phrase.

Judge Mary Libby Payne wrote a concurring opinion. I was the only person to join her. A concurring opinion adds some other thoughts to the majority's statement or may even disagree with the majority's reasoning, though not with the result. There is language in the concurring opinion that the mother was free to "choose any activity in which to engage; however, I also am aware that such person is not thereby relieved of the consequences of his or her choice." That language was not an assault on the idea that a person who is gay or lesbian has made a choice and presumably can later decide not to be gay or lesbian. The opinion was discussing Mississippi Supreme Court law that allowed a judge deciding custody to consider whether one of the parents *chose* to engage in "immoral" conduct, meaning having sex outside of marriage. Usually that conduct would be an intimate heterosexual relationship, but the principle would apply here, too.

I remember reading Judge Payne's opinion several times before voting on it. I was convinced that what she said at the beginning of her opinion was a crucial omission from the majority's opinion. She wrote that the Mississippi Legislature "has made clear its public policy position relating to particular rights of homosexuals in domestic relations settings." She discussed an enactment in 2000, prohibiting adoption of children by same-sex couples. In 1997 a prohibition on same-sex marriage was passed. Her observations were critical because the legislature is the policy-making branch subject only to constitutional limits. Not to mention the legislature seemed to me to ignore the main point.

I will again quote a few comments from Ed Whelan. On the issue of the consideration of the mother's relations with another woman, "the court of appeals majority cited and applied governing Mississippi supreme court precedents [which he names] that held that a parent's homosexuality may properly be considered as a factor (though not the sole factor) in custody determinations."

> Without even addressing the Mississippi supreme court precedents that the majority relied on, the dissent somehow drew "the inescapable conclusion that the issue [whether a parent is gay] has no bearing absent a conclusion that such has or will have an adverse impact on the child."
>
> The dissent elicited a separate response from Judge Payne, in a concurring opinion that Southwick also joined. [She wrote] that "the dissent has delved into an area where our State legislature has made clear its public policy position relating to homosexuals in domestic relations settings," and it briefly presents several provisions of Mississippi statutory law. . . .
>
> As for the supposedly "troubling" language of ["homosexual lifestyle"]: In *Lawrence v. Texas*, Justice Kennedy's majority opinion, joined by Justices Stevens, Souter, Ginsburg, and Breyer, used the same phrase that [is now

seen as] so nefarious. . . . And President Clinton used the plural of the same phrase—"homosexual lifestyles"—in his July 1993 speech announcing his "Don't Ask, Don't Tell" policy on gays in the military.[6]

Likely I protest too much. I was reluctant to review the opinions in this book, though I had to. Nothing I write satisfies the political disagreement with either outcome. Both applied controlling law as I tried my best to understand it. That is what appellate judges are supposed to do regardless of the politics of an outcome. If an election, or the U.S. Senate, or some other quintessential political arena lies ahead, there may be a necessary price to pay.

On Wednesday, the day before my hearing that would likely explore these cases, I flew to Washington with Sharon. My first duty was to attend a mock hearing session at the Justice Department. District court nominees Janet Neff and Liam O'Grady were both there too. Janet and I had our controversies, while Liam just needed to keep his head down.

The questions from the mock interrogators were harsh, both in tone and in substance. I am not sure how much good the practice round did. I remember someone from the White House, perhaps Legislative Affairs, stopping one practice answer I was giving. The question challenged my sense of racial justice, and I was responding at that level. The staffer insisted I avoid any discussion of personal feelings and just give a narrow legal explanation. Her opinion was informed, but it was not perceptive. In hindsight, it is clear the battle was waged over the kind of person I was.

I arrived early for the hearing the next day, held in the Judiciary Committee's usual hearing room in the Dirksen Office Building. Just before the hearing began, I talked to Senator Lott in the back of the hearing room, trying to avoid being close enough for reporters to overhear us. Lott indicated that it was unclear what impact the criticisms from outside groups would have. The next day, the Jackson newspaper's story about the hearing had a photograph of my miniconference with the senator. I was rapidly getting pulled into a place I did not want to be: the middle of a political fight.

At the hearing, all the senators who would be introducing their home-state nominees sat together at a table in front of the committee's high bench. I was introduced by Senators Cochran and Lott. They could not have been more supportive and glowing in their remarks. After they and the other senators were finished, they left. I was called up to the wide table, covered with a dark green cloth, where those speaking to the committee sat. After being sworn, I sat down by myself at the table. A cameraman was on the floor between the high bench for the committee and the much lower level of the witness table, taking pictures as I made my best effort to stay calm.

Senator Whitehouse chaired the hearing. He was the only Democrat in the hearing room when we started. Senator Orrin Hatch was there for the Republicans. Senator Whitehouse asked if I had an opening statement. My only one was to introduce Sharon, who was sitting a few rows behind me in the audience. I named the other family members and said they were there in spirit.

Senator Whitehouse opened with some observations about separation of powers and the role of the courts. He had been attorney general and the U.S. attorney for Rhode Island. My later meeting with him convinced me he was knowledgeable and concerned about the law. I stated that judges needed to stay in their proper role among the three branches.

He then turned to the controversy about the opinion I had joined on the state court of appeals that had used the phrase "homosexual life-style." He indicated that many considered it to be a pejorative phrase. I responded that I had not been aware that there was anything objectionable about the language. It seemed in common enough use without it being used as an epithet. As would be pointed out later, President Clinton and the U.S. Supreme Court had both used that phrase without any charge that it was being used in a negative way.

More generally, I explained how it was part of my makeup to treat all who came before the court with respect. I mentioned the state bar's Judicial Excellence Award that I had won in 2004. One of the stated reasons was that I treated all those who were in the court, whether in questioning during oral argument or in my opinions, with dignity. I mentioned also that a handout I give to each year's new law clerks stated that any draft opinion written for me should treat all the litigants respectfully, including a criminal defendant whose conviction we affirmed.

Senator Hatch was next. He started with kind remarks about my record on the court and in the military. He mentioned the ABA's rating and stated his opinion that the group was not known for its bias toward conservatives. I gave short answers to various points he made. He then went through the five cases that had been the subject of the criticisms by the outside groups. I responded to each of them.

I was focusing on Senator Hatch, seated to my left, and not paying attention to anything occurring on the right side, where the Democrats sat. When we began, only Whitehouse and Hatch were there. With respect for the delightful Senator Hatch, who was being extremely helpful to my nomination, at the time I remember wishing he would hurry up and finish. Perhaps I could leave before any angry questioner showed up. As he no doubt knew, there was no chance of that.

When Hatch finished his questions, I looked back to the right, and there sat Senator Russ Feingold of Wisconsin. No matter how quickly Hatch had finished, I have no doubt someone would have been waiting on the Democratic side. Other senators would come out later from a waiting area outside the committee room. Only one Democrat at a time was at the bench, though, other than today's chairman, Whitehouse.

Senator Feingold jumped right into asking questions about the five cases. His tone and questions made me think he felt I was a criminal in the dock, and he saw himself as the virtuous prosecutor, ready to break me before the jury.

It was a slow tennis match, with the ball on one side for ten minutes while a Democrat asked questions, then back to my left to have a Republican ask questions. I, of course, was the ball being whacked. Temporary chairman Whitehouse had gone first, then Senators Hatch, Feingold, Tom Coburn of Oklahoma, and Ted Kennedy of Massachusetts. There was not another Republican immediately after Kennedy, so Democrat Dick Durbin went next. He too thought it would be better to indict than to confirm.

Durbin's opening comment was interesting, as in my view it admitted what was behind the effort to characterize a few opinions as disqualifying:

> *Senator Durbin*: Judge Southwick, thank you for joining us today. I think it is very clear that the context of your nomination is a big part of our deliberation, and I think you must understand that from some of the questions that have been asked of you. It is my understanding that President Bush has submitted 10 nominees for the Federal bench in Mississippi, 7 at the District level, 3 at the Fifth Circuit, and not one has been an African-American. Mississippi being a State with more than a third of the population African-American, you can understand why the African-American population feels that this is a recurring pattern which does not indicate an effort to find balance on the court when it comes to racial composition, or even to give African-Americans a chance in this situation.[7]

My answer to one question would form the basis for some later speeches he gave. He mentioned U.S. District Judge Frank Johnson of

Alabama. I agreed that he had the courage of his convictions to follow Supreme Court directions diligently during the civil rights struggles. Senator Durbin then asked:

> So when you look back at your career in public service, can you point to an example of something that you have done, on the bench or otherwise, where you really stepped out and subjected yourself to criticism for taking an unpopular view on behalf of the dispossessed, or minorities, or poor people where it may have subjected you to criticism for showing courage in trying to side with a position that you thought was right and might not have been popular?
>
> *Judge Southwick:* I wish those came readily to mind. Perhaps I just didn't keep enough of a catalog of experiences. You mentioned Frank Johnson, a conservative Republican, but probably never a member of the Federalist Society.
>
> *Senator Durbin:* An Eisenhower Republican. Yes.
>
> *Judge Southwick:* Alabama Republican. And I—not because of this hearing, or not because of anything else, but judges, and Federal judges, and Fifth Circuit judges, fascinate me. I read *Taming the Storm* by Jack Bass on Judge Johnson just a few months ago. His career is an inspiration to anyone who wants, no matter their political background, no matter what they have done before arriving at the bench, to apply the law even-handedly and imaginatively to the issues that come before him. I don't want to get into analogies [earlier made by] former colleagues of yours, U.S. Senators. I'm no Frank Johnson, I know that.
>
> *Senator Durbin:* None of us are. But can you think of a time in your life or career where you did bend in that direction, to take an unpopular point of view on behalf of those who were voiceless or powerless and needed someone to stand up for their rights when it wasn't a popular position?

As he was asking that question, I remember thinking that the best example of being willing to take an unpopular stand despite knowing it could adversely affect me politically, and I was being proved correct at that exact moment, was my decision on the racial slur case. I remember analyzing that possible answer very quickly and deciding I could not safely phrase it. I feared being condemned by something along the lines of "Southwick equates himself to civil rights hero Frank Johnson when he protects racial slurs." So after a slight, or longer, pause, I said only this:

I hope that a careful look—and the answer is, no, I cannot think of something now. But if I can give you this answer. I cannot recall my opinions, and I don't think of them in those terms. I think of them in terms of not considering the reaction, not looking at the result and working backward, but following through and, no matter how popular or unpopular the decision may be, to come to the conclusion that I think is compelled by controlling authority.

Several times in the months ahead, Durbin would characterize my answer as indicating that I could not think of any time in which I stood up for an unpopular cause.[8] That was fair under the unfair rules that apply to political debate. And in fact, I had not named any case.

Senator Durbin was the last of the rotating questioners. Senators Hatch and Whitehouse gave closing remarks. Senator Whitehouse tasked me with doing an Internet search on the phrase "homosexual lifestyle" and reporting to the committee on what the first fifty entries were like. His point was that the phrase had at some stage become one often used by those opposed to the goals of activists for gays and lesbians. I later respectfully reported my findings to the committee.

Senator Hatch and I had a lengthy conversation in the hallway after the hearing. I was struck by how tall and thin and tastefully dressed he was, including what I considered an overly colorful tie, but style sense is another of my weaknesses. He seemed totally committed to my success. For someone of his national renown to take such an interest in me was an honor and a relief. Later, after seeing that when Democratic nominee Justice James Dennis had his confirmation troubles in 1995, Hatch crossed party lines to assist him, I became even more impressed with the senator.

The Jackson newspaper's headline was "Bush's Latest Pick for Appeals Court Grilled by Senators." I was honored to have the paper's clever cartoonist, Marshall Ramsey, draw me tied and horizontal, held over the edge of a volcano by four human-shaped donkeys: "Yet another Bush 5th Circuit nominee from Mississippi receives a warm reception from Democrats in Washington."[9]

At my age, it was not exactly refreshing to see my name muddied for the first time. Yet it was only a small part of the cost of being a nominee to this court from my state. Of course, to my critics, the cost was incurred only because of my shortcomings.

14

The Sorting Out

I was discouraged. I had hoped that what in my view were simplistic and political criticisms that did not take account of the limited role of an appellate judge would not have any effect on the senators. Could the Democratic senators really believe the harsh things they were saying?

The Senate had a narrow Democratic majority, and thus so did each committee. The Judiciary Committee membership was ten Democrats and nine Republicans. As the controversy about me became more serious, I worried that even some Republicans might not support me. That did not occur. But I would need at least one Democrat to join the Republicans, or else I would be stuck in committee as Judge Charles Pickering and Justice Priscilla Owen both had been in 2002.

A fair indication of my worries was this note to family:

I think the issue of confirmation is in doubt. The state NAACP came out against me last week, saying it is time for a black person to be named. There was also some reference in their reasoning to the case in which I am said to show racial insensitivity. Sen. Leahy, chairman of the committee, has all year been saying that there needs to be more diversity on the Miss. federal bench and will continue to be concerned about my race, which continues to be what it has always been.

Sometime last summer, after the delay on my earlier nomination was starting to cause some anxiety, I printed out to put on my desk the lines from Proverbs 3:5, "Trust in the Lord with all your heart, and rely not on your own understanding. In all your ways be mindful of him, and he will make straight your paths." My sense is that it was more than coincidence that the verse listed in my pamphlet of daily meditations (the *Upper Room*), that I read as I went to bed the night before the hearings, was Proverbs 3:5. Of course, where the path is going may be different than I had in mind, but that is fine too.[1]

The Jackson newspaper remained supportive. "Here we go again" was how the editorial started.[2] The problem was that I was "caught in the ongoing partisan battle in the Senate over judicial nominations, a battle that has seen abuse on both sides of the aisle and a battle that increasingly is damaging to the federal bench."

An explanation for this awful process was suggested later by a new federal judge from Kentucky, Amul Thapar. "Peter Keisler once told me that being nominated to a judgeship is like parachuting into Ireland or the Middle East—there are a hundred years of disputes that you have nothing to do with and now you are right in the middle of them."[3] Peter nailed it. Until the week of the hearing, it appeared that the key participants in both parties had agreed I would be allowed to go on through without difficulty. Now significant outside groups that support Democrats declared that I needed to be stopped. Could their opposition change the course on which so many had already agreed?

The week after the hearing passed slowly. A talented recent graduate of the Mississippi College Law School in Jackson, Michael Bentley, offered to perform the Internet search for me to answer Senator Whitehouse's question about "homosexual lifestyle." Michael prepared a summary on the first fifty Web site links that resulted from the search. I reviewed and revised the wording and felt profuse gratitude for getting some initial help on what likely lay ahead.

On May 16, a column appeared in the *Houston Chronicle*, written by the same person who had so savaged Mike Wallace. He considered me vile. One blog called me a "vicious racist KKK slug." A more imaginative slur was "goosestepping hillbilly." I was starting to worry about my soul. Would I become angry, vengeful, or hateful? Was the goal worth it?

Rees called at 10:00 p.m. that same night to say that his brother Jim had encountered Senator Leahy in Washington earlier in the day. Jim had asked Leahy whether he was going to get me confirmed. Leahy said, "We're working on it." Jim Barksdale, an extraordinarily successful businessman and entrepreneur, was well known in Washington. His speaking informally with Senator Leahy at least twice on my behalf surely helped restrain the opposition.

On May 17, one week after the hearing, one of the senior Justice Department attorneys involved with judicial selection, assistant attorney general Rachel Brand, left a voice mail around noon, saying she wanted to talk "about an issue relating to your nomination." My notes said this: "Among my worries when calling was White House wavering. But Brand said, confidentially, that [Senator Mitch] McConnell is pushing very hard for me to get an immediate committee vote and confirmation within three weeks. What a roller coaster. She said the minority leader's hard push for me was 'huge.' She said that I was not in nearly as bad a shape as several nominees. She did not want to sound as if she was guaranteeing me anything, but she thought I would be confirmed."

On May 17, I submitted the draft response to Senator Whitehouse's Internet search query. At noon on Friday, May 18, the questions from a few other committee members were delivered to the Justice Department. Senators Leahy, Kennedy, and Durbin all submitted questions. They were basically all the same, just different ways of asking how I could possibly have joined in or written the five opinions. Nothing from Senator Feingold, surprisingly.

The questions were going to take all weekend to answer. They needed to be submitted on Monday for the committee to vote on me that Thursday. In the committee's terminology, my nomination would be on "markup," that is, on the agenda for a vote at the next business meeting of the committee on May 24. The one requirement was that my answers to all the written questions needed to be submitted. I needed some help, so I turned to Michael Bentley again, whose only known job at the moment was to study for the bar exam in July.

On May 18 I received an e-mail from Charles Pickering: "I know what you are going through. I think you will probably be confirmed. However, in this environment, anything can happen as you are aware. One of the encouraging things from your perspective is that when I saw Thad briefly, he told me that he was going to have to do some spade work, but he thought everything would be ok. I thought that was a very positive sign."[4]

In the warm and supportive messages I occasionally received from Judge Pickering, he would talk about faith and often a specific scripture. This is what he wrote this time: "Early on in my proceeding, my pastor preached from the book of Habakkuk. The prophet concluded the book of Habakkuk by saying, and I paraphrase, 'though there be no fruit on the vines, no grain in the fields, nor cattle in the stalls, yet will I praise God.' I concluded that I was to be content whether I was confirmed or not confirmed. That was a great comfort." His memory was remarkable, as he gave a close paraphrase of chapter 3, verses 17–18.

On Sunday, May 20, I sent my draft responses to the Justice Department for their review. On Monday, Senator Feingold finally submitted his questions. I worked until about 7:30 that evening on finalizing a response, as I was told that if the answers were submitted to the committee early Tuesday, I was likely to get a vote on Thursday.

Senator Cochran's counsel wrote me concerning his knowledge of what lay ahead. "Senator Cochran has been personally and insistently working on Senator Leahy to support your nomination in the Committee. Senator Cochran seems optimistic. If I learn more, I will let you know. Senator McConnell's staff yesterday reported favorable conversations as well."[5]

My notes on the day for my committee vote started this way: "May 24. This is the day, especially, that the Lord has made." I expect this meant that I began the day cautiously optimistic.

Sometime that morning, I heard from someone who felt confident that efforts to name a black lawyer to the district court vacancy had likely failed. I felt such a selection would be of huge assistance to me. I had been told by numerous people, black and white, that the opposition to me was largely based on the insistence that it was time for more black judges on the federal bench in the state. The letters sent by the five Mississippi black leaders to Senators Cochran and Lott on March 23 had offered such a selection as the means to "rectify" the concerns about my nomination. According to my friend, neither of the senators, in conversations in the last few days with a leading black lawyer, had accepted the suggested names because they felt others were more qualified

Another extremely important and negative development was that the Congressional Black Caucus, consisting of the forty-three black members of Congress, announced on the day of my scheduled vote that they opposed me. The head of the caucus, the delegate from D.C., Eleanor Holmes Norton, said that I had a "very fixed, right-wing world view and intolerant racial views."[6] I wrote in my journal early on the day of my expected vote: "I still feel able to accept whatever comes. Still praying, though, that what comes will be success in this. 'Let my will be Yours' is probably where I am. But also 'Thy will be done regardless.'"

The business meeting was to start at 10:00 a.m. in Washington. I would not learn until almost noon that no vote was taken. On the afternoon of May 24 I e-mailed my siblings.

Nothing about this is ever easy. I was called about 12:45 CDT and told that Sen. Feingold wanted my nomination held over until the next committee meeting. The chairman agreed. The next meeting, because of the Memorial Day/week recess, is not until 6 or 7 June.

The one encouraging news, and it is quite positive, is that the Democratic chairman of the committee, Sen. Leahy, appears ready to support me. Leahy told Thad Cochran today that he was "likely" to support me and will encourage everyone else on the committee to do so. A little while ago, the D.C. reporter who covers these stories for the Jackson newspapers called to ask for comment. [She] told me that the information she was getting from committee staff is that I would be confirmed in two weeks, that Leahy is for me and that will bring most of the Democrats on the committee along. Of course, much can sometimes happen in two weeks' time.[7]

As the week passed, no senator announced opposition. On May 31, I wrote in my journal that reporter Ana Radelat called. She "said that a teleconference had been held by Nan Aron, a black Texas congressman [Al Green], and a few others. Aron challenged the [Judiciary] committee, saying I am the first controversial nominee since Democrats took control. Are they willing to stop me? Ana said she had to call, and told me she would say the usual, 'Southwick would not comment since the nomination was still pending.'" The reporter, at least in discussions with me, thought that the press conference had arisen from concern that no senator had yet taken up the battle against me.

On this troubling day, I got a wonderful e-mail from one of my former judicial colleagues, Tyree Irving.

> I just wanted to take a moment to let you know that I have been thinking about you during your trying times. Although it does not help your situation, I really believe the real opposition is not directed at you personally, but could not find a way to attack the real problem (the lack of racial diversity by the President in the judicial appointment process) without attacking you as a beneficiary of the President's insensitiveness. Stay encouraged.[8]

I replied on the same day:

> I cannot tell you how grateful I am to hear from you. This has been a difficult few weeks, something I had long worried would happen but hoped would not. How the arguments would be made I did not know, but I felt it quite possible something from my opinions, my law journal articles, or something else would be used to show I did not merit confirmation.

I have long wanted to be a Fifth Circuit judge, a statement that will not surprise you. But these labels, this anger directed at me, are taking the joy out of the prospect of gaining this position. Faith and family. The rest hardly matters when compared to those basics.[9]

Later on May 31, I learned that I was scheduled for the next business meeting of the committee on June 7. That was the good news, particularly with silence from the Democratic senators on the committee. But then the silence began to end. Around 5:45 p.m., Ana Radelat called a second time. She said that a senator named Barack Obama had come out against me that day. In mid-2007, Obama was not yet considered to be a likely president. Hillary Clinton seemed the Democrat most likely to succeed. But Senator Obama was certainly a growing force in the Democratic Party. He issued a press release, saying that I had a "disappointing record on cases involving consumers, employees, racial minorities, women, and gays and lesbians." The release also said that he "shared the concerns of his fellow members of the Congressional Black Caucus that Judge Southwick would not adequately defend the rights of workers and enforce civil rights laws."[10]

Obama was the first senator to oppose me. I had considered until then that it was possible he would support me. He was among the senators whom I hoped the White House could have gotten me in to see. Perhaps Senator Obama would want to seem more moderate by discounting the charges and saying that though he would never have nominated me, he saw no disqualification. Because I did not believe these criticisms were justified, I had hoped that Senator Obama, as a lawyer, would see that. He saw something quite different, though.

As the next Judiciary Committee business meeting date of Thursday, June 7, approached, more criticisms appeared. The *New York Times* wrote a scathing editorial, calling me "An Unacceptable Nominee."[11] It focused on the racial slur case. Another sign that a quiet and speedy confirmation would not occur was that I was a recurring story in the three Washington strictly politics newspapers, *Roll Call*, *The Hill*, and *Politico*. On June 4, *Roll Call* reported troubles but found my chances still good.[12] The story began by remarking that after "six months of steadily supporting President Bush's top-tier judicial nominations, Senators this week may be head for their first partisan battle over the bench," unfortunately meaning me. The administration was reported to be solidly backing me and to "believe there is enough Democratic support to clear Southwick through the chamber." The "only Democratic Senator to publicly oppose his nomination is Sen. Barack Obama," who was described as being a Congressional Black Caucus member and presidential candidate. He would become better known later.

After it became clear that a battle lay ahead, the Justice Department and White House asked me to give them contact information for people who might write to support my nomination. The charge was racial prejudice. Those who would have some credibility if they disagreed were needed. I did not make the contacts myself, as that might be seen as undue pressure on them to assist. Instead, on June 1, I gave the Justice Department lawyer an initial list of about twenty people.

I hated to think of friends and colleagues in these terms, but I categorized them—blacks and whites, Democrats, those who knew me through charitable work, law school colleagues, military friends, nonlawyers with whom I had some sort of professional relation, and many others. A wonderful attorney at the Justice Department, Tessa Platt, contacted them all.

Several letters became part of the debate. Supportive blogs mentioned them, and some were quoted on the Senate floor. Two of the letters became the most frequently quoted in the battle.

The first well-publicized letter was from one of my first law clerks at the Mississippi Court of Appeals, La'Verne Edney. Several years earlier, she had graduated from Alcorn State University and went to work, eventually, at the state college board. She had two children by the time she decided to go to Mississippi College School of Law. I became aware of her when she worked at the court the summer before her last year in law school. She impressed me. She was diligent and smart and reflected her Christianity through compassion and humility and a genuine interest in others. In the fall, she accepted my offer of a clerkship. She was superb. After leaving her one-year clerkship, she began work at the Brunini law firm, where I used to work. By 2007, she had been a partner there for many years. On June 5, she wrote the committee.

> Dear Senators:
>
> I am an African-American partner at the law firm of Brunini, Grantham, Grower & Hewes, PLLC, where Judge Southwick was once a member. I believe in fairness for all people and salute our leaders for giving their lives to assure that fairness. While I share the sentiments of other African-Americans that the federal judiciary needs to be more diverse, I believe that Judge Southwick is eminently qualified . . . and write in support of his nomination.

I met Judge Southwick during my third year of law school when I interned with the Court of Appeals of Mississippi. That internship allowed me an opportunity to work with most of the Judges on the bench at that time. I was most impressed with Judge Southwick because of his work ethic and his serene personality. When I finished law school in 1996, I believed that my chances for landing a clerkship were slim because there was only one African-American Court of Appeals judge on the bench at the time and there were very few Caucasian judges during the history of the Mississippi Supreme Court or the Court of Appeals (which was fairly new) who had ever hired African-American law clerks. In spite of the odds, I applied for a clerkship. Judge Southwick granted me an interview and hired me that same day. While Judge Southwick had many applicants to choose from, he saw that I was qualified for the position and granted me the opportunity.

During my tenure as clerk with the Court, Judge Southwick thought through every issue and took every case seriously. He earned a reputation for his well thought out opinions and his ability to produce the highest number of opinions in a term. It did not matter the parties' affiliation, color, or stature—what mattered was what the law said and Judge Southwick worked very hard to apply it fairly. Judge Southwick valued my opinions and included me in all of the discussions of issues presented for decision. Having worked closely with Judge Southwick, I have no doubt that he is fair, impartial, and has all of the other qualities necessary to be an excellent addition to the United States Court of Appeals for the Fifth Circuit.

Over the years, Judge Southwick has earned the reputation of being a person of high morals, dignity, and fairness. It is unfortunate that there are some who have made him the chosen sacrifice to promote agendas and have set out to taint all that Judge Southwick has worked so hard to accomplish. I am prayerful that those efforts will not preclude Judge Southwick from serving as our next Judge on the United States Court of Appeals for the Fifth Circuit.

A. La'Verne Edney

Other former clerks wrote as well. I do not include their letters here, though they meaningfully encouraged my confirmation. I can only thank them.

The other letter I will quote came from the adjutant general of Mississippi, Major General Harold A. Cross. He was the head of the Mississippi National Guard, a wonderful leader, and in many other ways the epitome of the citizen soldier. He wrote on June 1.

Dear Senators:

I am writing you concerning Leslie H. Southwick, who serves under my command as a Lieutenant Colonel in the Mississippi National Guard. During my tenure as Adjutant General, I have had the pleasure coming to know LTC Southwick personally.

LTC Southwick joined the Army Reserve in 1992—obtaining an age waiver to allow him to join, even though he knew from the outset his age would necessarily prohibit him from serving long enough to vest a military pension. In 1997, then-Captain Southwick transferred into the Mississippi National Guard.

While LTC Southwick was originally assigned to what was then called State Area Command, in 2003, Southwick volunteered to transfer into the 155th Separate Armor Brigade, a line combat unit. This was a courageous move, as it was widely known at the time that the 155th was nearly certain to mobilize for overseas duty in the near future.

In fact, in August 2004, the 155th mobilized for duty in support of Operation Iraqi Freedom, as the 155th Brigade Combat Team. From August 2004 to January 2006, LTC Southwick served on active duty, distinguishing himself as Deputy Staff Advocate at Forward Operating Base Duke near Najaf—and later as Staff Judge Advocate for the 155th, located at Forward Operating Base Kalsu. After his service in Iraq, LTC Southwick transferred back to Joint Force Headquarters, Mississippi National Guard.

Both before and after his service in Operation Iraq Freedom, LTC Southwick has worked directly with me on numerous matters of significance to the Guard. I have always found his counsel sound, his bearing exemplary, his judgment exceptional and his character beyond reproach.

While there are many core qualities critical to a successful military officer, one attribute I have found particularly important during my many years of service is sound temperament. In that regard, LTC Southwick has both a considerate and measured personality. I can tell you without hesitation that I have always found LTC Southwick to treat everyone with whom he comes into contact with both kindness and respect.

I hope you find this information useful, as you consider matters coming before your Committee. Thank you for permitting me the opportunity to correspond with you concerning LTC Southwick.

Harold A. Cross,
Major General

These letters were indispensable in countering many of the criticisms. Opponents were also gathering letters with a rather different message. I will quote one of those at length later.

Besides letters, Tessa Platt was also acquiring useful information. She asked me to give her statistics on my opinions. I sent her the following on June 4. "This is what I have determined on my reversal rate: Total opinions for court—823. Reversed—21."

I may have missed a few, but the numbers were as accurate as I could make them. Reversal rate is considered one indication of how well a judge is doing. My number, less than 3 percent of my opinions, is quite small. If my nerves were not so frayed, I would have found it hilarious a few months later when a critic talked about my abysmally high reversal rate.

The vote was scheduled for Thursday, June 7. The administration wanted as many letters sent to the committee by then as possible. The day before, I e-mailed Tessa Platt. "I got a call from former Miss. Supreme Court Justice Jimmy Robertson this morning. Down here, his reputation is as a liberal Democrat. He wants to help, and was prompted by reading the *New York Times* editorial, which he described in a voice mail message with a strong expletive. I sent him some information about the cases."[13]

One incredibly important offer of a different kind of assistance came from a colleague at Mississippi College. I was about to embark on a time-consuming campaign to save my nomination and my reputation. Yet I was also scheduled to teach a summer course.

On June 6, I received a welcome e-mail from Jeff Jackson with the subject line "Substitute Teaching." "I write to offer again to substitute teach for you this summer if you find you need me to do so. Late notice is not a problem as long as know what problems you are covering in ethics. I do not know how to help you on confirmation. However, if I can help with your class or in any other way, please let me know. Be assured that the people who know you know what a good judge you have been and will be, and are rooting for you."[14] I would need Jeff's help a lot.

On June 7, the morning of the business meeting, the *Wall Street Journal* ran an editorial titled "Judicial Speech Code."[15] The title was explained in the first paragraph. "Move over, *Roe v. Wade*. The latest liberal judicial litmus test is whether the nominee is willing to repudiate the phrase 'homosexual lifestyle.' Believe it or not, that's one of the two raps against Leslie Southwick, whose nomination for the Fifth Circuit Court of Appeals comes before the Senate Judiciary Committee today." What the editorial said about my prospects for confirmation was accurate. "His nomination looked safe enough until two weeks ago, when liberal critics, having scoured his 7,000-plus rulings on the Mississippi appeals bench, uncovered two allegedly hanging offenses."

As had happened on the night before my hearing, the message in a daily meditation book for June 7 was directly on point. "I trust the best outcome will develop in the perfect way and at the optimum time." What had been on course to be simple was shifting to a difficult if not impossible route. I needed to trust that this new course was the perfect one, leading to the best outcome at just the right time. What outcome, and when, was a mystery. My willingness to trust the timing was immediately put to the test, as no committee vote took place on this day. "Pennsylvania Sen. Arlen Specter, the top committee Republican, said he thinks the committee will approve Southwick's nomination." A different key senator was beginning to reveal doubt. "However, committee chairman Patrick Leahy said objections from a number of civil rights groups about Southwick's rulings in a handful of cases raise questions about the 57-year-old nominee's commitment to equal justice. Leahy, D-Vt., gave little indication of how he would vote. He noted that, in his 30 years as a Judiciary Committee member, he usually deferred to a nominee's home state senators."[16]

Republicans reacted strongly to my not getting a vote. Senator Trent Lott spoke about a "major meltdown" of the Senate, and GOP leader Mitch McConnell said he was mad about my treatment and believed these tactics could cause a "total shutdown here pretty soon."[17]

June 14 was now the target. I continued to field questions from the Justice Department. Occasionally I got some wonderful calls from people saying they wanted to help. I sent an example to Tessa at the Justice Department. "Former Miss. Democratic Governor William Winter wants to send a supportive letter for me. One of his law partners left me a message to that effect an hour or so ago, and asked me to call and leave the necessary information about addresses, etc."[18]

June 14 finally came. An editorial in the *Clarion-Ledger* said that I was being opposed because of the desire for a black judge to be appointed.[19] Not long after reading the morning paper, I got news from Senator Cochran's counsel Brad Davis. "Right now it does not look encouraging. Sen. Specter thinks that he might be able to get some movement my way with a little more time. Recently there was a conversation between Thad and Leahy about moving me to the district court seat. Thad said I had made that choice already." Brad asked whether I would agree to another delay. I told

The Sorting Out / 177

him that if those helping me thought it was a good idea, then I was all for it, too.

Later Thad called and said this was one of the most discouraging and surprising things that had happened to him in the Senate. He had thought Herb Kohl, Dianne Feinstein, Leahy, or even Durbin might be helpful, as Durbin had been saying things earlier as if he were helping. No longer. Thad told me that Senator Leahy had agreed not to have a vote until Thad was ready. That agreement was honored for six weeks, and the delay was indispensable.

The next day, Senator Specter was quoted as saying that it was "clear to me that Mr. Southwick would be rejected if a committee vote is called." He wanted "another week to spend my time—perhaps waste my time" to persuade Democrats on the committee. Senator Leahy agreed, but a *Congressional Quarterly* headline indicated he thought the time would be wasted: "Judiciary Chairman Says Court Nominee Will Not Get Out of Committee."[20] Senator Leahy had written the White House, urging the president to withdraw my name for the Fifth Circuit and nominate me again for the district judgeship. He also urged the nomination of black U.S. district judge Henry Wingate in my stead. On June 13, the article said, White House counsel Fred Fielding passed along a refusal to consider switching me. This was the first I had heard of this rather important matter. It may be usual, though, for a nominee to be kept in the dark about high-level discussions.

Dave Illingsworth, an Air Force JAG who had been a blogger while he was finishing law school, wrote to inquire about events. I responded with some personal thoughts.

> Every spring I go for three days to a Catholic retreat house in Louisiana called Manresa. The approach of the retreat was designed by the founder of the Jesuits, St. Ignatius of Loyola. We are encouraged to strive in our lives to be "indifferent," i.e., not to care, whether we find riches or poverty, success or failure, praise or insults. Though we should not—and I do not—want what is negative in life, we should not mind. At least to Ignatius, that is what the Beatitude means about being "poor in spirit"—to have spiritual poverty is to be detached from the riches of the world. To be condemned and to receive insults is to experience what Christ experienced. I am being condemned for doing what I thought was right, which in a very small way does make me identify with the sufferings of worthier people. I would feel spiritually worthier if the insults were due to my faith, but I have not achieved that.

Regardless of what happens, I am certain that God's plan is to make me better for my experiences if I will let that benefit come. I am trying.[21]

Each Thursday to Thursday, my hopes and anxieties grew, and then the committee failed to vote. Patience was the most needed virtue. "Thursday, June 21. Went to jog at 7:15 a.m. Decided that I did not want to agree to shift to the district judgeship if that was the compromise. Trust in the Lord, and my trust would require that I let Him act. I am not sure if that is faith or my sense of self."

At 3:00 p.m., Justice Department lawyer Beth Cook "called to say that the Republicans were avoiding having a quorum because of the Democrats' desire to issue subpoenas [to White House officials]. Sen. Specter is trying to arrange a meeting for me with some of the more reasonable senators. So far, he has had no one agree. I will likely not be on the agenda next week, because there are too many other matters right now. The following week is a recess for July 4." Senator Specter's suggestion of having meetings would in coming months turn into my dominant role in the confirmation struggle.

Senators Specter and Leahy talked to the administration about shifting me back to the district court and nominating a black judge to the Fifth Circuit.[22] In March some Mississippi black leaders had suggested that placing a black judge to the district court would "rectify" the naming of another white (me) to the Fifth Circuit. Now Senator Leahy wanted to rectify the situation in the opposite direction, a black judge for the Fifth Circuit and moving me to the district court.

Leahy's friendship with Thad may have been what led him to offer a congenial outcome for me as opposed to just urging my defeat. Opposition senators in a judicial confirmation battle can at times show some compassion.

15

A Pause, and a New Approach

Among those following my lack of progress were my former secretary at the state court and three prospective law clerks, all of whom by late May had an offer to join me at the Fifth Circuit, contingent on my getting there myself. One of my occasional status reports was sent at this time.

> I am writing you collectively, as each of you has been offered a position for working with me should I become a Fifth Circuit judge. The odds of success look rather long, but there are reasons not to give up hope.
>
> Sen. Specter has tried to arrange meetings for me with individual senators on the committee. He has not had much success, but the effort continues. I will be in Washington on Tuesday through Thursday (26–28 June), to meet with the two senators who have so far agreed to see me and with anyone else who does so. It is not thought that I will be on the committee agenda again until the week after the July 4 recess. I am told that the immigration bill, committee subpoenas, and several other angry issues make it advisable to leave me off the next agenda.
>
> My advice would be not to depend on my confirmation, but not to abandon the possibility either. Clear?[1]

Of course, the only thing clear was that I was in deep trouble.

As I noted to my potential future staff, Senator Specter's efforts to arrange meetings were bearing fruit. On June 22, the day after the fourth postponement of a committee vote, the Justice Department said that two committee members would see me, Democrat Herb Kohl of Wisconsin and Republican Jeff Sessions of Alabama.

A timely piece of information made much less expensive the eight separate trips over the next four months that I did not yet know would be needed. I contacted a JAG about his finding a substitute for some National Guard duty that I had earlier in the day agreed to handle before learning of the need to go to Washington. I got the substitute, and more. Major Mark Majors e-mailed me on June 22: "Great news about the meetings! I'll find someone else to cover. Did you know you can fly Space-A to DC on our C-17s from Jackson to Andrews AFB? Flights are on Mondays and Fridays."[2]

The answer to his question about whether I knew about these flights was no. These were called "space-available" flights because a military service member was entitled to fly on them if there was space left over from the mission being performed. For example, on my first flight, a military retiree friend, Ben Piazza, and his family were flying to Germany for a vacation.

The flights were on huge C-17 cargo planes, based at the Air National Guard facility on the grounds of the Jackson airport. The air wing at the base flew the planes to Andrews Air Force Base outside Washington, then to Germany, then to Iraq to pick up wounded. The plane returned with injured soldiers first to a military hospital in Germany. Those more seriously injured were brought back to Andrews Air Force Base for transfer to Walter Reed or other area military hospitals. Burn victims were flown to San Antonio, requiring a detour from the direct flight home to Jackson. Of the eight trips ahead, I flew on military airplanes five times and commercial on three.

I contacted Peter Keisler. I wanted to let him know I would visit the Civil Division again. "I apologize, as the controversies about me have stopped you. Each delay in my vote gives the Democrats a chance to delay everyone else. Right now I am the stopper in the bottle."[3]

Peter's response was generous and gentlemanly:

> One stopper does not need to apologize to the stopper located right beneath it in the same bottle. I'm under no illusion that, if I were up right now instead of you, I would be having any easier a time—or that I will have an easier time if and when they get to me in the future. To the contrary, I've always believed, and still do, that you have a stronger case for confirmation than me.
>
> So no apology of any sort is remotely necessary. I've been shocked and dumbfounded at what's been happening in your case. It's not right. I'm rooting hard for you.[4]

We were rooting for each other. We still do.

One of the most talented and humorous people I have ever known is Stuart Schiffer. He was a career lawyer at the Justice Department at the time I was there and had only recently retired. Stuart also wrote me at this time:

> Please don't blame Peter for giving me your email address. I was standing next to him earlier today when he was looking at a message he had just received from you. He couldn't pretend to have lost your address.
>
> I wrote a couple of letters to committee members on Peter's behalf (without consulting him) before I left the Department. Not only were they not acknowledged, but I assume that they were a major reason why his nomination has not moved. As a result, I have done you the favor of not repeating the exercise on your behalf.
>
> I know that what is going on isn't fun, and I hope that you are bearing up okay.[5]

Unsolicited messages like Stuart's meant a great deal to me. As strangers were criticizing, it was encouraging to hear from those who knew me that they remained supportive.

"Monday, June 25. Sharon took me to Air National Guard facility at 4:00 p.m. Plane left at 6:10 p.m., a C-17 with about 25 people. Arrived at Andrews Air Force Base at 9:00, EDT." I stayed at a nearby motel that first night.

On Tuesday, June 26, I went to my friend John Hamre's office first. John was the president of the highly respected Center for Strategic and International Studies. He let me work out of a spare office and stay at their house. He and his wife Julie provided meals, too. I would avoid imposing in the future.

"Wednesday June 27. Went to White House and escorted to Fred Fielding's office. Outgoing Deputy Counsel Bill Kelley [heading to Notre Dame Law School], incoming Deputy J. Mike Farren, Kate Todd and Cheryl Stanton all there. Fielding said he wanted me to know that the White House was fully behind me. He had either read the two challenged opinions or just read about them, and the opponents' characterizations of them made him angry."

"Karl Rove came in, and I stood and saluted; he returned it. Goofy, but I felt as if someone in command had come in." My eighteen months on active duty was recent enough that perhaps a salute to authority was still an instinct. "He invited me to go by his office when I finished. I did, but he was on a 'long' conference call. Perhaps the invitation was just a gesture on his part, but I appreciated it." This was just a courtesy meeting with the White House counsel, but it encouraged me. Thad was completely supportive, but the administration's support was more conditional.

White House legislative affairs staffer Andrea Looney, Kohl's counsel Seth Bloom, and I met with Senator Kohl. "I said that I could answer whatever questions he might have, or just start with a summary of my background. He said something like 'go ahead.' I talked about my life in Texas, went to Miss. for a clerkship, then stayed." I mentioned various endeavors, both professional and charitable. He had to leave after about ten minutes and wanted me to talk more with Seth.

The next day, I sent my friend Lanny Griffith a report on my meeting.

> Sen. Kohl could not stay long—he came late from voting on the latest immigration matter, then left after about ten minutes for another vote. The senator said very little, but at the end told me something along the lines that I was a good man. Maybe he meant something, maybe he was just trying to be kind in my obviously difficult predicament. My meeting with Seth then went on for another twenty minutes. He was very kind, receptive, and noncommittal.
>
> As I had been told, [Kohl] is a man of exceptional reserve. He became animated only when I mentioned professional basketball, as he is the owner of the Milwaukee Bucks franchise. My comment as I was standing to leave was to mention the Bucks, then to admit (with good humor, I hoped) that I was actually a huge San Antonio Spurs fan. He with equal good humor praised the Spurs organization and we discussed basketball for a few minutes.[6]

On Thursday, June 28, I met with Trent, who told me that "Leahy and Reid had told him without qualification that I would be reported out of committee and confirmed by Memorial Day, and that is when Trent called me. He mentioned how strong Mitch McConnell was, and how angry."

I went to the Justice Department to meet with attorney general Al Gonzales. "Gonzales seemed tired and even discouraged. This was the day he was dealing with subpoenas. Really not much substantive said, though I was there 10–15 minutes." I had a great deal of sympathy for the troubles he was having, much more important than my own.

These meetings made it obvious that although I had started as an unknown nominee from Mississippi, sponsored by the enormously well-liked Senator Cochran, thought to be on an easy path to confirmation and therefore of little political importance, I was quickly becoming a person of interest to both sides of the political battle. Senator Orrin Hatch was the first (I think) to give lengthy remarks about me on the Senate floor. On June 28, he spoke for several minutes and several pages of the *Congressional Record* on my behalf. His focus was on what he called "these wrong tactics, these inappropriate methods, and illegitimate means" used to vilify me.[7]

Finding a Democratic senator on the Judiciary Committee to vote for me was now the goal. To find a Democrat, I needed strong Republican assistance. No Republican was likely to more helpful than Senator Arlen Specter of Pennsylvania. A moderate, even liberal, Republican, he was not popular among conservatives. Senator Lott had told me in my morning meeting that Specter would see me that afternoon, a meeting arranged only after I got to Washington.

The ConfirmThem Web site posted Specter's responses to press questions that morning:

> *Question:* Where are you at now? Does this guy have a chance?
> *Specter:* Well, I'm meeting with Mr. Southwick this afternoon. He's meeting with some of the Democrats on the committee, I'm told. And I want to talk to him in some greater detail about those couple of comments in those two opinions, to see what there is to it. If we can't confirm Southwick, I don't know anybody we can confirm.
> *Question:* Is there a compromise here that puts him in a district position?
> *Specter:* No. No. The president is not going to cede his authority to name circuit judges, not going to do that. Thank you all.

Andrea Looney took me to the vice president's private office in the Capitol. "The meeting with Sen. Specter was at 5:00. Andrea and I went into a small reception room. Sen. Specter came in with Sen. Hatch. Specter had three or four of his staff." Specter was seventy-seven, vigorous, mentally sharp, looking much younger than his years due partly to a diligence about exercise. He would adopt me as a project, and I am greatly in his debt. Gregg Nunziata headed the Republican staff on the committee. He was young, bald, intense, and skilled in the ways of the Senate. He and the other lawyers who worked with him were wonderful. My salutation for Gregg in my e-mails was the "Great One," because I felt that way about him and the staff.

"Specter sat on a small sofa and told me to sit next to him. Specter asked Gregg what the language was in each case that was considered improper. Gregg underlined something in the *Richmond* [racial slur] case and handed it to the senator." After reading the key section, "Specter said some magical words to Nunziata that I still remember vividly—'is that all there is?' Incredulity was certainly the reaction I wanted. Specter said he would go to Sen. Feinstein, maybe Kohl and Leahy, and talk to them about this. We [also] talked about the custody case."

"Sen. McConnell came in. I stood to shake his hand. He asked if I was willing to stick this out, and I said that I was. I did not phrase it as convincingly as he expected, and he questioned me a bit." His concern about whether I had the spine for all of this struck me at the time, and even more as my troubles mounted. Some senators were going to work very hard for me, and the GOP leader wanted to make sure I would stay the course."

"When Sen. Specter and I were finished, we were told that Fox News was waiting for us to come out. A Specter aide asked if I wanted to walk out with Sen. Specter. I asked the senator what he wanted. He said for us to do it. The cameraman was there, but no questions were asked."

A few days after my meeting with Senator Specter, *Roll Call* labeled him "chief" among my backers.[8] The paper quoted him as saying that after reviewing my record, "there's absolutely no reason not to confirm Judge Southwick." I grew, quickly, truly to like this man. My first awareness of him had been in 1967. Philadelphia district attorney Specter was favored to win the mayor's race, something a Republican just did not do in that city. Specter did not either, but it was close.[9] My interest in politics as a teenager inclined toward Republicans in unlikely places. Nowhere was as unlikely as in the South and in big cities. I continued to follow Specter's career. He had many more defeats than victories until he was elected to the Senate in 1980. His remarkable perseverance after recurring defeats would in 2007 prove vital to my judicial hopes.

Thanks in large part to Senator Specter, I flew home on Friday with some revived hope.

◆ ◆ ◆

Senator Thad Cochran was my constant supporter, encouraging colleagues in his behind-the-scenes way. As my nomination seemed to be heading toward defeat, one Washington newspaper headline read, "Thad Cochran Tries to Rescue Bush Nominee." The first sentence said that he was "making a last-ditch effort to save" me by working with Senator Specter to get Democrats to meet with me. Thad was quoted as saying he had asked both Senators Kohl and Feinstein to meet me. The warmly supportive head of one group, Curt Levey of the Committee for Justice, said that they were the "most open-minded Democrats on Judiciary." Another newspaper said that civil rights groups had "pressed Cochran and Lott to recommend a minority candidate," and quoted Levey as believing opposition was based on the demand that a black person be nominated.[10]

In the weeks ahead, I would get questions through Tessa Platt, the Justice Department lawyer assigned to assist me. Once she also gave me an unusual request. Someone had asked for information about one of my ancestors, Rebecca Nurse. She was a many-times great-grandmother who had been hanged as a witch in 1692 during the Salem hysteria. Nurse is often a character in Salem movies. One of the earliest, *Maid of Salem* (1937), had a few scenes in which Nurse was portrayed by Lucy Beaumont. In *The Crucible* (1996), Elizabeth Lawrence played Nurse. In a 2002 television movie, *Salem Witch Trials*, Shirley MacLaine played her.

I describe Nurse on a résumé that I use for various purposes, including material to be used by anyone needing to introduce me. I did not remember giving a copy to the Justice Department, but I must have. I would find out later why that inquiry was made.

The decline in my fortunes was becoming clear. A story in one of the Washington political newspapers suggested that my confirmation was slipping away.[11] "Judiciary Chairman Patrick Leahy (D-Vt.) said late last week that as it currently stands Southwick's nomination wouldn't make the cut. 'He'd lose now,' Leahy asserted. 'That's probably why they want more time.'"

Another trip to Washington was needed for the week of July 9–13. Again I flew up on Monday on the C-17 to Andrews Air Force Base. For the first time, I stayed at transient officer quarters at Andrews. I also got down my routine. I would walk about three-quarters of a mile to an exit from the base. Across the street was a bus stop on a route that would take me to a Metro Green Line stop. Then into Washington I would go on the Metro.

The next day I had the most important meeting in the entire ordeal. It also was a double anniversary of my seeking a position on the Fifth Circuit. In my diary, I wrote, "Tuesday, 10 July. Sixteen years today since this started," meaning that I learned on July 10, 1991, that Judge Charles Clark was retiring. In addition, the 1991 date was exactly sixteen years after I wrote my July 10, 1975, letter applying to clerk for Judge Clark.

In the afternoon, I went to the office set aside for the vice president in the Dirksen Senate Office Building. It contains a large conference room and a small office. It is an outpost for the executive branch in a Senate building. It was my retreat on those days when I was on Capitol Hill. I was to meet senator Dianne Feinstein, one of only two members of the Judiciary Committee who was considered reachable by the merits of my credentials and character—such as they were. For thirty minutes, Harold Kim and Dianna Dunne discussed what to expect.

"Met with Sen. Feinstein in her conference room at 2:40–3:30. Harold and Dianna with me, and two senatorial staffers. She was angry at President Bush and the Supreme Court. She found last term's decisions to be outrageous. She also said that both Roberts and Alito misled the committee about what they would do in 'following the law' and not being activists. She no longer thought that anything that a judicial nominee said was reliable. She also indicated that nominees would be better served not to deal with [White House] Legislative Affairs, and just testify 'from the heart.' She said that when a nominee is a borderline one such as myself, she may be less likely to vote for them because of her experiences with Roberts and Alito."

It was not an encouraging meeting. She was a decent and thoughtful woman but incensed at the president and his recent nominees. She had been mayor of one of the most liberal cities in the country, San Francisco, had lost a race for governor, and had been in the Senate since 1992. The racial slur and lesbian mother cases must have been particularly hard for her constituents to understand. I later learned she was seventy-four, which astounded me, as she looked much younger. When we were not discussing her disappointments, she was considerate and friendly. We had a long discussion at the end, after I stood to leave. I asked her what else she was dealing with that day other than controversial judicial nominees. She discussed a southern California, northern Mexico public works project. She showed me a map of the project, which was probably already lying on a table. I asked just how many meetings she thought she had on average per day. I forget her exact answer, but it made her job sound awful. I was not exactly at risk of becoming a senator, but the risk of my becoming a federal judge was increasingly minimal, as well.

Back at Andrews, I wrote my final notes on the day. I was thinking of Churchill's placing in perspective a few successes Britain had in 1942 in

World War II after so many years of bloodshed. He knew there would be much still to be decided. He said that the recent success was "not the end. It is not even the beginning of the end. But it is, perhaps, the end of the beginning." My battle was further along than that. I wrote at the time, and remain convinced it was the correct perception, that the "sixteenth anniversary of the start of this quest became the beginning of the end, though what end remains to be seen."

The next day I had some more meetings. "Saw [GOP] Sen. Lindsey Graham in V.P.'s reception room. He seemed preoccupied with Iraq issues of the day and was tired. He asked what he could do, and I mentioned my awkward meeting with Sen. Feinstein. I was concerned she might declare against me and hoped he would talk to her soon. The senator thought timing was the key, and this was not the best time to be getting me through" the Senate. Later that day, I also met with Senator Sheldon Whitehouse of Rhode Island, who had chaired my hearing in May.

On July 12, *Politico* ran a front-page, above-the-fold story about me, with a large photograph of Senator Specter.[12] It reported that on July 10, the day I met with Senator Feinstein, "representatives from about 15 organizations, ranging from Concerned Women of America to the Family Research Council, gathered in Specter's office to plot strategy for pushing President Bush's nominees," including me.

The Hill reported that majority leader Harry Reid had told Senator Cochran that I "had no hope of confirmation." Senator Specter charged that Reid and Judiciary Chairman Leahy had broken their promises about me.[13] "Sen. Leahy told me that he was prepared to voice vote Southwick out of committee," Specter said. "Feingold raised an objection. In the intervening time, the positions hardened." He told the conservative activists that "he was prepared to battle Democrats and asked if they also had an appetite for a fight, according to several people who attended the meeting." The attendees accepted the challenge.

Specter seemed correct about events. Democratic senators first saw me as uncontroversial and knew they had to confirm a few Bush judicial nominees while seeking to preserve vacancies for the future. So I was accepted as the next confirmation. It was outside groups who researched my record for the best criticisms that could be given their Senate allies. This was the kind of consultation that had been the subject of well-publicized memos in 2003 regarding nominees Miguel Estrada, Priscilla Owen, and others.[14] After the criticisms burst into public view in the week of my hearing, Democratic senators initially seemed reluctant to abandon the agreement. Commitments in politics, though, have an implied escape clause for changes in the political landscape. I felt as if a volcano had erupted. That will change the landscape.

For all the difficulties the outside groups caused—though they would say my rulings caused my troubles—their delay in announcing opposition was absolutely vital to me. Perhaps they were surprised that I got the hearing in May and had not yet looked for reasons to condemn me. Had they made their opposition to me clear before Senator Leahy agreed to schedule my hearing, I might have joined all those other Bush nominees who never received a hearing. Instead I was the only nominee in that Congress to be filibustered.

At the Specter meeting was Wendy Long, counsel for the Judicial Confirmation Network. She said that Specter "thinks it would be wise to fight, he is ready to fight, he is eager to fight and he wants to know if we would do the same. Every person in the room was very enthusiastic about a fight." Another attendee was Tom McClusky, vice president of government affairs at the Family Research Council. He said that the response to Specter's call for a fight "was a unanimous 'Yes!'"

Ed Whelan, president of the Ethics and Public Policy Center, was insightful. "There are folks who didn't care squat about Southwick in the beginning who now feel he is a good man and he's being treated unfairly. Now they feel this is the right fight to fight." I had been unknown to anyone involved in the national political battles, a stranger to both parties and their allies. No more. Whelan had also defended me effectively in many articles on *National Review Online*, two of which I have already quoted. I was very appreciative, and when I got home, I e-mailed him: "I read your several *National Review* online analyses. Your descriptions of the two challenged cases are far clearer and more persuasive than what I have been able to say to senators at the hearing and in my meetings. I would also say the descriptions are exactly correct, but I hardly am objective. How can so many make so much out of so little?"[15]

He replied: "As you are probably aware, there are plenty of hardened Senate staffers who are particularly appalled by the unfair treatment that you are receiving. Although there are significant challenges ahead, I remain hopeful that you will be confirmed."[16]

Thursday, July 12. On my last full day in Washington, "I did not have any meetings scheduled. After seeing Thad, I went toward the Catholic Church on Capitol Hill to attend mass at 12:10 p.m. Hugh Gamble from Trent's staff called [before mass started]. He said Trent wanted to talk with me. Trent said he had been on the sidelines, and Specter was leading the team. Trent would come off the bench if Specter said it was time. Trent [said, in answer to my question] that the goal still very much was my confirmation and not just making some political points using a doomed nominee." My resolve was weakening as I feared my allies were changing their goal.

As soon as the phone call ended, I walked into church. "Reading from Gospel was about disciples not taking anything on their missionary journeys and just to rely on what God provided. Priest's homily was on point too, as he talked about all the objects that we seek that are fine so long as kept in perspective. But fame, prestige, power cannot be the goals, only the consequences."

After church, I went to the Justice Department. Peter Keisler joked about creating a twelve-step support group—"Hi, my name's Peter, and I was blocked for the D.C. Circuit. Hi, my name is Leslie . . ." The first step to recovery could be to admit what obsessed us to others similarly obsessed. I enjoyed Peter so much, even when just sharing our miseries.

After this trip, there was a new and vital person in my life. He was the incredible Harold Kim, assigned as my handler by the White House after Andrea Looney went on maternity leave. Harold was early in his career, knowledgeable and effective in his dealings with me and senators. His physical features reflect his Korean heritage, handsome, somewhat serious in his demeanor. He was splendidly organized and gave me wise counsel. With great respect to Harold, I expect he was not always candid because he needed to help me avoid emotional meltdown.

Despite the involvement of so many new people, my prospects were bleak. The title of a *Roll Call* article, "Southwick May Stymie Senate," was bad.[17] Its first sentence was worse: "Barring an unlikely confirmation of Leslie Southwick to the 5th U.S. Circuit Court of Appeals by the Judiciary Committee this week, Senate GOP leaders have privately mapped out a retaliatory plan that involves blocking passage of Democratic legislation from now until the August recess." Senator Cochran said, "There's a small chance a Judiciary Committee Democrat or two would consider advancing Southwick to the floor." Thad was losing confidence, and so was I.

On July 17, Harold called. There was a new plan to put pressure on the Democrats. "Harold said that the 'leader' [McConnell], Thad, Trent, and many of the Republicans on the Judiciary Committee met today. He mentioned Graham, Specter, and Cornyn. They decided to seek the agreement of as many Democrats as possible—particularly from the

Gang of 14—to agree to vote for a 'sense of the Senate' resolution that I should get a floor vote."

"Apparently the feeling is that Leahy will not let me out of committee, and this should pressure Democrats to allow a floor vote. Sen. Graham [who was one of the Gang in 2005] in particular will be trying to convince them to meet with me next week."

A strong signal that the GOP leadership was taking up my cause was Senator Specter's floor speech on July 17.[18] He reviewed the contentious recent history on judicial nominations. There had been two decades "of partisanship on judicial nominations," and it was time for the Senate to stop. He discussed the two cases on which the opposition to my confirmation was largely based, saying that "they show there is not any reason this man should not be confirmed. I discussed these cases with him. I met with him at length and talked with him about his judicial career and his service in Iraq. He is a mild-mannered professional who is a confident man—not flamboyant and not overstated. We talked about legal issues. He is a solid lawyer and has been a solid judge."

He then reviewed some of the letters that had been sent. I learned for the first time of one from an old high school friend. "Jose Alberto Cantu, a self-described lifelong Democrat, expressed outrage over what he considered to be the unfair characterization of his friend from Edinburg, Texas. After reading an article in the *Houston Chronicle*, he wrote, 'I was shocked to read about the opposition to his nomination on this basis [racial animosity]. I was a classmate of Judge Southwick in high school and knew him very well. I always found him to be extremely polite and absolutely fair with everyone. . . . The Valley has a large Hispanic population, and Leslie never showed the type of discriminatory attitudes that were implied in the article. To the contrary, I remember him as treating everyone fairly and with respect.'"

The day after Specter's speech, I taught my course at the law school from 6:00 to 8:00 p.m. Sharon was home by herself and watched the Fox News program *Special Report with Brit Hume*. Hume segued to the first commercial break with this: "Coming up next, the story of a judge. You may never have heard of him, but there is a fight over him, and you will hear of him." Sharon thought the judge might be one she had heard of and kept watching. After the break, a clip from Specter's speech was shown, which revealed the report was on me. Hume then gave these initial questions to his panel: "So who is this guy, and why should we care about him? And what is up with him?"

Fred Barnes started by stating background. He mentioned both Judge Pickering and Mike Wallace as prior nominees. "Now Southwick comes along, who is not so hard core conservative. This is not Scalia in Mississippi clothing. Here is a moderate conservative, and was about to sail through." Then the outside groups announced their objections. The panelists described the criticisms and dismissed them. Charles Krauthammer called them a "smear campaign," while Mort Kondracke said they were "over the top."

The lengthy segment on me ended with each panelist responding to Hume's question "And so you think he will get through?"

> *Krauthammer:* I'm not sure, I don't think [so].
> *Kondracke:* I don't think he is going to get through.
> *Barnes:* I am afraid not.[19]

It was a shock for Sharon to hear commentators, who for nearly ten minutes had spoken so supportively, abruptly close by saying I would fail. She did not mention their predictions to me until months later. We both had our silent discouragements in addition to the many we did admit to each other.

16

Desperation, and Witches and Martyrs

The nature of my problem with Senator Leahy became public on July 19. He released a statement, posted on the committee's Web site.[1]

> I have urged the White House to work with Senators of both parties and to fill the 5th Circuit vacancy from Mississippi with the nomination of the Honorable Henry Wingate. Judge Wingate would be the first African American from Mississippi to serve on the 5th Circuit. He was appointed to the federal bench in Mississippi by President Ronald Reagan. He has served with honor and distinction for more than 20 years, since we helped confirm him in 1985. He has served as the Chief Judge of the District Court since 2003.
>
> I cannot imagine why an experienced judge appointed by Ronald Reagan would be unacceptable to this White House. But if for some reason he is, I will work with the White House, the Senators from Mississippi, the Senate's Majority and Republican leader and our Ranking Member, the senior Senator from Pennsylvania to identify another worthy candidate.

Such tactics put Henry Wingate in an exceedingly awkward position. Henry was a gentleman and a friend throughout. My guess, and it is only a guess, is that he had the same struggle I did when Judge Pickering and Mike Wallace were named: wishing for fairness to the nominee, but if politics would not allow success, then hoping to be the next in line. Henry may well have done a better job of avoiding those thoughts than I had.

Thad usually worked behind the scenes. On July 19, though, he went to the Senate floor to give long and impassioned remarks on my behalf. His first lines sound perfectly like Thad. "I have been very deeply disappointed with the response of Senate Democratic leaders to the President's nomination of Judge Leslie Southwick to serve as a judge on the U.S. Court of Appeals for the Fifth Circuit. I had expected that his nomination would move expeditiously through the Judiciary Committee and the Senate."[2]

My sense of Thad is that he is a nearly vanished kind of senator, one who is not particularly partisan, who realizes there are political points that senators need to make from time to time, but who expects that on matters of great personal importance to a senator who had good friendships among his colleagues, politics will not be played with the issue. He was genuinely surprised and I think offended by the course of events that began two days before my hearing. "It never occurred to me at any moment," he said, "that there would be any question raised about the integrity, the sense of fairness, the qualifications, or the fitness to serve as a U.S. Court of Appeals Judge during the consideration by the Senate of this nomination."

He gave our background together, saying he had known me for thirty years. He read from many of the letters sent to the committee on my behalf. He said, "I hope you can sense the sincerity and seriousness of purpose of those who have written and the high quality of the people who have authored these letters." Thad seemed both perplexed and indignant. A sense of Thad's dismay can be seen in his comments that "it is a dark and sad day in the Senate if . . . the Judiciary Committee is considering recommending that Judge Southwick not be confirmed. . . . It is unthinkable."

The next day, the Jackson newspaper headline was "Cochran's Plea Aims to Shame Dems Who Oppose Southwick Nomination."[3] With all the good quotations from Senator Cochran's speech, another view was expressed by Wade Henderson, president of the Leadership Conference on Civil Rights. "Leslie Southwick's confirmation would be a slap in the face to African Americans and people of good will. His views on workplace discrimination are, at best, questionable, and at worst, indifferent to the dignity of minority workers."

A law school colleague, Professor Matt Steffey, wrote me about an article that had mentioned Senator Kohl and his professional basketball team, the Milwaukee Bucks. The article concerned Kohl's interest in trading for some players from the San Antonio Spurs. I responded: "Thanks for putting Sen. Kohl's concerns in perspective. Leahy and the NAACP want me to be black. Sen. Kohl might be more favorable if I were tall."[4]

On Monday, the *Wall Street Journal* weighed in with a very supportive editorial titled "The Southwick Stonewall."[5] It discussed the two problem cases and found each to be a reasonable decision based on the role of an appellate judge.

My troubled mind kept searching for a way to change the dynamics of the struggle. Senator Leahy was barring the door because he wanted an African American. A few days before my meeting with him, a plan began to form that might give something to all as a compromise.

Sunday, July 22. "At 2:00 a.m., woke up and could not stop thinking about a recess appointment plan. It seems clear that [Leahy] is concerned about nothing other than diversity. His posting last Thursday of the suggestion that Wingate be named, and his statements that were premised on the futility of my cause, may have been what prompted this increased thinking on the subject. Rees will likely take senior status on 8 Aug. 2009. So the problem is that there is not yet, but the opportunity is that there soon will be another vacancy with which to pair my confirmation."

My idea was that I would receive a recess appointment in August, that the president, Cochran, and Lott would agree "that the next vacancy would go to someone who would satisfy the Democrat majority's concerns," and finally that the Democrats would agree "that my confirmation could proceed at that time [2009] in tandem with the other."

"The positives include these: (1) Democrats gain a commitment, which is verifiable, that a black appointee will get the next vacancy and perhaps soon. (2) Republicans get my immediate appointment, with a commitment that is sort of verifiable that I will be confirmed if the contingency [of a black named to the next vacancy] occurs. Negatives avoided: (1) Whatever threats the GOP could actually carry out to slow Senate business, and any possible negative publicity from blocking me, do not occur. (2) GOP is not made to appear obstructionist, and (3) I am not defeated."

I realize now that such a plan was too bold or too fanciful, with too many people to satisfy. I explained it to Harold on Monday. "He said it was a possibility, but he was not enthused." He still saw hope that I could be confirmed without any agreement like this.

Senator Leahy agreed to meet with me. His opposition was firm and public, so I was being summoned to play my part in some ritual. I agreed.

Tuesday, July 24. "Early flight to D.C. Upon arriving at Reagan National airport, I went straight to the Capitol." My first meeting was with eighty-nine-year-old senator Robert Byrd. "He could stand and sit only with difficulty. Mentioned Philip and Cathy having each received Byrd scholarship. I said each child should have Byrd's picture, or maybe their parents should." I discussed my life and mentioned the two controversial cases. "I also said that another vacancy from Mississippi would open up in the summer of 2009, when my friend Rhesa Barksdale had already indicated he would retire. So the door would be open for another new judge soon." This was my first effort to point out that this vacancy was not the last chance for a black judge for a long time. The White House would soon rebuke me, as to them it sounded as if I was implying a deal could be made. I was.

It was a favorable meeting, but there was no commitment.

At 2:30, I "went to Sen. Ben Nelson's office. As we walked down the hall to his office, a cameraman in front of his office filmed us. It was a Fox News camera, as that network had staked out Nelson's office after asking the White House for my schedule. There was a picture of Omaha in waiting area. I mentioned early in my conversation with Sen. Nelson that the previous year I had gone there for the College World Series. No aide sat in with us. Nelson said he had read the two cases, that he had been insurance commissioner before he was governor, and he very much understood the limited role for courts in agency review. Neither case concerned him, and he indicated support. This is the first Democrat who had done so. Shame he is not on the committee."

I would talk with Senator Nelson several times in the coming months, though this was the only time in his office. He was sharp, always seemingly in command, somewhat like Trent Lott in never having a hair out of place. He looked physically strong. He was also one of the few who consistently sought to bridge the gap between the parties, perhaps because he was a Democrat from a conservative state.

"Fox News had sent word that they wanted a statement, and the senator and I walked out together. I shook his hand for the camera, then walked off with Harold. Nelson had told me he would tell reporters that our meeting was a useful informational opportunity, and he would not state any support at this time. Harold thought that made sense, as he does not need to become a target."

"Meeting with Sen. Ken Salazar [Colorado] at 3:10. We talked about both cases, and he did not seem to have a problem. The senator indicated that he thought this was really for the committee initially, and was wondering why we were seeing him. I answered that if I were fortunate enough to have the nomination get to the floor, it was useful for me to have met with him and others to build confidence about me beyond the committee."

Wednesday, July 25. I went to Justice Department, but I had no meetings until the one with Senator Leahy. "Supposed to meet with Harold Kim at 3:00, at Dirksen. As was walking [from Union Station to Dirksen], got call from Bret Gerry [acting head of the Office of Legal Policy at the Justice Department]. He set up a call with various lawyers who worked on nominations—Kate Todd, Beth Cook, and Cheryl Stanton—on other phones." I was standing in a park between Union Station and the Dirksen Building.

My callers were concerned that I would discuss a deal with Leahy. The day before, I had mentioned to Senator Byrd that another vacancy was anticipated in 2009. I had not referred to my recess appointment idea, though. The latter made no sense for me to negotiate but instead was something for the White House to pursue if it seemed beneficial. I hoped that would occur, but even Harold had been unreceptive. The callers insisted that I not mention again any future vacancies. They also said that Leahy would mention the possibility of shifting me to the district court. I did not know then how much Harold had told them about my recess appointment suggestion, but the idea died. Later I learned that he had the good sense not to mention it to anyone. So what had triggered this stern warning was my mentioning to Senator Byrd that another vacancy was ahead.

These lawyers seemed to believe I was getting too independent as I was struggling to survive. The administration still wanted me confirmed, but my success was clearly not as vital to them as it was to me. For the first time, I realized how my interests and those of the White House diverged. It had rejected out of hand an arrangement to move me to a district court nomination without even telling me, because that would surrender its authority on a Mississippi seat to a Vermont senator. Despite my doubts as I stared into the jaws of defeat, I always returned to the conviction that it was better to give my all for the Fifth Circuit and lose than to give up and succeed for the district court. It just would have been nice for someone to ask for my thoughts.

Whine, whine.

"Went to Leahy's office in Russell with Harold. Bruce Cohen sat in. Sen. Leahy started with his offer to shift me to the district court, and that he was being falsely accused of having made a promise to get me out of committee. I said that when I was given a choice about the district or circuit in January, I eagerly accepted the Fifth Circuit. [An appellate court] is where my experience has been, and where I am most suited. I thanked him for the effort."

Before my meeting, my image of Senator Leahy was of a man who was usually scowling, criticizing Republicans and asserting the purity of the Democrats. Many senators did comparable things. That sense of him, whatever its truth, was tempered by the fact that he was Senator Thad

Cochran's close friend. Leahy had doubled in age in the Senate, first elected at thirty-four, and now he was sixty-seven. He was fairly tall, balding, and had far more power than most senators to decide my fate. I wanted to find a basis on which we could understand each other.

"I talked too long, trying to think of every example of political moderation in my career." The conversation drifted. Likely Senator Leahy's only purpose in having a meeting was to get me to agree to being shifted back to the district court. After I quickly rejected that idea, there was not much else to do. The courtesies required more than just a few minutes, though. At the end, Senator Leahy said that I had an impressive record, and the meeting was over.

While I was meeting with senators, some of the groups supporting me organized a coalition of supporters, sent a letter to each Judiciary Committee member, and issued a press statement on Wednesday, July 25. The version of the press release forwarded to me from Senator Cochran's office, sent to him by Curt Levey, executive director of the Committee for Justice, had this caption: "Sixty Groups Demand Judiciary Committee Do Its Job on Judges; Decry Character Assassination of Iraq War Vet Southwick."[6] The sense of the press release can be seen in its first paragraph.

"WASHINGTON, DC—Today, a coalition of about 60 organizations, including the Committee for Justice, delivered a letter to each of the 19 members of the Senate Judiciary Committee expressing deep concern that a lack of progress in reporting judicial nominees out of committee . . . has made it impossible for the Senate to fulfill its constitutional duty of advice and consent in good faith." The effort was focused on the general lack of progress by the Judiciary Committee on nominees, but I was the current project. Other versions of the press release were captioned "Keisler Is 'Highest Priority"—as made sense. At least I was the current priority.

There were sixty signatories. They included the Christian Coalition of America; Paul M. Weyrich of the Coalitions for America; Wendy Wright, Concerned Women for America; Richard A. Viguerie, Chairman, ConservativeHQ.com; Phyllis Schlafly, President and Founder, Eagle Forum; Family Research Council; Focus on the Family; Wendy E. Long, Judicial Confirmation Network; Judicial Watch; Dr. Don Wildmon, Founder and Chairman, American Family Association; Christian Legal Society; and the National Legal Foundation.

More support for my cause came from the Senate Republican Campaign Committee. It issued a press release on July 26, calling me an "extraordinarily accomplished individual." Highlights from many of the letters sent on my behalf were quoted; statements and comments from a few publications appeared. It was all quite complimentary, but I did not know to what effect.

Back to Andrews for the night. The next day, I flew home, very discouraged.

A news story on July 26 reported that the old Gang of 14, which had broken the deadlock on circuit nominees in 2005, might be reformed. The agreement itself said it applied only to the 2005–6 Congress, but perhaps the spirit of compromise could be revived. *Roll Call* stated that GOP senators were seeking to reenlist and enlarge the Democratic half of the Gang to break the impasse over me.[7] The story said that several of the Democratic seven did not believe the group would gather soon, but I had met with Senator Nelson that week and he "may already be on board." He was, but he was the only one I could count on so far. The story went on to say that Senator Leahy had indicated he would hold a vote on me whenever Senators Cochran and Lott requested.

As the war became hotter, I was thrilled to see the most satisfying article published during the confirmation struggle. It appeared on July 30 in the *National Journal*, the *Atlantic*, and the *Legal Times*.[8] Stuart Taylor, the columnist, started by observing that if either Hillary Clinton or Barack Obama was elected president, their opposition to me would not give them much standing to complain about Republican filibusters of their nominees.

Taylor wrote a beautifully supportive line:

> Southwick, who is a professionally well-qualified and personally admirable Bush nominee for the U.S. Court of Appeals for the 5th Circuit, . . . is the latest victim of a judicial confirmation process that has steadily become more degraded by partisan warfare in recent decades.
>
> Of course, liberal groups and Senate Democrats don't admit to opposing Southwick simply for being conservative. But their detailed complaints boil down to just that, as do scurrilous insinuations that Southwick is a bigot—insinuations denounced by, among others, his former law clerk La'Verne Edney, an African-American. "It is unfortunate," she has written, that "there are some that have made him the chosen sacrifice to promote their agenda." Some astute Democratic thinkers privately agree.

He noted that the criticisms focused on two opinions I did not write. He agreed with Senator Specter that even if the decisions "might have been articulated differently, might have been more sensitive, [they] certainly are not disqualifiers." He said that Specter had "often bucked his party in the judicial wars. But he angrily deplores what Democrats are doing to Southwick." Taylor reviewed each case at some length and decided I was simply a conservative, not a hater.

He closed by saying that "Republican senators will take their revenge on well-qualified liberal nominees during the next Democratic administration. The confirmation process will continue to become an ever-uglier ordeal."

The article was just too uplifting for me to ignore its author. Though I believed that his credibility was improved by not having any contact with me, I nonetheless sent him an e-mail:

> As you may appreciate, when someone is being drowned by events that are
> both unexpected and overwhelming, anyone who throws a life preserver
> of any size becomes immensely important. You may be wrong and the crit-
> ics right, but I would like to think that what you wrote captures the real-
> ity about me. I will not thank you, as that may suggest you did something
> beyond just writing about these events as you saw them. I will say, though,
> that you have brightened my day. Week, too.[9]

Republicans were building a case for me, trying to reach Democrats not on the committee in case no committee Democrat broke with the party. On the Senate floor on July 30, Senator Hatch gave a lengthy speech presenting my credentials, describing opponents' criticisms as mischaracterizations of the role of appellate courts in reviewing lower-court decisions.[10]

The floor speeches, meetings with outside groups, and the other pieces of the strategy had not yet gained for me even a private commitment from a Democrat on the committee. My Republican advocates decided it was time to implement their plan to force all Democrats to declare whether they agreed with letting my nomination die in committee.

On Wednesday, August 1, Senators McConnell and Specter offered a resolution on the floor. It had twelve numbered paragraphs, each called "findings." They dealt with my career, including highlighting my military service, and with the actions of the Senate since my nomination had been submitted. The last part of the resolution read: "It is the sense of the Senate that the nomination of Judge Leslie Southwick to the United States Court of Appeals for the Fifth Circuit should receive an up or down vote by the full Senate."[11] Senator McConnell spoke at some length on the floor in support of the resolution. Senator Specter spoke for several minutes in a plea for fairness. Senator Lindsey Graham also spoke. Before the resolution was introduced, Senator Lamar Alexander of Tennessee spoke.[12] Republican senators had taken up my cause. I was immensely pleased. I had first heard of this idea two weeks earlier.

An article in *Roll Call* stated that this maneuver was intended to build pressure for a confirmation vote. According to the article, a vote on the resolution would occur no earlier than Friday. Senator Reid would try to table the resolution Wednesday afternoon. The resolution would be nonbinding, but it might put Judiciary Committee members in an awkward box if they ignored it. In fact, the resolution would be withdrawn on Thursday without any vote being taken.[13]

On Tuesday, the day before the Sense of the Senate resolution was introduced, I learned that Louisiana senator Mary Landrieu had agreed to meet with me. I left Wednesday on a 6:00 a.m. commercial flight. Upon arriving in Washington, I learned that Senator Leahy had put me on the business meeting calendar for Thursday. Instead of just meeting with a senator, I was going to be in Washington when the Judiciary Committee voted. Senator Leahy released a revised calendar less than an hour after Senator McConnell's press release about the Sense of the Senate resolution.

Fox News reported that Senator Leahy "met McConnell's move with one of his own. Mentioning nothing about the actual substance of the nominee, Leahy announced on the Senate floor that despite not having received a request from Republicans to bring Southwick up for a vote in committee, as is common practice, he will hold a vote in the committee on Thursday." The *Congressional Quarterly* reported the death of my hopes: "Detente Over, and So Is Southwick's Chance for Senate Confirmation." The story believed that Senator Leahy had "retaliated" against the resolution and I would be rejected "along strict party lines."[14]

I had been in the air on the way to Washington when news of my being on the next day's calendar was released. ABA representative Kim Askew generously wrote me after she saw the schedule. I saw the two e-mails at the same time, though they had been sent an hour apart.

Kim's message, under the subject line "Best Wishes," read: "Just wanted you to know you are in my thoughts and prayers. Great strength and dignity are gained during the tough times. Hang in there. Kim."[15] Thank you, again.

"I called Thad. He said that he asked Leahy that morning for the reason. Leahy said he was tired of getting beat up by Republicans for doing what Thad wanted, so he put me on agenda. He told Thad that I was 'likely to be reported out of committee.'" Thad asked what Democrat would vote for me, but Leahy did not say.

"At 3:00, met Harold at Dirksen. We briefly discussed Senator Landrieu. Walked to her office for 3:30 meeting. A Fox News crew filmed me walking there. Sen. Landrieu's aide said that she was willing to have the crew film me in her office, talking about innocuous things. We joked a bit about LSU and Mississippi football teams and discussed her family and mine while the cameras were there. When they left, I finished discussing my family. I also talked about the two cases. It was a very friendly meeting, without any commitments."

I then went to Thad's office to decompress among friends. "Talked to Brad Davis, who knew what Leahy had said. They were taking it as an honest revelation of a break for me and speculating about who it might be. I then went back to DOJ. While I was talking to Peter, at little before 5:00, Harold called to say that Sen. Feinstein wanted to talk with me and that I should get down to the vice president's office in Dirksen. I thought it was for a meeting. I took a cab, still carrying my luggage [as I had not checked in at Andrews]. As I was walking into Dirksen at the security point, Trent called. So I walked out of the building again, still talking to Trent on the phone."

Trent said that Feinstein wanted a letter in which I acknowledged that the racial slur case was a mistake. Soon after I got to the Dirksen office, Senator Feinstein called. We talked for perhaps ten minutes. "She said that she was leaning toward voting for me, but she wanted me to say the racial slur opinion was a mistake. I said that I could not do that. She wanted me at least to say that the phrase in the opinion was a mistake," meaning, as I understood her, that the opinion's analysis of the significance of the racial slur was erroneous. She wanted the letter that night.

What I clearly needed to do is explain myself in a way that would convince her that the racial slur opinion did not reflect an unacceptable attitude about race.

Harold thought the vice president's office at the Capitol would be the place to work. We went there on the Senate subway. I worked on a computer for a while, initially writing a lengthy section on the usual explanation of standard of review and other legal concepts. Then after thirty minutes or so, I got to my feelings on the use of the slur. Trent called while I was working; perhaps Senator Feinstein told him I would not characterize the case's result as a mistake. He encouraged me to make the letter as strong as I could, because it was key to getting her support. Trent also urged me, pleasantly, to hurry up. I ended up removing all the legal explanation of the opinion's reasoning. Though I could not honestly say I believed the result in the case was wrong, I now believed the opinion should have explained something better. The following was the key language in my draft: "What I now see as a mistake and a significant flaw in the opinion is that the court failed to express clear repudiation of the word." The draft went to Beth Cook at the Department of Justice, who sent it to Fred Fielding, the White House counsel. They would review.

"About 30–45 minutes later, Beth called. She quoted Fielding as agreeing [with her] that the 'mistake' language needed to come out, because at my hearing I had said that I thought the opinion was well-written. I told her that the intervening months had convinced me that in an opinion like this, something more needed to be said to prevent such willful mischaracterization. I got a little sharp with her, and she said that Fielding was adamant and would oppose (some such word) sending a letter like this to Feinstein in light of my testimony. I said that I would need to think about their comments, and would get back to them."

After hanging up, I talked to Harold about what had been said. I finally accepted the changes and sent them to Beth. "The principal additional change was that I had first written that the opinion 'should' have said more about the viciousness of the racial slur. The final version said that the opinion 'could' have said more. On such points do lawyers and politicians dispute among themselves." Considering its importance, I include most of the letter here.

August 1, 2007
Dear Senator Feinstein,

Thank you again for making time in an incredibly busy schedule to talk with me about my nomination. As you made clear to me today, one of your principal concerns is about an opinion that I joined which evaluated the use of a racial slur by a state employee. With your indulgence, I would like to give as complete an explanation as I can of my thoughts on the slur itself and how it was discussed in the opinion.

The court said that the use of the word "cannot be justified" by any argument. It could have gone far beyond that legalistic statement. Captured in this one terrible word is a long, dark, sad chapter in our history. This racial slur is unique in its impact and painful to hear for many, including myself. I said at my hearing that this is the worst of all racial slurs. Its use is despicable. All people of good will should make their rejection of the word clear. The opinion had an opportunity to express more fully and accurately the complete disgust that should greet the use of this word. Such a statement would certainly be consistent with my own beliefs that this is the worst kind of insult. As I testified, everyone took this issue extraordinarily seriously. I regret that the failure to express in more depth our repugnance of the use of this phrase has now led to an impression that we did not approach this case with sufficient gravity and understanding of the impact of this word.

Since this opinion has been considered by some to be the window into my own beliefs, a peek into my soul, allow me to give you some events in my life that reflect my strong beliefs in fairness and opportunity for all and my rejection of racial insults. I always tried to treat everyone who came before me as a judge with respect. I gave a memorandum to each of my law clerks that they were to use no disparaging words toward anyone in a draft opinion, no matter what the appeal was about. [I went on to mention charities that focused on the inner city in which I had participated.]

From the bench and in my opinions, I followed that same rule. I believe that everyone whom I encounter, whether as a judge or in some purely private capacity, is deserving of my respect. I took a broad view in looking for staff. I was one of the original ten judges on the Court of Appeals, taking office in January 1995. In my second year on the court, I became the first white judge to hire an African-American law clerk on that court. I could not have been more pleased with her work, and she went on to be a partner in a major Mississippi law firm. I was equally pleased with the two additional African-American clerks I hired before I left the court. . . . [I then mentioned some of my volunteer activities that refuted any suggestion of racial hostility].

Until the last two months, my fairness and temperament had not been subject to criticisms. The recent concern may have arisen from the fact that only one piece of evidence was being used, namely, the racial slur opinion. A much better explanation of my own abhorrence of this slur clearly could have been written. I have tried in this explanation to express my disgust for the use of that word and to present some of the evidence from my own life to prove my commitment to furthering the civil rights of all.

Thank you again for your effort to understand not just the words in an opinion, but my heart.

Harold printed, I signed, and he faxed the letter to Senator Feinstein's house at perhaps 10:00 p.m. Now it was time for me to check in to a hotel. My stays at Andrews Air Force Base were as a "space-available" transient officer, which did not allow me to make an advance reservation. By the time we finished the letter at the Capitol, there were no longer any rooms at Andrews. "I asked Harold if I could impose on him just for a sofa for the night. Harold called his house, and all was well. On the drive home, he ignored calls from the counsel's office. Finally [associate counsel] Kate Todd called my phone and asked to speak to Harold. There was disagreement about having sent the letter to Feinstein without the protocol of a copy to Leahy. Legislative Affairs wanted it kept secret from Leahy and thought that was their decision" to make. Feinstein would have been under extreme pressure before the vote had the letter been disseminated, but that is exactly what the counsel wanted. The gap between my interests and those of some in the White House was widening. I was tired and worried, making the call triply irritating.

We got to Harold's house in Arlington at 11:00. His wife Amy was kind. She should have been put out because of all the straightening I expected she did with six-month-old J.J. and three-year-old Evie. I had a mattress on the floor of the basement, all made up. Harold was going in to work early the next day, and Amy graciously agreed to take me later when she went to her law firm.

As the final hours played out before the vote, one that could end my dream or keep it alive, quite a bit was occurring. The four principal GOP candidates for president all issued public statements urging my approval by the committee.

Former Massachusetts governor Mitt Romney said that rather than "playing typical Washington games with nominees, Democrats must act to give Judge Southwick a fair up or down vote." Former New York mayor Rudy Giuliani issued a statement: "Judge Leslie Southwick is a distinguished and qualified candidate with a long record of service to his country who deserves an up or down vote." Arizona senator John McCain wrote the committee that allowing my nomination to languish was particularly unfair because of my military service.

The most unique of the statements urging my approval came from former senator Fred Thompson of Tennessee. On August 1, he posted a statement on his Web site.[16] I now knew why the Justice Department had made inquiries about my Salem ancestor. Senator Thompson wrote:

You've probably never heard of Rebecca Nurse, but bear with me for a moment. Nurse arrived in Salem, Massachusetts in 1640. There, despite being known as a woman of virtue and piety, she was accused of being a witch. On July 19, 1692, she was hanged.

Now almost 315 years to the day later, one of Nurse's descendants is suffering through a witch hunt of a more modern variety. I'm talking about Judge Leslie Southwick, whose nomination to the long-standing vacancy on the United States Court of Appeals for the Fifth Circuit is being thwarted by Senate Democrats. [Thompson found no evidence to justify the attacks on me.] . . . Judge Southwick's reward for being a qualified judge, and by all accounts a good citizen, is a Senatorial inquisition meant to besmirch his professional and personal reputation.

Senator Thompson's bringing in "grandma" was one of the charming parts of the experience. I have long been interested in genealogy. That research uncovered Rebecca Nurse, one of twenty people hanged in 1692 as witches in Salem, Massachusetts, while another was crushed to death. She was seventy-one, a respected woman in Salem. She was arrested, tried, and found not guilty by the jury. There was no Bill of Rights in colonial Salem, though. The presiding judges emphasized certain evidence to the jurors and sent them back to deliberate again. The verdict the second time was "guilty." After she was hanged, outrage over her death helped end the insanity.[17] The house in which she lived in Danvers is operated today as the Rebecca Nurse Homestead.

I found Senator Thompson's analogizing my situation to hers to be a pleasant and thought-provoking effort. No one was on the verge of actually hanging me, of course, so my trials were far easier than what my ancestor went through.

My genealogy search uncovered another example of persecution. My first ancestors in America were Lawrence and Cassandra Southwick. Lawrence arrived in Salem in about 1630 from England. Later his wife and children came over. They were Quakers at a time when followers were considered to be heretics by the Puritans in the Massachusetts Bay Colony. Many communities had laws against the practice of the Quaker faith. Imprisonment and even execution were the penalties for being a Quaker. England became concerned about the treatment of Quakers in the colonies and in 1660—too late for Lawrence and Cassandra—ordered all who had been arrested for this offense to be sent to England.[18]

Lawrence was arrested for the first time in 1656 or 1657, apparently for failure to attend the approved church. He and Cassandra were both arrested again in 1658 and imprisoned for twenty weeks. They and three other Quakers wrote from their jail in Boston, beseeching the authorities, "if the Spirit of Christ did dwell and rule in you," to free them. Released, they were again arrested in March 1659. They appeared before a court and refused to renounce their beliefs. They were banished to Shelter Island, a small island off the eastern end of Long Island, New York. They died of exposure, within three days of each other. A large stone monument with their names and those of other martyrs who met the same fate remains a landmark on the small island.

Another part of their story is that when they were banished, their twenty-two-year-old son, Daniel, and their eighteen-year-old daughter, Patience, each owed fines for their Quaker offenses, but they had no money. Captains of ships in Boston Harbor were ordered to sell the two into slavery either in Virginia or in Barbados. The captains refused. In 1849, the Quaker poet John Greenleaf Whittier wrote about the events, highlighting the failed slave sale. Poetic license was used to give the daughter and the poem the evocative name of the mother, Cassandra Southwick.[19]

These Southwicks and Rebecca Nurse were models for me. Faith before all else. Do not yield to the world. Dealing with the attacks without being embittered required constant tending of my soul. The day of decision in the Judiciary Committee would challenge me as had no other.

17

The Committee Speaks

Because I was in Washington, I did not see the morning Jackson newspaper. That was for the best. A front-page story was subtitled "Southwick Nomination Not Expected to Pass Committee Muster Today."[1] The article said that no Democrat was expected to vote for me. Photos of Henry Wingate and of me were atop the article. The reporter said Senator Leahy had suggested Wingate take my place as the Fifth Circuit nominee. The tone of the article was that I would be stopped, and Judge Wingate was next.

"Thursday, August 2. I was worried, even discouraged, that the letter would not say enough. I slept fitfully. Amy took me to DOJ. At Civil Division, called Sharon. She was going to 8:00 church. I sent an e-mail report to the family. I closed the note by saying, 'I am hopeful. I am also praying for peace no matter the outcome.'" Both Philip and Cathy responded. Philip wrote: "We are praying for your protection—from negativity and misunderstanding—and that a decision can be reached." Cathy said: "Good luck Dad!! I am thinking about you!"[2]

My first notes for the day state: "Harold called to say that the original letter [i.e., not a faxed copy] needed to be gotten to Feinstein. I printed out a new copy, signed it, and took a cab. I got to Dirksen perhaps at 9:30. Dianna Dunne [from the White House] came in for the letter a little after 10:00." Later I went to St. Joseph's Catholic Church, thinking the result might be known before the 12:10 service began. I heard nothing.

While I was walking, drinking coffee, and the like, the committee had a hearing from 10:00 until almost noon about the controversial firing of several U.S. attorneys. Presidential adviser Karl Rove had been called as a witness. As expected, he refused to appear. The other witness, presidential assistant J. Scott Jennings, did appear at a contentious session.

The business meeting at which my nomination would be voted on was supposed to start at 11:30. Instead the committee recessed for two hours.[3] As I wrote to one friend, I hoped that no one was "too grumpy" after the first battle.

"Harold called me when I was walking back to Union Station [after church], and told me the business meeting had been postponed until 2:00." The new problem was that no committee was to begin meeting more than two hours after the start of a day's session without authorization.[4] If someone raised that objection, the meeting would end. "If Feinstein would vote for me today, it would be difficult for her to maintain that decision through the August recess. Harold agreed that today needed to be the day." Now added to my worries was that the vote would be postponed.

"I went back to DOJ. I tried to take a nap [in the office loaned to me in the Civil Division area] at about 2:00. Peter came in to say that the meeting was on, but it was another issue. I told him that I did not want to hear the speeches, or at least only half of them. So I stayed in the office without a television." I eventually got up and just started responding to e-mails without yet going to watch.

I also made some handwritten notes about my thoughts. "Waiting for Committee, 3:10. Prayer, contemplation. Useful visit to church at noon. 'Do not judge another person's *soul*.' God judges that, though we can find right and wrong in their actions. I felt a special eagerness when I took communion at church today, a real sense and a real need for the body and blood of Christ."

"3:35. How long are speeches? Have they even gotten to me yet? Might they even not vote? Probably will, since Senator Leahy says he was tired of being criticized. At least the 'two-hour' rule must have been waived."

"3:50 p.m. Surely I am on their minds by now. Surely. Will it be much longer? Trust in the Lord with all my heart, and expect a miracle. I do. But I worry about whether God had the miracle *I* have in mind. Thy will be done."

"4:00. It would seem a good time. It has been two hours since the start. I am afraid to get too hopeful, and afraid not to be completely hope-filled. Believe, trust, expect."

What had been occurring was this.[5] When the committee convened for its business meeting at 2:13 p.m., Senator Leahy complained that Republicans had boycotted previous meetings. He welcomed by name some of the Republicans who had missed earlier meetings. The agenda was long, he said, because for the last two weeks no committee business could be accomplished owing to the absence of a quorum. Apparently the morning meeting had created some grumpiness.

Ninety minutes were consumed discussing and voting on crime-related bills. The nomination of the U.S. attorney for Puerto Rico was reported favorably to the floor. Two district court nominations were pending, those of Sharion Aycock of Mississippi and Richard Jones of Washington. Senator Leahy said that those nominations would be held over, as they were on the agenda for the first time. The last item, he then announced, was my nomination.

Senator Leahy explained that "we've held that off several times [scheduling a vote on me] at the request of the Republican leadership and Republican Senators from the State. When I heard that—because I was following what the Republicans asked me to do, I was also, as often happens, being criticized by the Republicans for doing what the Republicans asked. We put it back on." His complaint about being unfairly criticized for delaying my vote seemed justified to me.

Senators Hatch and Cornyn each put prepared statements into the record. Senator Specter then supported my nomination with a strong speech. He was followed by Democrats Ben Cardin, Leahy, and Chuck Schumer, who said my votes on the contested opinions disqualified me.

The next speaker was senator Dianne Feinstein. Her first words revealed she was not following the script. "I don't quite see this the same way and I want to point how and why I don't." She had reviewed my record, read the transcript of the committee hearing, and read the letters. She had "a full and very lengthy meeting with him in my office. What emerged was an appreciation on my part that Judge Southwick is a qualified, circumspect person." She believed I had made a mistake on my votes in the two cases, but there was no hatred in my heart.

In the past, Republicans had not treated some nominees fairly. Her "hope is that we can put these days behind us and that we can give people a fair hearing, and that we can move them on. I think what sometimes gets lost in our debates about judicial nominees is that they are not just a collection of prior writings or prior judicial opinions, they are, first and foremost, people." There was extraordinary decency in those words, rare decency.

While she was talking, Peter Keisler came to tell me she would vote for me. I waited a few moments, said a prayer of thanks, and then went to watch. Senator Feinstein spent some time remarking on my military service. She said that may not count to some people, but it did to her.

She informed the committee that we had spoken the day before. She read the letter I had just written. When she finished, she announced that she would vote to report my nomination to the floor. While she was reading the letter, I went back to the office I was using to send an e-mail to Philip, Mary, and Cathy.

> C-SPAN 3, which is available here, shows that my nomination is now being debated. Sen. Feinstein said in her remarks that she will . . . WILL . . . vote for me. She spoke for about 10 minutes, then started reading the letter that I sent last night to her, after spending 3–4 hours preparing it, getting comments, etc. I did not want to hear all that, so I went back to my loaner office to write you.
>
> I only needed one Democrat. It would be great to get one or two more. A month ago I wrote a friend—one of the Michigan nominees with whom I had my hearing last year, and who had his own long delays—that I was trusting in the Lord, and expecting a miracle.[6]

I had the miracle.

Among the speeches I missed were those ending the hearing, by Senators Durbin and Kennedy, with the vote following. A transcript of the hearing showed what happened. First, all the Democrats were polled in order of seniority, except for Senator Leahy, who as chairman was the last senator to vote. Five of these first nine Democratic votes were by proxy. Only four, including Feinstein, were cast in person. I had received only one vote after the first nine Democrats finished, but it would be all from them I needed this day. Then the nine Republicans were polled. All were present, and all voted "aye." Then Senator Leahy voted "no." It was 10–9 in favor.

Television coverage of the meeting showed that the room had been packed. After the vote, many who had come for my defeat lingered to talk to members of the committee. One of those was congressman Bennie Thompson, who went up to the bench to speak to Senator Leahy.

Even before the vote was concluded, I started to get phone calls. Governor Haley Barbour called. I was deeply honored he was following my struggle. I got an odd call from an associate White House counsel. I could not hear much of what was said in all the commotion in the room, but my sense was that this was a call to say "all is forgotten" from our disagreements from the night before. I was told "how much they were supporting me."

There were calls from friends and family. Unforgivably, I had forgotten to call Sharon in the release of emotions when I learned of Senator

Feinstein's vote. But she forgave. She was not able to access the broad-cast from our home in Jackson and did not know what had occurred. Our friend Pete Perry called to express congratulations. "For what?" was her response. Sorry (again).

Later news reports said that Senator Feinstein, though encouraged by friends on the Republican side such as Trent Lott and Arlen Specter to support me, had not told anyone of her vote before she cast it.[7] I never asked her if that was accurate.

There was briefly a hope that the momentum of the surprising vote would carry on into Friday, which was the last day before the Senate recessed until after Labor Day. It did not happen. The next day, after spending the night at Andrews, I went back to DOJ.

"Friday, 3 August. Harold had lined up a call with Sen. Specter. When he answered, I said, 'Is this the incredible Arlen Specter?' He said, with a laugh, 'No, but it is Arlen Specter.' I told him how thankful I was for his energetic support. I am sure he was instrumental in getting Sen. Feinstein's vote. He said many people helped, but the key person was me and how I came across to people. Nice. He had been asked earlier in the day whether he thought there would be a filibuster, and he responded that he did not. He also said that if there was, it would all-out war."

"Harold set up a time for me to call Sen. McConnell. Called about 11:15. McConnell said there is reason to be optimistic, but should take nothing for granted. There are 10–15 Western and Southern Democrats who will be reachable. If it takes a cloture vote, I will probably win it."

One of the e-mails I responded to before catching my plane was from Judge Pickering. He wrote just to congratulate me. He is a most decent man. I responded: "Yesterday's was not the only hurdle, but I am told that it was the highest one. You have been at this position before yourself, and I too will face the prospect of a filibuster. Whether it will be attempted remains to be seen. Trent, Thad, and others are guardedly optimistic."[8]

My notes had this: "Harold arranged a call with Sen. Feinstein. She called as I was leaving DOJ at 1:30. I told her she was my new favorite senator, but please not to tell Thad or Trent. I expressed regret that helping me was causing her criticism. She said that senators were elected to make decisions like that."

I had to get back to Andrews to catch a C-17 for home. "Sen. Hatch called at 5:00 or so [while I was waiting for the plane]. Fifteen-minute call and a very friendly one. He thought the floor vote against me would be fairly large, but not to be discouraged. Most of the people do not dislike me. The tactics being used are terrible. I said this was just what I feared, this allegation of racism. Hatch said that it would not last as a label, that most would be forgotten once I started serving."

The next day's Jackson newspaper quoted the head of the Leadership Conference on Civil Rights, Wade Henderson, that reporting me was a "slap in the face of African Americans and people of good will everywhere." The Washington political newspapers gave prominent coverage to Senator Feinstein's dramatic vote. A filibuster was noted as a possibility, so the challenges ahead remained uncertain. *Roll Call* said the vote "marked a major turning point in Southwick's previously stalled appointment, one that many Senators believed was all but dead just days ago." The caption to a press release by the Committee for Justice, a group supporting me, was "Southwick Win Is a Huge Setback for Dems, but Fight Is Not Over."[9]

President Bush said he was pleased with the fact that I would "soon" get a vote from the full Senate. I hoped his sense of timing was good. The Senate majority leader, Harry Reid, issued a statement that he would schedule a debate and vote despite his opposition to my confirmation.[10] The worry that the Democratic leader would not even schedule a vote was removed even before I had a chance to realize I should be worried.

It had been so very, very close to the end of all my hopes. By the pre-vote calculations of most people, it should have been the end. I had wondrously survived to journey on.

18

A Lull: Would There Be a Storm?

An encouraging news story appeared in *Roll Call* on August 6. It had a terrific title, "Gang May Reunite for Deal on Southwick."[1] It started with this line: "As Republican Senators prepare for a possible September stand-off with Democrats over their choice for the 5th U.S. Circuit Court of Appeals, the remaining members of the bipartisan 'Gang of 14' say they may have to come together to help referee the fight." Senator Ben Nelson was identified as a key Democrat wanting to avoid a return to the dark days of filibusters of judicial nominees. Senator Cochran, trying to belittle the idea, was quoted as saying that he did not believe an effort to filibuster me was likely.

My surprising survival of the Judiciary Committee experience briefly got national publicity. Columnist Robert Novak's *Human Events* newsletter identified my victory as one that caught both parties "off-guard." Novak said that Senator Leahy had expected a "party-line defeat" for me.[2] Likely only Senators Feinstein and Lott had known what was going to occur.

Another sign of my brief national notoriety was a column by George F. Will. He wrote about the not-yet-likely Democratic nominee for president, Senator Barack Obama.[3] Will found Obama's early opposition "disappointing. . . . His candidacy kindled hope that he might bring down the curtain on the long-running and intensely boring melodrama 'Forever Selma.' . . . It was hoped Obama would be impatient with the ritualized choreography of synthetic indignation that degrades racial discourse. He is, however, unoriginal and unjust regarding the nomination of Leslie Southwick to the 5th U.S. Circuit Court of Appeals." Will wrote that critics say my "defect is 'insensitivity,' an accusation invariably made when specific grievances are few and flimsy."

Removing one worry was the kind reception I received at the law school. On August 14, I received a proposal from Dean Rosenblatt, endorsed by the faculty. I would remain a visiting professor. "Judge South-wick is twixt and tween right now until his confirmation," the dean wrote. "In my opinion it would be an appropriate courtesy to extend his term as a visiting professor through the fall semester and take him through the confirmation process."

On Saturday, August 18, Stuart Schiffer, the career deputy assistant attorney general whom I met when working at the Justice Department, sent a link to the morning's *Washington Post*. On the home page was a color photograph of me and the caption "Give this man a federal judge-ship." That sounded as if I were desperate, which I was, but the *Post*'s choice of words was amusing

The highlights of the editorial included its title, "Qualified to Serve."[4] It discussed my ABA rating, my years on the state court, and then the two cases. It basically found my positions to be acceptable if not quite what the writers might themselves have done. Then it got to the heart of the matter. "Adding to the discomfort of many civil rights advocates is the fact that President Bush has once again nominated a white man to a court lacking in significant minority representation: Only 1 of 19 sitting judges on the 5th Circuit is African American, even though the three states forming that federal appeals court—Texas, Louisiana and Mississippi— have between 30 percent and 40 percent non-white residents, according to the 2000 Census."

The *Post* accepted that race was a factor. "For that reason, and because of his relatively pinched approach to judging, Judge Southwick wouldn't have been our first choice for this vacancy. Nor do we like the results in the custody and racial slur cases. But we cannot find fault with Judge South-wick's narrow but ultimately legitimate interpretation of the law in those cases, and we do not find in his record the anti-gay, anti-worker caricature his opponents have drawn."

It was not nearly as enthusiastic as I could have written ("pinched?"), but it was more than I expected. It was good news, which seemed to be mounting. Perhaps as compensation for an endorsement of my confir-mation, three days later the *Post* made space for my first accuser, Nan Aron of the Alliance for Justice. The title of her column said it all: "An Unjust Judge."[5]

I continued to get national publicity, a sign of a slow news months with Congress in recess. Short pieces appeared in three issues of *National*

Review magazine, criticizing the Democrats and finding no merit to the charges. The conservative *Washington Times* joined the liberal *Washington Post* in endorsing my confirmation. The *Times* said that I was being "Borked." The editorial discussed the two cases, finding that they were not even "objectionable, much less 'highly disturbing.' Opposition to Judge Southwick is more about politics than qualifications. Anyone willing to take a fair look at Judge Southwick's record—like Sen. Dianne Feinstein, whose vote moved the Southwick nomination out of the Judiciary Committee, and the editorial board of *The Washington Post*—says he deserves a fair shake in the Senate."[6]

The Congress was in recess for all but the first few days of August. As Labor Day passed, Ana Radelat, the Jackson newspaper's Washington reporter, had a new story. A filibuster was my remaining risk, she wrote. "But opposition to Southwick has not reached the level it had for previous nominees for that seat whom the Democrats were able to block from Senate confirmation—Mississippi Judge Charles Pickering and Jackson lawyer Mike Wallace."[7]

Republicans were staying focused on my plight. In the Republican leader's opening-day speech on September 4, he listed my nomination as one of the key issues to resolve: "He deserves a vote and he deserves it soon." The next day, Republican senators Arlen Specter and Orrin Hatch joined various organizations and individuals for a press conference about my nomination. On an easel was a large blowup of a photograph of me in my army uniform. Gregg Nunziata from Senator Specter's staff had earlier asked me for the digital image.[8]

A Web site that was following my ordeal posted a summary.

Senators Specter and Hatch held a press conference in support of Leslie Southwick's nomination. They were joined by the principals of various organizations involved in the judges fight. In addition to the senators, a few principals spoke, as did Jim Warner, an attorney and Vietnam veteran with 2 Purple Hearts.

"I think that with sufficient enthusiasm, and candidly, with sufficient pressure, we will get Judge Southwick confirmed."—Sen. Arlen Specter.

"We hear a lot talk these days about how the justice system is supposedly being politicized. If those Senators who protest about this most loudly are sincere, they should put their votes where their mouths are and support Judge Southwick's nomination. What could be more politicizing than the demand that a judge must rule for certain parties or promote certain political interests in their decisions? That's what Judge Southwick's opponents are demanding."—Sen. Orrin Hatch.

The next day I was told of some other developments. "September 6, 2007. Harold Kim called at 1830, Thursday. Said that Lindsey Graham had gotten Sen. Dorgan (ND) to agree to meet with me, and I am also meeting with Sen's Lieberman and Lincoln. Harold also had learned that Reid had committed to a vote before the recess the second week of October."

I needed to fly to Washington to meet with the senators who were agreeing to see me. Worrying that I could not make a reservation at Andrews, I asked Harold if he could. It occurred to me, and perhaps I should not have sought it, that a call from the White House might help. Harold said he would take care of it. He also invited me to a ceremony on the South Lawn of the White House on Tuesday morning, September 11, to observe a moment of silence with President and Mrs. Bush.

A few days before I went, I got a call from Robert O'Brien, a California lawyer with whom I had attended the army basic course in 1992. "He had gone to a dinner at which Sen. Feinstein spoke. He went up to thank her. He said that he knew me from Army basic course, that I was a scholar, a gentleman, and a 'sweet man.' She beamed, and said that there was someone she wanted him to repeat those statements to. She took him to an editor of the *Los Angeles Times*. The paper had been quite harsh toward her due to the vote for me."

I took a military flight on Monday afternoon, and stayed at Andrews.

On Tuesday, September 11, I attended the ceremony on the White House lawn commemorating 9/11. "Saw Pres., VP, and wives come out of White House. Military band playing on balcony on first floor. Chimes sounded that started the moment/minute of reverence."

Then Harold and I went to Sen. Lieberman's office for a 10:00 meeting. "I had planned a spiel, but Sen. Lieberman had questions. We discussed both the racial slur and child custody case. It seemed to go well. At the end, I mentioned the book that I wrote" on defeated presidential and vice presidential candidates, published in 1998. I gave him a pamphlet that updated the book with his and other biographies for the 2000 election. "He said the idea [of the book] was a good one, and hoped that I thought well of his campaign." I had and was ready to think even more of him.

Wednesday, September 12. At noon, I went with Harold to Sen. Blanche Lincoln's office. "She had two aides with her. I learned she had first cousins John Allin and Kelly Butler in Jackson. [I knew John, and also knew Kelly's husband, Thorne. I met with the Butlers when I returned, and they agreed to help me with cousin Blanche.] I discussed both cases. I said I had not been around people who used the 'N' word. She had, once being called a 'N-lover' at a campaign stop. I said that the child custody case confused me a bit, as at times it seems that the principal argument is that the phrase 'homosexual lifestyle' was gratuitously insulting. I laughed at some stage, and said that some of what is said about me is so different from how I am known in Mississippi that laughter seems about all that I can do." I wonder, though. Knowledge of how someone is perceived by others can be the most difficult truth to learn.

"Went with Harold to see Sen. Byron Dorgan at 3:15. The two cases did not bother him, but the allegation that I had sided too often with business was something he wanted me to discuss." We discussed that for a few minutes, and I left with some optimism about him.

That was the end of my meetings this trip. They had left me encouraged.

I was thrilled to learn on September 17 that President Bush had named Peter Keisler to serve as acting attorney general. The president nominated retired U.S. district judge Michael B. Mukasey to be the new attorney general, but his confirmation would proceed slowly.

On September 21, Cochran's counsel Brad Davis called. "He said that Sen. McConnell had called a meeting of GOP senators to [prepare] for a vote [on me] in the last two weeks before the recess. He said Trent, Thad, Specter, and Graham were the most energetic in my behalf and others might get assignments for lobbying. Thad wanted me to know this was being planned, and to make sure that I thought it was time. I was ready if those helping me thought it was time."

As my cause was moving, a poignant article appeared in the Jackson newspaper about Judge Pickering.[9] Sid Salter, a friend of us both, had interviewed him. "Seeing former state Court of Appeals Judge Leslie Southwick getting close to a Senate confirmation vote . . . , retired federal judge Charles W. Pickering must feel like Moses on the mountainside overlooking the land of Canaan."

"September 26. Brad Davis called at 3:15, Wednesday. He said that Thad has asked him to pass on certain information. On Tuesday at 5:30, Trent, Thad, McConnell, several Jud. Comm Republicans, and perhaps others met to plan how to get me through the rest of the way. All agreed that there was no reason to wait any longer. Decisions were made as to which Republicans would contact which Democrats. McConnell would go to Reid to get the vote scheduled before the recess on Friday or Saturday, 5–6 October. I should plan to go up on Monday."

"September 27. Hugh Gamble called at 1300 Thursday. He said that Sen. Carper (Del) had agreed with Trent to meet me, and that based on what Trent was saying was receptive to voting for me. Trent wanted to clear the hurdle by 'more than just a couple,' so the meeting was important. I said my trip up is planned for late Monday."

"Harold called at 1330. He said six senators had agreed to meet: Bingaman, Conrad, Carper, Inouye, Webb, and Bill Nelson. I should plan on being there Monday by noon, and not Monday night. No firm count on filibuster will be available because senators are not going to be willing to commit. Also said no date has been set, that McConnell will go to Reid close to the date for a vote and tell him. That way, there is less time for the Democrats to prepare."

Because of the need to be there on Monday, I was flying on Sunday, September 30. Peter Keisler volunteered to have me stay at his house on Sunday night. I flew to Baltimore-Washington airport, then took the commuter train down to Union Station. He met me there to take me to his house. He was not alone. As acting attorney general, he had as significant a security detail as would any Cabinet officer. It was something of, as we say in the South, a hoot to be escorted by sunglasses-wearing security agents to two black SUVs. Fortunately Peter vouched for me. At the house were his wife Sue and their children Sydelle, Alex, and Philip. "They had made chocolate chip cookies, though quite a few were gone already. We all had some."

"Monday, 1 October. Slept on large window bench." The next day, I was available for meetings, but no senators set up any. "Went to Andrews Air Force Base at 5:00. Was surprised to be given Distinguished Visiting Officer Quarters for some reason. The Roosevelt suite in Building 1350. The White House arranged. Dianna Dunne called Monday to say she had arranged reservation, so perhaps that is the reason. Pretty sweet."

"Tuesday, 2 October. First meeting at 9:30 with Senator Bob Casey (Penn.). Two aides. Seemed to go well. He knew about some of the disputes, and asked about cases. I explained, giving him the usual summary. He asked how judges were selected, and I mentioned my elections. Started to say something about my 1996 race, and about namesake son of governor beating me out. Caught myself in time. [Casey is son of prominent political father.] I just said that in a judge's race, name identity is everything. He made some joke about being the son of a famous politician does not hurt. He seemed to accept my explanations about the cases and about me."

"Harold drove back to his office at White House, and I went with him. Had lunch in Mess with Associate White House Counsels Kate Todd and Cheryl Stanton. I said that the last time I had lunched there with White House Counsel office personnel was when I was under consideration for the Fifth Circuit in 1992, with Boyden Gray." That earlier lunch had not gone well.

At 3:00 I had a meeting with senator John Tester of Montana. "I talked about myself, my background. Took a while to get to controversy. He was about to dismiss me, saying how much he appreciated my taking the time to come see him. So I said that perhaps he would find it useful to have me review some of the controversies. I went over the two cases, probably saying that there was no controversy at all until the Monday before my hearing." I felt good about my reception.

"Kent Conrad (ND). Met at 4:00 in Senate Hart office. He needed to go to a vote, so we walked and rode train, and split outside Senate chamber. Aides took [Harold and me] to his hideaway office. He joined us fairly soon. Several aides there, perhaps three, one just passed Missouri Bar. Conrad familiar with issues, and specifically asked about the two cases. After I answered, he then said there was another question regarding whether I favored defendants too much. I responded with saying the issue was whether I was an 'ideologue.' He smiled, and said he would not have used that word. We talked for perhaps thirty minutes. He then said he was satisfied that I was a good choice, and he would support me. I was almost choked up, and as I rose to shake his hand, I could not for a moment speak clearly."

"This was by far—well, maybe Ben Nelson—the most satisfying of my meetings. He was not part of the Gang of 14, so if that group held, we would be at 58 without anyone else. And there are plenty of other possibilities."

One of the political newspapers, *Roll Call*, had a front-page story about my hunt for votes.[10] It reported that "a key group of GOP Senators and at least one Democrat will huddle today to talk strategy and gauge support for the 5th U.S. Circuit Court of Appeals hopeful. At the same time, Southwick himself has begun holding a series of private meetings with a handful of Democratic Senators whom the White House has targeted as possible swing votes."

The article also identified the "significant Democratic opposition working" against me, including majority leader Harry Reid, majority whip

Dick Durbin, Pat Leahy, and Charles Schumer. Senators Cochran and Lott were identified as my "most forceful advocates." Republican senators were said ready to discuss me at their policy lunch that day.

"Wednesday, 3 October. At 10:15 on way to Russell [Senate Office Building], saw Sen. Ben Nelson walking out as I was walking in. I went up to him and said it did not seem proper to come to Washington without saying 'hello.' He said that there were meetings about working some things out, on other matters he injected, that would allow me a vote."

I prepared handwritten notes to each senator after a meeting. Often I wrote them the night after my meetings and delivered them the next morning. For someone with whom I had connected, I would be rather personal. The black-and-white photo on most of the cards was from 1900. It showed a man waiting in front of the old Capitol in Jackson for the streetcar to stop. I referred to the picture in my note to Senator Conrad, who was the rare senator to announce his support during the meeting. "I hardly know what to say, though certainly a heart-felt 'thank you' is an inadequate beginning. This at times has been a hard journey. The picture on the note suggests a slightly different image—the journey has not even started as I am continually waiting for the train that will never come. I definitely need some help to get moving and am so grateful that you have agreed to give me an assist." I took it to his office before my next meetings.

By the time I arrived at the vice presidential office in the Dirksen building, Harold had some news for me. "He said that Sen. Warner was in hospital, and there was concern about going forward with me absent that sure vote. He also mentioned Sen. Domenici being back in NM explaining his decision not to run for reelection. Jennifer Elrod [another Fifth Circuit nominee, from Houston] had been told a week ago that she might get the vote this week instead of me. Harold thought I had a safe margin, but others were less optimistic. It would look bad for leadership for me to lose by one vote with Warner absent." A decision had not yet been made.

My next meeting was with Max Baucus, who met us at his hideaway office in the Capitol. "Baucus came after about 10 minutes. Three aides in all. He said that Specter had asked him to see me, and he thought, 'Why not?' Not a very encouraging start. He asked the usual questions." He also asked my view of pending legislation concerning intercepting of suspected terrorist phone calls, a major legislative controversy at the time. I said it was impossible to give a legal opinion without a close study of a statute, and I had not been following this issue. He apparently found that unacceptable, and we had an awkward closing to my visit. His questions were more apt for attorney general nominee Mukasey. Maybe he had his meetings confused.

"Jeff Bingaman. Meeting at 1100. Went to his Hart office, and was taken back to his personal office. He was somewhat familiar with the controversy, and the discussion seemed to go all right. No pledge of support, and he is a chairman so part of the leadership."

"My final meeting was not until 3:00. I went to see Paul Fassbender, a friend of someone I know at Mississippi College Law School. He got me in to see his boss, Republican Sen. Bob Corker of Tennessee. The senator [said he was] part of a group trying to form a 'Gang of 20,' then caught himself as if he was not supposed to say that. I mentioned my conversation with Sen. Nelson, and said that seemed related. Paul later said the senator should not have used that term."

"This gave me a great deal of encouragement, that a written agreement may give me release from the risk of a filibuster. Corker's referred to a new 'Gang.'" A "gang" seemed to be just what I needed. Senator Corker was so supportive and open that he seemed to be an old friend. Most of my conversations with senators were guarded, trying my best to say only the right thing. I was very relaxed with Corker. "My note to him later said that seeing him was an oasis in a desert."

I went back to Andrews Air Force Base for the night. Harold called at 9:00 p.m. to say that the decision had been made to wait on me. That night I e-mailed Sharon, Philip, and Cathy. "The Senate will not be voting on my nomination this week. Last night I was called, that because of the hospitalization of GOP Senator Warner of Virg., that it was considered too risky to go forward with my nomination. A woman from Houston, who is the only other circuit nominee ready for a vote, will be confirmed today instead. The Senate is in recess all next week. There are some things occurring, meetings and efforts at agreement on a range of issues by a bipartisan group of senators, that may help me. I feel pretty sure that I will be confirmed, but how and when remain ambiguous."[11]

In the *Congressional Record* for the day, October 4, I later read of Senator Cochran's moving the confirmation of Sharion Aycock of Tupelo, Mississippi, to be a U.S. district judge. She would become the first female federal judge in the state's history.[12] Senator John Cornyn of Texas then spoke in support of the confirmation of Jennifer Elrod, who had been moved into the spot on the agenda that had initially been for me.

The first vote was announced this way: "The question is, Will the Senate advise and consent to the nomination of Jennifer Walker Elrod of

Texas, to be United States Circuit Judge?" The Senate did, unanimously. I was happy for Jennifer, disappointed that it was not my name in the question, but confident that those who decided to have me wait were correct that delay improved my chance to succeed.

The day's *Roll Call* reported on Senator Lott's meeting with Republicans and with Senator Ben Nelson.[13] It discussed a new "Gang," which Senator Corker had been reluctant to discuss with me in explicit terms. "Senators said they vetted ways to work through upcoming fights," including on my confirmation. It mentioned the effort to get sixty votes for cloture, but that it was believed we were "still shy of meeting that mark against powerful Democratic opposition."

"Went to Trent's office. He went through list of senators, and said he had 57 or 58 he felt pretty good about. Trent asked me who I had seen. I named some, but could not remember the rest. He got a envelope out of his pocket and went through names. I did not remember all his targets, but I later tried to tell Harold as many of the names as I could."

Trent, with a smile, said he was "wasting" a lot of chits on me. I suggested "investing" was a better word. He later repeated "wasting."

"Jim Webb, to meet at 4:15. Met Harold in Dirksen office. Met first with a member of his staff, Nelson Jones, a Houston native, black man, high schools still segregated when he graduated in 1968. Webb graduated from Naval Academy in 1968, but was still there some when Nelson started that summer. After the Vietnam War ended, Nelson did not continue in naval career. Started at Georgetown law school with Webb in 1972. Been pals ever since."

"Webb came in after ten minutes. I mentioned Navy, but Webb corrected that he had been a Marine. I asked if I had already blown it and if I might as well leave. Webb smiled. We talked about his son's service; I mentioned having seen [in his waiting room] the boots that were his son's and that Webb had worn during the campaign."

"Nothing seemed bothersome. He had to leave for a roll call. An aide came in and said others were waiting to talk with him. Still, we continued for a while longer. When he left, he asked that I continue with Nelson. Nelson asked why the NAACP and others were so adamant, because the cases did not seem to justify. I said that I had been perceived as a moderate, as the consensus choice after two failed prior nominations. Harold had earlier told me that I should say 'consensus,' not 'compromise.' I mentioned the desire for a black nominee, that there was a news story calling my nomination an 'outrage' because it was time for a black" judge.

"We talked for a long time. As we left, he mentioned something about my being a judge in the future. I said that I really needed his senator's help in getting me there."

It was back to Andrews for the night, then home on a C-17 the next day.

19

The Final Two Trips

The Senate was in recess for a week. On Sunday, October 7, the Jackson newspaper quoted Thad as saying that senator Harry Reid, who as majority leader had the authority to schedule votes, had agreed to delay my vote, saying, "I'll call him up when you want me to call him up." That concession was hugely important and controversial. Months later, I read a newspaper article that said that "liberal Democrats have felt they were rolled before by Reid, who publicly opposed the nominations of both conservative Judge Leslie Southwick and Attorney General Michael Mukasey while working behind the scenes to set up floor votes for them."[1] I expect that Senator Reid of relatively conservative Nevada did have a difficult time with the largely liberal caucus that he headed, given the issues my controversy presented. For all the negative things he said about me, I am indebted to him.

"October 12. Harold Kim called at 11:15. He said that various outside groups were [involved in a phone call to let them know] they should push for an 'up or down vote' sometime next week. All have agreed, including Sen. McConnell, that next week is the time. Still need to get the Mississippi senators' reaction."

Of course, more was occurring than my small personal journey. I was touched by something Rees Barksdale sent me. Rees had served a tour in Vietnam, where his courage earned him a Silver Star. On October 13, he forwarded me a story about General Peter Pace, the marine who had just retired as chairman of the joint chiefs of staff. The message was by an earlier writer in the e-mail chain:

> I wanted to share with you what we saw in Washington DC last week. At the Vietnam Wall we saw something unbelievable. We noticed three small index

cards at the base of the Wall. I knelt down for a closer look and noticed that a 4-star general's rank was pinned to each card. The cards were personally addressed and said something like:

These are yours—not mine!
With Love and Respect,
Your Platoon Leader, Pete Pace

The Chairman of the Joint Chiefs had laid down his rank for his boys who died in Nam just the day before! I later found out that 1 Oct was also the same day he stepped down as chairman.

General Pace honored the members of his platoon who went to Vietnam and then never grew old. Compared to the dangers men like this faced, my service was tame. That is one of the reasons I am moved by sentiments shared among those who risked so much for their country.

I received word that a meeting had been scheduled with Senator Carper. It would likely be an important one. I went up a day early to be available for any other meetings.

"Wednesday, October 17. In afternoon, went to Russell Senate Office Building." A tunnel leads from the Russell basement to that of the Dirksen building. "In the tunnel, saw Trent coming toward me with an aide. He said, 'Who is that?' He almost immediately pulled a list from pocket. He had written names on something the size of an envelope; maybe it was one. I know Salazar's name was circled, and perhaps Lieberman's. He counted nine as 'committed.' My best recollection is they were Lincoln, Landrieu, Byrd, Lieberman, Conrad, Ben Nelson, Feinstein, Pryor, and Salazar. He also said that Bill Nelson and Dorgan were likely. That constitutes the eleven that I need. I mentioned that I was seeing Carper. He thought having some insurance votes would be really helpful. Also on his list, perhaps meaning he saw them as possibilities, were Casey and Inouye. There may have been one or two more. Apparently not on his list were Webb, maybe not Tim Johnson. But I did not remember all the names, and he did not give me a copy."

Trent also told me there would be "no vote this week—Sen. Warner out again with health problems, and McCain is iffy. But he feels pretty good about having the votes. Nothing definite. 'Completely confidentially,' he would like to have a vote early next week, at least Tuesday. Me too."

"Saw Harold by 4:30. I had printed out Carper's bio by then. We talked about what Trent had said. Went down to Carper's office in Hart. Carper came in from outside hallway with an aide. He greeted Harold first, as if he knew him. Then Carper and I introduced ourselves. We went into his personal office. Chris Pentergast, from Missouri, was the lawyer-aide in the meeting."

"I discussed the two cases, and Chris may have asked some questions about them. The senator was amusing, and took things with less than total seriousness. The discussion seemed to go well, with no apparent problems. Carper said he wanted to talk to some people in Miss. before deciding. He may have mentioned cong. Bennie Thompson by name, then former congressman Mike Espy, and I think he mentioned [congressman] Gene Taylor. Harold said we would get good phone numbers for them. I considered but decided not to mention that Thompson and the black groups in Miss. were insistent on having a black nominee, and that was what started this problem. He may vote for me, or not, but he could not have been friendlier and less confrontational."

Once back at Andrews, I was able to talk to Mississippi congressman Roger Wicker, whom I had known for years. I told him Carper wanted to talk to Gene Taylor, and asked if Wicker could help me with Taylor. Roger said he would do whatever he could.

"Met with Thad at 10:00 a.m. I went over list of senators whom it might be good for him to contact. I discussed the Carper meeting, and that it might be good if he talked to Gene Taylor." Thanks to his work, Daniel Akaka was willing to see me. This was a hopeful development, because Senator Akaka was not someone who was counted on to support me.

"Friday. Met Harold at Dirksen office at 9:50. Went to Hart. The senator's aide Tulsi Gabbard met us. She talked about being in the Hawaii National Guard for five years, and had just transferred to D.C. Guard. The senator started by saying that he had heard so much about me, that I am talked about a lot in the Senate. Some who talk to him rate me at a 10, and some at a very low number. Seeing me would help him make up his mind. He mentioned that among the very positive points was my military service, and he thanked me. He also knew about the ABA rating. I would allude to that several times as the best objective measure available, before the controversies started."

"I had mentioned being 'fair' at some point. He asked me what I meant by that. As I have gotten older, it has become clear to me that perspective is incredibly important in understanding the reality around us. He talked at some length about the diversity in Hawaii, and the difficulty of the different cultures understanding each other. He gave the example of a primitive person who was accused of stealing, but from his society there were no property rights—all was shared. I talked about fairness at some length, then apologized for giving such a long answer to such a simple question. Harold threw in that it showed I had given it much thought." My answer may not have shown any such thing, but Harold was a huge help all along the way.

Back at the Justice Department, I wrote my family about the trip and told them a vote was likely the next week. Philip responded. "Thank you for sharing, scary and confusing though it may be. In past meetings of our men's group, we have prayed for your protection during this process. This latest meeting, I prayed to set my bitterness aside. I am not pleased about the length of time and the number of people involved in deciding whether to schedule a vote on whether to make a decision."[2] His words, and those of other family, were always so helpful.

On Friday, *The Hill* reported on what was ahead. "The vote will likely be close. Republicans say they appear to have a majority support in the Senate for the nomination, but are not sure if they have the 60 votes that appear to be needed for his confirmation."[3]

"Caught the plane home from Baltimore-Washington home. [The name of former Democratic congressman Mike Espy was among those given to Senator Carper. Espy was on the plane.] He got in after I did, sat in front of me. After about an hour, I went up to sit by him. He did not seem eager, but he was friendly. He talked about Congressman Thompson, and Espy clearly supported the effort to block me. He thought Henry Wingate should get the nomination and did not understand why he had not. Still, Mike said if Carper called him he would be positive, or nice, or something to indicate that he would not disparage me personally." At least in speaking to me, he indicated his opposition was due simply to his belief that a black judge was needed.

Once home, I wrote in my notes: "God is always up to something. Please God, show me your hand here at the end."

I needed to be available in Washington for any meeting a senator might want on short notice. After spending the weekend at home, I left on an early Monday morning flight, with a layover in Charlotte. While there, I went to the USO and sent some e-mails.

"The fellow in the seat next to me on the plane had the paper, and I saw the headline the same time that he did."[4] I had left the house that morning before the newspaper came, so I had not seen it until my fellow passenger started reading his paper. It was something of a shock to see myself from the adjacent seat as the lead story. "Judicial Nominee Vote Near."[5]

Once in Washington, I called Hugh Gamble on Lott's staff. "He said Trent's focus is to be sure everyone is present at time of vote. He had talked to Harold briefly today, and list of contacts went to Carper. Went out to Andrews to check in to lodging, since there were no meetings."

That night, Congressman Thompson and three other members of the Congressional Black Caucus spoke for an hour in the House, sharply criticizing my nomination. Thompson began by noting that despite the state's large African American population, no black judge was on the circuit from there. He praised the past role of the federal courts in furthering civil rights but found that I was the kind of person who found it to be "all right" to use the worst of all racial slurs. He called my nomination "an affront to people of color, and an affront to people of good will."[6]

On Tuesday, October 23, the lead story in *Politico* was titled "A Troubled Southern Courtship."[7] The first sentence struck home. "Few seats in the federal judiciary carry this kind of baggage." It mentioned a letter sent to Senator Leahy in May by Carlton Reeves, the president of the Mississippi black lawyer association, the Magnolia Bar. To balance the long quotations I earlier made from two favorable letters, I also extract the strongest language in what was perhaps the most frequently mentioned condemnation of me. The letter was dated May 30, 2007.

> Leslie Southwick's nomination continues a stark pattern of racial discrimination and racial exclusion in appointments by President Bush to the Fifth Circuit and to the federal judiciary from Mississippi. If the Senate Judiciary Committee approves this nomination, it will perpetuate this pattern of exclusion and will, in our view, bear equal responsibility for it. Moreover, Judge Southwick's record as a state court of appeals judge in Mississippi suggests that he is not the right person for the Fifth Circuit Court of Appeals at this time in our history, and that his presence there could lead to an improperly narrow interpretation of the constitution and the civil rights laws. There are many others from Mississippi who would make good federal judges, some of whom are African-American. We ask that you not approve this nomination, but instead allow President Bush to reconsider and perhaps nominate someone who will add to the Fifth Circuit's stature, diversity, and sensitivity to the need to enforce fully the civil rights laws.
>
> Several organizations have already expressed concern about the decisions of Judge Southwick and whether he will fairly and properly interpret the law with respect to the civil rights of all. We share those concerns.

Particularly troubling is the decision Judge Southwick joined in the case of *Richmond v. Mississippi Department of Human Services.* The Mississippi Court of Appeals does not review many cases involving racial issues in employment. This is not a situation where this decision is an outlier in what otherwise is a progressive record on issues of race in the workplace. . . . This decision . . . seemed to send a message that the Court of Appeals majority did not believe state officials should have the power to eliminate this sort of behavior from the workplace.

We question whether Judge Southwick will properly enforce the law when it comes to the rights of those who are unpopular and who are marginalized by the political process. The Fifth Circuit needs a moderating influence at this point in history, but it appears this appointment will have the opposite effect.

He urged the Senate to "keep the seat open."[8]

Fox News reported that the Senate was "headed for an extremely close vote Wednesday on the controversial nomination" of the guy from Mississippi.[9] The story reported that Senator McCain, campaigning in New Hampshire in advance of that state's Republican presidential primary, had canceled his campaign events and was returning to Washington for my vote.

Judge Pickering sent me an e-mail on this next-to-last day, encouraging me. I responded. "Your message means an enormous amount to me. Almost no one can fully appreciate what this ordeal is like, but you certainly can. Indeed, you endured worse than what I have had to experience. A while back you referred me to *Habakkuk.* I have reread the passages from time to time, and looked at them again after getting your e-mail. I am nervously optimistic, but I will strive to rejoice in the Lord even if there ultimately are no blossoms on the tree."[10]

Extremely encouraging was a message from Senator Lieberman's chief of staff. Certain people made me less guarded than was my norm. Senator Lieberman and his chief of staff, Clarine Nardi Riddle, were among those. They seemed so genuine.

"Judge, Hope all is well with you. Good luck today, you are going to do fine. We are working on our statement and can't find anywhere the total number of opinions you have been a part of in total. Do you have a good number?"[11]

First I answered her questions: (1) total opinions by the court, 6,750; (2) majority opinions I wrote, approximately 800. Then I responded from the heart. "Thanks for writing not just with the request, but with some positive thoughts. I am encouraged. If you do not mind my injecting this, and I may even have mentioned it before, my continuing contemplation for several months is a personalizing of Proverbs 3:5, trust in the Lord, and expect a miracle."[12]

Clarine wrote: "Judge. Thank you so much. Great verse from Proverbs. My brother, also a judge in Indiana, just e-mailed me and reminded me that 'God has a sense of humor' and he, too, is right. I truly believe this is going to be a good day for you. Clarine."[13]

I replied: "God's sense of humor is something else that I have thought much about because it is so relevant. One way I had heard that expressed is that on Judgment Day, we may be surprised at who among those we thought had mistreated us will be marching in ahead of us. We all have our misguided and sinful actions; we all need forgiveness. He will have forgiven many people that we will still be struggling to forgive."[14]

At 11:00 I walked to Dirksen. "Harold called at about 11:00, and I was in front of Archives. He said vote is tomorrow, and Tim Johnson (South Dakota) will vote for me. Also said [Bennie] Thompson met with some group of Democratic senators this morning and said I had refused to meet with him and NAACP. [Harold] asked if that had happened. I responded that I was unaware of any request, and I certainly never rebuffed him. He will check with DOJ as to whether there was a request."

No meeting request from the congressman or the NAACP was found. In fact, I had not met with any House member. Congressman Thompson may have seen my failing to ask to see him as the equivalent of a refusal. It would have been wise to emulate my mentor, Charles Clark. When he was being considered for the Fifth Circuit in 1969, he asked for a meeting with a potential adversary, NAACP chairman Aaron Henry. I asked Harold to send a request now to Thompson. It was too late, of course, but I thought it proper to ask. Thompson immediately rejected the offer.

"Went to church. Tried to focus, but mind often wandered. Still, I was eager for communion, to be infused by His spirit and for Him to guard my words and acts."

"Tuesday 2:30. Harold called to see if I had a courtesy meeting with any Mississippi congressmen, and I did not. Told him the first contacts I made were phone calls beginning Friday to reach Wicker, Chip Pickering, Taylor," because Senator Carper would call them. He was responding to concerns that I met with the others but not Thompson. Harold "said there would be four hours of debate, half tonight, half tomorrow. Feinstein will speak for me." When I learned Senator Feinstein was yet again going to speak for me, I became emotional. The controversy was getting increasingly harsh, but she was not wavering. I was deeply honored.

My good friend starting with the 1980 Bush campaign, Lanny Griffith, called me. He said former New York mayor and current presidential candidate Rudy Giuliani wanted to telephone me from New Hampshire. I was not sure this was in my best interest. A mutual friend, Chris Henick, was working for Giuliani. Later "Chris Henick called, wanted to have Mayor Giuliani call. I was worried about partisan issue at this stage. He then said if asked, mayor would just say he had called to wish me well. I responded with the Bennie Thompson story. I could see the reaction—I won't meet with Thompson, but I have time to talk to Giuliani. Chris pointed out that McCain canceled an event to be here. So Giuliani needs something to grab the story too. I said no. I did not like being that self-absorbed, because I liked Chris and Giuliani. Just not enough to risk this."

"5:00 p.m. As I left the vice president's office in the Senate office building where I had been making calls, I decided to go to Thad's office. Doris Wagley [Thad's assistant] in hall. She said 'congratulations.' She just felt this was going to happen. Saw Thad, told him that Senator Carper wanted to see me again at 9:30. Thought at least meant he was still a possibility."

I headed back on the Metro to Andrews. One last night before the answer.

"7:00 p.m. Hugh Gamble [on Trent's staff] called, said Senator Salazar wanted to see me at 7:30 a.m. He said Trent had been working on him for a while. (I had been counting on him, so this is discouraging that I need to see him now). Still, I certainly have a chance still."

Harold and I talked once I got to my room. We set up that I would got to the Department of Justice by 6:30 a.m., then meet Harold at 7:05 to go to Salazar.

I was amazed that the Andrews rooms did not have C-SPAN as a station. So I missed the Tuesday night debate. Three opponents and five supporters talked.[15]

Senator Leahy started the debate. His used the word he always joined with my name, calling me the "controversial" nominee. He contrasted his view of how he had treated my nomination and the way in which Republicans had treated President Clinton's. Senator Leahy went through the disputed opinions, quoted from and introduced letters in opposition, then closed with a lengthy discussion of the need for more black nominees to the federal courts.

"When viewed against his record on the bench, the importance of this seat on the Fifth Circuit, and the troubling lack of diversity on that court, I am not convinced that he is the right nominee for this vacancy at this time." Senator Leahy was not excessive in his description of how my confirmation would be a setback for justice. He said I was the wrong nominee "at this time." His friendship with Senator Cochran may have moderated his language.

Senator Specter went next. He described my professional career. He mentioned my service in Iraq, quoting from General Cross's letter. He addressed the criticism of only two cases out of the thousands on which I voted. Specter quoted from the letters sent by my former law clerks La'Verne Edney and Patrick Beasley, countering the charges about lack of concern for equal rights.

Two more Democrats spoke, Ben Cardin of Maryland and Barbara Boxer of California, urging my defeat. Then Senator Feinstein spoke. Her words this night, as did those ten weeks earlier when she explained her committee vote for me, brought tears when I heard them later. My emotions were fragile. Both times, my plight was desperate. Both times, she showed compassion.

She started by saying that there had "seldom been an appellate nominee to whom I have given more thought than I have given to Leslie Southwick." She explained her thoughts at more length than perhaps any other speaker that night. She had reviewed the opinions; she had met with me; she had received the August letter explaining the racial slur case. All of that had convinced her I was not the person portrayed by my opponents. She listed three factors that convinced her: "First, the qualifications and character of the judge himself. Second, the need to fill this long-time vacancy in the Fifth Circuit which the judicial branch has designated as a judicial emergency. And third, my very strong belief that when a future Democratic president sends up a judicial nominee who becomes controversial, the test should be whether the nominee is within the judicial mainstream and is qualified by education, experience, and temperament." The senator found that I passed all three tests.

Senator Lott was the next speaker. He praised Senator Feinstein and discussed how they had worked on various legislative projects in the past. Some were successful, some not, but they had tried to do what was right for the country. He commended her for taking "that first step that can lead to other steps, and we will stop this slide I have observed occurring more and more each year for 10 years. Now maybe this is the moment, maybe this will be the catalyst that will lead to other steps . . . so that we will treat these nominations and legislation in a proper way."

He quoted from a letter sent by former Mississippi governor William Winter. Lott described Winter as a friend but also said that he would be considered "one of your more moderate to liberal Democrats." Lott then read from the letter.

> I further know him to be a very intelligent, conscientious, ethical and hard-working member of the legal profession. I have a great deal of personal respect for him and based on my association with him, I believe he will reflect fairness and objectivity in his approach to all matters which may come before him as a judge.

Senator Lott closed with a lengthy discussion of the Senate, of the need to avoid filibusters and his successful efforts under President Clinton to move two controversial nominees near the end of his administration. "This isn't just about Judge Leslie Southwick. This is about the standard that is being set for the future."

Senator Cochran spoke briefly. He would speak more in the morning. His dismay was obvious. He saw my problem as being the burden of history that Mississippi had not overcome.

Senator Brownback of Kansas, who had been the only senator at my district court hearing a year and a lifetime ago, spoke last. He noted I had been unanimously approved by the committee in 2006 but now was undergoing such criticism. He put a chart on an easel that showed the diversity on the Fifth Circuit. I did not see the chart, but the *Congressional Record* has his oral summary. It was a comparison of the sex and race of President Bush's appointments to the Fifth Circuit and those of President Clinton. Brownback thought that Bush had cast a wide net, with three women and one Hispanic male having been confirmed. One more woman would be confirmed later. President Clinton had nominated only men.

A wonderful young man—our daughter Cathy's future husband, David Brown—wrote on Tuesday night to wish me luck. "In the event that you check your e-mail before tomorrow's vote, I wanted to wish you good luck! Cathy and I watched tonight's Senate debate, that is, if you can even call it a debate. Your supporters' comments I thought were highly impressive. Senator Specter's remarks had a rationalizing effect unmatched by any of your detractors, and Senator Feinstein's speech I thought was particularly moving. Our one critique is that we thought Senator Brownback's chart would have been more effective had he replaced his statistics with a picture of your daughter."[16]

It would not be until Sunday that I had the opportunity to reply. "You were very kind to write on the eve of the vote. This was quite an experience, and having the encouragement of family and those close to family was hugely important to me. If you see that young woman today whom we are both so fond of, please give her a hug for me. And one from you too."[17]

20

The Beginning of the Last Day

The next morning, back I went to Capitol Hill. For better or worse, the end was near.

At the beginning of the book, I described the morning up until the time the vote began. There had been two early morning meetings, the first with Colorado senator Ken Salazar at 7:30, the other with senator Tom Carper of Delaware at 9:30. Then I went to a secretarial area for the vice president in the Capitol, adjacent to a large ceremonial waiting room just off the Senate floor.

What I did not earlier describe were some events I learned about later. The Jackson newspaper had me as a front-page story. The headline was "Senate Debate on Southwick May End Today."[1] It described the debate schedule and the procedures for cloture.

> The Senate is made up of 49 Democrats, 49 Republicans and two independents who caucus with the Democrats. If all 49 Republicans vote for Southwick, as expected, 11 Democratic votes would be needed to end debate on the nomination and then hold an up-or-down confirmation vote.
>
> If the Senate votes to end debate, it's likely the senators would vote to confirm Southwick.

All true. Other news coverage, also not seen until later, was fairly hopeful from my perspective. *Roll Call* had a great headline, "Deal Struck on Southwick Vote." The "deal" allegedly included a "hands-off posture by Senator Majority Leader Harry Reid (D-Nev.) and promises from key Republicans to help smooth the way on outstanding appropriations bills appears to be the right recipe" for my confirmation. I never did learn if there were any truth to that. Senator Lott was cryptic when he said, "Good-faith efforts on one side beget good faith efforts on the other side." Another story discussed how "red-state Democrats" were the target of Republicans, with a picture of North Dakota senator Kent Conrad accompanying the article.[2]

I did not see any press releases that morning, but one came out shortly before the vote at 11:00. Clarine Nardi Riddle sent it to me, and I saw it later.

Wednesday—October 24, 2007, 10:55 a.m.
FOR IMMEDIATE RELEASE

Lieberman Statement on Southwick Confirmation Vote
Today I voted to confirm Judge Leslie Southwick to the U.S. Court of Appeals for the Fifth Circuit. Judge Southwick served honorably on the Mississippi Court of Appeals for nearly 12 years, the American Bar Association has twice rated him "well qualified" to serve on the federal bench and the Senate Judiciary Committee has twice voted out his nomination favorably, the first time by a unanimous vote just last year.

Opponents of Judge Southwick's nomination point to two decisions out of the more than 6,500 opinions that he opined on over the course of his tenure on the bench to assert that Judge Southwick said it was acceptable to use a racial epitaph in the workplace and that gay and lesbian Americans are not fit to be parents. Had Judge Southwick said either, I would conclude that he was not fit for the federal bench. But I have read those two opinions, neither of which Judge Southwick wrote himself, and concluded that that is not what they stand for. In each case, Judge Southwick did his job as an appellate judge. He reviewed the application of the law to the facts under the relevant standard of judicial review to determine whether the lower court and agencies had erred.

As a Senator, I take my advice and consent duties very seriously and will not vote to confirm nominees who are not qualified or who demonstrate a judicial philosophy hostile to the rights afforded by the Constitution. Judge Southwick is qualified to be a judge on the Fifth Circuit and has not exhibited a judicial philosophy that would lead him to undermine those rights.

Press releases supporting me were issued by former governor Mitt Romney and former mayor Rudy Giuliani. Senator John McCain gave a laudatory speech on the floor. Former senator Fred Thompson had posted a blog two days earlier, also calling on the Senate to confirm me.[3]

My great friend Andy Taggart sent an e-mail as the voting started.[4] His message was uplifting, even if brief: "Go! Go! Go! Hebrews 12:1." I looked up the verse: "Therefore, since we are surrounded by such a great cloud of witnesses, let us throw off everything that hinders and the sin that so easily entangles, and let us run with perseverance the race marked out for us." Amen.

All along, I had very little control over my fate. Now, this morning, after my meetings with Senators Salazar and Carper, I had none at all. I was a spectator. On the Senate floor, Arlen Specter again spoke. He responded to the diversity issue. "It is the American way to consider Judge Southwick on the merits as to what he has done and as to what he stands for."[5]

Then Democratic senator Robert Menendez spoke. He said I was unfair to racial minorities and to all who needed someone to speak for them. His speech was angry and dismissive. I heard some of it when I was writing the letter to Senator Salazar in the Judiciary Committee staff office.

Senator John Cornyn, a former Texas Supreme Court justice, had warm words in my support. He mentioned the favorable reviews of my record by Stuart Taylor for the *National Journal*, and by the *Washington Post* when it said in August to "give this man a judgeship" (which is one of the few amusing events along the way).

Senator Durbin went next. Then Senator Whitehouse, who had chaired my hearing, added to the collection of negative letters to be inserted into the *Congressional Record*. Senators Feingold of Wisconsin and Levin of Michigan offered more letters and urged my defeat. Additional senators speaking in my behalf were John Kyl of Arizona, John Warner of Virginia, and Mel Martinez of Florida. Too much good, and too much bad, was said to be able to summarize it all.

Senator McCain, fresh from the presidential campaign trail and immediately to return to it after the vote, also spoke. I was greatly moved by his comments about my military service. He said my "decision to join the army is a model of self-sacrifice." As a prisoner of war for so long, he knew about real sacrifice. My service was not even an imitation. McCain urged that both parties abandon the idea of using a filibuster to prevent votes on judicial nominees. "This is an important decision right now, which I think is larger than just the future of this good and decent man."

Senator Graham was colorful. He called various charges against me "ridiculous" and "garbage." I loved his style.

Senator Chuck Schumer of New York gave the most quoted of the speeches of my opponents. He began with the claim that senators needed to consider the "history behind the seat to which the candidate has been nominated; the ideological balance within the court to which this nominee aspires; the diversity of that court; the demographics of the population living in that court's jurisdiction; the legacy of discrimination, injustice, and legal controversy in that jurisdiction."

He reviewed the history for a while, including the failed nominations. He then turned to my record, discussed the cases, and said he could have no confidence that I was a moderate and wise judge. He blamed me for not meeting with the black lawyer association or the black congressman from Mississippi. I wish I had, though it would simply have been a meeting to say we had met. The president of the Magnolia Bar Association declared my nomination an "outrage" the day it was made. Though nothing I said could remove the basic objection, I could have shown a willingness to talk. Senator Carper had made that point in our morning meeting, as it would at least have avoided any charge now that I had refused to meet.

Senator Hatch again spoke at length. I had grown quite fond of this man, who seemed such a decent soul. He spoke about the cases, defended my decisions as proper interpretations of the law, then asked rhetorically: "Are judges supposed to be legally correct or politically correct?" He articulated what I had long seen, from my biased perspective, of course, as the real criticism.

Senators Lott and Cochran both spoke again. I earlier wrote about Senator Lott's Tuesday night remarks. I will give some attention to Senator Cochran's on this Wednesday morning. He first summarized the criticisms. Then he said: "It is so inconsistent—all of that—to those of us who know this nominee compared with the harsh, shrill pronouncements being made on this floor of the U.S. Senate by leaders of the opposition to this nomination." He urged senators to look at what was being said by people who actually knew me, as opposed to the comments from outside groups. Thad seemed disgusted. Watching his speech later, I was yet again saddened that I had been the cause, unwilling though I was, of the events that had discouraged him about the Senate.

Cochran mentioned having spoken on the floor two or three earlier times on my behalf, and having introduced supportive letters then. He had one new letter to include, one that was on his desk that morning. "At 9:01 a.m. it was received in my office. It is from the Secretary of State of Mississippi, Eric Clark." He read it into the record, slowly and with much emphasis.

Dear Senator Cochran and Senator Lott:

I sat at home last night and listened on C-SPAN to the debate on Judge Leslie Southwick, and I feel compelled to write you this letter.

I am the senior Democratic elected official in Mississippi. I have been elected to office eight times as a Democrat. I am retiring from politics in January, so I have no ax to grind by commenting on this debate. During my entire career in public service, I have aggressively promoted the inclusion of all Mississippians, and particularly African-Americans, at the decision-making table in Mississippi. I take a back seat to no one in promoting inclusion in our state.

It has been my pleasure to know Leslie Southwick for more than twenty years. If I had to name one person who is kind, fair, smart, thoughtful, and open-minded, it would be Leslie Southwick. For any Senators who have been told or who have concluded otherwise, that is wrong—as wrong as it can be.

We in Mississippi are quite accustomed to being the objects of negative stereotyping. Of course, it is much easier to believe a stereotype about someone than to make the effort to get to know that person. It is perfectly clear to me that this is what is happening to Judge Southwick.

It seems to me that what is being decided in this case is not whether Leslie Southwick would be a good and fair judge—we could not have a better or fairer one. What is being decided, I think, is whether the United States Senate considers judicial nominees based on truth and merit, or based on politics and partisanship.

Let me make my point as plainly as I can: Leslie Southwick is the polar opposite of an ignorant and bigoted judge—the polar opposite of that stereotype. I hope that the Senate passes the test of recognizing the truth and acting accordingly.

Sincerely,

Eric Clark, Secretary of State of Mississippi

I went to see Eric when I got home. Just as he had written to Thad, he had been watching the debate on Tuesday night, became incensed, and wrote the letter at home. I was enormously touched. Eric and I know each other, as people in a smaller state, both in public office, would know each other. We had never done anything together socially, but we were friendly acquaintances.

The final two speeches were by the party leaders. Senator McConnell emphasized the kind things said about me by various Mississippians.

He talked about Stuart Taylor's article and the ABA rating. My troubles, McConnell asserted, were simply the result of politics.

The majority leader, Harry Reid, spoke last. His remarks were not lengthy, but he discussed the racial slur case. Racial intolerance was too significant a legacy of our country's past to overlook the troubling parts of my record.

Almost twenty senators spoke in the two hours allotted that morning. I missed them all, other than the snippet I heard while working on the Salazar letter, and then later the conclusion of Senator Reid's statement. Senator Reid was talking when I went into the vice president's secretarial area, near the Senate floor.

Senator Reid concluded by urging "all my colleagues to join me in voting 'no' so we can find a candidate truly benefiting this important lifetime appointment—a candidate who will give the people of the Fifth Circuit the confidence they deserve that their claim to justice will be heard with the respect and equality every citizen deserves."

For whatever reason, senator Carl Levin of Michigan then asked, "How many votes are required to invoke cloture and end the debate on the pending nomination under the rules and precedents of the Senate?" Surely Levin knew, but asking such a question before an unusual vote may be a Senate ritual. "The Presiding Officer: It will be three-fifths of the Members duly chosen and sworn, that being 60."

"Mr. Levin: I thank the Chair."

21

The Vote

The end of a sixteen-year journey was near. The destination was thirty minutes away, but looking toward it revealed nothing. Looking back, though, I could see so many things:

A decade and a half of hopes and disappointments, then a call from my dear friend Thad Cochran saying I would be nominated that day.

Being called by Senator Lott in late April to be told that I was the next nominee who would be given a hearing and would be confirmed by Memorial Day.

A campaign against me beginning on the eve of my hearing.

Expecting, then week after week not receiving, a committee vote.

In July, four flights to Washington to meet with senators.

The difficult meeting with Senator Feinstein.

The August miracle of Senator Feinstein's voting for me.

Four more flights, and meetings, and all those questions, the same questions.

Two meetings just this morning, with the last one again questioning my character.

The vote on my dream job was about to be held. Would I wake up tomorrow, aware it had only been a dream? I felt like a pawn but did not know which team had made the smarter moves.

The presiding officer, senator Ben Cardin of Maryland, called for a reading of the resolution on which the vote would be taken. An assistant legislative clerk read:

Cloture Motion

> We, the undersigned Senators, in accordance with the provisions of Rule XXII of the Standing Rules of the Senate, do hereby move to bring to a close debate on Executive Calendar No. 291, the nomination of Leslie Southwick to be United States Circuit Judge for the Fifth Circuit.

The clerk noted that nineteen senators, all Republicans, had signed the resolution.

> *The Presiding Officer:* The question is, Is it the sense of the Senate that debate on the nomination of Leslie Southwick to be United States Circuit Judge for the Fifth Circuit shall be brought to a close? The yeas and nays are mandatory under the rule.
> The clerk will call the roll.

The vote would take almost twenty-five minutes. The first time through, almost no one voted. Eventually most would go down to the "well" of the Senate, adjacent to the raised benches in the front of the chamber. There several Senate staff members made a record of what was occurring. A thumbs-up or thumbs-down by a senator, a yes or no, or some other indication was given. I later got the tally sheet on which a clerk was recording the votes. Printed names of the Democratic senators on the left, Republican senators on the right, with a line in the right box to indicate the vote.

I sat on a window seat, nervously half listening. As I remember, no one talked to me. But my memories are far from clear about these career-altering minutes.

A video of the vote shows all the names were read alphabetically, with only a few senators voting. Then the teller restated the names of senators as they appeared in the well ready to vote. Among them: "Ms. Landrieu," the teller called. A slight pause, then repeated, "Ms. Landrieu . . . no." Louisiana senator, personable, second term. She was one of those I had met, sensed was sympathetic to my plight, but she voted against me. She can be seen in the video walking into the range of the camera, catching the attention of the teller, then leaving before her vote was announced. Senator Lott, standing on the opposite side of the well, heard the announcement of the negative vote five seconds after it was cast. He looked around to find her, then he too walked out of the view of the camera. He apparently talked to her hurriedly, then returned to his post.

I was told—which does not make it so—that a contingent of my opponents showed up in her office that morning, insisting that she vote no. Even without such pressure, though, she may have by then agreed with those who found me unworthy of support. A news story a week after the vote said that she had "defied her most powerful and perhaps only GOP Senate ally," Trent Lott, by breaking a commitment she had made to support me.[1]

I heard a few others. "Mr. Nelson, of Florida." The pause. Then, "Mr. Nelson . . . no." My heart sank. I had not met Bill Nelson, but Senator Lott said he would vote for me. Lott later told me that Nelson credited Congressman Thompson's claim on Tuesday that I would not meet with him with changing his mind. There was not much cushion, perhaps none at all.

The video reveals that very few senators were in the chamber when the voting started. Soon Senator Lott positioned himself near the lower bench. Senator Cochran stood like a sentinel at the center aisle on the last wide step down to the well. Senators Specter and McConnell were nearby. The number of senators grew, most of them appearing to vote, then staying in clusters of conversations. It was a confused scene, with Senate tellers occasionally straining to see through the mass of other senators if the next senator who wished to vote did not make his or her way through the knots of colleagues. Some just gave a long-distance thumbs up or down.

Near the end, Senator Carper went to Trent, who was standing near the teller who at the end of the vote would show the results to the presiding officer to announce. Carper walked up from behind and put his hand on Trent's back, causing Trent to turn. Carper said something. Trent looked down at the paper in his hand, then spoke to Carper. After twenty seconds of discussion, Carper took a step toward the bench and cast his vote.

The teller said, "Mr. Carper. Mr. Carper . . . aye." Within the next twenty seconds, Senators Byrd and Warner voted for me. Senator Baucus, with whom I had such an odd meeting, closed the voting with his no.

In the room where I was not watching, one of the vice president's staff, Margaret B. Stewart, was keeping a tally of the Democratic senators voting for me. I think she was the one, but at about this point, someone said, "He's got it!"[2] Then someone else said, "Only if all the Republicans are here." I needed sixty votes under the cloture rules. If any Republican failed to vote, it would be the same as if he or she had voted against me. I did not let my hopes get too high yet.

After Warner cast his vote, giving me all that I would receive, Senator Lott left his station next to the bench and walked out into the open area on the floor. The consummate vote counter, he knew before it started within just a few votes what the outcome would be. But the doubtful few, the ones who he had more than once told me could not be counted until they voted, would make the difference between victory and defeat. Trent joined Dianne Feinstein and Ben Nelson, who had been talking to each other in the well. Senators Lott and Feinstein remained in conversation for the several minutes it took to prepare the announcement of the official vote. Majority Leader Reid by then was at the lower bench, perhaps confirming the outcome. Judiciary Committee Chairman Leahy came up. Reid gave him a slight nod. Leahy lingered briefly, then walked away.

Finally the long sheet of paper, with the senators' names and their votes, was complete. The teller recording the votes stood, then turned around to face Senator Cardin, who was seated higher and behind her at another bench. She held the roll out where he could read it.

Senator Cardin looked around the chamber, rapped on the desk twice, paused, then twice again. He then read: "Is there any senator in the chamber who desires to record a vote or change a vote?" He looked up briefly. Watching later, knowing the outcome, that request for more or changed votes still makes me uncomfortable.

Senator Cardin then looked down at the paper before him and said, "On this vote, the yeas are 62; the nays are 35. Three-fifths of the senators duly chosen and sworn having voted in the affirmative, the motion carries." The sixtieth vote cast for me had been Carper's, that gentle man I had seen less than two hours earlier. Then Byrd and Warner gave me the small cushion.

From my notes later in the day: "There was no joy, or any particular emotion. There was an emptiness, a numbness. Then relief seemed to appear." Those in the room came up to congratulate me. The nomination vote was under way, but I was not hearing it. Senator Cardin: "Under the previous order, the question is, Shall the Senate advise and consent to the nomination of Leslie Southwick to be United States Circuit Judge for the Fifth Circuit. Those in favor," he said, then was stopped by Majority Leader Reid. "I ask for the yeas and nays." Without the request, there would have been a voice vote. Cardin: "Is there a sufficient second? There is a sufficient second."

The calling of the roll began. This vote took only fifteen minutes. Many senators, still in the chamber, were voting when their names were first called. It was anticlimactic. The sixty votes for cloture had been the challenge, but still I was concerned about this last vote. When it came time to state the final tally, senator Jim Webb of Virginia was presiding. I would have preferred his vote, but all I got was his reading the official results of my confirmation. He announced: "The yeas are 59, the nays are 38, and the nomination is confirmed. Under the previous order, a motion to reconsider is laid upon the table. The president is notified of the Senate's action."

The last three senators to vote were Carper, Whitehouse, and Salazar. Whitehouse had chaired my hearing and this morning twice left chairing another hearing to vote no.[3] Only Senator Inouye joined Carper and Salazar in voting for cloture but against confirmation. I had seen the latter two that morning. I wonder if my meetings secured their first vote or lost their second.

Within a few minutes, Trent came to the room where I had been watching to congratulate me. We had a photo taken that I would see on the news. Judiciary Committee staff members who had been working tirelessly wanted their pictures, too—so did I, as I want to remember Gregg Nunziata, Chris Mills, Blair Latoff, Elizabeth Hays, Gabe Bell, and the others. I was taken to see Senator McConnell. I received phone calls from old friends, such as former state GOP chairwoman Ebbie Spivey. I talked to her just after talking to McConnell, while still standing in the hallway next to a statue of Chief Justice White of Louisiana. Thad came and gave me a hug. He was relieved and quite pleased. Me too. He had been my first and constant and best ally.

Harold and I decided that I should call all Democrats who voted for me and all Republicans who spoke for me over the last few days. Back in the vice presidential staff office, I did that. Dianna Dunne would place calls and hand the phone to me.

A sixteen-year struggle had ended, one containing many defeats along the way, brief discouragement, then decisions to try again when the opportunities arose. My persistence was hardly unique. A better man with a similar history was William Winter. He first ran for Mississippi governor in 1967, led in the first Democratic primary, then lost in the runoff. He was elected lieutenant governor in 1971, perhaps comparable to my being elected to the state court of appeals after my first effort for the Fifth Circuit failed. He ran again for governor in 1975. He once more led in the first primary but lost in a runoff. In 1979, with some (including me) finding his decision quixotic, he filed again for the gubernatorial primary just two hours before the deadline. When he won the runoff for the nomination, after coming in second in the first primary, the Jackson newspaper headline read: "After 12 Years, Winter Celebrates End of Long Quest." One line also aptly described my circumstances almost thirty years later: "Winter, who has plenty of practice accepting defeat," now had a chance to accept congratulations.[4] He later won the general election.

I was among the lucky ones who, in a difficult and lengthy quest, got the one more chance needed. This had surely been my last chance, win or lose.

22

A Victory Lap

Senator Specter and his staff organized a reception for me in the Senate Judiciary Committee hearing room at 5:00 that afternoon. Republican senators Kyl, Hatch, and Cornyn were there. So was Senator Feinstein. It was a soft-drink reception until Senator Feinstein had California wine brought over from her office. There were perhaps forty people, including representatives from some of the outside groups that had been so helpful. I finally got to meet Ed Whelan, Curt Levey, David Keene, Wendy Long, and others. Senate staff were there, dear people, who had been allies and now were friends. And so was Harold, the indefatigable Harold Kim, whose last semi-official duty was to escort me there.

I left the party at about 6:30, heading back to the Justice Department. Walking down the hall to the exit, I passed Oregon senator Ron Wyden's office. I twice had an impromptu conversation with him. The hurdles of politics and regional perceptions always meant he was unlikely to support me. He did not, but I wanted our brief connection to close on a positive note. I went into his office, told the receptionist who I was and asked to talk to her senator. He came fairly soon with his counsel. We had an enjoyable chat in a small conference room. He graciously said he might have been wrong in his vote. He generously did not say he might have been right.

After my victory, one of the indispensable people issued a press release.[1]

THE WHITE HOUSE
Office of the Press Secretary
For Immediate Release October 24, 2007

STATEMENT BY THE PRESIDENT

The confirmation of Judge Leslie Southwick to the U.S. Court of Appeals for the Fifth Circuit is a victory for America's judicial system and for the citizens of Louisiana, Mississippi, and Texas. Today's bipartisan vote resolves a long-standing judicial emergency and will help ensure that the Fifth Circuit can operate more effectively. Judge Southwick is a man of character and intelligence who will apply the law fairly. I appreciate the Senate's approval of his nomination.

That night, Chip Williams, a good friend and Jackson lawyer, wrote a brief letter to me. "Today, in a 'five-lawyer deposition,' news of your confirmation came by text message to one of the lawyers who announced it to all. Everyone cheered, Leslie." I include this comment because it describes what I hope was the reaction of many people in Mississippi who knew about me but were not friends, who were plaintiff lawyers and defense counsel, and who perhaps widely but surely not universally believed I was deserving of this position. Of course, to be the one lawyer in the room who did not cheer the new federal judge would have been awkward.

The next morning I had a few hours before my flight. I went by some Senate offices to express my thanks. As I was walking toward one of them, Senator Whitehouse came up behind me. I heard an initially unrecognized voice asking me, "Are you taking a victory lap?" We had a positive and only slightly awkward conversation. I then met a few senators in their offices.

An extremely enjoyable phone call was with former judge Charles Clark. He said my only mistake was to pass on the better judgeship, which was for the district court. This great former chief judge of the Fifth Circuit told me that he would have preferred being a trial judge. But he knew, as he put it, the "Fifth was in my heart."

I returned to the Justice Department briefly before catching my flight home. Acting attorney general Peter Keisler made time in his schedule to see me in his office. Peter was far better read than I. He said the battle scars I had received reminded him of Shakespeare's play *Coriolanus*, where it was necessary for those who would lead to display their battle wounds to the crowd to prove themselves worthy. If scars were needed for a judgeship, I was surely qualified.

On the Monday after my confirmation, my commission was ready to be signed by the president and the attorney general. Peter wrote a note that was included with the commission. He said that nothing he had signed in his five years at the department, including his six weeks as acting attorney general, gave him as much pleasure as signing my commission. What a wonderful thing to write.

Congratulations came in by e-mail. Andy Taggart was succinct as usual: "Hooray! Hooray! Hooray!" He then actually added a full sentence. Even so, "Hooray" was the key thought.

I responded. "What a journey, one neither fully expected nor certainly wanted, yet also one that may prove to be one of the most useful to me in my personal growth. Greater patience, chances for forgiveness, bearing the insults of (part of) the world and trying to rise above them, all of those are benefits of this process. Thanks, old friend, for everything."[2]

I wrote La'Verne Edney, saying that there had been "many contributors to my victory, but very few had your impact. I expect that your letter was quoted far more than anyone else's. I was extremely honored by your comments and your willingness to inject yourself into such a controversy. You are a dear person, and a dear friend."

I also wrote Ed Whelan, who had written often and well about me for *National Review*. " 'Tis done. No one came close to your intensity and quality of work in researching and then explaining the truth about the arguments concerning the disputed opinions. Though the cause does not deserve the analogy, you were my *Publius*, describing with zeal and with greater clarity than could be found in the original materials that were being defended."[3] *Publius* was the joint pseudonym of Alexander Hamilton, James Madison, and John Jay, who wrote the *Federalist Papers* between October 1787 and August 1788, to explain the Constitution and encourage its ratification in the states.

"The myths of a formidable opposition had to be demolished. No one was more instrumental in providing the weaponry for the assault on those myths than you."

The sentence in my e-mail about myths had been plagiarized from a wonderful letter I received a few days after confirmation. It had been sent by a political science professor at Rice from whom I had taken some classes and also for whom I had been an exam grader my senior year. "Doc C," known to those who do not know him well as Dr. Gilbert Cuthbertson, was just about every political science students' favorite professor when I was there. He started with a challenge to my powers of recollection by quoting the *Aeneid*, without attribution. "What a struggle to found the race of Rome," both Doc C and Virgil wrote. The hardships of building an empire were a bit more epic than mine, but I loved the analogy. Doc C congratulated me and gave his sympathy for what I had endured. He then gave me another piece of history to contemplate.

> The situation for some reason reminds me of [Texas] Senator Wigfall's flee-
> ing Richmond [as the Confederate government collapsed in 1865]. He got to
> Arkansas where the ferryman told him that as a Unionist he would like to hang
> Jeff Davis and Wigfall from a sour apple tree. Wigfall, who was traveling incog-
> nito, agreed, saying he'd be "pulling harder at the rope than anyone else."[4]

Indeed, he would be required to put all his weight into it. No hanging for me.

News coverage of the victory closed my time of national notoriety. Clearly supportive was the *Wall Street Journal*. It said that I was the tar-get of racial politics because of an insistence for more black judges on the Fifth Circuit.[5] The political newspapers in Washington gave their final words. The *Politico* called Senator Feinstein my "unlikely heroine."[6] The story described the press conference held within minutes of my confirma-tion. Present were Republican senators Thad Cochran, Trent Lott, Arlen Specter, Mitch McConnell, Orrin Hatch, and Lindsey Graham. Willing to join them was Senator Feinstein. "This may be out of precedent," Specter said, "but if I may, with the concurrence of the home-state senators, yield to the hero—the lady—of the day, Sen. Feinstein."

She began by saying, "I don't know about this heroine business." She was worried about the future. "In this body, what goes around comes around. I have been on the Judiciary Committee for fifteen years, and I have watched it go around and come around, and it has got to end. Some-body has to be part of an effort to step forward and try and see if that can happen." Senator Lott was emotional at the press conference. He said his state—our state—had been "maligned" in this and other instances. Sena-tor Feinstein put her hand on his shoulder in a sign of friendship.

Roll Call thought that Majority Leader Reid, though opposing me, "did little to whip his party against him." Instead some argued that "Reid made a clear effort to tamp down the opposition rhetoric on his side of the aisle." That seemed accurate, and I appreciated it. The news stories quoted several opponents. Some "deplored" my confirmation, some were "incred-ibly disappointed," and some even promised to "publicize the people who turn their back on black people."[7]

A sign of the bitterness was that a few weeks later, Senator Feinstein had to beat back an effort to censure her at a meeting of the Executive

Board of the California Democratic Party, held in Anaheim on November 16–18. The basis of the censure was "her shameful votes" on me and then on Attorney General Michael Mukasey, who was confirmed on November 8. The petition said that she had voted to confirm me, despite my "clear record of racism and gender discrimination."[8] Political courage invites censure, hence its rarity. Fortunately her opponents failed.

My wife taped a lengthy news report that day on my confirmation. Appearing on the screen when the story was announced was "Here Comes the Judge." Brit Hume on Fox News introduced the story, then turned to the reporter, Major Garrett. For the first time, I saw the tape of my walking down a Senate office building hallway with Harold Kim, probably when we went to see Senator Ben Nelson. Excerpts from some favorable speeches were shown, including that of Senator McCain. Senator Schumer's comments about two hundred years of history were repeated. Parts of the Specter-Cochran-Lott-Hatch-Graham-McConnell-Feinstein press conference were shown. The segment closed with excerpts of an interview with George Washington Law School professor Jonathan Turley. He said there was no evidence "whatsoever" that I was a racist. As to the racial slur case, Professor Turley believed I had just followed what I thought to be the law. The reporter closed by stating that the president had called Senator Lott to thank him but "did not telephone Senator Feinstein." The next day, the same program reported that Bush had expressed his thanks in person when Senator Feinstein flew with him on Air Force One to see the damage caused by wildfires in California.[9]

The Jackson newspaper editorialized on the journey, saying it was not "Southwick who was being judged, but the dark days of our region." The editorial closed: "This should be a day for celebrating—a judge and a region as they are, not what they once might have been."[10]

My cousin George Tarpley sent me an e-mail soon after the vote. "Gloria and I have just finished watching the Wednesday morning session of the Senate debate and ultimately confirm your nomination. I cannot imagine how you—or any relatively rational and accomplished human—put up with the process, but am absolutely delighted with the confirmation. Congratulations."[11]

In a postscript, George added, "I think you are quite capable of carrying 200 years of accumulated history on your shoulders, but I don't think that's exactly what our friendly Democrats meant."

I learned a few details about the events of that last day, not reported in the press, as time went by. One of the more intriguing I was told a month later as I waited in line at a coffee shop in Jackson. Ahead of me was Donald Clark, a lawyer and friend. Donald practices law with Mike Espy. He said that on the day of the vote, he was given a call from Senator Tom Carper, who was trying to reach Espy. Donald thought the senator was on the Senate floor, trying to get some advice before the vote. Donald was unable to locate Espy. After he and Carper hung up, Donald called one of the lawyers for Governor Barbour, Paul Hurst. Donald suggested the governor or someone else do something. "We're on it," was Paul's quick response.

I also later learned from another brand-new Mississippi judge, Sharion Aycock, that she had months earlier expressed her regret to Brad Davis, Senator Cochran's counsel, for the hardships I was facing. She told me Brad responded, "He will be okay; he is a soldier." That was not how I saw myself, but I was honored that someone else saw me that way.

The best congratulatory writing was from my wife Sharon. We passed each other in the Jackson airport on Thursday, as she needed to fly to Houston while I was returning home. She gave me the car keys, told me where she had parked, and we went our separate ways.

At home, on our dresser, I found she had set up a display. Forming a semicircle were framed photographs of my mother, father, and stepfather, all long deceased; of her parents, one of them now gone, too; of our children; and of her, a picture from long ago just as our joint journey began and our route could not be foreseen. A sheet of paper was in the center, on which she had written: "Congratulations from all of us! We are so proud of you." I remain deeply touched by the idea of all those people peacefully smiling at the result.

Now that I was home, my chore was to do the paperwork to allow the White House to get the president to sign my appointment. The most important item was a letter resigning from my position as a visiting professor at Mississippi College. I was told to write that the resignation was effective upon the president's appointment. Though the resignation was directed to the dean of the law school, the more important transmittal was by fax to the White House counsel.

I was told on Friday that the president might sign the appointment on Monday. The difficulty was that he was only going to be in Washington in the morning, then was flying to Cincinnati to meet, coincidentally, my brother Larry and several hundred other contributors for a fund-raising function for an Ohio congressman.

The president did sign the commission on Monday. Then he was off to see Larry. "I got to talk to Mr. Bush just fine," Larry reported in an e-mail. "He worked the 'rope line' and probably half of the attendees talked to him, got his autograph, got a picture, or had something really important to say—as I did! He said you were a 'good man.' Finally, as for your twenty-year quest for reaching a high goal in your profession, a hearty CONGRATULATIONS!"[12] Now, Larry, it was not *twenty* years. Just sixteen.

Around noon on Monday, I got a call from the White House Counsel's Office to inform me that the president signed the appointment. I could be sworn in immediately. My first thought was of a small event in the office of one of the other Fifth Circuit judges, with Sharon and my new staff in attendance. That grew over the next twenty-four hours to an event in a courtroom with about thirty people, including all the judges in the courthouse, the retired Fifth Circuit judge Charles Clark, who got me to Mississippi thirty years ago, and others. I invited the two nominees who had fallen by the wayside during the Bush presidency. I called each of them and said that I could not quite discern whether I would have wanted to attend had our roles been reversed, but I wanted each to feel welcome. Each came. My success over similar obstacles may have given them some closure.

Several weeks later, a good friend, Margaret Patterson, thoughtfully organized the most enriching celebration of all. She arranged for retired bishop William Houck, along with priests Mike O'Brien and Ben Martinez, to celebrate a mass in my honor in her backyard with several dozen of our friends. She and her husband Dave then served a marvelous dinner. The ceremony sealed the achievement spiritually. Now it was up to me to be deserving of all that had happened.

23

Reflections

Less than a week after my vote, the *Boston Globe* columnist Peter Canellos wrote that many opponents had been infuriated at my victory. He then wrote sensitively about the perspective of nominees who go through such experiences. He discussed the personal cost to the nominee, a point he quoted Senator Feinstein as having made in one of her speeches about me. He closed his column with the opinion that the savaging of nominees "has made them very bitter."[1]

Thankfully, I was able to avoid bitterness. I prevailed, which surely helped. I hope it would have been possible to avoid resentments even had I been defeated. Being tested in the fire can either consume a person or, with luck and perseverance and understanding, instead help to purify.

Among the insights I gained is that well-intentioned people, from the perspectives formed by their backgrounds, could take a careful look at my record and come to the conclusion that I was fatally flawed as a potential judge. I hoped that most careful observers, regardless of the biases we all have, would have thought the criticisms unfair. But that hope indicates my own prejudgments.

Whether people accepted the criticisms of my record or not, the battle would likely not have been so difficult if not for the insistence that there needed to be more African Americans on the Fifth Circuit. Surely no one should be excluded from consideration for a judgeship because of race. On the other hand, one line ought never to be crossed: no person should be opposed because of race. The line between supporting greater diversity but not opposing someone of the wrong race is not just a matter of semantics. As long as a choice is being made among different individuals, a desire for diversity is saying yes due to race. Once a choice is made, though, opposing that person is saying no due to race. We should be discarding those attitudes, not picking them back up. My conclusion, though, may simplistically express my painful memories. It is at least a point others might wish to add to their own reflections.

My predecessors as nominees and targets of national attention were extremely gracious. Judge Pickering congratulated me warmly at the ceremony when I was sworn in. Mike Wallace did, too, then sent me a generously complimentary note. He and his wife Barbara had kept my wife and me in their prayers, he wrote. I wish there had been some way for all three of us to succeed, and Bob Galloway too. Months later, Bob drove all the way from the coast to attend a reception for me.

I thought about all the people to whom I owed my success. My political career was long in my past. But there was someone whom I had not seen in years, for whom I had worked in 1970, 1980, and 1988, who had given me the foundation on which I built my public career. On December 17, I wrote former president Bush in Houston.

"It is to you that I largely owe this success." I told him of my work on his 1970 Senate campaign.

> You were the first public official who inspired me. You continued to do so throughout your career. For twenty years your campaigns or your administration were the focus of so much of my energy and emotion. My public association with you was vital to my electoral success. The exemplary character of your service was a spur to my own efforts. And it was in working for you that I got to know the honorable man who is now serving courageously as our president.
>
> In this small, belated, and perhaps curious way, I wanted to note the incalculable debt I owe you. That debt existed even had I never been considered for this judicial position, but my recent success makes me acutely conscious of my obligation.

The former president replied: "Your letter was one of the nicest I have ever received. Thank you for those very kind sentiments, and thank you for your loyal support to the Bushes."

Former Fifth Circuit judge Charles Clark was as important as George Bush in starting me on the road that led to this destination. In 2009 I wrote him a letter, one of many to be given him at a reunion of his former law clerks. I expressed my affection and respect, then wrote, "You gave me an interview, a clerkship, and a foundation for a wonderfully varied and rewarding career in your native state, which beginning with our meeting gradually became my home."

Stuart Taylor, the *National Journal* writer who wrote an extremely positive article about me in late July, sent me an e-mail after the turmoil was over. He casually inquired about my reactions to what had happened. I then deluged him with words in reply.

> As I was considering last January whether to agree to be redirected to the circuit court nomination from my relatively calm voyage as a district court nominee, I was hardly oblivious to the storms that my predecessor nominees had encountered. Whatever legitimate concerns could be raised about any of us, there was a viciousness in some of the criticisms of Charles Pickering and Mike Wallace that set the tone for what might be ahead for me if I changed course. The decision to accept the higher-court nomination was composed of perhaps equal parts of hope that the process would not be too difficult and of conviction that the circuit court was the proper place to use whatever judicial skills I vainly believe I possessed.
>
> A part of my thinking, but not as dominant at some times as others, is that I did not want the ordeal to be so personally offensive that I would become permanently resentful. I had decided to withdraw if I ever thought that the process was trapping me in animosities from which I was not likely to escape once the journey was over.
>
> For the two months after the hearing, there seemed uniformly grim news about the prospects of success. I was trying very hard to trust and have faith, but I was not certain if optimism about confirmation was the proper attitude. A different conviction was that I should constantly try to understand others and their motivations, to put in context that what was occurring to me was different only in specifics to what had occurred to others, and always, always try to forgive those who wanted no forgiveness. There was even a thread of guilt through it all, because during the previous several years as prior Miss. nominees were subjected to their ordeals, in the back of mind—as hard as I fought it—was the realization that their failure might redound to my benefit. So I also saw my being put through the fire in 2007 as a useful penance for the attitudes I had not been able to avoid in previous years, relating to previous nominees.
>
> If I could maintain that emotional balance, I was convinced that blessings of personal growth and faith would come. I needed at all costs, even the cost of the nomination, to avoid the tempting but destructive emotions that can be generated by unfair criticisms.

I put the final result in terms of my faith as well. Dianne Feinstein was one of the wonderful people who, in my conception of the world, was available to provide the miracle that I needed. So many other people had to work to cause that miracle to occur, and that was providential. When the August recess was over, it became clear that I would need almost as great a miracle to stop a filibuster. That too was provided, because some delightful people did what was necessary.

One of the truly surprising and indispensable instruments of the miracle was Trent Lott. We had never been close (though not adversaries in any way, if someone in my various minor roles could ever rate as an adversary of a U.S. senator). He likely had doubts about my judicial philosophy. But my sense of what motivated him is that he hated the way Mississippi was by extension being condemned when I was condemned. He liked to battle, particularly a battle that with the energetic application of his insider skills, could be surprisingly won.[2]

My point about Lott had been highlighted in a *Washington Post* article when he announced his resignation almost exactly a month after my vote. An aide said that Lott had "wondered aloud why he was working so hard for a man [me] he did not really know and for someone who was much more closely allied" with Senator Cochran. "You just like the process," the aide responded—the struggle and the opportunity to win. Lott "just smiled."[3]

Continuing my e-mail to Stuart Taylor: "What again was your question? Oh yes, what are the continuing effects of all I experienced? I sincerely believe that the effects are positive ones. I told a group of friends that had a celebration for me about a month ago, that if I had been given the choice early in the process of being confirmed easy or being confirmed hard, I would have immediately taken the easy path. Now that it is over, I am glad for personal reasons that it occurred the way that it did."

I did not include the following verse in my e-mail to Taylor, but this passage from Malachi 3:3 captures what I was trying to say to him. It refers to the Lord coming with a refiner's fire:

He will sit refining and purifying silver, and he will purify the sons of Levi, Refining them like gold or like silver that they may offer due sacrifice to the Lord.

A refining is what I hoped I gained. "I believe that I am more understanding and forgiving, more conscious of my faith, a better person in important ways. Though many criticized me simply because of politics, there were a great many others who must have been genuinely concerned that I was a judicial ogre. The experience of 2007 reminds me of how constantly I have to be aware of the insidious effects of preconceptions." I closed my e-mail with thanks for what Stuart had contributed.

One effect of preconceptions is a temptation to categorize people because of One Big Thing. We use that one thing as proof of a person's worth. The one big thing may be the person's region of the country, or political party, or opinion about some public issue, or who is supporting or opposing the person. It may be more personal, such as one thing the individual did or said.

Expressing concerns about such habits was a former member of President Lyndon Johnson's Cabinet, John Gardner. In 1969 he said that "one of the most corrosive of social delusions is the conviction on the part of the individual that he and his kind of people are uniquely faithful to the true American morality but that others who are morally less worthy are bringing the nation down."[4] I agree. The most insidious of today's sins is feeling morally superior to all with whom we disagree. That attitude justifies victory at all costs because everything the opponent stands for is anathema. There cannot be respectful discussion because there is no respect.

Similarly, those who seek political office promise if elected to fight for their beliefs, not just debate as a person of goodwill in support of those beliefs. A too-rarely followed approach is to practice verbal nonviolence. Instead, in American politics, the first rule of engagement can be to attack opponents with the entire arsenal that words provide.

Partisan excesses have seemingly always been with us. They were noted even at the close of one of the most dramatic exchanges ever heard in the Senate, that of March 1830, when Massachusetts senator Daniel Webster urged "Liberty and Union, now and forever," against the protests of South Carolina senator Robert Hayne, who charged that a Congress dominated by the North was making the "grass grows in our streets; our very fields are scathed by the hands of injustice and oppression." When Webster and Hayne ended their debate, another orator arose, New York senator Edward Livingston.[5] He spoke at length on the excesses of party often displayed in the Senate. What he feared were the "indulgence of passions," which would find expression in the trifling as well as in the serious—"the liberties of a nation, or the color of a cockade [ribbon in a hat], are sufficient to excite it." Partisan indulgence "creates imaginary, and magnifies real causes of complaint; arrogates to itself every virtue—denies every merit to its opponents; secretly entertains the worst designs, publicly imputes them to its adversaries."

Livingston closed his laments with the prayer that "from these evils, may Heaven, in its mercy, preserve our beloved country: but, that this prayer may be heard, we must begin by correcting in ourselves every approach of the passions which lead to them. . . . I am no censor of the conduct of others; it is sufficient for me to watch over my own."

I too am guilty of not adequately watching over my own attitudes, of indulging passions. There are not two kinds of people—"my kind," who are virtuous because they see the world as I do, and everyone else. I accept the truth of Aleksandr Solzhenitsyn's words in *The Gulag Archipelago* that "the line separating good and evil passes not through states, nor between political parties either—but right through every human heart—and through all human hearts."

I am what I am, flawed. My confirmation journey needed to be hard. I needed an unsparing penance for my lack of sufficient Christian sympathy for what Judge Pickering and Mike Wallace had to endure. My intellect and emotions and character had to be refined in the fire.

In the Judiciary Committee, as the partisan flames grew increasingly intense, my dream should have been destroyed. Most objective observers were certain it would be. In confirmation warfare, the nominee rarely matters nearly as much as partisan gain or loss. Seeing my hopes so nearly ended, then having them survive because of the diligence of Trent Lott and the decency of Dianne Feinstein, is the most miraculous event of my professional life.

C. S. Lewis wrote years ago in words that describe why, if I were going to reach the goal I had so long wanted, this was the best route.

> Everyone has noticed how hard it is to turn our thoughts to God when everything is going well with us. We "have all we want" is a terrible saying when "all" does not include God. We find God an interruption. As St. Augustine says somewhere, "God wants to give us something, but cannot, because our hands are full—there's nowhere for Him to put it." Or as a friend of mine said, "We regard God as an airman regards his parachute; it's there for emergencies but he hopes he'll never have to use it." Now God, who has made us, knows what we are and that our happiness lies in Him. Yet we will not seek it in Him as long as he leaves us any other resort where it can even plausibly be looked for.[6]

I am a blessed man.

Epilogue

The political turmoil that greeted each white male nominee to a federal court in Mississippi since the late 1980s arose from the insistence that more black judges had to be named. With Barack Obama's election in 2008, the demand would be answered.

The U.S. District Court vacancy for which I had been selected in 2006, then to which Meridian lawyer Rick Barry was nominated in 2008, was still unfilled when President Bush left office. It took more than another year, but Carlton Reeves, a Jackson lawyer, black male, and former first assistant U.S. attorney under President Clinton, was nominated in April 2010 and confirmed that December. Carlton is a longtime acquaintance. He became the head of the Magnolia Bar Association in Mississippi in 2007 and sought to block my confirmation.

At Reeves's confirmation hearing in 2010, Republican senator John Kyl of Arizona asked about the letter that Reeves sent to the Senate in 2007. Reeves indicated he still thought the judgments he expressed about me then were accurate.[1] His stance was a reminder of what had not changed. Some who had opposed me still felt I did not belong on the court. Reeves was honest that he could not accept my explanations for the parts of my record he found disqualifying. Honesty is a good foundation on which to build years of a positive association between us. I do not know if there is a splinter in his eye about me. My attention needs to be only on the beam in my own.

A new vacancy was created on the Fifth Circuit when my friend Rhesa Barksdale announced in August 2008 that he would retire from active service in August 2009. My knowledge of how the new nominee was chosen is limited and potentially incorrect.

Because both Mississippi senators were Republicans, the Obama administration turned to others for advice. One of the most important was Secretary of the Navy Ray Mabus, a former Mississippi governor and early

Obama supporter. Sometime by mid-2009, he provided a lengthy list of possibilities. Three names I heard were Mississippi Supreme Court justice James Graves, my former state court of appeals colleague Leslie D. King, and Jackson attorney Doug Minor, all of whom are African Americans. Another was Brad Pigott, who served as U.S. attorney in Jackson when Bill Clinton was president. Pigott was a white male and may not have been a serious possibility. Representative Bennie Thompson apparently encouraged nomination of black state circuit judge Winston Kidd of Jackson.

It took a while, but James was finally told his nomination would be made on May 9, 2010. He waited for the public announcement, but nothing happened. The reason became clear the next day when Elena Kagan was nominated to the Supreme Court. James's nomination was delayed an extra month, but it was finally made. He had a hearing late in the session. He received no vote that year, was renominated in January, then was confirmed in February 2011.

James is immensely intelligent, a truly gifted public speaker, and a warmhearted man. It was a sign of the tremendous change in the South since 1869 when William Woods was named the first circuit judge of the Fifth Circuit Court, and since 1891 when Don Pardee became the first circuit judge to serve on the Fifth Circuit Court of Appeals, that Graves was nominated to fill the Woods-Pardee seat. John Minor Wisdom, later Alvin Rubin, and most recently Rhesa Barksdale were others who filled the position with sound judgment, integrity, and, when necessary, courage. Now James has a turn to do his best and let history be his judge.

History's verdict, though, just like that given by senators, is a matter of perspective.

Appendix: Selection of Fifth Circuit Judges, 1869–2012

Circuit courts were created by Congress in the first Judiciary Act, adopted in 1789. They were a hybrid: a trial court with responsibility for the more significant criminal and civil cases and an appellate court to hear appeals from district courts where the less important cases were handled. For eighty years, with a sixteen-month exception, no judges were named to serve solely on the circuit courts. Instead a Supreme Court justice was assigned to each circuit and jointly presided twice a year in each district over circuit court cases with a district judge. The exception began in 1801, when the lame-duck Federalist Party majority in Congress created sixteen circuit court judgeships, most of which were then filled by president John Adams during his last two weeks in office. Those judicial positions were eliminated in 1802 by the Jeffersonian majority in Congress, and the old law was revived. An example of a two-judge circuit court trial was that of former vice president Aaron Burr for treason. In 1807, chief justice John Marshall and Virginia district judge Cyrus Griffin jointly presided over Burr's trial in Richmond. Burr was acquitted. Eventually district judges usually presided alone over the circuit courts and had their district court duties too.[1]

In 1869 Congress authorized a single circuit court judge in each circuit. In 1891 it allowed a second judge for each circuit. Also in 1891, Congress created a court of appeals for each circuit, separate from the trial-level circuit courts. The circuit court judges served on both courts. The judges continued to have their trial court duties, but they now also served on three-judge panels to hear appeals, sitting with district judges from the states in their circuit and even Supreme Court justices at times. The circuit judges' trial court duties ended in 1912 when the circuit courts were abolished, and the district courts became the only trial courts. Circuit judges thereafter served only on the courts of appeals. After a second judge for each circuit was authorized in 1891, Congress added new judgeships to individual circuits as needed. The Fifth Circuit now has seventeen positions.[2]

The number and boundaries of the circuits changed through the years. In 1789 the states were divided into three circuits. By 1866 there were nine circuits. The Fifth Circuit contained Texas, Louisiana, Mississippi, Alabama, Florida, and Georgia. On October 1, 1981, the western three states became the new Fifth Circuit. The eastern three states became the Eleventh Circuit.[3]

The following summarizes Senate consideration of every nominee to a Fifth Circuit judgeship. It reveals that two of the first four nominees faced strenuous challenges. Then for almost a century, the Senate with a few exceptions acted within weeks of receiving a nomination, and often within days. Almost always, the action was approval by voice vote or unanimous consent. Mississippian James P. Coleman in 1965 received the first votes cast in opposition to a motion to advise and consent on a nomination to the Fifth Circuit. Only two more nominees since Judge Coleman have had a divided vote on confirmation. One was Priscilla Owen of Texas in 2005. I was the other in 2007. All three of us were confirmed. No Fifth Circuit nominee has ever lost on an actual floor vote. The defeats occurred earlier: nine nominees failed to emerge from the Judiciary Committee, and one was stopped by a filibuster on the floor of the Senate. Thus a total of ten nominees were not confirmed. So far.

Circuit Judges of the Fifth Circuit Court (1869–1912) and the Court of Appeals for the Fifth Circuit (1891–2012)

The first range of dates in the parentheses shows years of birth and death; the second indicates the years of service on the Fifth Circuit. If a judge took senior status, the initial date range shows the judge's active service, and the final year is when the judge left the court.

Names in italics were nominated but not confirmed. The italicized name with an asterisk had a recess appointment but was never confirmed.[4]

1869: Congress authorized one judge in each circuit.

Woods, William Burnham, of Alabama (1824–87; 1869–80). Nominated on December 8, 1869, and confirmed by voice vote on December 22, 1869. Woods was appointed to the Supreme Court on December 21, 1880, the only Fifth Circuit judge so far to be elevated to that court.

Billings, Edward Coke, of Louisiana (1829–93; not confirmed). Federal District Judge Billings of New Orleans was nominated by outgoing president Garfield on January 24, 1881. Within two weeks, reports stated that the Democratic Judiciary Committee chairman did not move the Billings nomination because of charges he had made a decision as a judge that was unfairly ruinous to a railroad. Supporters said that Billings had not even been a judge at the time of his alleged ruling. He was also said to have allowed an extravagant fee to be paid to the trustees who had taken over the same railroad. A New Orleans Democratic newspaper said that the charges were contained in "one of the most malignant and false documents that we have perused of late. The pen which wrote it could not have been guided by the hand of an honest man; the brain which inspired it was a very weak one, and the heart which nerved the movement was filled with malice." Five different charges were discussed in the article, and each was rebutted.[5] The Senate Judiciary Committee never voted on his nomination, and it lapsed on March 3, 1881, when Congress adjourned.

Pardee, Don Albert, of Louisiana; moved to Georgia in 1899 (1837–1919; 1881–1919). Nominated on March 14, 1881, and confirmed unanimously on May 13, 1881. Pardee was nominated for the U.S. District Court in 1875 but was blocked, and Edward Billings was then nominated and confirmed. Their roles were reversed in 1881.

1891: Circuit Courts of Appeals created; two judges authorized for each circuit.

McCormick, Andrew Phelps, of Texas (1832–1916; 1892–1916). The bill creating a second judgeship in each circuit passed on March 3, 1891. Congress went into recess that day, returning on December 7; nominations could not be made during the recess. U.S. District Judge McCormick was mentioned as a strong contender by June 1891. Late that year, the Justice Department investigated allegations that he had appointed his son to a lucrative position as a court master to handle a railroad receivership. It was Judge Pardee who made the appointment. By the time McCormick was nominated on January 5, 1892, opponents may already have been preparing. On February 17, the House approved Alabama representative John Bankhead's motion that the Judiciary Committee investigate three charges that could be used to impeach McCormick as a district judge; a fourth was added a few days later. A Dallas newspaper thought that Bankhead's motives were to allow his candidate for the Fifth Circuit, U.S. attorney and former Alabama governor Lewis E. Parsons, to be nominated. The investigation was of the receivership question, other claimed financial improprieties, and a claim that he had once declared before trial that two criminal defendants were guilty and he would ensure their conviction. The judge submitted a lengthy defense, denying the charges and giving the rest of the story on the relevant events. On March 15, the House committee "unanimously decided that the evidence on the charges against Judge McCormick was not sufficient."[6] The Senate unanimously confirmed him on March 17, 1892. McCormick was the first native of one of the Fifth Circuit states (Texas) to serve on the court.

1899: Congress authorized three judges in the Fifth Circuit.

Shelby, David Davie, of Alabama (1847–1914; 1899–1914). Nominated on February 21, 1899, and confirmed unanimously on March 2, 1899.

Circuit Courts were abolished in 1912; the Circuit Courts of Appeals remained.

Walker, Richard Wilde, of Alabama (1857–1936; 1914–1930, senior–1936). Nominated on October 2, 1914, and confirmed unanimously on October 5, 1914.

Batts, Robert Lynn, of Texas (1864–1935, 1917–19). Nominated on January 17, 1917, and confirmed unanimously on February 5, 1917.

Bryan, Nathan Philemon, of Florida (1872–1935; 1920–35). Nominated on April 23, 1920, and unanimously confirmed on the same day. Confirmation without a hearing for former U.S. senators was a tradition. Bryan had been a U.S. senator from 1911 to 1917.

King, Alexander Campbell, of Georgia (1856–1926; 1920–24). Nominated on April 29, 1920, and confirmed unanimously on May 24, 1920.

Foster, Rufus Edward, of Louisiana (1871–1942; 1925–42). Nominated on January 3, 1925, and confirmed on January 13.

1930: Congress authorized four judges in the Fifth Circuit.

Sibley, Samuel Hale, of Georgia (1873–1958; 1931–49, senior–1958). Nominated on December 20, 1930, and confirmed unanimously on January 13, 1931.

Hutcheson, Joseph Chappell, Jr., of Texas (1879–1973; 1931–64, senior–1973). Nominated on December 20, 1930, and confirmed unanimously on January 13, 1931.

Holmes, Edwin Ruthven, of Mississippi (1878–1961; 1936–54, senior–1961). Nominated on August 23, 1935. Senator Theodore Bilbo opposed him because in 1923 District Judge Holmes had jailed Bilbo for ten days for contempt. The Senate Judiciary Committee delayed a vote until Bilbo was ready to present witnesses on March 5–6, 1936. The committee unanimously reported Holmes favorably. On March 19, at a floor debate, Bilbo spoke for five hours. Bilbo's motion to recommit the nomination to the committee failed on a 4–59 vote, with 33 not voting. Holmes was then confirmed by a voice vote.[7]

1938: Congress authorized five judges in the Fifth Circuit.

McCord, Leon Clarence, of Alabama (1878–1952; 1938–51, senior–1952). Nominated on June 9, 1938, and confirmed unanimously on June 15.

1942: Congress authorized six judges in the Fifth Circuit.

Waller, Curtis Longino, of Florida (1887–1950; 1943–50). Nominated on February 18, 1943, and unanimously confirmed on March 9, 1943.

Allred, James Burr, V, of Texas (1899–1959, not confirmed). Nominated on February 18, 1943. He had been Texas attorney general from 1930 to 1934, governor from 1934 to 1938, and a U.S. district judge from 1938 to 1942. At President Roosevelt's urging,

Allred resigned as judge and ran against Senator "Pappy" O'Daniel in the August 1942 Democratic primary. Allred lost with 433,000 votes to O'Daniel's 451,000. Six months later, Allred was nominated to the Fifth Circuit. In the Senate of the 1940s, a senator could generally stop a nominee from his own state who was "personally obnoxious" to him. O'Daniel found the nominee to be obnoxious and claimed that Allred had been promised a new judgeship if he ran against O'Daniel and lost. Attorney general Francis Biddle testified at the hearing that no such commitment had been made. Allred also testified at his own request to refute the claim of a deal. A different objection was offered by the first witness at Allred's hearing, Louisiana senator John Overton. He insisted that the seat belonged to his state, which had no judge on the court, whereas Allred would give Texas two judges. Louisiana senator Allen Ellender submitted a written statement that he and Overton believed that Louisiana Supreme Court justice Archie T. Higgins should be named. On March 22, 1943, the committee refused on a 9–9 vote to report Allred to the floor. The next day, the Louisiana senators added their state's four district judges as recommendations. In May, Allred wrote the president to request that his nomination be withdrawn.[8] After O'Daniel retired, Allred was appointed as a district judge and served from 1949 to 1959.

Lee, Elmo Pearce, of Louisiana (1882–1949; 1943–49). Nominated on November 5, 1943, and confirmed unanimously on November 30. Lee received the position that Allred had sought.

Borah, Wayne G., of Louisiana (1891–1966; 1949–56, senior–1966). Nominated on October 15, 1949, and unanimously confirmed on October 19.

Russell, Robert Lee, of Georgia (1900–1955; 1949–55). Nominated on October 15, 1949, and unanimously confirmed on October 19.

Strum, Louie Willard, of Florida (1890–1954; 1950–54). Nominated on September 14, 1950, and confirmed unanimously on September 23, 1950.

Rives, Richard Taylor, of Alabama (1895–1982; 1951–66, senior–1981; Eleventh Circuit, senior 1981–82). Nominated on April 12, 1951, and unanimously confirmed on May 1, 1951.

1954: Congress authorized seven judges in the Fifth Circuit.

Tuttle, Elbert Parr, of Georgia (1897–1996; 1954–68, senior–1981; Eleventh Circuit, 1981–96). Nominated on July 7, 1954. His initial hearing on July 16 was a formality. Then the subcommittee was contacted by a widow who criticized Tuttle's legal work on her husband's estate. A second hearing was held on July 30. As soon as both the widow and Tuttle testified, the three members of the subcommittee unanimously reported the nomination favorably. Tuttle was confirmed unanimously on August 3, 1954.[9]

Cameron, Benjamin Franklin, of Mississippi (1890–1964; 1955–64). Nominated on February 18, 1955, and unanimously confirmed on March 14, 1955.

Jones, Warren Leroy, of Florida (1895–1993; 1955–66, senior–1981; Eleventh Circuit, senior 1981–93). Nominated on March 4, 1955, and unanimously confirmed on April 19, 1955.

Brown, John Robert, of Texas (1909–93; 1955–84, senior–1993). Nominated on April 25, 1955. A perfunctory Judiciary Committee hearing was held on May 25. Then on May 31, nationally syndicated columnist Drew Pearson wrote about Brown's actions on behalf of a client after a cargo of government-owned fertilizer exploded in the hold of a ship in the harbor at Texas City in April 1947. The explosion killed five hundred people, injured another five thousand, and destroyed two adjacent ships, one of which was owned by Brown's client. Pearson claimed that soon after the explosion, Brown "erased the warning 'explosive' which the government had stamped on the ship's papers." A Senate subcommittee hearing was held to examine the charge on July 15–16. Brown testified that he had insisted that the bills of lading, which had not been finalized before the explosion, accurately state the form of ammonium nitrate. No warning was deleted. A Justice Department lawyer investigated and found no wrongdoing. Two of Brown's future colleagues, Chief Judge Hutcheson and Judge Rives, sent letters to the committee calling Pearson's claims "libelous." The Judiciary Committee unanimously reported the nomination favorably on July 21. Brown was confirmed unanimously on July 22, 1955.[10]

Wisdom, John Minor, of Louisiana (1905–99; 1957–77, senior–1999). Nominated on March 14, 1957. A Senate judiciary subcommittee held four days of hearings, starting in Washington on April 29, 1957, and then in New Orleans on May 11, 21, and 22. A biographer detailed the allegations and identified most of the opponents as segregationists who were concerned about Wisdom's work with the Urban League in support of civil rights. The committee unanimously reported him on June 24, and he was confirmed unanimously on June 26.[11]

1961: Congress authorized nine judges in the Fifth Circuit.

Gewin, Walter Pettus, of Alabama (1908–81; 1961–76, senior–1981). Given a recess appointment on October 5, 1961. Nominated on January 15, 1962, and confirmed by unanimous consent on February 5, 1962.

Bell, Griffin Boyette, of Georgia (1918–2009; 1961–76). Given a recess appointment on October 5, 1961. Nominated on January 15, 1962, and confirmed by unanimous consent on February 5, 1962.

Thornberry, William Homer, of Texas (1909–95; 1965–78, senior–1995). Nominated on June 22, 1965, and confirmed by unanimous consent on July 1, 1965. On June 26, 1968, President Johnson nominated Thornberry to take the place of associate justice Abe

Fortas on the Supreme Court. The president had nominated Fortas for chief justice. No vote on Fortas was ever taken, and both nominations were withdrawn on October 4, 1968.

Coleman, James Plemon, of Mississippi (1914–91; 1965–81, senior–1984). Nominated on June 22, 1965. Mississippi senator and Judiciary Committee chairman Eastland initially scheduled a hearing on June 29, but it was delayed until July 12–13 because Coleman was hospitalized for a week due to a painful attack of kidney stones. The NAACP opposed him, and several black leaders testified against him at his July hearing. President Johnson sent attorney general Nicholas Katzenbach to testify. Katzenbach tried to place Coleman's record in the context of the racial politics of his state. Coleman's politically courageous endorsement of John Kennedy for president in 1960 may have kept senator Ted Kennedy from opposing him. The committee reported him favorably by a 13–2 vote. A floor debate occurred on July 26, and he was confirmed by a 76–8 vote. These were the first votes cast against a motion to confirm a Fifth Circuit judge.[12]

1966: Congress authorized thirteen judges in the Fifth Circuit.

Goldberg, Irving Loeb, of Texas (1906–95; 1966–80, senior–1995). Nominated on June 28, 1966, and confirmed by unanimous consent on July 22, 1966.

Ainsworth, Robert Andrew, Jr., of Louisiana (1910–81; 1966–81). Nominated on June 28, 1966, and confirmed by unanimous consent on July 22, 1966.

Godbold, John Cooper, of Alabama (1920–2009; 1966–81; Eleventh Circuit, 1981–87, senior–2009). Nominated on June 28, 1966, and confirmed by unanimous consent on July 22, 1966.

Dyer, David William, of Florida (1910–98; 1966–76, senior–1981; Eleventh Circuit, 1981–98). Nominated on August 16, 1966, and confirmed by unanimous consent on August 25, 1966.

Simpson, John Milton Bryan, of Florida (1903–87; 1966–75, senior–1981; Eleventh Circuit, 1981–87). Nominated on October 11, 1966, and confirmed by unanimous consent on October 20, 1966.

Clayton, Claude Feemster, of Mississippi (1909–69; 1967–69). Nominated on October 16, 1967, and confirmed by unanimous consent on October 26, 1967.

1968: Congress authorized fifteen judges in the Fifth Circuit.

Morgan, Lewis Render, of Georgia (1913–2001; 1968–78, senior–1981; Eleventh Circuit, 1981–2001). Nominated on July 17, 1968, and confirmed by unanimous consent on July 25, 1968.

Carswell, George Harrold, of Florida (1919–92; 1969–70). Nominated on May 12, 1969, and confirmed by unanimous consent on June 19, 1969. He was nominated to the Supreme Court on January 19, 1970. Critics expressed concerns about his civil rights attitudes and charged that he was a mediocre lawyer and judge. On April 8, he was rejected by the Senate on a 45–51 vote. Twelve days later, Carswell resigned from the Fifth Circuit to run for the U.S. Senate from Florida. He lost in the GOP primary. Carswell was the second Fifth Circuit judge in less than two years to be nominated to the Supreme Court and not be confirmed; the earlier one was Homer Thornberry.

Clark, Charles, of Mississippi (1925–2011; 1969–92). Nominated on October 7, 1969, and confirmed by unanimous consent on October 15, 1969.[13]

Ingraham, Joe McDonald, of Texas (1903–90; 1969–73, senior–1990). Nominated on December 2, 1969, and confirmed by unanimous consent on December 17, 1969.

Roney, Paul Hitch, of Florida (1921–2006; 1970–81; Eleventh Circuit, 1981–89, senior–2006). Nominated on October 7, 1970, and confirmed by unanimous consent on October 13, 1970.

Gee, Thomas Gibbs, of Texas (1925–94, 1973–91). Nominated on June 11, 1973, and confirmed by unanimous consent on July 13, 1973.

Tjoflat, Gerald Bard, of Florida (1929–; 1975–81; Eleventh Circuit, 1981–). Nominated on November 3, 1975, and confirmed by unanimous consent on November 20, 1975.

Hill, James Clinkscales, of Georgia (1924–; 1976–81; Eleventh Circuit, 1981–89, senior–). Nominated on May 4, 1976, and confirmed by unanimous consent on May 19, 1976.

Fay, Peter Thorp, of Florida (1929–; 1976–81; Eleventh Circuit, 1981–94, senior–). Nominated on June 11, 1976, and confirmed by unanimous consent on September 17, 1976.

Rubin, Alvin Benjamin, of Louisiana (1920–91; 1977–89, senior–1991). Nominated on August 16, 1977, and confirmed by unanimous consent on September 16, 1977.

Vance, Robert Smith, of Alabama (1931–89; 1977–81; Eleventh Circuit, 1981–89). Nominated on November 4, 1977, and confirmed by unanimous consent on December 15, 1977.

1978: Congress authorized twenty-six judges in the Fifth Circuit.

Kravitch, Phyllis A., of Georgia (1920–; 1979–81; Eleventh Circuit, 1981–96, senior–). Nominated on January 19, 1979, and confirmed by unanimous consent on March 21, 1979.

Johnson, Frank Minis, Jr., of Alabama (1918–99; 1979–81; Eleventh Circuit, 1981–91, senior–1999). Nominated on April 2, 1979; confirmed by unanimous consent on June 19, 1979.

Garza, Reynaldo Guerra, of Texas (1915–2004; 1979–82, senior–2004). Nominated on April 30, 1979, and confirmed by unanimous consent on July 12, 1979.

Henderson, Albert John, of Georgia (1920–99; 1979–81; Eleventh Circuit, 1981–86, senior–1999). Nominated on April 18, 1979, and confirmed by unanimous consent on July 12, 1979.

Reavley, Thomas Morrow, of Texas (1921–; 1979–90, senior–). Nominated on May 17, 1979, and confirmed by unanimous consent on July 12, 1979.

Politz, Henry Anthony, of Louisiana (1932–2002; 1979–99, senior–2002). Nominated on May 3, 1979, and confirmed by unanimous consent on July 12, 1979.

Hatchett, Joseph Woodrow, of Florida (1932–; 1979–81; Eleventh Circuit, 1981–99). Nominated on May 17, 1979, and confirmed by unanimous consent on July 12, 1979.

Anderson, Robert Lanier, III, of Georgia (1936–; 1979–81; Eleventh Circuit, 1981–2009, senior–). Nominated on April 18, 1979, and confirmed by unanimous consent on July 12, 1979.

King, Carolyn Dineen Randall, of Texas (1938–; 1979–). Nominated on April 30, 1979, and confirmed by unanimous consent on July 12, 1979.

Tate, Albert, Jr., of Louisiana (1920–86; 1979–86). Nominated on July 31, 1979, and confirmed by unanimous consent on October 4, 1979.

Johnson, Samuel Dodson, Jr., of Texas (1920–2002; 1979–91, senior–2002). Nominated on August 10, 1979, and confirmed by unanimous consent on October 4, 1979.

Clark, Thomas Alonzo, of Florida (1920–2005; 1979–81; Eleventh Circuit, 1981–91, senior–2005). Nominated on August 28, 1979, and confirmed by unanimous consent on October 31, 1979.

Jefferson, Andrew Leon Thomas, Jr., of Texas (1934–2008; not confirmed). Nominated on October 11, 1979, and received a hearing in the Judiciary Committee on November 8, 1979. Two representatives from the newly formed Houston Police Patrolmen's Union testified against him, saying that while a state judge, Jefferson had demonstrated "an unreasonable disdain for law enforcement agencies and a corresponding unjustified sympathy for criminal defendants resulting in the release of dangerous and violent persons contrary to the best interests of society."[14] The politics of a presidential election year likely prevented his receiving a vote in the committee. The nomination was returned on December 16, 1980, with the adjournment of the Congress.

Williams, Jerre Stockton, of Texas (1916–93; 1980–90, senior–1993). Nominated on April 14, 1980, and confirmed by unanimous consent on June 18, 1980.

Garwood, William Lockhart, of Texas (1931–2011; 1981–97, senior–2011). Nominated on September 17, 1981, and confirmed by unanimous consent on October 21, 1981.

October 1, 1981: Fifth Circuit encompassed Texas, Louisiana, and Mississippi, with fourteen judges.

Jolly, Elbert Grady, Jr., of Mississippi (1937–; 1982–). Nominated on July 1, 1982, and confirmed by unanimous consent on July 27, 1982.

Higginbotham, Patrick Errol, of Texas (1938–; 1982–2006, senior–). Nominated on July 1, 1982, and confirmed by unanimous consent on July 27, 1982.

Davis, William Eugene, of Louisiana (1936–; 1983–). Nominated on November 1, 1983, and confirmed by unanimous consent on November 15, 1983.

Hill, Robert Madden, of Texas (1928–87; 1984–87). Nominated on June 4, 1984, and confirmed by unanimous consent on June 15, 1984.

1984: Congress authorized sixteen judges in the Fifth Circuit.

Jones, Edith Ann Hollan, of Texas (1949–; 1985–). Nominated on September 17, 1984, and had a Judiciary Committee hearing on September 26. Congress adjourned without voting on her. Nominated on February 27, 1985, and confirmed by unanimous consent on April 3, 1985.

Smith, Jerry Edwin, of Texas (1946–; 1987–). Nominated on June 2, 1987, and confirmed by unanimous consent on December 19, 1987. The six-month delay was largely due to arguments from senators from other states that the seat should not go to a Texan.

Treen, David Conner, of Louisiana (1928–2009; not confirmed). He was nominated on July 22, 1987, but was opposed by civil rights groups owing to his membership in the States' Rights Party early in his career. He never received a vote in the Senate Judiciary Committee, and he asked that his name be withdrawn. It was on May 10, 1988.[15] Treen had been a congressman from 1973 to 1980, and governor of Louisiana from 1980 to 1984.

Duhé, John Malcolm, Jr., of Louisiana (1933–; 1988–99, senior–). Nominated on June 27, 1988, and confirmed by unanimous consent on October 14, 1988,.

Wiener, Jacques Loeb, Jr., of Louisiana (1934–; 1990–2010, senior–). Nominated on June 27, 1988, the same day as Duhé, but did not receive a hearing before the end of that Congress. Nominated again on November 17, 1989, and confirmed by unanimous consent on March 9, 1990.

Barksdale, Rhesa Hawkins, of Mississippi (1944–; 1990–2009, senior–). Nominated on November 17, 1989, and confirmed by unanimous consent on March 9, 1990.[16]

1990: Congress authorized seventeen judges in the Fifth Circuit.

Garza, Emilio Miller, of Texas (1947–; 1991–2012, senior–). Nominated on April 11, 1991, and confirmed by unanimous consent on May 24, 1991.

DeMoss, Harold Raymond, Jr. ("Hal"), of Texas (1930–; 1991–2007, senior–). Nominated on June 27, 1991, and confirmed by unanimous consent on November 27, 1991. The delay was likely due to Justice Thurgood Marshall's announcing his retirement on the day that DeMoss was nominated. The Senate's judicial focus was on Clarence Thomas until he was confirmed on October 15.

Fitzwater, Sidney Allen, of Texas (1953–; not confirmed). Nominated on January 27, 1992. He never got a Judiciary Committee hearing, and the nomination was returned to the president on October 9, 1992, when Congress adjourned. Fitzwater was one of eleven circuit court and forty-six district court nominees stopped in that Congress. As the *New York Times* put it in September, circuit court nominees "are undergoing greater scrutiny, especially those who are identifiable conservatives." Fitzwater was identifiable, and he was on a list of eight circuit court nominees criticized by the Alliance for Justice, a coalition of groups that opposed many Republican judicial nominees.[17]

Benavides, Fortunato Pedro ("Pete"), of Texas (1947–; 1994–2012, senior–). Nominated on January 27, 1994, and confirmed by unanimous consent on May 6, 1994.

Stewart, Carl Edmond, of Louisiana (1950–; 1994–). Nominated on January 27, 1994, and confirmed by unanimous consent on May 6, 1994.

Parker, Robert Manley, of Texas (1937–; 1994–2002). Nominated on January 27, 1994, and confirmed by unanimous consent on June 15, 1994.

Dennis, James Leon, of Louisiana (1936–; 1995–). Nominated on June 8, 1994, had a hearing in the Judiciary Committee on September 14, 1994, but never received a vote. His nomination lapsed at the end of that Congress. Nominated again on January 31, 1995. He was reported favorably by the committee on July 20. On September 28, Mississippi senator Thad Cochran filed a motion to recommit the nomination. He argued that the seat, formerly held by Charles Clark, a Mississippi judge, belonged to his state. Cochran also criticized Dennis's failure to recuse himself in a recent case on the Louisiana Supreme Court. After a lengthy debate, the motion to recommit failed by 46–54. Dennis was then immediately confirmed by unanimous consent.

Rangel, Jorge Cantu, of Texas (1948–; not confirmed). He was nominated on July 24, 1997, but never received a Judiciary Committee hearing. The nomination was returned to the president on December 19, 1998. Rangel was in private law practice in Corpus Christi, and a member of the ABA Standing Committee on the Federal Judiciary that rated judges. Texas senator Phil Gramm, by refusing to return his "blue slip" that would allow the nomination to proceed, may have been expressing displeasure with the ABA's rating of some of Gramm's past recommendations.

Johnson, Harry Alston, III, of Louisiana (1946–; not confirmed). He was nominated on April 22, 1999, but never received a hearing in the Judiciary Committee. The nomination was returned to the president on December 15, 2000. President Clinton renominated Johnson on January 4, 2001, after President Bush's election but before the inauguration. The nomination was withdrawn on March 19, 2001. There were no substantive objections to Johnson, but it was reported that majority leader Trent Lott was offering agreement to approve the president's friend in exchange for having a Mississippian nominated to another vacancy. No agreement was reached.

Moreno, Enrique, of Texas (1955–; not confirmed). He was nominated on September 16, 1999, but never received a Judiciary Committee hearing. The nomination was returned to the president on December 15, 2000. President Clinton renominated him on January 3, 2001, after President Bush's election but before the inauguration. President Bush withdrew the nomination on March 19, 2001. The committee that Texas Republican senators Phil Gramm and Kay Bailey Hutchison used to screen nominees recommended that Moreno not be supported, though a large number of the members did not participate in the decision.

Clement, Edith Joy Brown, of Louisiana (1948–; 2001–). Nominated on May 9, 2001. She was renominated on September 4, 2001, after all judicial nominations had been returned to the president on August 3, before a month-long recess. On November 13, 2001, she was confirmed by a vote of 99–0.

Prado, Edward Charles, of Texas (1947–; 2003–). Nominated on February 6, 2003, and confirmed by a vote of 97–0 on May 1, 2003.

Pickering, Charles Willis, Sr., of Mississippi (1937–; not confirmed; recess appointee, 2004). He was first nominated on May 25, 2001. Pickering received a Senate Judiciary Committee hearing on October 18, 2001, then had a second hearing on February 7, 2002. Controversy was made of his opposition to abortion, though he would have to follow Supreme Court authority. Some charged he was racially insensitive. On March 14, 2002, the Democrat-controlled Judiciary Committee, by 10–9 party-line votes, refused to report the nomination to the floor. The nomination remained pending and was returned to the president when the Senate adjourned on November 22, 2002. Judge Pickering was renominated on January 7, 2003. The now GOP-led committee did not require a third hearing. On a 10–9 party-line vote, he was reported out of committee on October 2, 2003. He was one of ten circuit judge nominees filibustered in this Congress. On October 30, 2003, cloture failed on a 54–43 vote. Judge Pickering received a recess appointment on January 16, 2004, which expired at the end of the Senate's 2004 session on December 8, 2004. Pickering was the third recess appointee to the Fifth Circuit. The other two, Bell and Gewin in 1961, were both confirmed in 1962.

Owen, Priscilla Richman, of Texas (1954–; 2005–). She was nominated on May 9, 2001, and had a Judiciary Committee hearing on July 23, 2002. On September 5, the majority Democratic committee voted 10–9 along party lines, refusing to report her to the floor. On January 7, 2003, she was again nominated. She had a second hearing on March 13, 2003, and was reported favorably by the then GOP-majority committee on a 10–9 party-line vote on March 27. Cloture failed on May 1, 2003, by a 52–44 vote; she needed 60 votes. Cloture was again rejected on May 8 (52–45), July 29 (53–43), and November 14 (53–42). She was nominated a third time on February 14, 2005. She was the beneficiary of the "Gang of 14" agreement of May 23, 2005, to end some Democratic filibusters. The next day, cloture was approved by an 81–18 vote. A day later, she was confirmed 55–43, four years and two weeks after she was originally nominated. Owen was criticized for being too conservative, with particular focus on one of her rulings on abortion on the Texas Supreme Court, where she had served from 1995 to 2005.

Wallace, Michael Brunson, of Mississippi (1951–; not confirmed). Nominated on February 8, 2006. On May 9, the ABA rated Wallace "not qualified." He is considered a superbly skilled attorney, but the low rating was based on an alleged absence of judicial temperament. From 1984 to 1990, he been a board member and president of the Legal Services Corporation. In that and other capacities, Wallace had disagreements with lawyers who in 2006 were prominent in the ABA; supporters thought that background created Wallace's ABA problems. Wallace had a hearing on September 26, 2006. No vote was taken before adjournment on December 9, when the nomination was returned to the president.

Elrod, Jennifer Leigh Walker, of Texas (1966–; 2007–). Nominated on March 29, 2007, and confirmed by a voice vote on October 4, 2007.

Southwick, Leslie Harburd, of Mississippi (1950–; 2007–). Nominated on January 9, 2007, and had a Judiciary Committee hearing on May 10. He was condemned for two opinions he joined while a member of the Mississippi Court of Appeals. Many opponents insisted that a black judge needed to be appointed. He was reported favorably on August 2, on a 10–9 vote. On October 24, 2007, cloture was approved by a 62–35 vote; he was confirmed 59–38.

Haynes, Catharina, of Texas (1963–; 2008–). Nominated on July 17, 2007, and confirmed by unanimous consent on April 10, 2008.

Graves, James Earl, Jr., of Mississippi (1953–; 2011–). Nominated on June 10, 2010, and had a Judiciary Committee hearing on September 29. He was reported favorably on December 1, but no floor vote was taken before the end of that Congress three weeks later. His nomination lapsed. Nominated on January 5, 2011, and confirmed by voice vote on February 14, 2011.

Higginson, Stephen Andrew, of Louisiana (1961–; 2011–). Nominated on May 9, 2011, and confirmed by a vote of 88–0 on October 31, 2011.

Notes

1. The Final Day

1. 153 Cong. Rec. S13284 (daily ed., October 24, 2007) (remarks of Sen. Schumer).

2. Beginnings

1. Alicia A. Garza, "Weslaco," in *New Handbook of Texas*, vol. 6, ed. Ron Tyler (1996), 883. Tarpley's photograph as superintendent in 1923 appears in Karen Gerhardt and Blanca E. Tamez, *Weslaco* (1999), 46.

2. "Republican Resurgence," *Time*, November 18, 1966; "New GOP Galaxy," *Newsweek*, November 21, 1966. The mention of Bush was in "The South: Toehold to Foothold," *Time*, November 18, 1966, 30.

3. Steve Jackson, "Federal Clerking: Hard Work, High Rewards," *Texas Law Forum*, April 15, 1975, 1.

4. "McFarland Resigns as Canal Zone Judge," *Jackson Daily News*, August 22, 1979, 7A. McFarland was appointed on July 12, 1978, and resigned on July 15, 1979. *Judges of the Federal Courts*, 469 F. Supp. vii, xiii (1979). Susan died on May 15, 1979. Resignation letter, Robert McFarland to Jimmy Carter, June 2, 1979, provided by Jimmy Carter Presidential Library. Louisiana District Judge Morey Sear was assigned the last Canal Zone cases while maintaining his other docket. "Panama to Honor N. O. Judge," *New Orleans Times-Picayune*, March 22, 1997.

5. "Mississippi: More toward Moderation," *Time*, October 13, 1967, 29–30. Jere Nash and Andy Taggart, *Mississippi Politics* (2006), 48. The final vote was 315,318 for Democrat John Bell Williams and 133,379 for Phillips. "General Election Returns, November 7, 1967, Governor," in *Mississippi Official and Statistical Register, 1968–1972*, (c. 1969), 460.

6. "General Election Nov. 7, 1978, for United States Senator," *Mississippi Official and Statistical Register, 1980–1984* (1981), 458–59. In 1977 I wanted to help Doug Shanks, a thirty-year-old Jackson city commissioner, become the city's first Republican mayor since John McGill in 1888. Shanks lost to Democrat Dale Danks. Bill Minor, "Danks

Spanks Shanks," *Jackson Capital Reporter*, June 9, 1977, 1. I could not legally participate, though, because I was a judicial law clerk. Thus Thad's 1978 campaign was my first venture into Mississippi politics.

7. A book consisting largely of Bush's letters to family, friends, and supporters reveals how prolific and personal his correspondence has been. George Bush, *All the Best: My Life in Letters and Other Writings* (1999). None of his notes to me made the cut. Heck.

8. Jo Ann Klein, "Bush to Visit State before GOP Primary," *Jackson Clarion-Ledger*, February 8, 1980, 8A; Klein, "Reagan, Bush Top Poll by State GOP," *Jackson Clarion-Ledger*, February 13, 1980, 1A.

9. Jo Ann Klein, "Candidates File for GOP National Convention Slots," *Jackson Clarion-Ledger*, April 5, 1980, 3A; Jo Ann Klein, "Reagan Runaway in State," *Jackson Clarion-Ledger*, June 4, 1980, 1A; Mississippi Secretary of State, Certificate of Official Returns, Mississippi Republican Primary Election and Delegate Selection Primary Election, June 3, 1980.

10. David Hampton, "Bush Slips into Town after Funds," *Jackson Daily News*, July 10, 1980, 1A; David W. Kubissa, "Bush Tactfully Short on Words in Jackson Visit," *Jackson Clarion-Ledger*, July 11, 1980, 3A.

11. Anne Q. Hoy, "Coleman Retires as Appeals Court Chief," *Jackson Clarion-Ledger*, January 30, 1981, 1A; letter, Coleman to the President, May 11, 1981, files of Fifth Circuit Executive.

12. Jolly's assistance to the Pickering campaign and congressman Jon Hinson's resignation are mentioned in Nash and Taggart, Mississippi Politics, 94, 122–26. Jolly, Ellington, and Cochran were good friends. Bill Minor, "State GOP: It's Hard to Handle Success," *Jackson Capital Reporter*, July 23, 1981, 3. When Thad endorsed Williams, he had to deny rumors that he really supported Ellington. Cliff Treyens, "Thad Cochran Says He Backs Williams," *Jackson Clarion-Ledger*, June 9, 1981, 3B. Democrat Wayne Dowdy beat Liles Williams in a runoff. "Special Election, U.S. House of Representatives, Fourth District," *Mississippi Official and Statistical Register, 1984–1988* (1985), 393. In 1979, Republicans contested four of nine statewide offices and three of seven Public Service Commission, Highway Commission, and Supreme Court seats, losing all; they had 47 nominees for 174 legislative seats, winning 8. *Mississippi Official and Statistical Register, 1980–1984* (1981), 517–26, 529–52.

13. Johanna Neuman, "Lott, Cochran Square Off on 5th Circuit Vacancy," *Jackson Clarion-Ledger*, July 3, 1981, 1A; Anne Q. Hoy, "In Dispute, Allen Sees GOP Health" and "Jolly Would Miss Politics and Privacy," *Jackson Clarion-Ledger*, July 6, 1981, 3A; Anne Q. Hoy, "At Least 9 Lawyers Being Considered for 5th Circuit Slot," *Jackson Clarion-Ledger*, July 14, 1981, 1A. The other reported suggestions were Chancery Judge James Arden Barnett of Jackson; Jackson lawyers Bill Goodman, Jerome Steen, and Phineas Stevens; Gulfport lawyer George E. Morse; McComb lawyer Norman Gillis; and Meridian lawyer Walter Epps. Interest in naming a Republican was understandable because in a state that Democrats had dominated for a century, no person who had participated in Republican

politics had been named a federal judge since Fifth Circuit judge Ben Cameron in 1954. Cameron's limited GOP activities are described in Jack Bass, *Unlikely Heroes* (1981), 85. Before Cameron, the last Republican appointed was District Judge Henry Clay Niles in 1891. Niles was a party leader and had been a GOP legislator. Frank E. Everett Jr., *Federal Judges in Mississippi, 1818–1968* (1968), 108–12.

14. Johanna Neuman, "Dissident State GOP Faction Moves to Oust Mike Retzer," *Jackson Clarion-Ledger*, December 6, 1980, 1A; Cliff Treyens, "GOP Gives Retzer Vote of Confidence, Shows Unity," *Jackson Clarion-Ledger*, December 9, 1980, 3A; e-mail, Harry Allen to the author, November 26, 2012; Brian Williams, "Jolly Prime Candidate for Court," *Jackson Clarion-Ledger*, August 21, 1981, 1A. The day before Allen called Cochran, a Washington newspaper reported that Jolly was Reagan's probable nominee. Nicholas D. Kristof, "Reagan's Federal Bench Team Is Conservative, White, Male," and "President's Choices," *Washington Post*, August 19, 1981, A2.

15. Loretta Pendergrast and David Hampton, "Judge Nixon Likely Nominee to 5th Circuit," *Jackson Clarion-Ledger*, October 6, 1981, 1A; Brian Williams, "Nixon Seems on Road to 5th Circuit Job with Little or No Republican Baggage," *Jackson Clarion-Ledger*, October 7, 1981, 1A; Lloyd Gray, "Lott: White House Suggested Nixon for Court," *Gulfport-Biloxi Daily Herald*, October 13, 1981, A12; Mike Retzer, telephone conversation with the author, December 7, 2012, and Wayne Drinkwater with the author, December 12, 2012; Bill Minor, "New Judge Appointment Waits on Cochran, Lott," *Natchez Democrat*, December 13, 1981, 4A; Had Grady become the chief judge of the Southern District of Mississippi, he could have served until he turned seventy in 2007. Instead Walter Nixon became chief judge, doing so in 1982 when the previous chief resigned early.

16. Lloyd Gray, "White House Suggested Nixon for Court," *Gulfport-Biloxi Daily Herald*, October 13, 1981, B1; Carol S. Lacy, "Walter Nixon Declines Appeals Court Seat," *Gulfport-Biloxi Daily Herald*, October 16, 1981, A1; e-mail, Walter Nixon to author, December 3, 2012.

17. Letters, Thad Cochran to the President, October 15, 1981, and Trent Lott to the President, October 27, 1981, both from Ronald Reagan Presidential Library. Cochran met with Reagan on July 14. Hoy, "Nine Lawyers Being Considered," *Jackson Clarion-Ledger*, July 14, 1981; Gary McElroy, "Barnett: Judge Must Be Refiner," *Jackson Daily News*, April 29, 1980, 3A; Joe Rogers, "Lee Garners Supreme Court Judge Position," *Jackson Daily News*, November 5, 1980, B5. Garwood had been appointed in 1979 as the first Republican since Reconstruction on the Texas Supreme Court. Robert E. McKnight Jr., "Will Garwood: Making the Grade," *Fifth Circuit Civil News*, September 2004, 1, 14. Had Barnett been elected, he would have had the same distinction on the Mississippi court.

18. Joy McIlwain, "State's Year-Old Vacancy on 5th Circuit Still Awaiting Break in GOP Stalemate," *Jackson Clarion-Ledger*, February 15, 1982, 3A. Letter, Trent Lott to the President, February 18, 1982, Ronald Reagan Presidential Library; Minor, "New Judge Appointment Waits," *Natchez Democrat*, December 13, 1981, 4A.

19. Mary Thornton, "Rep. Lott Forcefully Presents His Views to the Justice Department," *Washington Post*, February 19, 1982, A2; Cliff Treyens, "Thad Cochran Nominee Grady Jolly Apparent Winner of 5th Circuit Seat," *Jackson Clarion-Ledger*, March 17, 1982, 1A; Ron Harrist, "Attorney Jolly Tapped for Spot on 5th Circuit," *Jackson Daily News*, March 17, 1982, 1B; *Confirmation of Federal Judges, Hearings before the Committee on the Judiciary, United States Senate*, 97th Cong., 2d Sess., Serial No. J-97-52, Part 4, 61–62, 68–70 (1982); *128 Cong. Rec.* 15755 (daily ed., July 1, 1982) (nomination); 16001 (daily ed., July 14, 1982) (notice of hearing); 18008 (daily ed., July 27, 1982) (confirmation).

20. Shawn McIntosh, "Senate OKs Constitutional Referendum," *Jackson Clarion-Ledger*, January 23, 1987, 1A; Opinion, Leslie H. Southwick, "Don't Fight Constitution's Rising Tide," *Jackson Clarion-Ledger*, January 25, 1987, 1H; Shawn McIntosh, "Constitutional Reform Dead—for Now," *Jackson Clarion-Ledger*, March 13, 1987, 1A.

21. Danny McKenzie, *"A Time to Speak": Speeches by Jack Reed* (2009); the quote by Winter appears on the book jacket.

3. The Bush Administration

1. Roger Whittaker, *New World in the Morning* (BMG, 1971).

2. *Florida Coalition for Peace and Justice v. Bush*, 1989 WL 451627 (D.D.C.,1989); Malcolm Gladwell, "Space Shuttle Launched on Secret Military Flight," *Washington Post*, November 23, 1989, A8.

3. Charles McCoy and Paulette Thomas, "Ongoing Fiasco, Hundreds of S&Ls Fall Hopelessly Short of New Capital Rules," *Wall Street Journal*, December 7, 1989, 1; Linda Himelstein, "How Thrift Agency Brought Kaye Scholer to Its Knees," *Legal Times*, March 9, 1992, 1.

4. *Long Island Savings Bank, FSB v. Federal Savings & Loan Ins. Corp.*, No. CV-89-2699 (E.D. NY 1989); *Long Island Savings Bank v. United States*, 60 Fed. Cl. 80 (2004).

5. Norman Kempster, "Reagan Tapes Testimony for Poindexter Case," *Los Angeles Times*, February 17, 1990, A1; Lee Katz, "Reagan Told to Testify on Iran-Contra," *USA Today*, February 6, 1990, 1A; *United States v. Poindexter*, 951 F.2d 369 (D.C. Cir 1991) (reversal of conviction).

6. *Dellums v. Bush*, 752 F.Supp. 1141 (D.D.C. 1990). The case is discussed in Emily Barker, "Big Suits," *American Lawyer*, January–February 1991, 32. Another suit that I worked on was decided the same day by a different U.S. district judge in Washington. It involved a National Guardsmen who argued he could not be sent to war without congressional action. He was wrong. *Ange v. Bush*, 752 F.Supp. 509 (D.D.C. 1990).

7. Andy Kanengiser, "Judges: White, Protestant, Male," *Jackson Clarion-Ledger*, January 21, 1990, 1H.

8. Mark Ballard, "Bush Ready to Pack the 5th Circuit," *Texas Lawyer*, October 15, 1990, 1; "Et Al., Garza, O'Neill in Line for 5th Circuit," *Texas Lawyer*, January 21, 1991,

6; Gordon Hunter, "Swamped 5th Circuit to Get Relief," *Texas Lawyer*, July 8, 1991, 10; Mark Ballard, "Bush-Senate Standoff Ending," *Texas Lawyer*, February 3, 1992, 4.

9. Ralph Blumenthal and Robert F. Worth, "The Veterans: For Kerry's Chief Accuser, a Flashback to a Political Battle from 1971," *New York Times*, August 28, 2004, A10; Evan Thomas, *Election 2004: How Bush Won and What You Can Expect in the Future* (2004), 109–26.

10. Mark Ballard, "DeMoss on Fast Track to 5th Circuit," *Texas Lawyer*, October 7, 1991, 8.

11. Andy Kanengiser, "Respected Appeals Judge Plans to Retire After 22-Year Stint," *Jackson Clarion-Ledger*, July 10, 1991, 1B.

12. Frank B. Atkinson, *Dynamic Dominion: Realignment and the Rise of Two-Party Competition in Virginia, 1945–1980*, (2006), 403–34. Professor Atkinson wrote me that Obenshain had displayed grace comparable to Warner's in his own previous political disappointments. E-mail, Atkinson to Southwick, November 14, 2011.

13. U.S. District Judge Tom Lee, conversation with the author, February 22, 2013.

14. "Inadmissible: A Lott of Clout," *Legal Times*, January 27, 1992, 3. Mike Wallace's selection was also reported in Mark Ballard, "Bush-Senate Standoff Ending," *Texas Lawyer*, February 3, 1992, 4.

15. Bill Minor, "Jackson Attorney May Get Court of Appeals Nomination," *Jackson Clarion-Ledger*, March 29, 1992, 3G.

16. *Public Papers of the Presidents of the United States: George H. W. Bush, 1991*, book 2, p. 1712 (1992); 1992–93, book 1, p. 1251 (1993).

17. "Loser: John Roberts, Jr.," *Legal Times*, December 28, 1992, 10.

4. The Mississippi Court of Appeals

1. Emily Wagster, "GOP Lawyer Seeking Seat on New Court," *Jackson Clarion Ledger*, February 1, 1994, 5B.

2. Peter O'Connell, "Appeals Court Candidate Burning Plenty of Leather," *Natchez Democrat*, September 7, 1994, 1A.

3. Carmen McCullum, "Candidate Puts Heart and Soles into Campaign," *Jackson Clarion Ledger*, September 19, 1994, 1A.

4. "General Election, Nov. 8, 1994, Appellate Court Judge, District 4, Place 1," and "General Election Run-Off, Nov. 22, 1994, Appellate Court Judge, District 4, Place 1," in *Mississippi Official and Statistical Register, 1996–2000* (1997), 339, 354.

5. *Confirmation Hearings on Federal Appointments: Hearings before the Committee on the Judiciary, United States Senate*, 103d Cong., 2nd Sess., Serial No. J-103-28, Part 5, at 597–612 (1996). Senator Heflin expressed confidence that confirmation would proceed smoothly. *Id.* at 604–5. The Dennis segment of the six-nominee hearing is at 610–12. This document is available online at http://www.archive.org/details/confirmationhearo5unit.

6. Bruce Alpert, "Politics Gets in Way of Nomination," *New Orleans Times-Picayune*, October 30, 1994, B1.

7. The story of LBJ's 1948 Senate race is told in Robert A. Caro, *The Years of Lyndon Johnson: Means of Ascent* (1990), 209–67. Perhaps Caro considered the helicopter the most literal means of LBJ's ascent.

8. "General Election, November 5, 1996, Supreme Court Justice, District I (Central) Position," in *Mississippi Official and Statistical Register*, 1996–2000 (1997), 479. I wrote an article on all state Supreme Court elections and included many details of the 1996 race not mentioned here. Leslie H. Southwick, "Mississippi Supreme Court Elections: A Historical Perspective, 1916–1996," *Mississippi College Law Review* 18 (1997): 183–85.

9. *Garrison v. State*, 695 So.2d 603 (Miss. Ct. App. 1997) (Table), *rev'd*, 726 So.2d 1144 (Miss. 1998). Instead of a fifth trial, Melissa pleaded guilty because her sister was apparently finally going to testify against her. "Daughter Tried Four Times Pleads in Mother's Death," *Baton Rouge State-Times/Morning Advocate*, March 6, 1999, 4B. The court of appeals opinion is not published but appears on the court's Web site, linked with all the decisions for May 20, 1997, http://courts.ms.gov/appellate_courts/coa/coadecisions.html.

10. *Pearson v. Columbus and Greenville Ry.*, 737 So. 2d 390 (Miss. Ct. App. 1998). The first opinion in the case was handed down in 1995, and it sent the suit back for additional factual development. When the case returned to our court in 1998, the original opinion was published along with our new opinion. The 1995 opinion was the earliest one issued by our court to be published, though the publication was long delayed. I also wrote the first opinion of the court to be published as soon as it was released. *Hynson v. Jeffries*, 697 So. 2d 792 (Miss. Ct. App. 1997) (common law "open mines" doctrine was overridden by Mississippi statute).

11. *Dawson v. Townsend & Sons, Inc.*, 735 So. 2d 1131 (Miss. Ct. App. 1999).

12. *Speed v. Scott*, 1998-CA-01520-COA (Miss. Ct. App., Apr 25, 2000), aff'd, 787 So.2d 626 (Miss. 2001).

13. *Wolfe v. City of D'Iberville*, 799 So.2d 142, 148 (Miss. Ct. App. 2001) (Southwick, P.J., concurring).

14. Leslie Southwick, "Separation of Powers at the State Level [Part I]: Interpretations and Challenges in Mississippi," *Mississippi Law Journal* 72 (2003): 927; "Separation of Powers at the State Level, Part II: Service in a Civilian Public Office and in the National Guard," *Mississippi Law Journal* 74 (2004): 47.

15. Beverly Pettigrew Kraft, "U.S. Justice Speaks Out on Religion at MC Event," *Jackson Clarion Ledger*, April 10, 1996, 1A.

16. Ibid.; Joan Biskupic, *American Original: The Life and Constitution of Supreme Court Justice Antonin Scalia* (2009), 188–89. The "Fools for Christ" is from a letter by St. Paul, 1 Corinthians 4:10.

17. Paul Hendrickson, "Weeping Statues of the Bleeding Priest," *Washington Post*, March 13, 1992, F1.

18. Joan Biskupic, "Scalia Makes the Case for Christianity: Justice Proclaims Belief in Miracles," *Washington Post*, April 10, 1996, A1. Cartoon, Herb Block, "Worldly-Wise Guys," *Washington Post*, April 11, 1996, A22.

19. Scalia did not release a copy of his speech. Reconstructions of it can be found, e.g., on the Web site of Christian Action for Israel: "We Are Fools for Christ's Sake," *Israel Report*, June–July 1996,. http://christianactionforisrael.org/isreport/fools.html. Another, with criticisms of Scalia from a variety of news sources, is the Web site for Shalom Jerusalem, http://www.shalomjerusalem.com/heritage/heritage7.html.

20. Wesley Pruden, "A Kick in the Pants for 'a Fool for Christ,'" *Washington Times*, April 12, 1996, A4.

21. Larry Witham, "Do You Believe in Miracles?," *Washington Times*, March 26, 1992, E1.

5. Clinton's Fifth Circuit Choices

1. Jerry Urban, "Krueger Picks 10 for Federal Bench in Texas," *Houston Chronicle*, May 21, 1993, A27; letter, Jorge Rangel to the President, August 20, 1993 (copy provided author by Rangel); "Et al.: Overstreet, Rangel End 5th Circuit Bids," *Texas Lawyer*, September 6, 1993, 46.

2. R. G. Ratcliffe, "Lawmaker's Tip a Curve to Clinton," *Houston Chronicle*, November 18, 1993, A29.

3. Steve Cannizaro, "Two Recommended to Appellate Court; Pair Await OK from Clinton," *New Orleans Times-Picayune*, April 24, 1993, A27; Mark Ballard, "New Contenders for 5th Circuit," *Texas Lawyer*, September 13, 1993, 1; Courtland Milloy, "A Way to Judge How Far We've Come," *Washington Post*, May 22, 1994, B5 (column about Stewart by high school classmate).

4. Bruce Alpert, "La. Nomination to 5th Circuit Is in Jeopardy," *New Orleans Times-Picayune*, May 18, 1995; Bruce Alpert, "Nomination of Judge from La. Is Opposed by Miss. Senators," *New Orleans Times-Picayune*, June 29, 1995, B8.

5. *141 Cong. Rec.* 19688 (daily ed. July 20, 1995) (Judiciary Committee reports Dennis nomination favorably), 26781-97 (daily ed. September 28, 1995) (debate on nomination of James L. Dennis to the Fifth Circuit; reprints the *Times-Picayune* article of July 23, 1995); Cassandra Burrell, "Lott, Cochran Make Waves over Clinton Judicial Nomination," *Jackson Clarion-Ledger*, August 26, 1995, 3B; Dennis Camire, "Miss. Snubbed in Court Appointment," *Jackson Clarion-Ledger*, September 30, 1995, 13A. The recusal issue was raised in connection with a freedom-of-information case seeking records regarding tuition waivers at Tulane University. *Times-Picayune Pub. Co. v. Johnson*, 645 So. 2d 1174 (La. Ct. App. 4th Cir. 1994), *cert. denied*, 651 So. 2d 260 (La. 1995). Senator Biden's remarks on the floor give a good explanation of why recusal was not appropriate. *141 Cong. Rec.* 26783–85.

6. Richard Connelly, "Clinton Gets Four Names to Weigh for Southern District Judge," *Texas Lawyer*, March 17, 1997, 7. Rangel had also been considered for a district judge nomination in 1995. Libby Averyt, "Three's a Charm," *Texas Lawyer*, August 4, 1997, 1; Mark Ballard, "U.S. Judicial Hopefuls Have Long Wait," *Texas Lawyer*, June 24, 1991, 2; Tim Fleck, "The Insider: So Nice to See You Again," *Houston Press*, July 3, 1997, 2–3, http://www.houstonpress.com /1997-07-03/news/the-insider.

7. Senatorial courtesy and the blue slip process are described in Mitchel A. Sollenberger, *The President Shall Nominate: How Congress Trumps Executive Power* (Lawrence: University Press of Kansas, 2008), 23–24, 164–65.

8. Letter, Jorge Rangel to President, October 22, 1998, *149 Cong. Rec.* S11471 (daily ed. September 5, 2003). The letter was used in Senator Leahy's speech rebutting GOP criticisms of the filibuster against Miguel Estrada, the success of which had caused Estrada to withdraw the previous day.

9. S. C. Gwynne, "Judge Not," *Texas Monthly*, November 2000; *Ghosts of Nominations Past, Setting the Record Straight: Hearing before the Subcommittee on Administrative Oversight and the Courts of the Committee on the Judiciary, United States Senate*, 107th Cong., 2nd Sess., Serial J-107-78, (2003), 16–17, 31–32 (statements of Jorge Rangel and Enrique Moreno), http://judiciary.senate.gov/resources/ transcripts/107transcripts.cfm.

10. Peggy Fikac, "Nominee Seen as Political Casualty," *San Antonio Express-News*, May 15, 2000, 1A.

11. Joe Gyan Jr., "Baton Rouge Lawyer Nominated for 5th Circuit Spot," *Baton Rouge Advocate*, May 1, 1999, 1B.

12. "Baton Rouge Lawyer Nominated for 5th Circuit Court," *Mississippi Law Week*, May 9–15, 1999, 1.

13. E-mail, Bob Galloway to Leslie Southwick, July 8, 2009, in possession of author; telephone conversation between Leslie Southwick and Trent Lott, February 15, 2008.

14. I learned about Politz's planned retirement from a May 1999 newspaper article. However, those who knew where to look had prompt notice of his decision. His name soon appeared on a list of judicial vacancies posted on a Web site maintained by the Administrative Office of the U.S. Courts and updated as needed. The March 1, 1999, list titled "Future Vacancies in the Federal Judiciary" still appears on the Web site as one of the archived records. Politz's retirement on August 10 was listed. http://www.uscourts .gov/vacancies/03011999/futurevacancy.htm.

15. Wilson was nominated to the Court of Federal Claims on January 3, 2001, and recess appointed on January 19. She served until Congress adjourned November 22, 2002. Denis Steven Rutkus, *Judicial Nominations by President Clinton during the 103rd–106th Congresses*, CRS Report 98-510 (September 20, 2006), 32–33. On March 19, 2001, President Bush withdrew her nomination along with many others, including those of Enrique Moreno and Alston Johnson. 147 *Cong. Rec.* 3956 (Daily Digest, March 19, 2001). Failure of President Bush or Senate Republicans "to accommodate our request to consider [Wilson's] nomination for a continued position" was among Democratic

complaints about Bush judicial nominations. 149 *Cong. Rec.* S3020 (daily ed., March 3, 2003) (Remarks of Sen. Leahy).

16. Someone sent Bob Galloway a copy in 2000; Bob provided it to me in 2009.

17. Bruce Alpert, "Former Head of La. Democrats Finally Confirmed to Judgeship," *New Orleans Times-Picayune*, May 25, 2000, A8; Joan McKinney, "Sen. Breaux Hopes to Meet Clinton on 5th Circuit Nominee," *Baton Rouge Advocate*, July 12, 2000, 14A; Joan McKinney, "Breaux: Outlook for BR Lawyer Worsening," *Baton Rouge Advocate*, July 24, 2000, 9B.

18. *145 Cong. Rec.* S7246 (daily ed., June 17, 1999) (nomination of Elena Kagan to be U.S. Circuit Judge). Roberts was confirmed after his third nomination to the D.C. Circuit in 2003, then was elevated to be chief justice of the Supreme Court in 2005. Kagan skipped the circuit stop.

19. *Ghosts of Nominations Past, Setting the Record Straight: Hearing before the Subcommittee on Administrative Oversight and the Court of the Committee on the Judiciary, United States Senate*, 107th Cong., 2nd Sess., Serial J-107-78 (2003), http://judiciary.senate.gov/resources/transcripts/107transcripts.cfm.

6. A Hesitant Application

1. E-mail, Roger McMillin to Leslie Southwick, December 13, 2000, 9:21 a.m.; e-mail, Leslie Southwick to Roger McMillin, December 13, 2000, 9:31 a.m.

2. E-mail, Leslie Southwick to Roger McMillin, December 14, 2000, 9:49 a.m.

3. Beverly Pettigrew Kraft, "Pickering Pick for Fifth Circuit," *Jackson Clarion-Ledger*, February 1, 2001, 1A.

4. Bennett Roth, "Bush Submits 11 Names for Federal Bench," *Houston Chronicle*, May 10, 2001, A1.

5. Trent Lott, *Herding Cats: A Life in Politics* (2005), 211–16.

6. Ana Radelat, "Pickering Nominated for Federal Post," *Jackson Clarion-Ledger*, May 26, 2001, 1A.

7. Becoming a Soldier

1. *Confirmation Hearings on Federal Appointments: Hearings before the Committee on the Judiciary, United States Senate*, 107th Cong., 1st Sess., Serial J-107-23, Part 1, at (2002), 341–46, 397–99, http://judiciary.senate.gov/resources/transcripts/107transcripts.cfm.

2. "Sept. 14 Leads in National Draft Lottery," *Houston Chronicle*, December 2, 1969, 1; David E. Rosenbaum, "Lottery Is Held to Set the Order of Draft in 1970," *New York Times*, December 2, 1969, 1A; Selective Service System, History and Records, "The Vietnam Lotteries," http://www.sss.gov/lotter1.htm (accessed December 20, 2009).

3. An e-mail from Ron Mears, Rice's assistant sports information director, to the author on December 22, 2009, gave Myer's and Reist's birth dates. Reist also excelled on and off the court, as he got lottery number 302. Game time was 8:00 p.m. Bruce Spinks, "Knodel Loses Starter in Eve of Opening Game," *Houston Post*, December 1, 1969, sec. 4, p. 2. Rice lost this, their first game of the season, 89–86. Joe McLaughlin, "Too Little, Too Late and Owls Tumble," *Houston Chronicle*, December 2, 1969, 1. His coach called Myer "one of the best outside shooters in the country." Ford Hall, "Knodel's Knaves Know Kneeds," *Rice Thresher*, December 4, 1969, 7. The Myer-Reist luck and skill helped give Rice its only Southwest Conference championship in any major sport while I was a student.

4. Judy Keen, "Forty-nine Were on Active Duty in War Era," *USA Today*, August 24, 1988, 9A; "Quayle Episode Raises Long-Dormant Issue: Were You in the War?" *Wall Street Journal*, August 25, 1988, 1.

5. Arthur M. Schlesinger Jr., *The Imperial Presidency* 440 (2004). Schlesinger named secretary of defense Dick Cheney, House GOP whip and future Speaker Newt Gingrich, columnist Pat Buchanan, and former assistant of state Elliott Abrams as advocates of military force who had not served during the Vietnam War. Molly Ivins, "Return of the War Wimps," syndicated column, *San Francisco Examiner*, March 20, 1991, A17.

6. In 2010 a newspaper story discussed the toll on soldiers of their constant redeployments resulting from the small size of the military and the "vast majority of the American military-aged population" not serving. Greg Zoroya, "Repeated Deployments Weigh Heavily on Troops," *USA Today*, January 13, 2010, 1A. That story did not make me feel guilty. The wound was healed.

7. E-mail, Leslie Southwick to Greg Maggs, Wednesday, September 19, 2001, 1:43 p.m.

8. Mixed Judicial and Military Pursuits

1. *Confirmation Hearings on Federal Appointments: Hearings before the Committee on the Judiciary, United States Senate*, 107th Cong., 1st Sess., Serial J-107-23, Part 2 (2002), 241–62, http://judiciary.senate.gov/resources/transcripts/107transcripts.cfm.

2. Ana Radelat, "Senate Panel to Scrutinize Pickering," *Jackson Clarion-Ledger*, October 19, 2001, 1A.

3. *Confirmation Hearing on the Nomination of Charles W. Pickering, Sr., to be Circuit Judge for the Fifth Circuit: Hearing before the Committee on the Judiciary, United States Senate*, 107th Cong., 2d Sess., Serial No. J-107-57 (2003), http://judiciary.senate .gov/resources/transcripts/107transcripts.cfm.

4. Ana Radelat, "Senate Urged to Oppose Pickering," *Jackson Clarion-Ledger*, February 7, 2002, 1A; James Charles Evers, "A Brave Judge's Name Besmirched," *Wall Street Journal*, February 7, 2002, A16.

5. Ana Radelat, "Pickering Hearing Contentious," *Jackson Clarion-Ledger*, February 8, 2002, 1A.

6. E-mail, Leslie Southwick to Roger McMillin, Saturday, February 9, 2002, 9:05 a.m.

7. Stuart Taylor Jr., "The Politics of Picking: Senate Fights for Power to Change the Bench," *Legal Times*, February 18, 2002, 34.

8. Bill Sammon, "Bush Marshals Nominee Backers," *Washington Times*, March 7, 2002, A3.

9. Ana Radelat, "Senate Panel KOs Pickering," *Jackson Clarion-Ledger*, March 15, 2002, 1A; Audrey Hudson, "Panel Kills Bush's Court Choice," *Washington Times*, March 15, 2002, A1.

10. E-mail, Beverly Tarpley to Leslie Southwick, Monday, March 18, 2002, 8:18 a.m.

11. Jerry Mitchell, "Speculation Follows Defeat of Bush Pick," *Jackson Clarion-Ledger*, March 16, 2002, 1B.

12. "Pickering Confirmation," *Magnolia Political Report*, March 15, 2002, 1.

13. *Confirmation Hearings on Federal Appointments: Hearings before the Committee on the Judiciary, United States Senate*, 107th Cong., 2d Sess., Serial No. J-107-23, Part 4 (2003). The hearing on Owen begins at page 1013. The report is available at http://judiciary.senate.gov/resources/transcripts/107transcripts.cfm. Jonathan Groner, "Owen Faces Abortion, Judicial Activism Questions at Hearing," *Texas Lawyer*, July 29, 2002, 10; Chuck Lindell, "Senators Reject Owen for Appeals Court Seat," *Austin American-Statesman*, September 6, 2002, A1.

14. Trent Lott, *Herding Cats: A Life in Politics* (2005), 246.

15. Trent Lott, *Herding Cats: A Life in Politics* (2005), 243–60; Major Garrett, "GOP Looks to Re-nominate Some Bush Judicial Picks," *Fox News*, December 26, 2002.

16. *Setting the Record Straight: The Nomination of Justice Priscilla Owen, Hearing before the Committee on the Judiciary, United States Senate*, 108th Cong., 1st Sess., Serial No. J-108-6 (2003), http://www.gpo.gov/congress/senate/pdf/108hrg/89329.pdf. The committee reported Owen to the Senate. *149 Cong. Rec.* S4512 (daily ed. March 27, 2003) (report of Senator Hatch for Committee on the Judiciary).

17. Charles Hurt, "Memos Reveal Strategy behind Judge Filibusters," *Washington Times*, May 18, 2005, A14; Manuel A. Miranda, "The Memogate Papers: The Politics, Ethics, and Law of a Republican Surrender," *Texas Review of Law and Politics* 9 (2004): 147.

18. "Nominee Who Lost Supports Pickering," *Washington Times*, April 26, 2003, A2.

19. Jon Frandsen, "Democrats Block Pickering," *Jackson Clarion-Ledger*, October 31, 2003, 1A.

20. Ana Radelat, "Leaders Pushing Recess Option for Pickering," *Jackson Clarion-Ledger*, November 21, 2003, 1B.

21. E-mail, Leslie Southwick to Roger McMillin, Thursday, November 13, 2003, 10:17 a.m.

22. Ana Radelat and Andy Kanengiser, "Bush Sidesteps Dems," *Jackson Clarion-Ledger*, January 17, 2004, 1A; press release, "President's Statement on Appointing Judge Charles Pickering to Fifth Circuit Appeals Court," January 16, 2004 (copy in possession of author).

23. Ana Radelat, "White House Seeks Pickering Replacement," *Jackson Clarion-Ledger*, February 6, 2004, 2B.

24. E-mail, Leslie Southwick to Roger McMillin, Wednesday, April 28, 2004, 7:29 p.m.

9. Training and Pursuing

1. Ryan Clark, "Judge's Call-Up to Iraq Leaves Court Three Short," *Jackson Clarion-Ledger*, July 23, 2004, 1A.

2. Emily Wagster, "Appeals Court Judge Being Deployed for National Guard Service," *Biloxi Sun Herald*, August 6, 2004; Sandi P. Beason, "Judge Prepares for Tour of Duty in Iraq," *Northeast Mississippi Daily Journal* (Tupelo), August 10, 2004, 1A.

3. Ana Radelat, "Pickering's Fate Uncertain: White House Mum on Renomination," *Jackson Clarion-Ledger*, November 27, 2004, 1A; Charles Pickering, *A Price Too High: The Judiciary in Jeopardy* (2007), 211–13; press release, "Retirement Statement by Charles W. Pickering, Sr.," December 8, 2004 (copy in possession of author); Holbrook Mohr, "Pickering to Step Down from Bench," *Jackson Clarion-Ledger*, December 9, 2004, 1A.

4. E-mail, Leslie Southwick to Kevin Watson, Thursday, December 9, 2004, 4:30 p.m.

5. Ana Radelat, "At Least Five in Running to Replace Pickering," *Jackson Clarion-Ledger*, December 23, 2004, 1B.

6. E-mail, Dabney Friedrich to LTC Leslie Southwick, Friday, March 18, 2005, 12:44 a.m.

7. E-mail, LTC Leslie Southwick to Dabney Friedrich, Friday, March 18, 2005, 5:46 a.m.

8. E-mail, Dabney Friedrich to Leslie Southwick, Friday, March 18, 2005, 6:18 a.m.

9. E-mail, LTC Leslie Southwick to Dabney Friedrich, Friday, March 18, 2005, 8:22 a.m.

10. E-mail, Sharon Southwick to Leslie Southwick, Friday, March 18, 2005, 5:31 p.m.

11. E-mail, LTC Leslie Southwick to Dabney Friedrich, Sunday, March 20, 2005, 7:51 a.m. L. B. Cowman, *Streams in the Desert* (1925; Zondervan, 1997), 122–23.

12. E-mail, Leslie Southwick to Martha Ponder, Thursday, March 24, 2005, 8:17 a.m.

13. Ana Radelat, "GOP Chairman Says He's Not Top Pick for Court," *Jackson Clarion-Ledger*, April 23, 2005, B1.

14. Maura Reynolds and Richard Simon, "Compromise in the Senate," *Los Angeles Times*, May 24, 2005, 1; Jim Abrams, "Senators Let Judicial Nominee Move to Vote," *Stars and Stripes* (Mideast ed.), May 25, 2005, 8.

15. John Council and T. R. Goldman, "Senate Showdown Ends with Owen Confirmed—Finally," *Texas Lawyer*, May 30, 2005.

16. E-mail, Grant Dixton to Leslie Southwick, Tuesday, July 5, 2005.

10. A Year in Iraq

1. E-mail, Sharon Southwick to Leslie Southwick, January 26, 2005.

2. E-mail, Leslie Southwick to Sharon, Philip, and Cathy Southwick, January 27, 2005, 5:15 a.m.

3. E-mail, Leslie Southwick to Lloyd, Larry, and Linda Southwick, Saturday, February 12, 2005, 8:15 p.m.

4. E-mail, Leslie Southwick to Sharon, Philip, and Cathy Southwick, Monday, February 14, 2005, 10:53 a.m.

5. E-mail, Leslie Southwick to Linda Southwick, Tuesday, February 15, 2005, 7:10 p.m.

6. E-mail, Leslie Southwick to Maj. Christopher B. Walters, Thursday, March 3, 2005, 7:28 a.m.

7. E-mail, Leslie Southwick to Lanny Griffith, February 23, 2005.

8. E-mail, Leslie Southwick to Lt. Col. Roy Carpenter, Thursday, March 17, 2005, 8:42 a.m.

9. E-mail, Leslie Southwick to Sharon, Philip, and Cathy Southwick, Wednesday, April 27, 2005, 5:08 p.m.

10. E-mail, Leslie Southwick to Sharon Southwick, Friday, March 25, 2005, 5:15 p.m.

11. E-mail, Leslie Southwick to Sharon, Philip, and Cathy Southwick, Wednesday, July 27, 2005, 1:17 p.m.

12. The indomitable Dr. Bernhard returned to the war zone after his work with us. "Doc, 75, Leaves for War Again," *Jackson Clarion-Ledger*, June 17, 2006, 10A.

13. E-mail, Leslie Southwick to Sharon, Philip, and Cathy Southwick, Friday, August 5, 2005, 3:46 p.m.

14. E-mail, Leslie Southwick to Sharon, Philip, and Cathy Southwick, Wednesday, November 9, 2005, 3:30 p.m.

15. E-mail, Leslie Southwick to Dick and Beverly Tarpley, Friday, November 18, 2005, 7:57 a.m.

16. Joe Lieberman, "Our Troops Must Stay: America Can't Abandon 27 Million Iraqis to 10,000 Terrorists," *Wall Street Journal*, November 29, 2005, A18.

17. The Mississippi Bar published a revised version of the speech as part of a military symposium issue. Leslie H. Southwick, "To Iraq and Back," *Mississippi Lawyer* 56 (October–December 2009): 30. The Holmes quote is from Richard A. Posner, ed., *The Essential Holmes* (1996), 86.

11. Back Home and Breaking Through

1. E-mail, Mark Keenum to Leslie Southwick, Tuesday, January 24, 2006, 2:08 p.m.

2. Ana Radelat, "Bush Picks Jackson Lawyer: Michael Wallace Nominated for Seat on Court of Appeals," *Jackson Clarion-Ledger*, February 9, 2006, 1B.

3. E-mail, Leslie Southwick to Roger McMillin, Wednesday, February 15, 2006, 3:14 p.m.

4. E-mail, Roger McMillin to Leslie Southwick, Thursday, February 16, 2006, 1:40 a.m.

5. Ana Radelat, "Wallace Nomination May End Truce on Capitol Hill," *Jackson Clarion-Ledger*, March 2, 2006, 1A.

6. Jaribu Hill, "Magnolia Bar Opposes Wallace 5th Circuit Nomination," *Jackson Clarion-Ledger*, May 22, 2006, 7A.

7. Reuben Anderson, "Wallace Good Choice for Seat on 5th Circuit," *Jackson Clarion-Ledger*, March 13, 2006, 7A.

8. Ana Radelat, "ABA: Wallace Unqualified for Seat on Federal Bench," *Jackson Clarion-Ledger*, May 11, 2006, 1B.

9. Jonathan Allen, "ABA Rating of Wallace Riles Right," *The Hill*, May 23, 2006.

10. Kate O'Beirne, "Good Summary of the State of Play: What's the Holdup? More Stalling, Smearing, and Fumbling on Judicial Nominees," *National Review*, May 23, 2006.

11. E-mail, Leslie Southwick to Dick and Beverly Tarpley, Friday, May 12, 2006, 4:45 p.m.

12. E-mail, Leslie Southwick to Kim Askew, Wednesday, July 26, 2006, 3:49 p.m.

13. Jimmie E. Gates, "U.S. District Judge Taking Senior Status," *Jackson Clarion-Ledger*, February 26, 2006, 1B.

14. *Confirmation Hearings on Federal Appointments, Hearings before the Committee on the Judiciary, United States Senate*, 109th Cong., 2d Sess., Serial J-109-4, Part 6, at 345–50, 441–82 (2007), http://judiciary.senate.gov/resources/transcripts/109transcripts.cfm.

15. Ana Radelat, "Confirmation Hearing Cordial," *Jackson Clarion-Ledger*, September 20, 2006, 2A.

16. *Confirmation Hearing on the Nominations of Michael Brunson Wallace to Be U.S. Circuit Judge, and of Vanessa Lynne Bryant . . . , Committee on the Judiciary, United States Senate*, 109th Cong., 2d Sess., Serial J-109-115 (2008), http://judiciary.senate.gov/resources/transcripts/109transcripts.cfm.

17. "Judicial Nominee Defends Himself before Senate Panel," *Jackson Clarion-Ledger*, September 27, 2006, 1B.

18. E-mail, Hugh Gamble to Leslie Southwick, Thursday, September 28, 2006, 6:05 p.m.

19. E-mail, Leslie Southwick to Sharon, Philip, and Cathy Southwick, Friday, September 29, 2006, 11:31 a.m.

20. E-mail, Leslie Southwick to Bob Jonker, Paul Maloney, and Janet Neff, Saturday, September 30, 2006, 6:40 a.m.

21. E-mail, Leslie Southwick to David W. Clark, Friday, October 6, 2006, 4:53 p.m.

22. Ted Roelofs and Theresa McClellan, "Same-Sex Ceremony Stalls Judicial Nominee," *Grand Rapids Press*, October 7, 2006.

23. "GOP Senator Blocks Judge Pick over Gay Rite," *Washington Times*, October 6, 2006.

24. Ana Radelat, "Bush Judge Picks May Be Doomed," *Jackson Clarion-Ledger*, November 16, 2006, 3B.

12. The Fifth Circuit Shift

1. E-mail, Leslie Southwick to Brad Davis (Cochran) and Hugh Gamble (Lott), Wednesday, December 13, 2006, 5:08 p.m.

2. E-mail, Leslie Southwick to Brad Davis (Cochran), Thursday, December 21, 2006, 11:22 a.m.

3. E-mail, Leslie Southwick to Rhesa Barksdale, Thursday, December 21, 2006, 8:38 p.m.

4. Sid Salter, "Judicial Hopeful Steps Aside: Bush's Nominee for 5th Circuit Withdrawing amid Criticism," *Jackson Clarion-Ledger*, December 23, 2006, 1A; Sid Salter, "Now, Can Someone Give Wallace His Reputation Back?" *Jackson Clarion-Ledger*, December 27, 2006, 7A.

5. Julie Goodman, "Potential Judicial Nominees Studied," *Jackson Clarion-Ledger*, January 2, 2007, 1A.

6. Andy Kanengiser, "Bush Selection of Southwick for Appeals Court Criticized," *Jackson Clarion-Ledger*, January 10, 2007, 1A.

7. Mary Libby Payne, letter, "Southwick Will Be a Qualified Judge," *Jackson Clarion-Ledger*, January 15, 2007, 9A; editorial, "Southwick: Judge Qualified to Fill the Position," *Jackson Clarion-Ledger*, January 11, 2007, 8A.

8. *Confirmation Hearings on Federal Appointments: Hearing before the Committee on the Judiciary, United States Senate*, 109th Cong, 2d Sess., Serial J-109-4, Part 5, at 137, 189, 372 (2007), http://judiciary.senate.gov/resources/transcripts/109transcripts.cfm.

9. Pamela A. MacLean, "Lack of Black Bench Nominees Criticized," *National Law Journal*, February 14, 2007.

10. E-mail, Leslie Southwick to Philip and Cathy Southwick, February 24, 2007, 8:40 a.m.

11. E-mail, Leslie Southwick to Peter D. Keisler, Tuesday, April 17, 2007.

13. The Hearing

1. After the supreme court took the case, the Web link to our opinion was removed. The supreme court's opinion is *Richmond v. Miss. Dept. of Human Serv.*, 745 So. 2d 254 (Miss. 1999).

2. *May v. Mississippi Bd. of Nursing*, 667 So. 2d 639 (mem.), 93-CC-00765-COA (Miss. Ct. App. June 27, 1995). The opinion is not published, but much of its analysis of

state administrative law is restated in Southwick, "Administrative Law," in 1 *Ency. Miss. Law* § 2:66–2:68 (2001).

3. Joseph Ammerman, "Caucus Wants Appeals Court Abolished," *Jackson Clarion-Ledger*, August 14, 1998, 1B.

4. Ed Whelan, "Aron-neous Assault on Judge Southwick, Part 1," *National Review Online*, August 21, 2007, http://nationalreview.com.

5. *S.B. v. L.W.*, 793 So.2d 656 (Miss. Ct. App. 2001).

6. Ed Whelan, "Ridiculous Case against Leslie Southwick," *National Review Online*, July 11, 2007, http://nationalreview.com.

7. *Confirmation Hearing on the Nominations of Leslie Southwick, to be Circuit Judge for the Fifth Circuit; Janet T. Neff, to Be District Judge for the Western District of Michigan; and Liam O'Grady, to Be District Judge for the Eastern District of Virginia: Hearing before the Committee on the Judiciary, United States Senate*, 110th Cong., 1st Sess., Serial J-110-52, at 57–58 (2007), http://judiciary.senate.gov/resources/transcripts/110transcripts.cfm.

8. *153 Cong. Rec.* S13278-79 (daily ed. Oct. 24, 2007) (Statement of Mr. Durbin).

9. Ana Radelat, "Bush's Latest Pick for Appeals Court Grilled by Senators," *Jackson Clarion-Ledger*, May 11, 2007, 1A; Marshall Ramsey, Cartoon, *Jackson Clarion-Ledger*, May 17, 2007, 10A.

14. The Sorting Out

1. E-mail, Leslie Southwick to Larry, Lloyd, and Linda Southwick, Dick and Beverly Tarpley, Sunday, May 13, 2007.

2. Editorial, "Southwick: Consider Person, Not Politics," *Jackson Clarion-Ledger*, May 12, 2007, 9A.

3. E-mail, Judge Amul R. Thapar to Leslie Southwick, January 19, 2008, 4:23 p.m.

4. E-mail, Charles Pickering to Leslie Southwick, Friday, May 18, 2007.

5. E-mail, Brad Davis to Leslie Southwick, Wednesday, May 23, 2007.

6. Ana Radelat, "Senate Dems Win Delay of Southwick Confirmation Vote," *Jackson Clarion-Ledger*, May 25, 2007, 3B.

7. E-mail, Leslie Southwick to Lloyd, Larry, and Linda Southwick, Thursday, May 24, 2007, 2:39 p.m.

8. E-mail, Tyree Irving to Leslie Southwick, Thursday, May 31, 2007.

9. E-mail, Leslie Southwick to Tyree Irving, Thursday, May 31, 2007.

10. Ana Radelat, "White House Candidate Opposes Southwick Judicial Appointment," *Jackson Clarion-Ledger*, June 1, 2007, 2B.

11. Editorial, "An Unacceptable Nominee," *New York Times*, June 5, 2007, A22.

12. Erin P. Billings, "Nominee to Spark Showdown," *Roll Call*, June 4, 2007.

13. E-mail, Leslie Southwick to Tessa Platt, Wednesday, June 6, 2007.

14. E-mail, Jeff Jackson to Leslie Southwick, Wednesday, June 6, 2007, 3:24 p.m.

15. Editorial, "Judicial Speech Code," *Wall Street Journal*, June 7, 2007.

16. *Daily Word*, June–July 2007, 22; "Judicial Nominee Vote Delayed Again," *Jackson Clarion-Ledger*, June 8, 2007, 2B.

17. S. A. Miller, "GOP Eyes 'Shutdown' of Senate over Judges," *Washington Times*, June 8, 2007.

18. E-mail, Leslie Southwick to Tessa Platt, Tuesday, June 12, 2007, 3:21 p.m.

19. Editorial, "Southwick: Consider the Person, Not Politics," *Jackson Clarion-Ledger*, June 14, 2007, 8A.

20. Ana Radelat, "Southwick Vote Postponed," *Jackson Clarion-Ledger*, June 15, 2007, 2B; Keith Perine, "Judiciary Chairman Says Court Nominee Will Not Get Out of Committee," *CQ Today*, June 14, 2007.

21. E-mail, Leslie Southwick to David Illingsworth, Monday, June 18, 2007, 9:20 a.m.

22. "Vote on Southwick Delayed for Fourth Time," *Jackson Clarion-Ledger*, June 22, 2007, 2B.

15. A Pause, and a New Approach

1. E-mail, Leslie Southwick to Martha Ponder, Donald Campbell, Dean Korsak, and Michael Bentley, Saturday, June 23, 2007, 8:20 a.m.

2. E-mail, Major Mark Majors to Leslie Southwick, Friday, June 22, 2007, 3:17 p.m.

3. E-mail, Leslie Southwick to Peter Keisler, Sunday, June 24, 2007, 4:26 p.m.

4. E-mail, Peter Keisler to Leslie Southwick, Monday, June 25, 2007, 7:34 a.m.

5. E-mail, Stuart Schiffer to Leslie Southwick, Monday, June 25, 2007, 7:54 p.m.

6. E-mail, Leslie Southwick to Katie McHenry, Wednesday, June 27, 2007, 6:25 p.m.

7. *153 Cong. Rec.* S8657-59 (daily ed. June 28, 2007) (statement of Senator Hatch).

8. Erin P. Billings and Emily Pierce, "Divided GOP Looks for Unity," *Roll Call*, July 2, 2007.

9. Specter's surprising loss for mayor of Philadelphia was reported in the same issue of *Time* as Rubel Phillips's expected defeat for Mississippi governor. "Elections: The Cities," *Time*, November 17, 1967, 28; see also "The States," 28–29.

10. Alexander Bolton, "Thad Cochran Tries to Rescue Bush Nominee," *The Hill*, July 3, 2007; Ana Radelat, "Senate Tiff Likely over Delays in Judge Vote," *Jackson Clarion-Ledger*, July 6, 2007, 1A.

11. Billings and Pierce, "Divided GOP Looks for Unity."

12. Jeanne Cummings, "Specter Leads Right on Judicial Fight," *Politico*, July 12, 2007, 1.

13. Alexander Bolton, "Specter Says Dems Broke Their Promise," *The Hill*, July 12, 2007.

14. Charles Hurt, "Memos of Special Interest on Hill," *Washington Times*, November 15, 2003, A1.

15. E-mail, Leslie Southwick to Ed Whelan, Sunday, July 15, 2007, 10:10 a.m.

16. E-mail, Ed Whelan to Leslie Southwick, Sunday, July 15, 2007, 8:18 p.m.

17. Erin P. Billings, "Southwick May Stymie Senate," *Roll Call*, July 16, 2007.

18. *153 Cong. Rec.* S9310-12 (daily ed. July 17, 2007) (statement of Senator Specter).

19. Transcript, *Fox Special Report with Brit Hume*, July 18, 2007, from the WestLaw News Room database, 2007 WLNR 13694861.

16. Desperation, and Witches and Martyrs

1. Statement of the Hon. Patrick Leahy, July 19, 2007, http://judiciary.senate.gov/hearings/testimony.cfm?id=2871&wit_id=2629.

2. *153 Cong. Rec.* S9562-67 (daily ed. July 19, 2007) (statement of Senator Cochran).

3. Ana Radelat, "Cochran's Plea Aims to Shame Dems Who Oppose Southwick Nomination," *Jackson Clarion-Ledger*, July 20, 2007, 2B.

4. E-mail, Leslie Southwick to Matthew Steffey, Saturday, July 21, 2007, 7:48 a.m.

5. Editorial, "The Southwick Stonewall," *Wall Street Journal*, July 23, 2007, A14.

6. The letter appears at http://www.confirmthem.com/60_groups_demand_progress_on_judges (accessed August 19, 2012).

7. Erin P. Billings and Emily Pierce, "'Gang' Courted for Southwick," *Roll Call*, July 26, 2007.

8. These were different publications of the same column: Stuart Taylor Jr., "Opening Argument: Shortsighted on Judges," *National Journal*, July 28, 2007, 17; "The Gantlet for Nominees," *Legal Times*, July 30, 2007, 62; "Shortsighted on Judges," *Atlantic*, July 31, 2007, http://www.theatlantic.com/magazine/archive/2007/08/shortsighted-on-judges/306145.

9. E-mail, Leslie Southwick to Stuart Taylor, Monday, July 30, 2007, 10:24 a.m.

10. *153 Cong. Rec.* S10304-6 (daily ed. July 30, 2007) (Statement of Senator Hatch).

11. *153 Cong. Rec.* S10532-33, S10544-46 (daily ed. Aug. 1, 2007) (Remarks of Senator Alexander; Amendment no. 2599 to amendment 2530, plus statements of several senators).

12. *153 Cong. Rec.* S10548-51 (daily ed. Aug. 1, 2007) (Statements by Specter and Graham).

13. Erin P. Billings, "McConnell, Specter Push to Force Vote on Southwick Nomination," *Roll Call*, August 1, 2007; *153 Cong. Rec.* D1121 (daily ed. Aug. 2, 2007). In the odd ways of Senate procedure, the Sense of the Senate resolution was offered as an amendment to another amendment of children's health insurance, the hotly debated S-CHIP program. Keith Perine, "Judiciary Approves Southwick for 5th Cir. Despite Liberal Opposition," *Congressional Quarterly Today*, August 2, 2007.

14. Trish Turner, "Heat Turned Up in Senate on Nomination of Judge Leslie Southwick," *Fox News*, August 1, 2007; Keith Perine, "Detente Over, and So Is Southwick's Chance for Confirmation," *Congressional Quarterly Today*, August 1, 2007.

15. E-mail, Kim Askew to Leslie Southwick, Wednesday, August 1, 2007, 11:01 a.m.

16. Fred Thompson, "Judge Southwick Should Be Confirmed," posted on Townhall. com, August 1, 2007; copies of Thompson, McCain, Romney, and Giuliani statements in possession of author.

17. Paul Boyer and Stephen Nissenbaum, *Salem Possessed: The Social Origins of Witchcraft* (Cambridge: Harvard University Press, 1974).

18. Walter H. Southwick, *Early History of the Puritans, Quakers, and Indians, with a Biography of the Quaker Martyr Lawrence Southwick* (privately printed, 1931), 1–20; Lydia S. Hinchman, *Early Settlers of Nantucket* (1896; Rutland, VT: Charles E. Tuttle, 1980), 87–95; Thomas Jefferson Wertenbaker, *The Puritan Oligarchy: The Founding of American Civilization* (New York: Grosset and Dunlap, 1947), 212–23; James M. Caller, *Genealogy of the Descendants of Lawrence and Cassandra Southwick of Salem, Mass.* (privately printed, 1881), 1–63.

19. *Poems of John Greenleaf Whittier* (Thomas Y. Crowell, 1902), 37. The Quaker Whittier also wrote the inscription on a monument to Nurse that is in the Rebecca Nurse Homestead cemetery in Salem Village, now called Danvers. "Christian Martyr," by John Greenleaf Whittier.

17. The Committee Speaks

1. Ana Radelat, "Senate Panel Sets Vote on Judge," *Jackson Clarion-Ledger*, August 2, 2007, 1A.

2. E-mail, Philip Southwick to Leslie Southwick, Thursday, August 2, 2007, 8:54 a.m.; e-mail, Cathy Southwick to Leslie Southwick, Thursday, August 2, 2007, 9:15 a.m.

3. *Preserving Prosecutorial Independence: Is the Department of Justice Politicizing the Hiring and Firing of U.S. Attorneys? Hearings before the Committee on the Judiciary, United States Senate*, 110th Cong., 1st Sess., Serial No. J–110–14, (2007), 459–513, http:// judiciary.senate.gov/resources/transcripts/110transcripts.cfm.

4. Rule XXVI, 5(a), Rules of the United States Senate.

5. Executive Committee Meeting, Committee on the Judiciary, United States Senate, S. [2084] School Safety and Law Enforcement Improvements Act . . . To Consider the Nomination of . . . Leslie Southwick, to be U. S. Circuit Court Judge for the Fifth Circuit, 110th Cong., Aug. 2, 2007 (2007). My consideration is at pages 70–106.

6. E-mail, Leslie Southwick to Philip, Mary, and Cathy Southwick, Thursday, August 2, 2007, 4:25 p.m.

7. Manu Raju, "Senator Lott Drawing Fire Again on Race from Civil Rights Groups," *The Hill*, September 7, 2007.

8. E-mail, Leslie Southwick to Charles Pickering, Friday, August 3, 2007, 11:39 a.m.

9. Ana Radelat, "Southwick Nomination Cleared for Final Vote," *Jackson Clarion-Ledger*, August 3, 2007, 1A; Alexander Bolton, "Feinstein's Flip Sends Southwick to the Floor," *The Hill*, August 3, 2007; Erin P. Billings, "Judiciary Approves Southwick after

Feinstein Votes with GOP," *Roll Call*, August 2, 2007; Committee for Justice, press release, "Southwick Win Is a Huge Setback for Dems, but Fight Is Not Over," August 3, 2007 (copy in possession of author).

10. White House, press release, "President Bush Pleased Judge Leslie Southwick Will Soon Receive Fair Vote by Senate," August 2, 2007; Senator Harry Reid, press release, "Reid Statement on Judiciary Committee Sending Southwick Nomination to Full Senate," August 2, 2007 (copy of both in possession of author).

18. A Lull: Would There Be a Storm?

1. Erin P. Billings, "Gang May Reunite for Deal on Southwick," *Roll Call*, August 6, 2007.

2. Robert Novak, "ENPR: Week of August 8, 2007," from HumanEvents.com, August 8, 2007 (copy in possession of author).

3. George F. Will, "Can Obama Explain it?" *Jackson Clarion-Ledger*, August 12, 2007, 5G.

4. Editorial, "Qualified to Serve," *Washington Post*, August 18, 2007, A12. The editorial was a terrific thirty-fourth wedding anniversary present for Sharon and me.

5. Nan Aron, "An Unjust Judge," *Washington Post*, August 21, 2007, A15.

6. "The Week," *National Review*, August 13, 2007, 8; August 27, 2007, 8; September 10, 2007, 6. Editorial, "Borking Judge Southwick," *Washington Times*, August 29, 2007, A18.

7. Ana Radelat, "Derailing Southwick May Take Filibuster," *Jackson Clarion-Ledger*, September 5, 2007, 1B.

8. *153 Cong. Rec.* S11003-4 (daily ed. September 4, 2007) (Remarks of Sen. McConnell). The press conference was described by Curt Levey on the ConfirmThem Web site, http://www.confirmthem.com/southwick_press_conference (accessed August 19, 2012).

9. Sid Salter, "Judge Reflects on Ordeal," *Jackson Clarion-Ledger*, September 23, 2007, 1G.

10. Erin P. Billings, "GOP Still Hunting for Southwick Votes," *Roll Call*, October 2, 2007, 1.

11. E-mail, Leslie Southwick to Sharon, Philip, and Cathy Southwick, Thursday, October 4, 2007, 10:07 a.m.

12. *153 Cong. Rec.* S12756-62 (daily ed. October 4, 2007) (confirmations of Aycock and Elrod).

13. Erin P. Billings, "Lott Looking to Form New 'Gang,'" *Roll Call*, October 4, 2007, 1.

19. The Final Two Trips

1. Ana Radelat, "Southwick Allowed More Time to Garner Support," *Jackson Clarion-Ledger*, October 7, 2007, 1A; Emily Pierce, "Spy Bill Knots Up Senate," *Roll Call*, February 6, 2008.

2. E-mail, Philip Southwick to Leslie Southwick, Friday, October 19, 2007, 10:42 a.m.

3. Manu Raju, "Vote on Southwick Likely Next Week," *The Hill*, October 19, 2007.

4. E-mail, Leslie Southwick to Sharon Southwick, Monday, October 22, 2007, 8:11 a.m.

5. Ana Radelat, "Judicial Nominee Vote Near," *Jackson Clarion-Ledger*, October 22, 2007, 1A.

6. *153 Cong. Rec.* H11825-30 (daily ed. October 22, 2007) (Congressional Black Caucus).

7. Carrie Budoff Brown, "A Troubled Southern Courtship," *Politico*, October 23, 2007, 1.

8. *153 Cong. Rec.* S13286-87 (daily ed. October 24, 2007) (Letter of Carlton W. Reeves, Nomination of Leslie Southwick to be U.S. Circuit Judge for the Fifth Circuit).

9. Trish Turner, "Vote Expected This Week on Judge Southwick Nomination to Circuit Court," *Fox News*, October 23, 2007.

10. E-mail, Leslie Southwick to Charles Pickering, Tuesday, October 23, 2007, 9:06 a.m.

11. E-mail, Clarine Nardi Riddle to Leslie Southwick, Tuesday, October 23, 2007, 8:52 a.m.

12. E-mail, Leslie Southwick to Clarine Nardi Riddle, Tuesday, October 23, 2007, 9:27 a.m.

13. E-mail, Clarine Nardi Riddle to Leslie Southwick, Tuesday, October 23, 2007, 9:33 a.m.

14. E-mail, Leslie Southwick to Clarine Nardi Riddle, Tuesday, October 23, 2007, 9:42 a.m.

15. *153 Cong. Rec.* S13242-54 (daily ed. October 23, 2007) (Nomination of Leslie Southwick to be U.S. Circuit Judge for the Fifth Circuit).

16. E-mail, David Brown to Leslie Southwick, Tuesday, October 23, 2007, 10:42 p.m.

17. E-mail, Leslie Southwick to David Brown, Sunday, October 28, 2007, 2:02 p.m.

20. The Beginning of the Last Day

1. Ana Radelat, "Senate Debate on Southwick May End Today," *Jackson Clarion-Ledger*, October 24, 2007, 1A.

2. Erin P. Billings and Emily Pierce, "Deal Struck on Southwick Vote," *Roll Call*, October 24, 2007, 1; Manu Raju, "Republicans Target Red-State Dems on Judge Southwick," *The Hill*, October 24, 2007, 3.

3. Blog by Fred Thompson, October 22, 2007; press releases by John McCain, Mitt Romney, and Rudy Giuliani, October 24, 2007 (copies in possession of author).

4. E-mail, Andy Taggart to Leslie Southwick, Wednesday, October 24, 2007, 10:09 a.m.

5. *153 Cong. Rec.* S13273-13300 (daily ed. Oct. 24, 2007) (Nomination of Leslie Southwick to be U.S. Circuit Judge for the Fifth Circuit).

21. The Vote

1. Erin P. Billings, "Landrieu's Judge Vote Provokes Lott's Ire," *Roll Call*, October 31, 2007, 1. Senator Landrieu was considered vulnerable in 2008, but she won with 52 percent of the vote.

2. I had been in the office with Margaret Stewart several times in my trips. She gave me the tally sheet—and signed it at my request—on which she had marked the Democratic votes. She had checked Democratic senator Jim Webb's name, then scratched out the marking. I wonder if she was counting Webb when she (if it were she) called out, "He's got it."

3. *Confirmation Hearings on Federal Appointments, Hearings before the Committee on the Judiciary, United States Senate*, 110th Cong., 1st Sess., Serial J-110-8, Part 2, (2009), 309–11 http://judiciary.senate.gov/resources/transcripts/110transcripts.cfm.

4. David W. Kubissa, "After 12 Years: Winter Celebrates End of Long Quest," *Jackson Clarion-Ledger*, August 29, 1979, 1A.

22. A Victory Lap

1. Press release, White House, "President Bush Pleased by Confirmation of Judge Leslie Southwick," October 24, 2007 (copy in possession of author).

2. E-mail, Leslie Southwick to Andy Taggart, Sunday, October 28, 2007, 3:20 p.m.

3. E-mail, Leslie Southwick to Ed Whelan, Saturday, October 27, 2007, 3:38 p.m.

4. It was such a clever story that I looked for its origins. A variant appeared as early as February 1872, in "Editor's Drawer," *Harper's New Monthly Magazine*.

5. Editorial, "One Judge Makes It," *Wall Street Journal*, October 25, 2007, A22.

6. Carrie Budoff Brown, "Southwick Confirmed by Senate," *Politico*, October 25, 2007, 1. Lengthy excerpts from the press conference appeared in a news story my wife recorded from Fox News on October 24, 2007 (copy in author's possession).

7. Erin P. Billings, "Southwick Approved by Senate after Long Fight," *Roll Call*, October 25, 2007, 3; Manu Raju, "Southwick Saga Ends with Win for GOP," *The Hill*, October 25, 2007, 1; David Stout, "Senate Backs Disputed Judicial Nomination," *New York Times*, October 25, 2007, A17.

8. Couragecampaign.org (accessed October 27, 2009); Susan Estrich, "In Politics, Nastiness Doesn't Take a Holiday," *Fox News*, November 25, 2007.

9. Transcripts, "Fox Special Report with Brit Hume," October 24 and 25, 2007, from the WestLaw News Room database at 2007 WLNR 20995617, 20944521.

10. Ana Radelat, "Senate OKs Miss. Judge," *Jackson Clarion-Ledger*, October 25, 2007, 1A; editorial, "Southwick: Judge Judged by Region's History," *Jackson Clarion-Ledger*, October 25, 2007, 8A.

11. E-mail, George Tarpley to Leslie Southwick, Wednesday, October 24, 2007, 11:40 a.m.

12. E-mail, Larry Southwick to Leslie Southwick, Tuesday, October 30, 2007, 3:47 p.m.

23. Reflections

1. Peter Canellos, "Fury at Vote Reflects a Politicized Process," *Boston Globe*, October 30, 2007, A2.

2. E-mail, Leslie Southwick to Stuart Taylor, December 27, 2007, 12:50 p.m.

3. Jonathan Weisman, "As Lott Leaves the Senate, Compromise to Be a Lost Art," *Washington Post*, November 28, 2007, A4.

4. John Gardner, "A Call for 'Commitment and Cool Intellect,'" *Christian Science Monitor*, April 16, 1969, 9.

5. 6 *Reg. Deb.* 255 (Mar. 15, 1830) (speech of Sen. Livingston).

6. C. S. Lewis, *The Problem of Pain* (HarperCollins, 2001), 94.

Epilogue

1. *Confirmation Hearings on Federal Appointments, Hearings before the Committee on the Judiciary, United States Senate*, 111th Cong., 2d Sess., Serial J-111-4, Part 7 (2011), 253–55, http://judiciary.senate.gov/resources/transcripts/111transcripts. cfm.

Appendix

1. From 1789 to 1793, two Supreme Court justices sat with a local district judge; from 1793 to 1801, then from 1802 to 1869, one justice was usually sufficient. A description of circuit courts is given in http://www.fjc.gov/history/home.nsf/page/ courts_circuit.html. The politics of creating circuit court judgeships in February 1801, then eliminating them effective in July 1802, is engagingly discussed in Cliff Sloan and David McKean, *The Great Decision* (2009). Burr's treason trial in circuit court was depicted in a seventy-six-minute movie produced by the Judicial Conference of the United States, in association with Pittsburgh's WQED television, in 1976. E. G. Marshall narrated. *Equal Justice under Law: U.S. vs. Aaron Burr* (broadcast by PBS affiliate stations, c. Sept. 1976). This was one of four period-costume video dramatizations of significant Marshall Court decisions. The other broadcasts were on the Supreme Court decisions of *Marbury v. Madison, McCulloch v. Maryland*, and *Ogden v. Gibbons*.

2. Harvey C. Couch, *History of the Fifth Circuit, 1891–1981* (1981), 17–18. The change in number of judges in the Fifth Circuit is compiled at http://www.fjc.gov/history/home .nsf/page/courts_coa_circuit_05.html.

3. Couch, *History of the Fifth Circuit*, 4–5, 10–11, 187–92.

4. The nomination and confirmation dates and the basic biographical information come from the Federal Judicial Center's Web site: http://www.fjc.gov/history/home. nsf/page/judges.html. The judges are listed according to the date of presidential appointment. When the president signs the commission of more than one Fifth Circuit judge on the same day, seniority on the court is by age. 28 U.S.C. § 45(b) (adopted 1948). Same-day commissioning first occurred on October 21, 1949, when both Wayne G. Borah of Louisiana and Robert Lee Russell of Georgia were appointed. Borah was older and thus senior. The most named were on July 13, 1979, when President Carter appointed seven Fifth Circuit judges. The senior because he was the oldest was Reynaldo Garza, while the youngest and most junior was Carolyn Randall King.

5. "Outrageous Attacks upon the Judiciary," *New Orleans Daily Picayune*, February 6, 1881, 2; "The Billings Case: A Glimpse at the Charges against Mr. Hayes' Nominee," *Washington Post*, February 10, 1881, 2. The rulings likely were in this case later appealed to the Supreme Court. *Williams v. Morgan*, 111 U.S. 684 (1884).

6. *Congressional Record* 23 (February 17, 1892): 1262 (motion of John H. Bankhead), and 2121 (March 16, 1892) (report of House Judiciary Committee on McCormick). Early consideration and controversy are discussed in a number of articles in the *Dallas Morning News*: "Private in the Ranks," June 14, 1891, 12; "Col. Culberson Declines," December 17, 1891, 1; "Local Notes," December 18, 1891, 3; "All Wrapped in Mystery," January 5, 1892, 1. The most detailed stories on the charges and postnomination events are "Against Judge McCormick," February 18, 1892, 1; "More Charges Preferred," February 24, 1892, 1; "McCormick Charges," February 25, 1892, 1; "A. P. McCormick's Answer," February 25, 1892, 8; "Federal Judgeship," March 6, 1892, 3.

7. Chester M. Morgan, *Redneck Liberal: Theodore G. Bilbo and the New Deal* (1985), 107–16.

8. Joseph P. Harris, *The Advice and Consent of the Senate* (1953), 217; *Nomination of James V. Allred, Hearings before a Subcommittee of the Committee on the Judiciary, United States Senate*, 78th Cong., 1st Sess. (1943), on LexisNexis Congressional Hearings Digital Collection, HRG-1943-SJS-0001, -0002; Sheldon Goldman, *Picking Federal Judges: Lower Court Selection From [F.D.] Roosevelt through Reagan* (1997), 42; "Louisianans Add Four Names to Court List," *Washington Post*, March 24, 1943, 8; "Thirty-Seven Nominations Are Sent Back to White House," *Washington Post*, July 23, 1943, 9.

9. Anne Emanuel, *Elbert Parr Tuttle: Chief Jurist of the Civil Rights Revolution* (2011), 109–14; *Hearing on Confirmation of the Nomination of Elbert Parr Tuttle, Subcommittee of the Committee of the Judiciary, United States Senate* [Part 2], 83d Cong., 2d Sess. (1954).

10. Drew Pearson, "Washington Merry-Go-Round," *Washington Post*, May 31, 1955, 43. On the morning the Pearson column appeared, Eisenhower was asked whether he knew of the allegations before he named Brown. He said that nominees were thoroughly investigated, and "I never heard such a word about Mr. Brown." Transcript,

presidential news conference, May 31, 1955, http://www.presidency.ucsb.edu/ws/index
.php?pid=10246; "Brown Hearing Centers on Texas City Disaster," *Houston Post*, July
16, 1955, sec. 2, p. 15; "Senate Panel OKs Brown; 'Satisfied' on Texas City," *Houston Post*,
July 22, 1955, 4. The lawsuits against the government were dismissed. *In re Texas City
Disaster Litigation*, 197 F.2d 771 (5th Cir. 1952), *aff'd, Dalehite v. United States*, 346 U.S.
15 (1953).

11. Joel William Friedman, *Champion of Civil Rights: Judge John Minor Wisdom*
(2009), 98–111.

12. "Coleman Illness Muffles Protest; but Liberals Read Attacks on Him as Judge
Anyway," *New York Times*, June 30, 1965, sec. 1, p. 17; Harold W. Chase, *Federal Judges:
The Appointing Process* (1972), 169–73; Steven Michael Gentine, "The Mississippi
Freedom Democratic Party's Congressional Challenge of 1964–65: A Case Study in
Radical Persuasion," M.A. thesis (Florida State University, 2008), http://diginole.lib.fsu
.edu/etd/127.

13. Leslie H. Southwick, "Chief Judge Charles Clark: A Life Well Lived," *Mississippi
College Law Review* 30 (2012): 391.

14. *Selection and Confirmation of Federal Judges, Hearings before the Committee on
the Judiciary, United States Senate*, 96th Cong., 1st Sess., Serial No. 96–21, pt. 4 (1980),
648.

15. Sheldon Goldman, *Picking Federal Judges: Lower Court Selection From [F.D.]
Roosevelt through Reagan* (1997), 318; James Gill, "Treen Judgeship May Spark Battle,"
New Orleans Times-Picayune, March 18, 1988.

16. Leslie H. Southwick, "The Journey of Rhesa H. Barksdale to the Fifth Circuit: A
Friend's Perspective," *Mississippi Law Journal* 79 (2009): 241.

17. Mark Ballard, "Bush-Senate Standoff Ending," *Texas Lawyer*, February 3, 1992,
4; Mark Ballard, "Judiciary Panel Kills Texans' Nominations," *Texas Lawyer*, October 5,
1992, 6; Neil A. Lewis, "Waiting for Clinton, Democrats Hold Up Court Confirmations,"
New York Times, September 1, 1992, A1.

Index